This book is dedicated to Steve Hutchinson,
who taught me electronic sticklebricks.

Digital Media and Society:
An Introduction

ADRIAN ATHIQUE

polity

First published in 2013 by Polity Press
Reprinted 2013

Polity Press
65 Bridge Street
Cambridge CB2 1UR, UK

Polity Press
350 Main Street
Malden, MA 02148, USA

ISBN-13: 978-0-7456-6228-2
ISBN-13: 978-0-7456-6229-9(pb)

A catalogue record for this book is available from the British Library.

Typeset in 9.5 on 12 pt Swift Light
by Servis Filmsetting Ltd, Stockport, Cheshire
Printed and bound in Great Britain by Clays Ltd, St Ives plc

The publisher has used its best endeavours to ensure that the URLs for external websites referred to in this book are correct and active at the time of going to press. However, the publisher has no responsibility for the websites and can make no guarantee that a site will remain live or that the content is or will remain appropriate.

Every effort has been made to trace all copyright holders, but if any have been inadvertently overlooked the publisher will be pleased to include any necessary credits in any subsequent reprint or edition.

For further information on Polity, visit our website: www.politybooks.com

Contents

Figures and Boxes

Acknowledgements

A work of this kind, stemming as it does from many years of teaching and learning in the field of digital media, owes a considerable debt of gratitude to the many colleagues with whom I have worked on the various subject areas covered in this book. Accordingly, I would like to express a debt of gratitude to Doug Clow and James Aczel at the Open University, Geoff Cox, Phil Ellis and Phaedra Stancer at the University of Plymouth, Graham Barwell, Kate Bowles, John Robinson and Chris Moore at the University of Wollongong, and Michael Halewood, Berfin Emre, Richard Davis and Rebecca Ellis at the University of Essex. I would also like to thank other colleagues, past and present, whose work is referenced here, including Mark Andrejevic, Melissa Gregg, Lynne Pettinger, Gareth Schott and Graeme Turner. For their support in providing space for the development of a substantive programme in digital sociology at Essex, I would also like to thank Mike Roper, Rob Stones, Sean Nixon and Eamonn Carrabine. Thanks are due also to Michael Bailey, for taking up the charge. I would also like to recognize the important contributions made to this endeavour by all of the students that I have taught in Australia, New Zealand and the UK. I am confident that their contributions, in terms of testing, challenging and extending the ideas discussed here, will grow in significance over the years. Finally, I would like to express my profound gratitude for the support provided by my editor at Polity Press for this book, Andrea Drugan. Like so many of the authors that have worked with Andrea in recent years, I have been struck by her extensive knowledge of the field, her enthusiasm for critical pedagogy and her capacity to deliver sound practical advice consistently and in real time. I would also like to thank Lauren Mulholland, Clare Ansell and Helen Gray, along with the reviewers of the proposals and drafts and everyone at Polity Press who strived to make this book as good as I wanted it to be.

Introduction

Over the last two decades, our view of mass communication in modern society has been extensively reconfigured by the 'new media' applications stemming from the rollout of digital technologies. In so many different ways, the digital media has come to be seen as the definitive technology of our times. The powerful combination of mechanical calculation, electronics, binary code and human language systems touches us in almost every aspect of life. Quite literally, the digital media have become the 'operating system' of almost everything else. In everyday life, our interpersonal relationships are conducted in a large part through digital communications. The institutions of work and governance are finely regulated by the same inexorable logics of programmatic management that lie at the heart of the technology. Our access to the vast stores of human knowledge, to cultural expression and to significant events unfolding in societies across the world is overwhelmingly mediated through various forms of digital media 'content'. Digital media, then, take us close to the rhythm of social life across the broad scale of human affairs. To understand these phenomena fully we have to discover how a 'whole way of life', in all its complexity, becomes infused with the presence of digital systems. As such, the multifaceted relationship between digital media and human actions poses one of the most complex questions facing contemporary sociology, and one that impacts upon almost every academic discipline in one aspect or another.

Naturally, given the enormous breadth and scale of the subject matter, this book cannot encompass every possible instance or example of our encounter with the digital. My objective, instead, is to provide a relatively accessible and succinct account of some of the major areas of sociological concern. Accordingly, this book will examine a broad range of phenomena – from social networking and digital labour to the rise of cybercrime and identity theft, from the utopian ideals of virtual democracy to the Orwellian nightmare of the surveillance society, and from the free software movement to the seductions of online shopping. Many of these topics have been the subjects of recent works in their own right, and I would encourage you to read further in the areas that you find most germane or compelling. It remains important, nonetheless, to understand the intrinsic connectivity between them, and that is why I hope this book can provide a useful primer for those interested in understanding the digital media in depth. In taking this larger view, I will not put forward any single explanation or seek to predict the future evolution of digital society. The overarching aim of this work, instead, is to situate the rise of the digital media within the context of dynamic social interaction and to encourage a critical engagement with our complex and rapidly changing world. To put that more simply, I want you read this book and make up your own mind about what is going on.

In that light, I have chosen to approach the topics covered here from a range of sociological approaches that each have something to offer to readers willing to make their own assessments of the claims being made. In each case, this will not be the only possible approach to that topic, and you will also need to make your mind up about which sets of theories and models make the most sense to you. In the process, we will interrogate many of the classic questions of sociological inquiry in their digital manifestation: the competing forces of structure and agency, the predominance of conflict or consensus, the relationship between action and meaning and the interface of individual and collective experience. This necessarily entails a degree of eclecticism. The role of technological mediation has been at the heart of the major sociological theories of the past thirty years but, at the same time, a good deal of the sociological examination of the digital media has been conducted within other academic disciplines. Once again, the collation of all this work is naturally beyond the scope of this book but in bringing together what I can in brief, I hope that new light can be shed on areas both familiar and unfamiliar to your studies thus far.

I should also note that 'digital society', the term that I employ here, is not a term in common use. I am using it precisely because the other available terms are all in some sense partial or overlapping with the terrain that I wish to explore. Each of them favours the structure, usage or form of digital communication in different ways. Taking the broader notion of a digital society therefore allows us to consider their significance in more relative terms. My intention is also one of synthesis, since various approaches have currency and validity and therefore merit our attention. Arguably, it is also the case that all of these models tend to privilege the broader (macrological) forms of society. At various points in this book, I will do the same. However, I will also take pains to emphasize that society is something that we live in, and to which we all contribute at the level of everyday life (that is, the micrological). Human beings make digital technologies social, and that puts human beings at the heart of any digital society. There is also a notable anglophone bias to my presentation, a charge to which most studies of the 'information revolution' must also answer. Human societies are, of course, somewhat distinctive in both character and function, and we should expect their 'digitization' to reflect this. However, keeping within the art of the possible, I will not seek to account for the full order of cultural diversity. I will instead ask you respectfully, as a reader, to make sense of what is discussed here within your own social and cultural situation.

Adrian Athique
November 2011

Part I

Digital Histories

CHAPTER 1

Building a Digital Society

It is important that many of the structural possibilities of a digital society were foreseen in the early days of electronic computing (and even before). Others were either unanticipated or came more from the pages of fantasy novels than from the rational projection of technologists. Parallel processes were in play. This first chapter casts its eye firmly on the futurism of the past, specifically from the advent of modern computer science in 1936 to the crisis of undue complexity in 2007. In this brief history, I will recall how digital technologies, through a virtuous circle of mediation, came to reinforce and implement particular ways of conceptualizing and ordering society in the late twentieth century. As the application of digital technologies gathered pace from the 1970s onwards, the various imperatives driving technological change were also reshaping the dominant political structures in developed and developing societies. Because of the apparent confluence of technical and social change, it has become commonplace to argue that the impact of digital technologies is comparable to that of the Industrial Revolution (Castells 1996). An 'information revolution' is seen to mark an irreversible transition from physical to intangible (untouchable) commodities and actions, and from embodied to mediated social processes (Leadbeater 2000). More cautious scholars have argued that it is vitally important to recognize that there is a crucial element of continuity with the previous 'industrial' age in terms of a progressive technical automation of human functions and social organization (Webster 2006). In that respect, the digital media have a substantial and fascinating history, and it is worth situating these arguments against the past evolution of digital society.

Information Society and the Atomic Age

The digital technology of today finds its origins in the mechanical calculating machines invented during the nineteenth century. The 'analytical engine' conceived by Charles Babbage in the 1830s was the first machine intended to process and store information with multiple purposes and flexible configurations of usage (Swade 2001). A prototype of this machine was completed by the beginning of the twentieth century. The storage of information records on 'punched' cards was also an innovation of the nineteenth century that would later become a key component of computing in the twentieth century. In 1936, Alan Turing introduced the concept of the 'Turing machine', a device that would make calculations based upon a large store of printed information which could be selectively applied for mathematical processing (Petzold 2008). Turing took this concept further to demonstrate the idea of a 'universal machine' that could read the description of any computational process (an 'algorithm') and then simulate its operation. Turing was one of the most significant figures in modern mathematics and as a consequence, following the outbreak of the Second World War, he was recruited to work at Britain's secret code-breaking centre at Bletchley Park. Turing famously devised the 'bombe' machine in order to decipher the secret codes produced by the German cryptological machine (the 'enigma') (Copeland 2004).

The global conflagration that killed between 50 and 70 million people in the mid-twentieth century occurred on the cusp of several major scientific breakthroughs, including not only computational machines, but also modern electronics and nuclear physics. In that respect, the war years (1939–45) were as much a scientific and techno-logical contest as they were a military one. The most technologically advanced nations in the world, Britain, the United States and Germany, effectively conscripted their scientific talents and applied them relentlessly to military applications, culminating in the advent of computers, missiles and the atomic bomb in the 1940s. It is in that context that Konrad Zuse developed in 1941 the first programmable machine operated through information stored in binary code. The United States built the first electronic computer in 1941 and Britain developed an electronic device with limited programmability (the 'colossus') in 1943 (Copeland et al. 2006). In 1942, Britain took the momentous decision to share all of its scientific secrets with the United States, and the collaboration between the two countries enabled them to surpass Germany in the fields of logical computing and atomic weaponry. Needless to say, the atomic bomb, and its use against Japan in 1945, was an epochal moment in human history. The significance of the emergence of modern computer science, however, was kept under tight secrecy, and did not become fully apparent until a number of years after the war.

The United States Army built the ENIAC device in 1946 to aid in the successful deliv-ery of missile weapons, whilst Britain built the first programmable electronic comput-ers (the 'Manchester computers') between 1948 and 1950. Accordingly, the pursuit of electronic computing – in primitive but strategically important forms – by the major antagonists during the Second World War in the 1940s is commonly seen as heralding what has been called the 'information age'. The conflict had brought together large number of scientists, academics and technicians on an unprecedented scale and had demonstrated how major technical achievements could be made quickly through such systematic collaboration. It was this experience that underpinned the decision to mas-sively expand university and technical education in the post-war decades. In making his assessment of these developments for the future, Vannevar Bush, the director of the Federal Office of Scientific Research and Development in the United States, wrote an essay in 1945 in which he reflected on the growing specialization of knowledge and the new tools for managing information that would become essential in the post-war world. Famously, Bush projected the imminent arrival of a desktop information management machine that he called the 'Memex'. The Memex would facilitate the storage, retrieval and, most critically, the linkage of information customizable to the needs of each user.

A Memex is a device in which an individual stores all his books, records and communications, and which is mechanized so that it may be consulted with exceeding speed and flexibility. It is an enlarged intimate supplement to his memory. It consists of a desk, and while it can presumably be operated from a distance, it is primarily the piece of furniture at which he works. On the top are slanting translucent screens, on which material can be projected for convenient reading. There is a keyboard, and sets of buttons and levers. Otherwise it looks like an ordinary desk. In one end is the stored material. The matter of bulk is well taken care of by improved microfilm. Only a small part of the interior of the Memex is devoted to storage, the rest to mechanism. Yet if the user inserted

5,000 pages of material a day it would take him hundreds of years to fill the repository, so he can profligate and enter material freely.

Vannevar Bush (1945) 'As We May Think', *Atlantic Monthly*, 176(1): 101–8

The development of 'mainframe' computers in the 1950s and 1960s produced rapid leaps in the application of electronic computing to solving advanced mathematical problems. These machines were far from the desk-based device envisioned by Vannevar Bush, commonly taking up the size of an entire room or more. Mainframes required a massive amount of power and a large team to maintain and operate. Nonetheless, the energies spent upon the development of these machines stemmed from a widespread recognition that the concentration of information in forms that could be processed in any number of ways would open up enormous potentials for scientific development. Computerization would simultaneously solve the problem of memorizing and managing all that information. The speed of electronic processing promised to overcome the time- and scale-based limitations of human thinking. This step-change in efficiency could obviously be applied to scientific experiments, but also to any number of large and complex processes employed in military, bureaucratic and manufacturing applications. 'Information management' would no longer be a technique of making and maintaining records, but rather a dynamic process of experimentation that employed digitized records ('data') as its raw material.

Cold War and White Heat

The 1950s and 1960s were characterized by the onset of the 'Cold War', a period in which the wartimes allies of the capitalist West and communist East were pitted against each other in an intense scientific and technological contest to master the new technologies of the age. These (dangerous) rivalries were also expressed in their respective desire to demonstrate the supremacy of their opposing economic systems. As such, the potential of computing to improve the efficiency of industrial production was quickly recognized both by state-owned enterprises in the communist bloc and the private industrial corporations of the Western world, in which the United States had now become predominant. The pursuit of 'information technology' was intended to transform the productive process of global industry, with this modernization furnishing a capacity to rapidly develop and commercialize any number of new technologies. In 1963, the British Prime Minister, Harold Wilson, referred to the 'white heat' of a technological age. The focus of commercial competition was therefore shifting from territorial expansion to the pursuit of more efficient industries and markets via rapid automation. Three years before, US President Dwight D. Eisenhower had already spoken of the new institutional form of scientific research and its co-evolution with what he called the 'military-industrial complex' (1961).

It was the machinery of 'high technology' that caught the public imagination in the 1960s, via the 'space race', nuclear power and the domestication of electronics (notably television). The new centrality of information management, however, subsequently proved to be an equally profound development in the remaking of the modern world. By the 1970s we had entered an era in which vast stores of information appeared to hold greater significance than large volumes of physical resources. All forms of human processes, concepts and activities were being recorded as data that could, in turn, be applied and improved by the machinery of information technology. The perceived outcome of 'computerization' was that electronic calculation could increase both the scale and speed of almost any process repeatedly and infinitely. Thus, it was not simply the capacity of the computer to hold inconceivable amounts of information, but its programmatic capacity to select the right bits of data and process them in new combinations that was permanently revolutionary. In the process, computerization promised to make the conduct of almost any complex undertaking vastly more efficient. The Cold War militaries were playing with nukes, a dangerous game that required automation and the elimination of human error. Military applications thus took primacy in the paranoia of the 1950s, but by the end of the 1960s computer processing was also applied with enthusiasm to all the institutions of modern life. Universities, the traditional storehouses of information, were at the forefront of this process and were influential advocates of computerization.

The benefits of greater speed and efficiency in information processing were also immediately obvious to the various branches of modern government and to the commercial corporations of the day. Sociology, as a putative science of social organization and systematic observer of human behaviour, was a natural partner in the process of 'informationalization'. As a technology of record, the more information that could be collected about every aspect of society, the more efficiently society could be assessed and managed. Equally, there were clear commercial benefits in knowing more about the habits of consumption in mass society. Ever more complex industrial processes became conceivable, making automated mass production bigger, faster and more innovative. It is fair to say, then, that computerization in the era of the mainframe was overwhelmingly corporate in scale and instrumental in purpose. The possession of data and the means to process it was intended to confer advantages that were inherently competitive in intent and managerial in flavour. Efficiency became the watchword of the day. In order to achieve these aims, it was necessary in the first instance to put computer technology to work on itself, rapidly advancing the technology and automating the process of its own development. Thus, information about computing itself became a major objective of scientific research, and algorithms for the computation of information (the 'software') became a major constituent in the development of the electronic components (the 'hardware') intended to carry out those functions.

It was, without a doubt, the United States that led the charge in computerization. Their Soviet adversaries made huge efforts in developing their own mainframe systems, while Britain, with its diminishing resources, struggled to keep up. Other European countries pooled resources to stay in the 'high-technology' game. In the developing world, India was keen to commit to the development of computer science, while Japan (under the post-war tutelage of the United States) pursued this new technological and managerial paradigm with unparalleled enthusiasm. As a consequence, it is relatively unsurprising that when the information age was given structural expression in the model of an 'information society', this took the form of a political economy of which the major advocates were American (Drucker 1959; Bell 1973) and Japanese (Masuda 1990). This emerging perspective on social structure has seen many different iterations in theory, but the hallmark of information society theory is social organization via data processing. In Robert Hassan's definition: 'At the broadest level of conceptualization, we can begin by saying that the information society is the successor to the industrial society. Information, in the form of ideas, concepts, innovation and run-of-the-mill data on every imaginable subject – and replicated as digital bits and bytes through computerization – has replaced labour and the relatively static logic of fixed plant as the central organizing logic of society' (2008: 23).

Box 1.1 Characteristics of an information society

- **Knowledge displaces skills** – fundamental importance of guiding processes over physical actions
- **Mechanical archives** – complete automation of informational processes
- **Social life as data** – unprecedented collection and collation of information on human activity
- **Purposeful knowledge** – value is extracted from the application of information rather than its meaning or essence
- **Continuous innovation** – configuration of data in new forms becomes the basis of knowledge production
- **Competitive velocity** – the accelerated speed and efficiency of information techniques constitute an advantage in all fields of activity
- **Exponential change** – The primary goal of the 'information revolution' is the total transformation of human affairs

---

The Flowering of Electronic Revolutions

The co-evolution of computerization and electronics was marked by a series of important hardware developments. The biggest breakthroughs were the transistor and the subsequent development of the integrated circuit (silicon chip), which allowed for the photolithographic production of millions of tiny transistors in cheap, powerful and extremely small computer processors. Many of these innovations had far wider applications than the rapid upscaling of computing machines. The post-war decades were also the era in which the Western democracies pursued the dream of a society in which productive efficiency put mass consumption at the heart of everyday life. As such, the fruits of electronic technology became rapidly available in the form of affordable consumer devices that quickly came to transform the domestic environment. This was an era of new 'labour-saving' devices that automated everyday chores and paved the way for women, in particular, to use their increasing free time to enter the paid workforce. This, in turn, increased the spending capacity of the family unit and further accelerated the purchase of devices designed to support a faster and more mobile way of life. The most striking domestic electronic device, however, was the television. Television brought an unprecedented range of information and popular entertainment into living rooms, irrevocably shifting the primary terrain of cultural consumption from public to private spaces. Along with the transistor radio, the electric record player and the telephone, the television quickly came to mediate our cultural environment (McLuhan 1964). Indeed, it was television that popularized the very term 'media' in everyday usage, and made media studies a logical proposition for academic study.

The culture industry, which Theodor Adorno and Max Horkheimer famously described in 1944, expanded rapidly to produce a vast array of accessible cultural works which could be enjoyed via the machinery of the home (Adorno and Horkheimer 1993). Thus, the era of electronics was also to be the era of the pop song, the soap opera and, along with them, domestic advertising. For the generation born in the twenty years after the end of the Second World War (the so-called 'baby boomers'), the new milieu of consumer electronics and mass consumption became an all-encompassing social environment. Since the realization of a computerized society took place simultaneously with the timeframe of their own lifespan, the baby boomers became critically important in the shaping of the digital present. By the end of the 1960s, the baby boomers were hitting their twenties. Due to massive public investments by the previous generation, they were far better educated on average and the long post-war boom in the West gave them ready access to jobs, housing, contraception and medical care. The fruits of the post-war dream thus fell into the hands of those who came to have quite different aspirations from their parents. Overall, they expected more material affluence, more individual freedoms (sexual, financial and cultural) and, by various means, they demanded unprecedented social mobility.

In their youth, the baby boomers also became particularly enraptured by the transformation of popular culture that took place as they were growing up. With the massive expansion of the cultural marketplace and the rising purchasing power of ordinary people, pop music, film, fashion, art and television were all newly accessible domains in which conscious and constant cultural experimentation was taking place. These developments, by their very nature, touched those in all walks of life, but it was the youth demographic in the educated classes that came to demonstrate (quite literally) their impatience to take up the reins of steering the information age. Their challenge to the old establishment and its values was expressed in the heady radical populism of 1968 (Doggett 2008). It was in the following decade, however, that middle-class baby boomers actually came to replace their predecessors in the professional domain. Nonetheless, the politics and revolutionary ambitions of the 1960s were reflected in the expression of a vague 'counter-culture' in the United States and Western Europe. This constituted a new view of social participation that valued self-expression above all else, and eschewed the old certainties and conformities of the 1950s (Roszak 1995). Baby boomers (in very general terms) placed their faith instead in technology, personal ambition and free speech as determinants for a better world. Many of the brightest of the generation, regardless of their wider politics, were infused with these values and it was logical, therefore, that many of them took a keen interest in computers.

What made the information revolution of the 1970s technologically different from the preceding era of the mainframe was that it was achieved in large part by 'distributed computing'. The twin rise of computerization and consumer electronics had driven a process of miniaturization that had begun with the demands of the space race. Electronic components had been subjected to a continuous process of refinement that made them smaller and therefore suitable for a wide range of new applications. In computing, this led to the recognition of 'Moore's law', which famously predicted that the processing power of a small integrated circuit would double every two years, reducing the size of computers and leading to exponential growth in computer power. While many of the larger technology corporations continued to concentrate on the supercomputers that were their stock-in-trade, the younger generation of computer technicians turned their attention to the possibilities of much smaller multipurpose devices, ushering in the era of the 'microcomputer'. These single-user devices could be assembled from basic components, were fully programmable and easily fitted on a desktop. A number of small companies were founded with the intention of commercializing basic microcomputers, including the now legendary Apple Computer in 1976.

Initially, microcomputers were sold as build-at-home kits for the technically minded and required knowledge of electronics and software programming. These were rare skills outside of the scientific community, but there was sufficient interest from the public to encourage the world's biggest computer corporation, IBM, to develop its own microcomputer design. In 1980, they commissioned a tiny company of microcomputer enthusiasts to write the operating software for this machine. This company, Microsoft, had the vision of putting a computer 'on every desk and in every home' (Gates 1995). The logic of this was that the concentration of computing power in large 'timeshared' devices would soon give way to a vast number of smaller machines that effectively distributed computing capacity amongst individual employees by giving them their own personal machine with software oriented towards their basic everyday tasks. The development of computer programs for 'word processing', 'spreadsheets' and basic 'databases' made microcomputers ideal for the modernizing office, and the affordability and versatility of microcomputers made them quick to deploy. Along with IBM, new companies such as Apple Computer marketed mass-produced 'personal computers' (PCs) that came straight out of the box with pre-loaded software. Before long, PCs were augmented with 'ethernet' technologies that allowed them to send messages to each other via an organization's internal telephone network. This made electronic mail (demonstrated in 1972) available on a mass scale and further accelerated the 'computer revolution' in the workplace.

As the counter-culture generation had shouted at the establishment in the West, the industrialized nations had been shaken by the oil crisis in 1973, which definitively ended the era of cheap energy on which their post-war economies had been founded. Throughout the 1960s and 1970s, the upheavals stemming from the decolonization of the old European empires also saw the antagonisms of the Cold War spread across the continents of Africa and Asia. Western capitalism was forced into a new era where costs rose, markets closed and profits inevitably declined. Simultaneously, Germany and Japan (having rebuilt themselves with astounding speed after their wartime defeat) had quickly put into place rapid advances in electronic manufacturing that introduced much more intensive competition into the global manufacturing economy. To respond to these twin challenges, American and British capitalism simply had to become more efficient. Given that information technology had already established itself as an available solution, its application throughout the economy was accelerated. In order to streamline the day-to-day operations of innumerable businesses, the business community and public administration turned to personal distributed computing with vigour. IBM, having neglected to insist on the copyright for Microsoft's 'Windows' operating system, saw their PC design widely copied by manufacturers across the globe, whilst Microsoft founder, Bill Gates, went on to become the richest man in the world.

The era of personal distributed computing was the moment in which software surpassed hardware in importance, and well-designed programs running on fairly simple computers could generate enormous revenues. Bill Gates was much more than a skilled programmer, however. He was also an ardent believer in, and advocate for, the information revolution. Gates believed that the efficiency savings of personal computers would overcome the contradictions and crises of capitalism and lead to a world where business worked well, and worked well for everybody (1995). He found a receptive audience, since the early fruits of distributed computing coincided with an equally revolutionary economic doctrine coming to the fore, which sought above all else to reduce workforces, streamline administration and invest in entrepreneurial projects. The new information technology (IT) companies fitted this bill quite nicely, and their products also made these objectives immediately plausible. Generational change in the political and business establishment brought another group of revolutionaries to the fore, in this case committed to the triptych of efficient capitalism, small government and computer science. Thus, in many different ways, the older institutional form of the information revolution became inflected with the various cultural and commercial revolutions of the day.

Revolutions, of course, require wide public participation and, throughout the 1980s, people from all walks of life embraced computerization with suitable fervour. In the home, computer gaming consoles and 'pocket money' machines such as the ZX81 and Commodore 64 encouraged children to learn computer skills from a young age. The cultural industries, always on the lookout for something new, 'got into computers' in a big way, with digital music and digital animation infusing the popular culture of the 1980s. Thus, it was machines of almost exactly the kind envisioned by Vannevar Bush that quickly came to dominate our vision of the future. It had taken thirty years, which, of course, is a very small space of time in the context of science and technology. During those intervening years, computers (real and imagined) had become part of the fabric of popular culture. From Captain Kirk's handheld communicator on *Star Trek* (1966) to the pathological computer in Kubrick's *2001 – A Space Odyssey* (1968), to 'R2D2' in *Star Wars* (1977), 'Orac' in *Blakes Seven* (1978) and countless others, the socialization of the information machine was widely reflected in our visions of the future. In the economic domain, fortunes were made and economies were remade. In the university system, the classicism of the past was replaced by a restless venture futurism, as a new generation of students went into business administration and computer science. All of this, however, was far from being the endpoint in the making of a digital society.

Box 1.2 Timeline of computerization

- Mechanical computers conceived in the nineteenth century
- Electronic computing developed during the Second World War (1939–45)
- Nuclear technology and the Space Race encourage development of massive 'mainframe' computers in the 1950s
- Computers spread beyond military applications to wider uses in universities and commercial corporations in the 1960s
- Less powerful 'microcomputers' are developed in the 1970s, with commercial build-at-home machines
- Mass-produced personal computers see widespread application in the workplace during the 1980s, with the coming of the 'spreadsheet' and 'email' software
- Apple Macintosh computers (1984) corner the commercial design market with advanced graphical capabilities
- Home computer ownership grows amongst the middle classes from the mid-1980s
- The advent of the World Wide Web and 'multimedia' capability in the mid-1990s heralds the era of 'new media'

- Domestic computer ownership and Internet connection becomes common across all social classes in developed countries during the 2000s
- In the 2010s, the personal handheld computer is an everyday accessory, along with a wide range of specialized digital devices

The New Media Age

By the 1990s, everything was in place for the next phase of 'informationalization'. A gigantic apparatus of cheap offshore manufacture was being constructed (mostly in Asia), there was a commercial standard in operating software (primarily via Microsoft's Windows platform) and there was an unprecedented boom in telecommunications (brought about by high-speed 'fibre-optics' and privatization). There were also boots on the ground, as basic operating skills became widespread and the personal computer became a fixture of everyday life in most developed societies. What brought all of these things together in a powerful new configuration was the development of the hypertext transfer protocol (http) by British computer scientist Tim Berners-Lee. Working at the European Organization for Nuclear Research (CERN), Berners-Lee had been concerned with improving the efficiency of information exchange in the scientific community. From the 1980s onwards, he worked extensively on the development of the 'hypertext' envisioned by Ted Nelson and Douglas Engelbart in the United States during the late 1960s. In a hypertext, related information in one electronic document is 'linked' to relevant information in other documents, allowing the reader to click through related sequences of information. What Berners-Lee envisioned in 1989 was the creation of a standardized 'hypertext mark-up language' (HTML) and the usage of the 'Internet' system to make a universal, global hypertext system.

The 'Internet' itself is a series of telecommunication linkages between the world's major computer networks. It began with the ARPANET in the United States in 1965 (which was initially designed to allow remote and dispersed command of a nuclear war) and was subsequently extended to integrate the computer networks being developed in America's top universities. As the operators of these networks became able to talk to each other in the early 1970s, email and live 'chat' were invented. The system became international with the connection to University College London, in 1973, which collaborated with Stanford University and the US Department of Defense in developing the 'transmission control protocol' and 'Internet protocol' (TCP/IP) that provided a standard mechanism for computer networks to 'talk' to each other using the telephone system (Cerf and Kahn 1974). Between 1975 and 1984, a number of large-scale networks were developed for civilian applications (TELNET, USENET and NSFNET). What effectively limited the capacity of users to work across these linkages was the lack of a software standard (both between networks and individual machines). Tim Berners-Lee's HTML provided this standard, along with his WorldWideWeb software for translating HTML into a visual display (the web 'browser') and the global address system (http:) that allowed users to easily 'visit' documents on any number of different networks and to 'browse' through information across the entire system of interlinked computer networks (the Internet). In combination with the TCP/IP telecommunications standard, this meant that anyone with a telephone connection and a 'modem' device could dial into the Internet system and start 'browsing' the web (Chandler 2005).

By choosing to put this software in the public domain, Berners-Lee also gave every user the opportunity to publish their own documents via the Internet. The impact of this was quite extraordinary, with the rapid development of a browser that could read pictures as well as text (1993) and the incorporation of a web browser into the predominant Windows operating system (1995). Within the space of five years, this experimental global hypertext system was being used by millions of people to both read and publish materials that could be accessed by computer terminals all over the world. The impact of this was seen as being so significant that a 'second media age' (Poster 1995) was proclaimed, the age of 'New Media' (Flew 2002; Giddings and Lister 2011). In many respects, this was not entirely true, because few of the technologies that were used in the World Wide Web were actually new. Rather, this was a new configuration of technologies. Similarly, most of the materials that people were accessing over the Internet were digital renditions of existing media of communication: text, photographs, video, telephone calls. What was entirely new was the sensory experience of using the Internet, since materials in a range of audiovisual formats became accessible in an 'interactive' digital state where their sequence of occurrence (via hyperlinks) and their form (the data itself) could be readily altered by the user (Negroponte 1995). Even more significant was the fact that the World Wide Web was not simply a medium of reception (for reading). It was also a system for communication between individuals, making it an entirely new form of social network (Scott and Carrington 2011). Equally astounding was the sheer scale of the World Wide Web, since the Internet gave it global reach, and the number of users grew exponentially to include a third of the world's population, some 2 billion people, in 2011.

The internet is above all a decentralized communication system. As with the telephone network, anyone hooked up to the internet may initiate a call, send a message that he or she has composed to one or multiple recipients and receive messages in return. The internet is also decentralized at the basic level of organization since, as a network of networks, new networks can be added so long as they conform to certain communications protocols . . . [it is] fascinating that this unique structure should emerge from a confluence of cultural communities which appear to have little in common: the Cold War Defense Department, which sought to insure survival against nuclear attack by promoting decentralization; the counter-cultural ethos of computer programming engineers, which showed a deep distaste for all forms of censorship or active restraint, and the world of university research . . . Added to this is a technological stratum of digital electronics which unifies all symbolic forms in a single system of codes . . . If the technological structure of the internet institutes costless reproduction, instantaneous dissemination and radical decentralization, what might be its effects upon the society, the culture and the political institutions?

Mark Poster 'Cyber Democracy – Internet and the Public Sphere', in D. Porter (ed.) (1997) *Internet Culture*, London and New York: Routledge, pp. 201–17

In the social sciences, the Internet is generally seen as intrinsically different from earlier 'mass media' technologies primarily because of its individualized interface and its decentred structure (see Cavanagh 2007; Fuchs 2008). Since the Web is a mediated social network, it has also been seen as heralding an era of entirely new social relationships, between individuals, between groups, between humans and machines, and between citizens and states. In the commercial domain, the aesthetics of the World Wide Web have been characterized by the predominance of popular culture modelled on the earlier mediums of print, television and computer games. Thus, having proclaimed the era of 'new media', a large number of 'old media' concerns have made extensive use of the system for delivering entertainment, providing information and communication services and promoting home shopping. The blank page of the 'electronic frontier' during the 1990s also inspired a vast array of entrepreneurial schemes to exploit this public system, making the Internet economy big enough to cause a global stock-market bubble that collapsed in 2000. The incipient era of 'new media', then, was primarily a gold rush, but the Internet itself has proved to be an enduring system. It is indisputable that the Internet has popularized computerized entertainment, dispersed unprecedented amounts of information amongst the (global) general public and created entirely new forms of sociability. The Internet and Web therefore constitute the major architectures behind contemporary personal computing.

The era of new media ran in parallel with the era of 'globalization' from 1991 to 2007, to which it contributed in important ways (Appadurai 1996; Giddens 1999). In 1991, the year in which the first web browser was released, the communist system in the Soviet Union collapsed spectacularly and the Cold War came to a close. There were many contributing factors, but it is worth noting that as effective as the Soviet system had been in collecting and collating information, its inherent paranoia and secrecy meant that the dispersal of information across society was unthinkable. As such, there was no information revolution, no cultural revolution and no distributed computing in the Soviet system. The USSR failed to make its heavy industries efficient or to create a self-sustaining market and its economic system subsequently collapsed, leaving a social and political vacuum. As a consequence of this collapse, the markets of the communist bloc were suddenly opened up to the Western capitalist economies. Capitalism itself was reinvigorated by the automation of its trading activities and rapidly re-established itself as a singular global system. Light-speed exchanges of vast volumes of capital and information across the world via the Internet, driven in large part by computer algorithms, came to define a post-communist world. Simultaneously, the dispersal of cultural forms to every corner of the globe, and the capacity of private citizens to communicate with their counterparts around the world, threatened to break down the national barriers of earlier media systems and appeared to suggest the emergence of a singular global culture characterized by connectivity, accumulation and consumption (Featherstone 1990).

Manuel Castells and the Network Society

Like any other era that has come and gone before, the era of new media has brought into being a language of its own (Hale 2006). We could easily fill a whole lexicon with these new words (if not an entire Memex) – some denote names of things, some summarize new concepts or proclaim new problems, and some facilitate new codes of communication and new ways of talking to each other. We will encounter many of these terms throughout the course of this book, focusing primarily on those that have already become common in everyday life. Many of the more technical terms will thus remain confined to classes for computer specialists (the so-called 'technorati'). In a large part, however, many of you will be familiar with a lot of these words, despite the fact that many of them didn't exist in the popular vocabulary ten years ago, and almost none of them existed twenty years ago. From a sociological perspective, there is more to the predominant language of networked computing than technical aptitude or cultural typology, since its arrival encourages us to think about the social world in particular ways (Van Dijk 2006). Manuel Castells, for example, is best known for his use of terminologies drawn from the era of mass computing in describing the role played by information technologies (1996). For this reason, the theoretical work of Castells provides a synergy for systematically establishing media and communications techniques as a force for social change at a number of levels.

Manuel Castells claimed that the impact of information network technologies upon human societies is so great that we now need to think of economic relations, nation-states and communities themselves taking the forms of networks. Hence, he claimed that we now living in a 'network society' (1996). The term 'network' provides an established metaphor for an entity comprised of connections between different points. It became central to mass communications and distributed computing because the connections between a large number of terminals can be mapped out as a graphical representation of the network, forming a spider-web pattern. In distributed computing, the network metaphor is augmented with the language of hydraulics, where the connecting cables are denoted as 'pipes' through which information 'flows', much like water, between different points in the network. The term 'node' is also used to describe any information-processing device that is connected to the network (a computer or file-server). Data thus traverses the network in flows that move between nodes. Thus, if society is to be described as a network (as Castells suggests), then it must be seen as being structured by dense interconnections between many different points, or nodes. For Castells, the nodes in the network society are the real or virtual places where information flows converge. The flows in the network society are comprised of channels of communication, financial data exchanges and increasing human mobility.

What is the Network Society? It is a society that is structured in its dominant functions and processes around networks. In its current manifestation it is a capitalist society . . . The Network Society is not produced by information technology. But without the Information Technology Revolution it could not be such a comprehensive social form, able to link up, or de-link, the entire realm of human activity . . . it resulted from the historical convergence of three independent processes, from whose interaction emerged the Network Society:

- The Information Technology Revolution, constituted as a paradigm in the 1970s
- The restructuring of capitalism and of statism in the 1980s, aimed at superseding their contradictions, with sharply different outcomes
- The cultural social movements of the 1960s, and their 1970s aftermath (particularly feminism and ecologism).

Manuel Castells (2002), 'An Introduction to the Information Age', in G. Bridge and S. Watson (eds) *The Blackwell City Reader*, Oxford: Blackwell, pp. 40–8

According to Castells, information exchanges now constitute the production of wealth, enable debate, manage populations and shape personal relations – all through the structural mechanism of the network society. In the process, vast quantities of information, wealth and people are recombined and redirected within the space of flows. A network society is a radically decentred social system where connectivity is everything. According to Castells, information technologies are removing the vestiges of Fordism and industrial conflict, and replacing manual labour and the 'organization man' with information work and the 'flexible woman'. The network society is a technologically functional political economy that is global in scale. It is not a utopia, since it is marked by new forms of division, being inhabited by expendable 'knowledge' workers (the networked), the information poor (soon to be jobless), and the networkers (a mobile, transient elite who inhabit the world of information flows). To exist within the network society is to be subject to ever-increasing pressures of mobility, ever-increasing volumes of information exchange and constantly shifting patterns of connectivity. To remain outside of these communication networks is to be excluded from the new social order, with information poverty quickly leading to social isolation and material destitution. Individual agency can only be achieved through the capacity to manage information, foster connections and manage the direction of communications. It is within these practices that the social world is being reconfigured. Castells concludes, therefore, that a reterritorialization of human relations has taken place in the form of the global network society.

Box 1.3 Characteristics of a network society

- **Digitization** – knowledge and meaning are 'informationalized' via binary code
- **Connectivity** – the capacity to transmit and receive information becomes a prerequisite for social participation
- **Nodes** – are represented by 'informational cities' where communication linkages and knowledge specialists are concentrated
- **Flows** – are social actions determined by the transfer of information and information workers between nodes
- **Power** – is de-centralized and diffused across the network
- **Space** – is reconfigured by the network structure, producing hot spots of connectivity and dark areas of information poverty where connectivity is poor or absent
- **Culture** – the network gives rise to its own symbolic codes of cultural expression through which democratic politics are contested

---

Living in a Digital Society

The metaphors of the 'information society' and the 'network society' are important because they point to the meeting point between technical ambitions and sociological understanding. They are closely related, but there are also some important differences between the two. Notably, the information society metaphor points us towards the content of the computer process whilst the network metaphor emphasizes its technical structure. Human beings are also situated quite differently in the two models. In an information society people come to be seen as biological computers. In a network society they come to be seen as somehow equivalent with data. In both respects, the two metaphors extend the logics of the machine society that preceded them, even as they simultaneously disavow the industrial society and the social theories that appeared equally compelling in that period. In that sense, we could see the two formulations as having an evolutionary relationship. The information society extends the industrial logic of 'Fordism'. The network society seeks to describe social structures in a post-Fordist era. The information society describes the push towards computerized automation and the network society grapples with its consequences. In our broad historical overview of modern computing, we can also see that the initial development of computerization was grounded in the intense competition between states, whereas in the world of today, information technology is characterized by 'collaborative competition' between global corporations. This is evidence of social change on a grand scale. It is important, therefore, that both theoretical propositions are overwhelmingly capitalist in perspective and economic in function. This is an area that I will return to in greater detail later in this work.

For now, it is equally important to note that the cultural dimensions of social life remain somewhat cursory in information society theory, but come to constitute a large part of the network society. Thus, we can also identify a more subtle, subjective, shift from a paternalistic and institutionalized worldview to a pervasive grassroots populism marked by new cultural, political and commercial forms of liberalism. This also reflects the 'cultural turn' in sociology that has, to a significant degree, been imposed by the electronic mass media. Certainly, there can be few technologies that have been so prevalent within popular culture as the computer (aside from the car). For half a century, the computer has symbolized ultra-modernity and the power of science as much as it has symbolized human anxiety, dependence and even obsolescence. As these technologies have moved steadily from the pages of science-fiction magazines into Hollywood scripts and eventually into our homes and into our pockets, the thing which they still most seem to symbolize is 'newness'. Computers, it seems, will always be in fashion. Images will always be seductive and talk always plentiful. How could the media not dominate in such a society? Certainly, computers have been destined to play a major role in our lives since before we were born. Digitization has already done much to ensure that the ways in which we study and play, in which we work (or avoid work) are markedly different from the experiences of the generations that have preceded us. Our social world has already become saturated with digital devices and the new social practices that surround them. For many of us, without any single causal explanation, this defines our experience of living in a digital society.

Think and Discuss

1. Key Terms
Can you describe in simple language what is meant by the following terms found in this chapter?

- Information society
- Algorithm
- New media
- Network society
- Internet

2. Critical Questions
Try answering the following questions, drawing upon your own understanding, experience and knowledge.

1. In what ways does computerization seek to improve the efficiency of human activity?
2. To what extent does the Internet personalize your usage of information?
3. What is the difference between data and knowledge?
4. How many terms can you think of that are derived from computing technology and now commonly used in everyday life?
5. How critical is digital connectivity in the conduct of your daily affairs?

Further Reading

Castells, Manuel (1996) *The Information Age: Economy, Society and Culture, Vol. I: The Rise of the Network Society*, Cambridge, MA, and Oxford: Blackwell.

Chandler, Alfred D. (2005) *Inventing the Electronic Century*, Cambridge, MA: Harvard University Press.

Gates, Bill (1995) *The Road Ahead*, Harlow: Pearson Education.

Hassan, Robert (2008) *The Information Society*, Cambridge: Polity.

Masuda, Yoneji (1990) *Managing the Information Society: Releasing Synergy Japanese Style*, Oxford: Blackwell.

Negroponte, Nicholas (1995) *Being Digital*, Rydalmere: Hodder and Stoughton.

Poster, Mark (1995) *The Second Media Age*, Cambridge: Polity.

Van Dijk, Jan (2006) *The Network Society: Social Aspects of New Media*, London: Sage.

Webster, Frank (2006) *Theories of the Information Society*, London and New York: Routledge.

Go Online

Bill Gates – http://www.microsoft.com/presspass/exec/billg/
Hobbes Internet Timeline – http://www.zakon.org/robert/internet/timeline/
The Information Society (journal) – http://www.tandfonline.com/loi/utis20
Intel Archives – http://www.intel.com/about/companyinfo/museum/archives/timeline.htm
MIT MediaLab – http://www.media.mit.edu/research
The Turing Archive – http://www.alanturing.net/
WorldWideWeb Consortium – http://www.w3.org/

CHAPTER 2

The Socio-technical Interface

As we have seen, the conceptual evolution of digital media and social change interacts with a rich and complex historical tapestry that blends the fantastic and the bureaucratic, the philosophical and the technical, the idealistic and the instrumental. In order to make sense of the multifaceted nature of the socio-technical interface that lies at the heart of digital society, we must carefully consider the intrinsic relationship between the technical apparatus and the wider social structures produced by collective human actions. To put that more simply, we need to understand how computer systems relate to human systems and vice versa. Putting things simply does not, of course, imply that easy explanations are close at hand. The nature of this particular socio-technical interface is highly complex and, as a result, the vast amount of information available to us provides support for very different forms of argument about human–machine relationships. We should not be surprised by this. The competing claims of natural science and human ingenuity represent a central challenge for any serious attempt to understand a technologically advanced society. Nonetheless, the broad parameters of the debate are within our reach, and we should make a modest start by recognizing the most influential contemporary accounts of the effective relationship between technology and society. We can then, in each and every encounter with the digital, consider the relevance of those arguments to a critical understanding of contemporary society and the 'rise of the machines'.

Technological Determinism

The very term 'digital society' is far from neutral, since it implies that it makes sense for us to begin with the technology. Starting with the first word appears to be self-evident 'common sense' (that is, until we stop to consider the arbitrary logics that structure the order of words and the naming of things). Of itself, digital technology has no innate preference for reading left to right (or top to bottom). Similarly, our starting point in this debate appears natural enough, but it is in fact arbitrary. That is, we will start with the technology because we must start somewhere, not because it makes any more or less sense than starting with the human dimension. You might wonder why I am trying so hard to muddy the water at this early stage. There are two vitally important reasons for me to emphasize the significance of our starting point in this chapter. One reason is that the conventions of the written word tend to imply that the final argument considered is the right one, and that will not necessarily be the case here. The other reason is that in order to make sense of this discussion, I need to try and step outside one of the most widely accepted ideas in modern history: the inevitability of scientific progress. In order to make this work effectively, you will have to grant me a measure of creative licence. First of all, you must pretend not to notice that my communication with you is technologically dependent, and second, you must temporarily assume that I am not, as a human being, inherently biased towards the importance of my own species.

With these objective caveats in place, I can now pose a fundamental question: what does technology actually do to society? By asking this, I mean more specifically: how does the use of a technology affect our capacity to do things and, in changing our capacity, how does the use of a technology change our social behaviours and our worldview? Your answer to this line of questioning may well be: 'That would depend upon the nature of the technology'. This is an eminently reasonable answer. It is also a symptom of a widespread general understanding of the world that is known as 'technological determinism'. Technological determinism in its strongest form is the belief that the social history of humanity has been driven first and foremost by technological developments. In the first place, this presents the events of the past as symptomatic of the impact of a series of advances, starting with the mastery of fire, pottery, metallurgy and the wheel in ancient times. From this perspective, the modern world emerges through a series of technological transformations unleashed by the Industrial Revolution, the atomic age and, right now, the binary computer. Technological determinism therefore claims that societies in the present are overwhelmingly shaped through their applied sciences. Logically, it follows that our future will be determined by the impact of further technological advances.

Marshall McLuhan on Media

One of the best-known theoretical accounts of modern media associated with a technologically determined viewpoint is the body of work produced during the 1960s by Canadian scholar Marshall McLuhan. McLuhan's central thesis was outlined in his book *Understanding Media: The Extensions of Man* (1964). It is here that most of the ideas for which he became famous are explained. Some of those ideas were published previously in the *Gutenberg Galaxy* (1962), and others were subsequently turned into a pop culture format in the best-selling *The Medium is the Message* (1967), composed in text, image and sound. *Understanding Media* was strongly influenced by Harold Innis's earlier works on communication technologies (1951, 1952) as a driving force in producing social change, as well as by Walter Ong's (1982) work on the significance of the shift from oral to textual communication in ancient times. McLuhan brought these ideas together at precisely the time that the (then) new medium of television was taking off, making the mass media a major focus of sociological inquiry. For this reason, McLuhan can be firmly located in the post-war traditions of anglophone scholarship.

McLuhan, however, was also intent on popularizing his ideas about the electronic media that were growing exponentially in Western societies at the time he was writing. His books were printed in popular editions, and he appeared on the covers of magazines like *Forbes*, gave interviews in *Playboy*, recorded a long-playing record and did cameos in cinematic features, along with numerous television appearances. McLuhan was, in that sense, a fully fledged 1960s 'media guru'. He deployed many of the catchphrases that have since become everyday references to the phenomenon of a mediated society in the era that we now live; although most of the nuances of McLuhan's arguments have been lost in the recital of his most famous aphorisms. For precisely this reason, Marshall McLuhan remains one of the most influential and controversial figures in debates on media technology.

McLuhan's popular touch was something which drew admiration from the younger generation of his day, but it also brought reproach from other scholars in the field who found his work variously apolitical, rhetorical, faddish and simplistic. McLuhan's work was at the height of its influence during the late 1960s, was generally discredited during the mid-1970s and then underwent a major revival with the coming of the Internet in the 1990s. This particular medium seemed to fit his theories of the media even better than the prevalent media of his own times. Accordingly, McLuhan's account of the media has enjoyed a major revival in the era of digital media, and he has become revered by the technologically minded as a 'prophet' of the electronic age (Levinson 1999).

Medium as Message

McLuhan believed that the major social effect of all media was the extension of our physical senses by technological means. Print media, for example, extended our capacity of speech. Photography and cinema extended our capacity of vision. Radio and the phonograph extended our capacity of hearing. In providing humanity with these sensory extensions, the media apparatus radically transforms both the scale of human society and our perceptions of that society. Simultaneously, it transforms our perceptions of ourselves and of each other. According to McLuhan's logic, any technology that extends the human senses can be considered a medium. As an extension of humanity, a media technology functions as a conduit for human activity. A media, in McLuhan's sense of the term, inevitably transforms (mediates) the way that sensory actions are performed in society. As such, the real significance of a communications technology is not found in the content that the technology is used to transmit, but rather in the new ways of speaking, reading and thinking that are made possible by the feat of transmission itself. This, according to McLuhan, is the true message of a medium, as expressed by its capacity to transform human affairs.

In a culture like ours, long accustomed to splitting and dividing all things as a means of control, it is sometimes a bit of a shock to be reminded that, in operational and practical fact, the medium is the message. This is merely to say that the personal and social consequences of any medium – that is, of any extension of ourselves – result from the scale that is introduced into our affairs by each extension of ourselves.

Our conventional response to all media, namely that it is how they are used that counts, is the numb stance of the technological idiot. For the 'content' is like the juicy piece of meat carried by the burglar to distract the watchdog of the mind. The effect of the medium is made strong and intense just because it is given another medium as 'content'. The content of a movie is a novel or a play or an opera. The effect of the movie form is not related to its program content. The 'content' of writing is speech, but the reader is almost entirely unaware either of print or of speech.

Marshall McLuhan (1964), *Understanding Media: The Extensions of Man*, New York: McGraw Hill, pp. 7–8

Whether the light is being used for brain surgery or night baseball is a matter of indifference. It could be argued that these activities are in some way the 'content' of the electric light, since they could not exist without the electric light. This fact merely underlines the point that the media are the message because it is the medium that shapes and controls the scale and form of human association and action. The content or uses of such media are as diverse as they are ineffectual in shaping the form of human association and action.

Ibid.: pp. 8–9

In order to illustrate this point effectively, McLuhan draws on the example of electric light (1964). Electric light has extended our sensory abilities by allowing us to see in the dark. In doing so, electric light has allowed human beings to turn night into day for the past century. This new capability has radically altered the rhythms of human life everywhere that is reached by electric current. The practical significance of this sensory extension is to be found in the new forms of human activity that have become possible, such as working or driving through the night. However, it is the annihilation of darkness that is the real message of this particular medium, not what we choose to do under electric lights at any given time.

If we apply this logic to the digital technology of the present, we might argue that the capacity to communicate with anyone in the world via the Internet is the real significance of email. Who we choose to speak to in any one instance, and what we have to say, is of much less importance than having the capacity to do so in the first place. Access to a global digital communication system inevitably transforms the scale of human social interaction and, for McLuhan, this would be the real message of the medium. Similarly, the capacity to retrieve information from an endless store of constantly updated knowledge is much more important than what we actually choose to read at any time. Following McLuhan's lead, we can therefore argue that the real message of the World Wide Web lies in its capacity to extend human sight, speech and memory to an exponential degree. It is this capacity-building which makes the Internet a media technology, not the fact that you can use it to wish me a happy birthday or read the news online.

Media Hot and Cold: The Interactive Dimension

According to McLuhan, each media shapes the human sensory experience through its particular technological form. In this sense, McLuhan did much to popularize the term 'media' as a way of referring to what in his day were previously seen as distinct practices of communication (press, cinema, television, radio), but he also consistently emphasized the particular qualities of each media – highlighting their technical differences and their distinctive effects. In *Understanding Media*, McLuhan made a distinction between different forms of media according to a metaphorical understanding of their interactive 'temperature'. For McLuhan a 'hot medium' is a technology whose message is linear, sequential and strictly controlled. By contrast, a 'cool medium' is one that favours participation, is multivocal and open-ended.

There is a basic principle that distinguishes a hot medium like radio from a cool one like the telephone, or a hot medium like the movie from a cool one like TV. A hot medium is one that extends one single sense in 'high definition'. High definition is the state of being well filled with data. A photograph is, visually, high definition. A cartoon is 'low definition', simply because very little visual

> information is provided. Telephone is a cool medium, or one of low definition, because so little is given and so much has to be filled in by the listener. On the other hand, hot media do not leave so much to be filled in or completed by the audience. Hot media are, therefore, low in participation, and cool media are high in participation or completion by the audience. Naturally, therefore, a hot medium like radio has very different effects on the user from a cool medium like the telephone.
>
> Marshall McLuhan (1964), *Understanding Media: The Extensions of Man*, New York: McGraw Hill, pp. 22–3

For McLuhan, media like radio, cinema and print can be considered 'hot' because their appreciation requires intense concentration by the audience. The audience is never left to 'fill in the blanks' or allowed to participate in their function. These are media technologies that require specialists to operate them and, in turn, favour a specialized understanding. By contrast, 'cool' media like telephones and television are not seen to require intense concentration by the audience. The audience is free to take breaks, to 'fill in the blanks' and to participate actively in their narrative function. Cool media do not require a specialized understanding to operate; nor do they require a high degree of media literacy to enjoy. McLuhan also drew parallel distinctions between hot and cool forms of behaviour, personalities and cultures. McLuhan believed that the social effect of the media was often determined by the interplay of hot and cool factors that surrounded its use in society. He believed that a hot medium might 'strike terror' in a cool society, whilst a cool medium would likely appear banal to members of a 'hot culture'. McLuhan suggested that a hot medium in a hot culture produced a 'hypnotic effect', whilst a cool medium in a cool society produced a 'state of hallucination'. He subsequently claimed that social order could be maintained by employing media technologies to balance hot and cold sensory effects (2001: 28).

In order to make sense of these statements, we need to recognize that throughout all his works, McLuhan remained committed to a single historical framework by which the Western world was seen to have progressed from a cool oral culture through a hot print society into a rapidly cooling electronic age. That is, McLuhan considered that the social imagination was essentially shaped by spoken communication before the advent of print technology. With the spread of the printed word, however, human beings developed a new relationship to knowledge and to each other. This was the birth of a 'hot' Western society – composed of rational, logical and detached individuals. According to McLuhan, other parts of the world mostly remained within an earlier 'cool' stage of development, where spoken forms of communication shaped a more collective, intuitive and emotive mentality. At the time he was writing, McLuhan believed that the new electronic media were essentially interactive and intuitive 'cool' systems that would encourage greater participation and interchange amongst their users. As such, he believed the new media would shift the Western world back into a 'cool' state.

The Global Village: Interconnectivity, Utopia and Conflict

In 1962, McLuhan coined the phrase 'the global village' in his book *The Gutenberg Galaxy*. He used this phrase to refer to the advanced stage of connectivity that the world had reached through modern technologies. He returned to this theme in *War and Peace in the Global Village* in 1968, where he elaborated (again in a graphically illustrated exposition of his ideas) on the media 'highway' that now ran through the remotest corners of the world, linking humanity in a 'global village' where everything was within earshot via one medium or another. This concept, of the increasing density of global communication intensifying connectivity and negating the significance of distance, was subsequently seen as being exemplified by the rise of computer networking (Giddens 2002: 11). The 'global village' thus became a celebrated phrase during the information technology boom of the 1990s.

McLuhan, by contrast, did not see worldwide media systems in entirely glowing terms. Greater connectivity between individuals, nations and societies inevitably favours the utopian proposition of a neighbourly world, or a 'brotherhood of man'. Nonetheless, McLuhan warned that the advent of the global village had also unleashed a mixture of collective sensorial phenomena with damaging effects. According to McLuhan, technology is of itself amoral and inherently neither good nor bad. Operating as an extension of man, however, technology has the capacity to enslave humanity in exactly the same way as an individual can 'fool' themselves. As such, the outcome of greater interconnectivity via the global village was the amplification of the socio-technical effects of new forms of mediated interactivity. Across the world, McLuhan saw the increased orality of cool electronic media as favouring not only the personal over the detached, but also as favouring emotive and irrational human instincts over reason. McLuhan concluded, therefore, that the contradiction of the global village was that vastly increased interconnectivity across the world was giving rise to the 're-tribalization' of human society and engendering heightened anxiety and conflict.

Despite these concerns, the notion of the 'global village' has been sustained in popular culture in its more utopian form. It was paraphrased as the 'global jukebox' in the satellite-enabled global benefit concerts, 'Live Aid', in 1985 and it has continued to be deployed in national and international policy objectives promoting media as a development spur. In the US, Democrat Vice-President Al Gore famously invoked the power of the 'information highway' in his promotion of the National Information Infrastructure (NII) initiative in 1993, and for its global extension in the Global Information Infrastructure (GII) pitch in 1994. These were both critical interventions in the popularization of the World Wide Web. The major public investments in the development of the Internet that followed were precisely intended to make good on the ideal of global connectivity by linking the socially and geographically isolated to the global repository of knowledge.

As we enter the third decade of the public Internet, however, we can also see some evidence of the more dystopian effects of connectivity (such as al-Qaeda online). Following McLuhan, we should remain attentive to the extent to which the mediation of distant events via words, sounds and images impacts upon our understanding of our place in the world, and upon public perceptions of personal safety and external threats (Giddens 1990; Beck 1999). The impending catastrophe of global climate change, for example, is only comprehensible due to the advent of the global village, and the interconnections it facilitates between natural disasters taking place across the globe. At the same time, the political battles being fought between different groups via digital media technologies are equally symptomatic of the tribalistic tendencies that emerge due to the heightened awareness of proximity between different cultures and social groups. For McLuhan, these would be human responses to the reorientation of our most basic senses via the expansion of media technologies.

McLuhan's Wake

After Marshall McLuhan died in 1980, many of his ideas were seen as belonging to the 1960s. Within two decades, however, the advent of the commercial Internet and the intellectualization of consumer electronics brought many of his ideas back into prominence. McLuhan's central tenet was that: if we wish to understand the social significance of the media, we must critically examine the cognitive effect of that technology upon human subjectivity. This remains the core of McLuhan's influence upon the sociology of media. It was in accordance with this emphasis upon the decisive role of technology in shaping social change that the technophile *Wired* magazine named McLuhan as its 'patron saint' during the 1990s. At the same time, within the equally wired academic domain, McLuhan's theories of media were being given a new lease of life as they were applied to the burgeoning realm of digital media applications, and to personal computing in particular (for example, Biro 1999; Bolter and Grusin 1999; Dery 1996; Horrocks 2000; Johnson 1997, 2001).

As a clear statement of technological determinism, McLuhan's arguments have been particularly amenable to scholars engaged in making projections on how the everyday presence of digital media will further transform modern society (Kroker and Kroker 1997; Landow 1997; Levinson 1999). McLuhan's distinctive psycho-social conceptualization of the sensory overload arising from the electronic extension of man was also forcefully taken up by 'postmodern' social theorists at the end of the twentieth century. His influence is notable in the work of Jean Baudrillard, and also contributes to the explanations of the digital media age put forward by Nicholas Negroponte, Mark Poster and Paul Virilio (Negroponte 1995; Poster 1995; Virilio 2000). Jean Baudrillard, the influential French theorist, was also attentive to McLuhan's claim that the mediating power of technology overwrites our sensory system to such an extent that rational, objective accounts of mediation are wholly ineffective, and arguably missing the point when it comes to the 'message' of the digital apparatus (1988).

In the present 'multimedia' era brought about by digitization, it has become apparent that McLuhan's earlier distinctions between the interactive 'temperature' of media forms have become hopelessly blurred. The 'hot media' of cinema, radio and the printed world are rapidly becoming forms of content within the interface of the personal computer, rather than being mediums in their own right. As such, McLuhan's observation that each media technology adapts the forms of previous media technologies for its content appears to have been validated. At the same time, McLuhan's attention to the distinctive nature of various mediums and his proposition of using a media mix to balance sensorial effects have clearly become obsolete. We can see, therefore, that the dominant idea of 'media' has moved since McLuhan's time from a plural reading of the term to something more akin to a monolithic apparatus of social communication. In contemporary society, the mass media operate as an aggregation and combination of technologies and social institutions. Therefore, in order to follow McLuhan's lead, we must approach them as a suite of interrelated technological effects: that is, as media.

The Social Shaping of Technology

Another of McLuhan's favourite sayings was that 'we shape our tools and our tools shape us'. It must be said, however, that he paid scant attention to the first component of the phrase. He had much to say about the ways in which technologies transformed the nervous system of human beings, but comparatively little to say about the role of human beings in the conception, design and implementation of those technologies. This places McLuhan at odds with a broad school of thought that has sought to emphasize the significance of human guidance over scientific development and to take note of the social imperatives that dictate the usage of particular technologies. This school of thought is broadly referred to as the 'social shaping of technology' thesis (or SST), and it brings together many different thinkers from both the sciences and the humanities (McDermott 1997; Williams 1974; Williams and Edge 1996).

The key principles of SST arise from an explicit rejection of technological determinism as a theoretical underpinning for understanding the socio-technical interface. For SST theorists, technology cannot be considered to come into being from a 'neutral' or 'pure' scientific process framed only by the inherent laws of natural science. Rather, the paths of inquiry taken by scientists and the subsequent trajectory of specific technological developments are seen as being influenced by human perspectives. Following this logic, the choices made in the sequence and application of technological innovation reflect the imperatives of human need, the ideological structures of human societies and the ambitions of the human beings who inhabit the institutions of scientific development. Consequently, SST foregrounds the argument that humans impact upon technology long before those technologies impact upon us, and do so for reasons that necessarily exceed the logics of science. Explorations of socio-technical interaction undertaken in this vein have also been attentive to the ways in which public institutions, market forces and popular demand all serve to determine how technologies are employed and accessed in their everyday usage.

Raymond Williams and Cultural Studies

In the field of media sociology, one of the most influential proponents of the SST approach was the British scholar Raymond Williams. A contemporary of McLuhan, Williams was a highly significant figure in the expanding sociology of culture during the latter half of the twentieth century. Williams wrote extensively on popular culture and on political aesthetics, paying attention to literature, advertising, film and television in a framework that was closely attuned to the historical trajectory of British society. Consequently, Williams is now widely regarded as the forefather of the inter-discipline of cultural studies, an interpretive tradition that takes the sociology of popular culture as its primary interest. During his lifetime, Williams also engaged closely with the more empirical mass communications tradition in North America, contributing *Communications* (1962) as a foundational textbook. As a counterpoint to the negative conclusions reached on post-war popular culture by the theorists of the Frankfurt School during the 1950s, Williams laid out an argument for how the institutions of mass communication could be usefully put to the service of strengthening democracy rather than undermining it.

Following this work, Williams returned to writing on literature for a decade before contributing one of his best-known studies of the media, *Television: Technology and Cultural Form* (1974). A groundbreaking work on the television medium, Williams's book cast a critical eye on the notion of 'media effect', where the content of the mass media was seen as being capable of reprogramming the social behaviour of its audiences. In the process, Williams responded critically to the popular accounts of media influence being offered by Marshall McLuhan. At one level, Williams put McLuhan's observation that 'the medium is the message' into practice by outlining the particular nature of television and ways in which that technology favoured certain structures of content (which Williams termed 'flow' and 'sequence'). At another level, Williams attacked McLuhan for his scientific mysticism and his alleged overstatement of 'technological determinism'.

Against Technological Determinism

The essence of Williams's critique of McLuhan's theory of media was grounded in a rejection of the idea that human society was shaped by the impact of technological advance, at least in ways that attributed technology with an internal logic that super-seded the importance of human inputs. Williams noted that technological determin-ism of this kind had come to operate in the modern world as 'an immensely powerful and now largely orthodox view of the nature of social change' (Williams 1974: 13). This view implied that technologies emerge from 'an essentially internal process of research and development' and subsequently determine 'the conditions for social change and progress' (ibid). With scientific advance in the driving seat, the nature of human progress becomes overwhelmingly defined by 'the history of these inventions', which are therefore seen to have 'created the modern world' (ibid). As a result, we become inclined to see social change as being dictated by the workings of technology rather than by human agency. Simultaneously, we are isolating the processes of scientific development from the rest of society, attributing them with their own unquestionable technical laws and insulating the 'inevitable' march of technological progress from moral or political questioning

The work of McLuhan was a particular culmination of an aesthetic theory that became, negatively, a social theory: a development and elaboration of formalism that can be seen in many fields . . . but which acquired its most significant popular influence in an isolating theory of 'the media'. It is an apparently sophisticated technological determinism which has the significant effect of indicating a social and cultural determinism, that is to say, which ratifies the society and culture we now have . . . For if the medium – whether print or television – is the cause, all other causes, all that men ordinar-ily see as history are at once reduced to effects. Similarly, what are elsewhere seen as effects, and as such subject to social, cultural, psychological and moral questioning, are excluded as irrelevant by comparison with the direct physiological and therefore 'psychic' effects of the media as such.

Raymond Williams (1974), *Television: Technology and Cultural Form*, London: Collins, pp. 126–7

In order that our sociological understanding of mass communications should not be reduced to a mere recording of the 'impact' of particular technological forms, Williams argued that we should continually bear in mind the development trajectory of those technologies. In doing so, it is necessary that we take note of the various actors who took part in their development and identify the intellectual objectives of the designers and patrons of the research process. Thus, in order to avoid what Williams saw as the trap of technological determinism, we have to understand where each technology comes from. In this respect, there are important confluences and divergences between scientific and sociological understandings of technology.

Scientific Problems and Social Problems

From the perspective of natural science, which has been replicated in the social sciences as positivism, technologies are derived from understanding and harnessing the power of the natural world and its inherent laws. This viewpoint is largely compatible with technological determinism, since the primary source of knowledge is seen as operating outside of human subjectivity. Taking a perspective more attuned to the pragmatic approaches of applied science, we could see the pursuit of technology as being directed towards finding solutions for problems faced by human societies. These may be new problems (such as 'peak oil') or newly apparent problems (such as 'climate change'). Equally, since technological development is also seen here as a sequential process, the impetus for new technologies also arises in the process of overcoming the limitations discovered in the application of existing technologies (such as the range of mobile phones). In this view, human needs and wants play a role in the direction of technological advance, but the technologies themselves are shaped by their own logics, that is, by what works. In general, this is the perspective most commonly replicated in the domain of information technology.

From a more sociological perspective, it is also logical to see technology as a response to a set of perceived problems. In an era of advanced mass communication, many of these problems are seen as being posed by social change rather than by natural barriers. In the interpretive tradition, the role of decision-makers in determining the nature, severity and priority of any particular problem of this kind becomes a major subjective constituent of technological development. From a materialist viewpoint, which emphasizes the politicized nature of the allocation of available resources, it is particularly important that technology emerges as a product of an institutionalized process of research and development. From this perspective, the development of all technologies is guided by the specific agendas of those who undertake and, more importantly, those who underwrite the research.

For this reason, Williams argued that we need to 'restore intention' to our understanding of technological development (1974: 14). In order to identify the problems that humanity has sought to overcome through the development of mass communications (such as scale, distance, interdependence and mobility), we need to understand how they came to be perceived as social, as well as technical, problems. Taking this route, the scope of the socio-technical interface is broadened from the arena of post-development 'effects' to include pre-development 'motivation'. In the process, the scientific domain becomes responsive to the wider patterns of social change that are guided by human dynamics. In this vein, Williams argued it was the forces which emerged from the institutionalization of capitalism in the making of modern societies (industrialization, urbanization and imperialism) that created new social conditions which, in turn, required new specialized means, and new technologies, of social communication.

Social Shaping of the Media

By the logic of SST, the forms of technological knowledge that are pursued (and the specific technical forms that subsequently emerge) are dictated to varying degrees by social forces. The form of any given society plays a major role in determining the new ways of doing things which are seen as being needed (or needing improvement) and which are, in the broadest sense, imaginable under those social conditions. Cinema, for example, can be seen as a technical practice that responded to new metropolitan social worlds and became viable as a commercial medium due to the rise of mass societies. Television, with its domestic location, can be seen as a communications technology that responded to the extension of Fordism and consumerism, and to the increasing mobility (and isolation) within society as exemplified by the nuclear family unit in the 1950s and 1960s. Because human societies are all characterized by particular structures of power in which some people rule over others, Williams was also keen to point out that the pattern of technological development is determined not simply by scientific facts or common social needs, but to a significant extent by the privileged interests within society. As he puts it: 'A need which corresponds with the priorities of the real decision-making groups will, obviously, more quickly attract the investment of resources and the official permission, approval or encouragement on which a working technology, as distinct from available technical devices, depends' (1974: 19).

Furthermore, since the world is presently configured within a system where different societies compete with each other for resources, 'We can see this clearly in the major developments of industrial production, and, significantly, in military technology' (ibid). Williams noted that all of the major developments in mass communication had arisen in the service of military and commercial operations, and that technologies lacking such potentials are frequently left to languish. Prior to the advent of a sophisticated consumer market, it was only as a by-product of these original usages that communications technologies became available to ordinary people (Standage 1998). We can also find this pattern replicated in the implementation of digital technologies, which were overtly military in their inspiration and were subsequently adapted to the needs of large commercial corporations, scientific institutions and government bureaucracies, well before they became available as a domestic medium for entertainment.

> **Box 2.1 Social shaping of digital media**
>
> Digital media technologies can be seen as being socially shaped prior to use:
>
> - Because technological research is an accountable goal-oriented practice directed by powerful interests with their own distinct objectives
> - Because advances in communications technologies are a necessary means of adapting to cumulative forces of social change
> - Because mass communication is an area of social practice where control over usage is exercised by certain interests, social conventions and legal mechanisms
> - Because the popularization of a technology in commercial societies implies design imperatives motivated by profit

Uses and Appropriations

As we can see, the primary purpose of the SST thesis is to break down the perceived separation of the scientific and social domains, laying claim to science and technology as a subject for sociological inquiry (Bloor 1991). In itself, this does not necessarily negate McLuhan's identification of the psycho-social effects of media technologies, but what it does do is insert a critical feedback loop into the socio-technical interface. This brings us more closely in alignment with the idea that 'we shape our tools and our tools shape us'.

Where SST stands in absolute opposition to McLuhan's position is in the notion that the content of media is more or less irrelevant. If the process of scientific development acts under the aegis of social forces, then we can expect the apparatus of entertainment and information to be equally subject to social dynamics. As such, media content could not be easily dismissed as entirely irrelevant to the intentions of media system designers, or to the sensory experience of media users.

Beyond a necessary focus on the origins of digital technologies, the logic of SST also compels us to ask to what extent the implementation of digital media applications has led to the identification of new usages that were unanticipated in the original purposes of design. As such, beyond the motivations of the groups that initially steered the direction of research, there is also the question of the agency that is subsequently exerted by the everyday users of digital media. This represents a further dimension of the social shaping of technology, one which takes place after the development process has been completed. It can be demonstrated empirically by the capacity of social actors to refine an application or to appropriate the technology for other purposes.

Through the popularization of digital technology for various purposes of entertainment, acquisition and interaction amongst the general public, its functional application has become responsive to needs which stem well beyond the founding interests of scientific possibility and of dominant social institutions. This reminds us that, while the mass media may 'work us over completely' (as McLuhan put it), ordinary people have consistently sought to explore the potentials of those technologies in pursuit of their own particular desires. As such, while certain technologies may have been developed, designed, produced and regulated with certain 'preferred' or fixed usages in mind, the social shaping of technology continues at the level of everyday use (Mackay and Gillespie 1992). This, in turn, produces recognizable social behaviours that have the capacity to influence future research and design, binding our understanding of the socio-technical interface into an even tighter feedback loop and breaking down any clear division between technology and society.

Box 2.2 Post-development social shaping of the Internet

- The Internet was not developed for the distribution of pornography or to promote the causes of radical or terrorist groups – but its infrastructure enables those activities
- The Internet was not developed for the perpetual surveillance of its individual users – but this is now a constituent feature of the system
- The Internet was not developed for the purpose of illegal file sharing, online shopping or orchestrating flash mobs – but its users have identified the potentials for these new forms of action

The Socio-technical Interface

The socio-technical interface can be usefully defined as the interactive process between human beings and their technical inventions analysed at a broad scale. This exchange can be seen as being a 'top-down' effect, as expressed in the strongest variants of technological determinism. Such socio-technical 'impacts' could be understood as being purely functional, or they could follow Marshall McLuhan's expression of psychosocial effects. By contrast, a 'social shaping' (SST) approach to the socio-technical interface emphasizes the human guidance of technology. This understanding could be constituted historically, as in Raymond Williams's work, or it could be conducted solely against the backdrop of present social conditions. An SST approach to digital media may choose to emphasize the guiding hand of dominant social institutions (such as government or market forces) in the development process, (acting either in concert or in contest). Alternatively, an SST approach may focus upon the post-development, or 'implementation', phase of an application. In doing so, you might choose to emphasize the shaping power of decision-makers or of the general public, or to seek to identify the meeting of the two.

In the social sciences, the SST thesis has been applied to the digital media under the heading of 'social informatics', which investigates the layers of negotiation between social actors as a framing process for technical development (Kling 1996). While there is a marked bias in social informatics towards understanding the development phase, a greater emphasis on the implementation phase can be found in studies emanating from humanities disciplines such as sociology and cultural studies (Bell 2006; Lievrouw and Livingstone 2005). Corporations that invest in commercial technical development and government agencies tasked with promoting the use of technology (such as the UK government's 'Race Online 2012' campaign) have typically adopted a 'Diffusion of Innovations' approach. This is broadly an applied science model that seeks to encourage the adoption of new technologies and to finesse applications to increase their uptake in society. Diffusion of Innovations approaches tend to be more technologically determined, although they may still seek to introduce a feedback loop into the design process (Rogers 2003). A further distinctive set of approaches has also emerged under the heading of 'Actor-Network Theory', which seeks to reconcile the competing claims made by technological determinism and SST models (Law and Hassard 1999).

All of these available approaches to understanding both the extent and the quality of the interface between technology and society are structured to some extent by the two very different viewpoints explored in this chapter through the work of Marshall McLuhan and Raymond Williams. In any sociology of mass communication, this debate becomes particularly pressing because the technology in question is not only a medium for human action, but also the primary arena of interaction, where ideas and meanings about society are produced and given expression. In the present era, the critical questions that arose with the early electronic media have been reframed by the rapid convergence of media forms and the incredibly varied applications of digital technology. As a consequence, this set of debates around the nature of the socio-technical interface will have a bearing upon all of the theories, models and topics that you will subsequently encounter in the rest of this book. Needless to say, it is crucially important that you are able to identify the competing influences of these viewpoints, and to formulate your own ideas about where you stand on this issue.

Think and Discuss

1. Key Terms
Can you describe in simple language what is meant by the following terms found in this chapter?

* Socio-technical interface
* Technological determinism
* The medium is the message
* Social shaping of technology
* Uses and appropriations

2. Critical Questions
Try answering the following questions, drawing upon your own understanding, experience and knowledge.
1. What claims have you heard about the ways in which digital media are 'transforming' society?
2. What evidence have you seen of new social behaviours influenced by digital technology?
3. To what extent do you think it is reasonable to claim that technological development is influenced by social forces?
4. To what extent do you think that the possible uses of your favourite digital devices were fixed before you bought them?
5. Can you think of any examples of people using digital media in ways that are either new, or distinctive from their original purpose?

Further Reading

Bell, David (2006) *Science, Technology and Culture*, Maidenhead: Open University Press.

Jordan, Tim (2008) *Hacking: Digital Media and Technological Determinism*, Cambridge: Polity.

Levinson, Paul (1999) *Digital McLuhan: A Guide to the Information Millennium*, London and New York: Routledge.

Lievrouw, Leah A. and Livingstone, Sonia (2005) *The Handbook of New Media: Social Shaping and Social Consequences of ICTs*, London and New Delhi: Sage.

McLuhan, Marshall (2001 edn) *Understanding Media: The Extensions of Man*, New York: Routledge.

McLuhan, Marshall and Fiore, Quentin (1968) *War and Peace in the Global Village*, New York: Bantam.

Poster, Mark (1995) *The Second Media Age*, Cambridge: Polity.

Rogers, Everett M. (2003) *Diffusion of Innovations*, New York: Free Press.

Williams, Raymond (1974) *Television: Technology and Cultural Form*, London: Collins.

Go Online

Marshall McLuhan – http://marshallmcluhan.com/
Social Informatics – http://www.social-informatics.org/
New Media and Society – http://nms.sagepub.com/
Information Technology & People – http://www.emeraldinsight.com/
Science, Technology and Society – http://sts.sagepub.com/

CHAPTER 3

Typing the User

We have begun to consider the fundamental debates that impact upon our understanding of what a digital society is. Thus far, our attention has been directed towards understanding society as a whole, often referred to as macro-sociology ('the big picture'). By contrast, this chapter will examine the socio-technical interface at the level of the individual, entering the domain of personal actions that constitutes the field of micro-sociology. Without a doubt, it is highly significant that the shorthand for the personal computer is almost always 'my computer', implying that the personal orientation of computing has become so taken for granted that we rarely stop to consider just how fundamental the 'personal' focus of the digital society is. The everyday commonality of our personal relationship to information technologies makes us forget just how recently and how extensively our lives have become organized in this way. Ask yourself: when did you as an individual become aware that you were part of a digital society? It may have been the moment that you first had a computer in your personal possession. It may have been during the period when you first had access to digital technology for your own usage. It might, instead, have been many years after these events that you first began to critically consider the significance of those encounters. Nonetheless, these first moments of engagement with information technologies were, are and will be moments when something happens to us as human beings. We are not born as, but instead become, computer users.

Defining a User

In the twentieth century, the word 'user' is one of the most common denotations of human activity. High-street consumers are 'end-users' to the designers of kitchen appliances, people suffering from chronic addictions are 'drug users' to therapists and legal enforcers, and citizens are rapidly becoming rebranded as 'users' of services provided or facilitated by governments. As widely as the metaphor has spread, it retains the commonality of denoting *the interaction with or consumption of goods or services for a specific intended purpose at the end of a design trajectory*. It is a very complicated term, then, since it implies that the actions of the user must be both purposeful and anticipated by the designers of the artefact or process. In that sense, the origins of the term 'end-user' in the systematic language of product designers, and designers of information technology in particular, is highly apparent.

Like previous media forms, digital technologies have generated a whole range of new things to do and new ways of doing them. The development of the new media around a one-to-one relationship between isolated individuals on single-user terminals presented a new challenge for interface designers and content developers: how to design a standard interface for a highly variable audience of one. Beyond the individuation of use, the inherent interactivity of the digital media meant that the reception of information was just one part of the equation. The ability of the end-user to manipulate the information flow and contribute to it added a further layer of complexity to the process of designing digital media platforms for a mass public. The need for a much more detailed behavioural understanding of information handling and processing quickly became apparent. Nonetheless, the need to accommodate widely divergent usages, motivations and approaches had to be balanced with the simple fact that mass communications systems only operate successfully with the imposition of a standard form. For that reason, one of the most fundamental challenges for information technology designers during the twentieth century was to encapsulate human diversity in one functionally plausible cognitive model – the 'user' (Sears and Jacko 2007).

Sherry Turkle and the Perfect Mirror

The sheer diversity of human communication means that it is highly improbable that even the best design team can successfully anticipate all possible variations of user inputs in any given application or system. That is why the phrase 'user error' is inevitably part of our everyday experience of digital technology. At the same time, the fact that incompatibilities between user inputs and algorithmic logic are expressed as 'user errors' is indicative of a complex power relationship that structures the way that human–computer interaction (or HCI) is understood from a design perspective. That is, real human users do things that are unanticipated, and therefore wrong (Rose 2003). Apart from a tendency to casually violate the logical integrity of a system, real human users are also driven by emotional tendencies that are antithetical to the tidy logics of programming. In her classic ethnographic research into the behaviour of computer users during the 1980s, Sherry Turkle witnessed not only fascination and pleasure but also a great deal of rage and frustration being engendered in the encounter between computers and their users. Turkle theorized that this occurred because computers show up too many of our own limitations.

> Itself seemingly perfect, the computer evokes anxiety about one's own perfectibility. There is pressure from a machine that leaves no one and no other thing to blame. It is hard to walk away from the perfect mirror, from the perfect test. It is hard to walk away from a video game on which you could do better next time, it is hard to walk away from a computer program with an undiscovered 'bug', it is hard to walk away from an unproofed text on the screen of a word processor. Any computer promises you that if you do it right, it will do it right and right away. People who try out video games and say they hate them, or who actively dislike their first experience with computer programming, are often responding to this same promise. Not everyone wants to be around the perfect mirror.
>
> Sherry Turkle (2005) 'Video Games and Computer Holding Power', in *The Second Self: Computers and the Human Spirit*, Cambridge, MA: MIT Press, pp. 65–90

At one level, Turkle's conclusion reminds us of that key disjuncture between human computer users (who operate intuitively and suffer from emotional fragilities like anxiety) and information systems (that simply process correct inputs and reject incorrect ones). At a deeper level, Turkle's argument is also indicative of the respect paid to automated information functions at the expense of human capacities. Turkle's confidence in the 'perfect' function of computers extends to the assertion here that even system 'bugs' are the product of human fallibilities rather than a system deficiency. There is some truth in this. After all, it was most likely a human programmer who made the original 'mistake' being reproduced by digital technology as a 'bug'. What we also have to remember is the original purpose of these machines. Modern computers were initially designed for solving mathematical problems, and their inherently problem-solving rationale has been reproduced in their subsequent usages. It is for this reason that most computer games, to take Turkle's example, are presented to us in the form of a problem to be attempted. For some personality types, problems of logic are perceived as an intellectual challenge with emotional rewards. For others, the same problems are experienced as inexplicable, coercive demands with little discernible purpose.

> Some people dislike what they experience as the precision, the unforgiveness of mathematics. Instead of being intrigued or reassured by the idea of there being a 'right answer' in their first arithmetic class, they found it intolerable. It was felt as a pressure, as a taunt, as a put-down. Mechanical objects (they work if you handle them right, they don't work if you handle them wrong) evoke the same anxieties. And when these people (in our culture, often women) meet the computer the problem is taken to a higher order. Here is a machine that goes beyond all others in its promise to reflect human competence. It is not always welcome. For some, its challenge may be felt as an alien contest. For others as a chance to finally test one's worth.
>
> Sherry Turkle (2005) 'Video Games and Computer Holding Power', in *The Second Self: Computers and the Human Spirit*, Cambridge, MA: MIT Press, pp. 65–90

Turkle touches upon something of fundamental importance here: not all end-users are equal in their logical capacity, and beyond that, not all end-users are psychologically inclined to favour the particular logics that operate in information technology systems. However, even if we gloss over what is clearly an indefensible gendering of technical 'incompetence', we can see evidence of a very clear example of the condescending view of human end-users that emerges from the perspective of those who possess a greater degree of technological literacy in the medium. This article of faith in the lateral perfection of technological development as a process, and a barely veiled frustration with the obvious behavioural flaws of human beings has dogged the development of human computer interfaces. It has also demarcated the power line between the computer experts and their lay public (Ensmenger 2010).

Determining Use

While Turkle's view is characteristic of one set of approaches to understanding end-users, there are a number of different points from which we might begin to conceptualize the critical human–computer relationship. In the first place, we have to decide whether to postulate from the perspective of the machine and its designers or from the perspective of the human user. Turkle, in her account, tries to do both things. On balance, however, it seems pretty clear that it is human beings, the users, who are positioned as responding to the presence of the technology. Arguably, this gives the computer (the perfect machine) the upper hand and leads to an explanation where human beings (imperfect and often illogical) either pass or fail the test of using the computer correctly (that is, in the manner in which correct usage was defined at the design stage). Drawing upon the debates covered in the previous chapter, we could certainly argue that Turkle's account is 'technologically determined'.

At first glance, it is logical that the use of a computer is defined in the first place by the design of the technology itself. The computer is intended for certain functions, such as calculation and communication, and it follows that the user will be engaged in those functions. The computer follows its own logical rules of operation, which the user needs to understand sufficiently in order to operate the machine competently. If the correct procedures are followed, the function will be successful and correct results will be obtained. Since each application of computer technology is designed to carry out a specified set of tasks, the computer user must also understand what those tasks are, or understand at least the parts of those tasks for which that user is responsible. At the most mundane level, the user needs to know how to input data correctly, and understand the anticipated output format well enough to spot anomalies or errors that would indicate an input error. If we extend this formulation from the functional to the conceptual level, we are inclined to understand that the correct manner of computer use is largely predetermined (either by hardware configurations or by the designers of the application in question). As such, correct use exists before the user becomes the user, and user behaviour has to be understood as a predetermined behaviour in which the user is instructed. User actions that transgress the anticipated input sequences represent incorrect behaviour, and therefore constitute 'misuse'.

Box 3.1 The determination of the user

We could define the fundamental approach to the computer user from a technologically determined perspective in the following statements.

1. The computer is designed to solve an information problem that is beyond human capacity.
2. The computer is designed prior to the user's encounter with it.
3. The user is anticipated in the design of the technology and its applications.
4. The user must therefore adapt to the technology by learning how to use it effectively.
5. The computer is a learning-machine and the user learns from the machine.
6. The more effective the learning process is, the more likely it is that the user will become trained for more advanced applications of the technology.

User Power

Taking the alternative 'social shaping of technology' view would inform our understanding of the computer user in a quite different way. That is, if the development of the technology is shaped by human factors beyond its own inherent technical logic, then it might well be the case that the technology can be modified for other uses that were not anticipated during its development. In this model, use is not wholly determined by design and this has very critical implications for the possibilities of the technology and for the balance of power between the designers and users of information systems. Don Norman, in his book *Psychology of Everyday Things*, argued that all designed objects have certain affordances, that is, properties which suggest certain applications and usages to human subjects: 'Affordances provide strong clues to the operations of things. Plates are for pushing. Knobs are for turning. Slots are for inserting things into. Balls are for throwing or bouncing. When affordances are taken advantage of, the user knows what to do just by looking: no picture, label or instruction is required' (Norman 1988: 9). However, such apparent possibilities for technological applications are also subject to the existing knowledge and capacities of the user. For this reason, the affordances of technologies are taken up in ways that users of varying technical literacy can understand in the context of their own lives. A user with limited, or unsuitable, technical literacy may not be able to comprehend the most significant affordances of a specialized technology. By contrast, a user with extensive technical knowledge might perceive a significant usage for a technology that was not even considered in its present design. Similarly, a user with a particular frame of social reference might detect affordances in their own social context that would not be perceived by other users.

The idea that end-users are capable of detecting design flaws through large-scale testing, and also of detecting new affordances for a technology has led to a conceptualization of 'user-centred design' (Norman and Draper 1986). This approach suggests that effective information systems develop in partnership with their users, each learning from the other, with users interacting with systems and feeding back their own suggestions for improvements in an iterative development cycle (basically, a feedback loop). More advanced approaches to understanding HCI in this way emphasize the importance of environmental considerations, and make extensive use of ethnographic methods intended to observe the behaviour of real users in genuine social environments where everyday computing takes place (Blomberg et al. 1991; Blomberg 1995). Arguably, it is the commercialization of computer technology that has encouraged the steady rise of user-centred design processes as a counterpoint to an old-fashioned system-design and training approach. Commercial designers need to understand what recreational users want to do with their systems, and then design applications which make those functions accessible and appealing to people in sufficient numbers to generate commercial returns in a competitive market. This can be seen as providing impetus for designing applications to serve a perceived consumer need that has no intrinsically technical rationale. This market-oriented approach has become characteristic of the IT economy since the 1980s, steadily entrenching the idea of the user as a consumer.

In that sense, the SST approach also requires us to take into account the power of social institutions as well as individual users. The market is one example where corporate and government entities regulate research, manufacture and exchange. In terms of actual usage, we would expect to see that certain affordances would be encouraged over others, and that there would be some sort of formal or informal regulatory regime put in place over the technology. It would be difficult to deny that a number of official and commercial institutions have succeeded in imposing their vision of how we will use our computers in both a formal and informal sense. At the same time, it has also been apparent that the digital media have proved much more difficult to regulate than earlier technologies in terms of what people have decided to do with them. This suggests a complex interplay between the power of social structures, the desires of ordinary users and the affordances of digital technology.

> **Box 3.2 Social shaping of the user**
>
> We could define the fundamental approach to the computer user from a social-shaping perspective in the following statements.
>
> 1. The computer is initially designed to perform operations perceived as socially valuable by decision-makers, including scientists.
> 2. The computer is initially deployed in the immediate interests of the most powerful social institutions.
> 3. The user interacts with the technology, identifying affordances on the basis of prior dispositions, formal learning and intuition.
> 4. The utility of computer is constantly extended and redeveloped to better suit new tasks that users wish to perform.
> 5. The more effectively computer applications are adapted to emerging user demands, the more popular information technology becomes, producing a virtuous circle of user-led development.
> 6. The achievement of critical mass in the domain of communication makes socially negative computer use a major concern for regulatory bodies.

The Evolution of the User Concept

In order to understand the evolution of the user concept, we also need to keep in mind the evolution of the computer concept. In the broadest terms, we can discern three different ideas of the human–computer relationship emerging from the scientific community between the 1950s and 1970s.

1. Computer as friendly robot (i.e., someone else).
2. Computer as extension of the intellect (i.e, an add-on to yourself).
3. Computer as interface to an interactive social network (i.e., a collective mediation with the self).

Each conception carries a different projection of use, and therefore implies users of a distinctive nature. Although generally sequential in their development, all of these three major conceptualizations of computer technology continue to influence our understanding of the relationship between computers and human beings. One of the reasons that one idea doesn't simply replace the other is that there is rarely an absolute consensus on the preferred use of a technology or the forms that it should take. Similarly, when we take a look at the ways in which the computer user has been conceptualized over the past half-century we can discern competing visions of the proper use of the technology as well as echoes of older ideas returning in latter-day models of the user. Nonetheless, there is a discernible historical process at work here as we have progressed from the theoretical ideas surrounding hypothetical users of these machines to the typologies that surround everyday users in the twenty-first century.

Stage 1: the reflexive user

In the early stages of development the computer user was a purely hypothetical construction. The term referred to someone who may perhaps employ a technology that at the present stage remains undeveloped, and who would use it for a broad range of unspecified tasks some time in the future. This hypothetical user is nonetheless imagined as having an identified need, or a potential application, for a machine offering a power of calculation much greater than the user's own. At this early stage, a wider need was already perceived for an information management machine that could extend the capacity to record, process and implement a hitherto inconceivable quantity of detail (Bush 1945). In this latter sense, what we can call the *reflexive user* is the imaginary human counterpart serving the intended purpose of the technology in the minds of its designers. This wholly imaginary person remains a constant presence in the minds of the designers throughout the development process.

By reflexive user we mean here the conceptual user resulting from the thought process of the designer antedating the potential use of his or her design. This anticipation is made possible by a set of representations understood both as cognitive practices creating an image of the user (a mental representation), and as political practices, a sketch of a strategic plan aimed at allowing the designer to speak and act in place of this user to be. In this strategic perspective, the reflexive user is a powerful construct, progressively shaped and transformed in order to ensure the designer's control in the process of realization of the user. But at the same time, as a cognitive construct, the reflexive user is a highly unstable, bound to eventually disappear and to be actualized in a separate living entity, the real user.

Bardini, T. and Horvath, A. (1995) 'The Social Construction of the Personal Computer User', *Journal of Communication*, 45(3): 40–66

Stage 2: the intellectual worker

Douglas Engelbart at the Stanford Research Institute in the United States promoted the idea of 'bootstrapping' during the 1960s, describing a process by which the learning cycle between designers and the machines that they were creating led to the improvement of both parties. Engelbart's goal was less the development of the computer per se, but rather the augmentation of the human intellect, a much more ambitious project for which computers were seen as a useful tool (Engelbart 1963). Engelbart saw the relationship between a computer and its users as one of 'co-evolution' and mutual improvement. This relationship of use was a mutually reinforcing learning process with machines and users playing an equal and complementary role. Engelbart defined the computer operator as an 'intellectual worker', a phrase that was later modified to 'knowledge worker' because the word 'intellectual' was perceived as having leftist overtones. In practice, the intellectual/knowledge worker was more or less explicitly a system designer seen as working in a 'pure' research environment (Bardini 2000). Similarly, J. R. Licklider famously compared a computer to a mechanical colleague (1960).

Stage 3: the programmer

Since the computer user would be required to learn the protocols of the technology in order to operate it correctly, it was obvious that they would need to understand the language of the technology. During the 1970s, it was not possible to use computers without knowledge of the specialized 'programming' languages that directed the operations of the various machines. As such, the potential knowledge worker required an extensive new literacy in order to carry out even the most basic tasks. Those who attained this goal constituted a new kind of professional, the computer 'programmer'. Since these skills were rare and in demand from the corporations that were seeking to invest in the new machines, computer programmers represented a new elite occupational class (Ensmenger 2010). The programmer was an expert operator who had acquired the language of a new specialist occupation.

Stage 4: the hacker

The advent of the microcomputer during the 1970s brought about a radical transformation in the accessibility of computing. Young computer technicians were quick to realize that the microcomputer would eventually mean that the world of large labs and their programmers would soon be augmented, or even replaced, by an army of 'personal computer' users. As Bill Gates, drawing on Alan Kay, famously put it, 'A computer on every desk and in every home'. Obviously, such a move necessitated new methods of operating computers that could be mastered by the amateur enthusiast. At the outset, the shift to the microcomputer was resisted by the established computer elite, and its development was largely undertaken by a new generation of programmers. Many of these young (mostly) men, were strongly influenced by their experiences of the so-called 'counter-culture' that flourished in the US during the late 1960s and early 1970s (Levy 2010). As such, the literature of the microcomputer was inflected by the language of 'radical' liberal democracy. Microcomputers were to be 'for the people' and would give them a new power over information that would lead to a more democratic society (Nelson 1974a/b). The role of the programmers, already skilled in the language of computing, was to direct their skills and their inside knowledge of the system towards building a free information society (in the first place amongst themselves). The hacker was a programmer with a radical liberal agenda.

Stage 5: the non-technical person

If the new vision of a society where computing was widespread was to be realized, then computing skills needed to be popularized and the everyday operation of the technology remodelled to make it easier for the non-technical person to master. This was not only a concern of the hackers, but also for the technicians who worked for the commercial research institutes owned by big corporations. Unlike the computer developers working in the more cloistered (in those days) world of academic research, people working in the research institutes were under pressure to develop computing into viable commercial applications. This meant that they had to consider the 'naive user' or 'non-technical person' at an early stage of development (Hiltzik 2000).

At a practical level, this meant redesigning the software to allow a non-programmer to use the machine. Thus, during the late 1970s, new operator 'graphical user interfaces' (GUIs) were developed that used lists of pre-designed functions (menus) as well as symbols that identified files, folders and other functions (icons). These could be selected by a naive user who 'clicked' on them using the 'mouse' technology (also developed by Engelbart and Bill English). Thus, for the first time, a non-programmer could use pre-written software to instruct the computer to carry out basic tasks. This kind of software (such as Apple's OS and Microsoft Windows) would become a massive commercial enterprise in the 1980s, allowing the 'non-technical' user to become a reality. From that point, the non-technical user was anyone with the inclination, and the $500 needed, to purchase one of the new mass-produced personal computer kits and follow written instructions.

Stage 6: Sally

In their new quest to understand the needs and attributes of the 'non-technical person' computer programmers needed to think about what people did in the world outside the research lab. In the first place, this entailed a quick peer round the door of the research lab: "Xerox was a commercial company, and we were thinking we'd better build these systems so the average person could use the technology . . . I think that the only model we had, again, were the people around us. Secretaries" (Bill English, *Xerox*, in Bardini and Horvath 1995). Designers working on the computer interface needed to understand what other people actually did in terms of work and how their tasks might be aided by computing. This entailed a stint of work placements for computer designers in a variety of companies where they could observe the kind of work being undertaken and the type of people doing the work. From this, they managed to identify the 'real user' in concrete terms. 'Sally' was a woman and she was an administrator.

> I felt that it was necessary to expose this collection of designers that I was hiring to real users. So they knew that Sally looked like this, talked like this, knew this kind of concept and didn't know other kinds of concepts. So all we did was develop a certain methodology where the designers were fanned out to various companies, and they would actually go and live there for a number of days, get to know the people, talk to them about what they did, come to understand their jargon, and try to abstract the concepts that they dealt with in doing whatever it is that they did.
>
> Charles Irby, (Xerox), in Thierry Bardini and August Horvath (1995), 'The Social Construction of the Computer User', *Journal of Communication*, 45(3): 56

Stage 7: computer gamers

As software (such as spreadsheets and word processing) was being developed in the late 1970s for administrative tasks in the workplace, the massive popularity of computerized games (following *Space Invaders* in 1978) amongst a whole generation of children brought software developers into direct contact with an entirely different kind of user, the child-enthusiast. Whilst the notion of the computer user as a child to be educated (or even programmed) went back as far as Alan Kay at Stanford in the 1960s, the commercialization of electronic games brought about a massive demand for computing knowledge from children who wanted to learn the ins and outs of this new technology. Ever keen to find new ways of encouraging learning, educationalists were quick to see the potential of microcomputers in the classroom and in the home (Suppes 1966). First of all, the computer could provide new ways of delivering traditional educational content. Second, but of no lesser importance, the skills being learned by children in the guise of educational games would underpin a widespread literacy in computing amongst an entire generation (Kafai 1994). The computer gamer was a child whose open mind could be more rapidly trained (even programmed) to adopt the problem-solving logics of computing.

Stage 8: networkers and the networked

As the software designed for Sally radically transformed the workplace during the 1980s, and as the first generation of digital whizz-kids grew up and joined the work-force, another dimension of human–computer interaction was coming to the fore. The desktop computer phenomenon of the 1980s made the extension of human capacity in the classroom and in the office an everyday reality. What it also did was to shift the focus of computer use from supercomputers to millions of individual workstations. The power of 'personal distributed computing', again first conceived in the late 1960s, was the interconnection of all these individual machines via a com-munication network (Goldberg 1988). This interconnection of individuals through their computers led to a new configuration of the user as a social entity as well as a productive unit. As the very nature of work becomes understood as a communica-tive and social process, the fundamental purpose of the computer workstation is to interlink with other users. The 'networker' was the technical specialist who facilitated sophisticated communications systems for transforming the organizational and logis-tical environment of the workplace. Those employees whose operational efficiency was now enhanced by, or even dependent upon, computer-mediated communication with other workers could be described as another category of user, the 'networked employee' (Castells 1996).

Stage 9: the client

The transformation of both work environments and domestic leisure activities through the expansion of information services was part of a much larger social and economic shift during the 1980s and 1990s. The diffusion of computing was an essential compo-nent of rapid economic change, as the growth of communication networks allowed the faster exchange of data and increased the speed of transactions (Hassan 2008). From the digitization of financial exchanges to the rise of teleworking and transnational 'outsourcing', the computer user was placed at the coalface of the new global economy. Computer literacy became vital for the management of business and an essential skill to maintain employability in an era where wealth was seen as being generated by informa-tion services. Accordingly, a whole new series of computer users were conceived in the era of the 'services economy'.

The impact of networked computing throughout the 1990s and 2000s was equally profound. It was the fateful merging of institutional networks with the World Wide Web in 1991 that launched the present era of hyper-connectivity. The provision of Internet access on a commercial basis to billions of new users led to a distinction between the 'server-side' architecture of the World Wide Web (run by a technical elite) and the 'client-side' (the point at which a new digital public accessed the Web). The user now became a customer or client of an Internet-service provider (ISP) that gave them access to information, whether they were shopping online, learning online or accessing crucial public services. In this sense, the conflation of the commercial and technical end-user concept was placed at the ideological centre of social change. The notion of the end-user as someone who consumes information services, as well as information about services, provided a new ideal citizen for a maturing digital society.

Stage 10: the Web surfers

As more and more workplaces were digitized, and an increasing number of employees networked, the prevalence of home computers offered an opportunity to create a fully networked society. The rapid growth of domestic subscriptions to the public Internet brought the first notions of leisure usage (outside of gaming) into being. With the advent of the web browser, the idea of 'surfing a wave' of hyperlinked information as a pleasurable activity was resurrected from McLuhan's *Gutenberg Galaxy* (1962). With the addition of images and graphics, surfing became the definitive conceptualization of Internet usage, and in its implementation constituted an entirely new form of reading (and thus, by implication, a new reader). The coming of the global Internet nonetheless raised serious media design issues for web developers. Graphical browsers, search algorithms and 'page' design had to be configured to facilitate rapid access to vast stores of data. Search mechanisms had to provide information the user was actively looking for, as well as offering relevant information that was unknown to the user. This information had to be presented visually in a form concise enough to be read straight from the screen. The navigational functions from one piece of information to another had to be readily comprehensible to an untrained user armed with the basic knowledge acquired from commercial operating systems like Microsoft Windows.

Since the Internet was a public system with no single originator, the establishment of conventions had to be established through trial and error. As such, a public consensus on the conventions of the Internet was forged in a live operating environment. Arguably, this has made the Internet the exemplar of Don Norman's human-centred design ideas (1986, 2002). Along with Jacob Nielsen, Norman was highly active in promoting the primacy of the user and the need to design web portals that took usability, rather than functional complexity or visual style, as their overarching design principle (Nielsen and Loranger 2006). The primacy of the user in contemporary web design processes reflects the reality of a relatively open and adaptive information system. From the outset, the public Internet brought a veritable army of 'real users' into existence. In the past two decades, more and more information has become available on the Web, applications for processing that information have become simpler and better designed, and tools for communicating with other Internet users have become much more sophisticated. As a result, new configurations of usage continue to emerge at a rapid pace, each with their attendant user profiles: from web designers to Internet predators, from 'bloggers' to online gamers, from 'silver surfers' to 'file-sharers' and many more categories of user that we will subsequently explore in the pages of this book.

Stage 11: the prosumer

For those of a critical mindset, the increasingly commercial nature of the contemporary Internet implies a citizen-as-customer mindset that raises the spectre of a pay-per-view information society (Mosco 1989). However, for those who see new possibilities for social agency in the elevation of choice, there is cause to see the networked client-society as a positive development. Being a client for a service is a more attractive proposition when you are able to make empowered choices armed with ready information. Like the hackers in the 1970s, liberal thinkers in the Internet era have seen the strengthening of consumer power as a guarantor of democracy in modern societies. Again, the computer

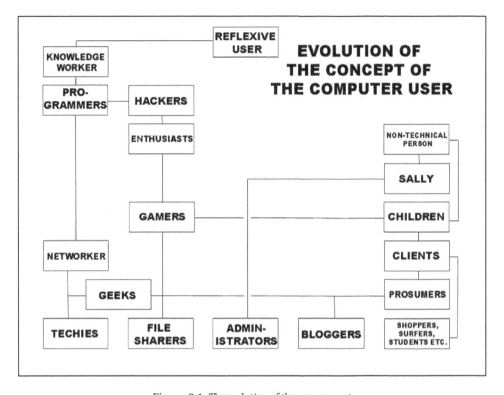

Figure 3.1 *The evolution of the user concept*

user has been heavily implicated in this model, since it is often assumed that access to electronic information is the proof-positive of an informed public. The idea of the digitally empowered citizen-consumer is encapsulated in Alvin Toffler's model of the prosumer (1980). Here, the information skills that have been transferred to the general public by the spread of computing are seen as enabling ordinary citizens to undertake for themselves many of the knowledge tasks that were previously professional domains. This inevitably leads to a blurring between the realms of work and leisure, between professional and amateur and between producer and consumer. A prosumer is not simply a consumer of digital services, but also a designer of digital artefacts, such as weblogs, digital music, video clips, game mods and so on.

Typology of the User Concept

This chapter has provided a brief summary of the evolution of the user concept as it has progressed from being a hypothetical concept to being a highly differentiated social body with various distinct models of usage that encompass the worlds of work, leisure and the spaces in between. The shift from scientists to skilled professionals, amateur enthusiasts, workers, children and, finally, to the elderly marks out a trajectory of the dissemination of computer technology (a trajectory inscribed with the power structures of our society). Such a journey is part and parcel of the popularization of any technology. In the process, the progression of the user concept has been determined by system designers for various reasons that encompass the technical, political and economic domains. However, there is plenty of evidence that the technical evolution of the computer concept has also responded to the social evolution of the user concept, providing support for more iterative perspectives of human–computer interaction. At the present time, the contemporary model of the user clearly demonstrates the extent to which today's actually existing computer users go far beyond the conceptual range of the system designers who hypothesized the reflexive user back in the 1950s and 1960s. Everyday computer users are now far more numerous than the technical elite of programmers and hackers could ever have become. As such, given human diversity and an almost infinite capacity for communication, there is no reason to assume that the user concept will not be further adapted to support new applications and to imagine future demands in computing applications. How we understand the evolution of this process depends, to a large extent, upon how we understand the balance of power within the socio-technical interface.

When we look beyond the functional dimensions of the user, however, we inevitably begin to encounter a broad range of 'deeper' associative meanings underpinning the characterization of computer-mediated roles in our society. This is where the user concept has become immeasurably multiplied and fragmented by its realization in actual human experience. At an early stage, the user was simply an imagined category referred to by the designers of digital technologies. Subsequently, as digital technologies were broadly applied across the domains of work and leisure, computer users came to constitute a large number of real people, who could be primarily classified against those who were not engaged with the technology (non-users). At the present time, however, the presence of digital technologies has become pervasive. That is, we find them wherever we turn. As a consequence, the foundational category of the user has come to represent such a broad base that it now enjoys similar status to other catch-alls like 'taxpayers', 'drivers' or 'citizens'. For sociologists of all kinds, effective categorization is the engine of social difference, and it therefore follows that the successful diffusion of information technology has necessitated a large series of more specific 'stereotypes' built around the interaction of human beings with computers. We now live in the age of the 'geek', the 'newbie', the 'teleworker', the 'eBay mum' and many others.

The basis of this more extensive typology is drawn from two major inferences. In the first instance, subcategories of the user are established by distinct forms of use (as with 'gamers'). In the second instance, subcategories of the user are established by the take-up of digital technologies by established social categories (for example, 'mums' or 'retirees'). In laying the foundations for much of modern sociology, Max Weber noted that sociological enquiry inevitably requires the purposeful construction of a typology. This process endows us with formal categories of notional human beings whose presence and actions within any given social phenomenon can be rationalized, and thus explained, at a general level (Weber 1949). A foundational process of 'typification' thus paves the way for an 'empirical' account of the subject, since it allows us to clearly identify, sort and enumerate (count) what is going on. All of the categories of computer user listed in this chapter are amenable to this purpose, as is the overarching concept of the user itself. This 'functional' use of typology is a favoured methodological approach for 'positivist' sociology, which takes the rational organization of facts as a given for a scientific understanding of society (Durkheim 1895). It is also a marked feature of media studies undertaken in the tradition of 'mass communications', which seeks to identify the structure and function of media technologies through observation and description (McQuail 2005).

From the perspective of the alternative 'interpretative' sociological tradition it is essential that we move beyond functional description in the pursuit of a deeper understanding of meaning in the social world (Husserl 1965; Schutz 1972). In order to do this, we must imbue our typology with plausible human motivations, emotions and responses. These more fleshed-out categories constitute the 'ideal types' with which interpretative sociologists commonly work. In media studies, this interpretative approach is most clearly seen in the domain of cultural studies, where the motivations of individuals and the underlying meaning of media content and its reception becomes the major focus of enquiry (Turner 2002, 2011). Even here, however, it is critically important to remain aware of the critical difference between hypothetical ideal types as the building blocks of a sociological language (the user) and actual individuals undertaking actions in the social world (you). An important, and necessary, gap persists between analytical categories and individual actors. You could think of this as the difference between the tools and raw materials of social inquiry. Ideal types (the tools) are purposeful constructs defined in relation to a specific action or question. Human beings (the raw material) are versatile and changeable individuals who operate simultaneously across any number of dimensions within social life. These are not, and cannot be, the same thing. Nonetheless, in seeking to investigate the operation of a digital society, we must first isolate the various relevant patterns of social behaviour and social relations from the versatility and unpredictability of any particular human subject. That is why a typology of computer users is important. From here on in, we can begin to build up 'generalizable' patterns of activity that can be comprehended within the broader field of social interaction. Users, as such, only make sense in relation to other users.

Think and Discuss

1. Key Terms
Can you describe in simple language what is meant by the following terms found in this chapter?

- Reflexive user
- Affordances
- Human–computer interaction (HCI)
- User-centred design
- Non-technical person

2. Critical Questions
Try answering the following questions, drawing upon your own understanding, experience and knowledge.

1. How would you characterize your own experience of becoming a computer user?
2. To what extent do you think that your own computer use is determined by the intentions of hardware and software designers?
3. Can you identify applications for digital technology that would be useful to you, but have not yet been realized?
4. Have you discovered patterns of user behaviour online that you consider broadly correspondent with certain types of computer user?
5. What does the graphical representation of user categories in box 3.1 suggest to you about the social relations between computer users?

Further Reading

Bardini, Thierry (2000) *Bootstrapping: Douglas Engelbart, Coevolution and the Origins of Personal Computing*, Palo Alto, CA: Stanford University Press.
Goldberg, Adele (ed.) (1988) *A History of Personal Workstations*, Reading: Addison-Wesley.
Jenkins, Henry (2006) *Convergence Culture: Where Old and New Media Collide*, New York: New York University Press.
Nielsen, Jacob and Loranger, Hoa (2006) *Prioritizing Web Usability*, Berkeley, CA: New Riders.
Norman, Donald and Draper, Stephen (eds) (1986) *User Centred System Design: New Perspectives on Human/Computer Interaction*, Hillsdale, NJ: Lawrence Erlbaum.
Norman, Donald (2002) *The Design of Everyday Things*, New York: Basic Books.
Rose, Ellen (2003) *User Error: Resisting Computer Culture*, Toronto: Between the Lines.
Sears, Andrew and Jacko, Julie (eds) (2007) *The Human–Computer Interaction Handbook*, New York: Lawrence Erlbaum.
Turkle, Sherry (2005) *The Second Self: Computers and the Human Spirit: 20th Anniversary Edition*, Cambridge, MA: MIT Press.

Go Online

Douglas Engelbart Archives – http://www.dougengelbart.org/
Human Computer Interaction Resources – http://hcibib.org/
NielsenNorman Group – http://www.nngroup.com/
Donald Norman User Advocacy and Human-Centered Design – http://www.jnd.org/
Palo Alto Research Center – http://www.parc.com
MIT Initiative on Technology and the Self – http://web.mit.edu/sturkle/techself/

CHAPTER 4

Audience as Community

The evolution of the user as a 'human standard' for computing applications tells us much about the foundational logics of digital technologies. Not least, it is important to note that for most of its history, the user concept was firmly focused upon the role of human beings as machine operators of various ranks and abilities. As a consequence, digital applications were consciously designed to address the user in ways that were task oriented and configured towards the inputs and outputs of the computational process. What is equally significant, as we have noted, is that the user is an ideal type. As such, the user denotes not only a standardized human role, but also implies a social body comprised of any number of individuals. At the level of the basic machine interface, the user exists in a singular form, but it is always recognized implicitly that the user is one of many. Thus, the term is inherently plural, and we always have to think of 'the user' as part of a group of 'users'. In that respect, the user concept serves to demonstrate the inherent duality of individuals playing roles within any broader social enterprise.

To take a less philosophical tack, we could probably say that the individual user was a more prominent reference point in digital technologies during the era of 'standalone' machines that existed before the rise of networked computing in the 1980s. By contrast, in the present era of social media and 'cloud computing', the user is only recognized as a constituent within a larger crowd of communicators. The 'user as crowd member' nonetheless remains a far more concrete category than the crowd itself, for reasons that we will seek to touch upon in this chapter. A further, and equally significant, shift in our understanding of users took place with the transition of computer technologies from the scientific domain and the workplace into the realms of entertainment and popular culture. An immediate consequence of this was the convergence of an evolving discussion in informatics (surrounding the nature of human–computer interaction) with another evolving discussion in media studies (surrounding the role of audiences in mass communications). The interaction between these two enquiries has since done much to shape the terrain upon which sociologists approach the critical question of community formation in a digital society.

Media Audiences

Earlier modern media forms in the twentieth century gave rise to many new practices of leisure and rituals of communication. There was the cinema audience, the radio listener and the television viewer. All of these various categorizations of media receivers were employed to describe members of society in ways that were previously unimaginable. As such, the ideal types of mass communication cast a series of particular mediated inflections upon our understanding of public participation and the underlying notion of the public itself. To take part in public life was to engage with media technologies, either as a producer or receiver of media content. This new centrality of social communication raised new possibilities for action in the public domain. Indeed, as Walter Benjamin noted in 1936, an intervention in the domain of visual culture had already become a necessity for political participation (1972). At a more functional level, the various technologies that constituted mass-media systems quickly gave rise to a number of specialist roles (from film producers to the TV 'weatherman'). The public conduct of mass communication subsequently made the mediated cult of celebrity a common culture, introducing many new kinds of social actors into our everyday experience (Marshall 1997; Turner 2004).

There is not sufficient space here to develop a typology of media professionals comparable to our previous analysis of the computer user. What is most pertinent to our present understanding of digital media is that all of these earlier media formats were understood primarily in terms of a powerful division between the producers and consumers of their content. There were the people in Hollywood and the people in the film theatres. There were people 'in television' and people who watched television. There was 'the press' and 'the public'. Thus, our understanding of all the early modern media was overwhelmingly structured around the 'top-down' transmission of information from a small professional class to a mass public. This is the basis of the popular notion of 'media power', which attributes the owners and operators of communications technologies with enormous persuasive power over the attitudes and activities of the rest of society. All of the early modern media were conceived around the centralized manufacture and 'broadcast' of media content to a mass public at a series of scales (from the urban populace to the national citizenry to the global battlefield of ideas).

Media Power and the Frankfurt School

In many respects, the twentieth century can be usefully understood as a period in which the central ideas of modern politics underpinned a series of military conflicts that were unprecedented in their scope and savagery (Hobsbawm 1995; Ferguson 2007). It was also a century in which the technologies of 'rational' government matured to such an extent that everyday life became subsumed by the 'micro-management' of the modern state. In this context, it was generally believed that the mass media possessed very considerable persuasive powers. The audiovisual media were widely seen as exerting much greater influence upon their audiences than the printed word had previously achieved. An assertion of this kind was more or less impossible to prove, but it was primarily grounded in the capacity of visual media to reach the less educated sections of society. The lower social orders were seen as lacking the capacity for critical literacy, and therefore as being particularly amenable to media influence. Accordingly, early interest in the use of media technologies to influence social behaviour came from the commercial sector and, by the middle of the twentieth century, mass advertising came to occupy a prominent role in the global economic system. During the same period, the 'new' media also came to be used extensively for propaganda purposes by most governments and political movements. Much of this material was crude in its approach, but sophisticated in its application. It provided the most visible terrain where many of the academic achievements of sociology and psychology were being put into practice. In turn, these applications of media technology in the wider world were fed back into university research. Systematic studies of the efficiency of media propaganda techniques were conducted throughout the 1950s, employing large-scale surveys and laboratory experiments designed to demonstrate the cognitive 'effects' of media exposure (that is, the power of media to change what we think and do).

For the German sociologists of the Frankfurt School, who had witnessed the rise of totalitarianism in Europe at first hand in the 1930s, the new techniques of persuasion were further evidence of the authoritarian tendencies that infused the modern world. Even within the comparative sanity of North America, Theodor Adorno and Max Horkheimer saw the twin rise of mass consumption and mass persuasion in almost entirely negative terms (Adorno and Horkheimer 1993). For them, the mass media were inextricably wedded to base motives of profit and a manipulative instinct that could only result in the intellectual subjugation of the population. A related aspect of this was the debasement of the cultural forms that the media industries were coming to monopolize through the technologies of mass reproduction (from music to drama, literature and visual art). From this perspective, the masses were dupes of commercial culture, and audiences were unwitting victims of the media that they consumed. What this (somewhat paranoid) vision of the coming media age shared with the fine-grained assessment of 'media effects' by those operating the machinery of persuasion was a commitment to the twin ideas of 'powerful media' and 'passive' audiences.

By the beginning of the 1960s, however, doubts were being raised surrounding the assumption of all-powerful media. Empirical research failed to prove conclusively that the mass media had a direct and quantifiable influence upon their audiences. Joseph Klapper concluded that 'mass communication does not ordinarily serve as a necessary or sufficient cause of audience effects, but rather functions through a nexus of mediating factors' (1960: 8). From this point onwards, the impact of media content was increasingly seen as being dependent upon the pre-existing social worlds inhabited by their audiences. People tended to accept messages that chimed with what they already believed, and they tended to be highly sceptical about messages that challenged those beliefs. As such, the 'effect' of mass communication was highly dependent upon who you were communicating those ideas to. This mitigation of media power encouraged the broad conclusion that the social positioning of viewers had 'primacy' over the intended meaning of media messages. The notion of media effect was not abandoned entirely, however, since the media (and television in particular) became an ever more prevalent feature of daily life. Nonetheless, theoretically at least, the capacity of the media to influence members of the public in a straightforward fashion was taken to be limited in important ways by the existing perceptions, opinions and social conditions that framed different social groups.

Active Audiences

A new understanding of the encounter between media content and its audiences was elaborated during the 1970s through Stuart Hall's model of the circuit of communication (1980). Here, the 'author' of the message is influenced by the wider cultural context of the society that they inhabit, as well as by their own social and institutional position. The meanings that they consciously 'encode' into each piece of media content are subject to the established 'language' of visual culture (which imposes meanings of its own). At the moment when the message is received (or 'decoded'), all of these layers of meaning are subject to interpretation by viewers who are inclined to read the message in different ways according to their own social experience. This much more complicated conception of social communication reflects two very important developments in the general understanding of media audiences. In the first place, the 'all-powerful' media of the 1950s has been replaced by a negotiated encounter with an 'active' audience. In the second instance, the 'top-down' transmission of messages has been replaced by a cycle of communication between producers and audiences. In the context of a social democracy, this is a far more optimistic proposition. The subjective domain of 'meaning' also becomes central to our understanding of media content. At the very least, Hall established that it is much easier to 'influence' audiences when you are telling them what they want to hear.

It is worth noting that this model of media reception rests upon the assertion that audiences are far from being homogeneous masses that 'read' meaning in the same way. The notion of the 'active' audience goes further in implying that each one of us is an intrinsic part of the collective process of social communication. Following on from this work, enthusiasts for the new model of the 'active' audience went as far as to embrace the notion that it was the audience that was all-powerful (Fiske 1989). In this reversal of fortunes, each individual was seen as selectively appropriating and creating the meanings that made most sense to them, regardless of the intentions of the author of the message. This school of thought has since become so orthodox within media studies that earlier notions of media power are frequently dismissed as anachronisms and historical oddities (Curran 2002). Nonetheless, the idea of the media as a powerful apparatus of psychological conditioning persists in the popular imagination. What unites both perspectives is their attempt to reconcile the democratic uncertainties of mass mediation in a social context where access to media platforms was necessarily limited by a number of structural factors.

In practice, for most of the twentieth century even the most 'active' audiences could not exert a direct influence over the final form of media content. All they could do was privilege their own social context in their personal assessment of the veracity or truth of the messages they received. Audiences, by definition, were not media producers. The narrow ownership of media institutions and their links to powerful interests of state and business was more or less incontrovertible (Wasko, Murdock and Soussa 2011). Numerous studies of media content confirmed systematic tendencies towards political bias and established social hierarchies (for example, Philo 1990). As such, the power of scepticism did not practically extend to the right of reply. For this reason, those who remained faithful to the more pessimistic viewpoints exemplified by Adorno tended to assert their 'active' reading of new audience theory by rejecting its claims for a more inclusive arena of social communication.

Digital Activity

Against the backdrop of these (often heated) arguments, however, the advent of digital media represented a 'game-changer' in a number of different ways. The video-game 'craze' that really got under way at the beginning of the 1980s introduced a new media technology with its own distinctive aesthetics and rules of engagement. Video games employed a one-on-one interface oriented towards a single player or to players by turn. As such, their mode of address was more akin to a newspaper than it was to broadcast media like television. Much more radically, they required a level of intense interaction between the player and the game for the narrative of play to unfold. In that sense, the players of games were required to be far more active participants in the medium than was the case with the established media (Taylor 2006). Of course, the fact that interactivity was a pre-designed requirement also meant that video games were heavily structured in ways that made the outcomes of player interaction quite limited. That is, you interacted in the right ways at the right moments and you 'won' the game. If you interacted outside of the rules of the game, you 'lost' and the game ended. Nonetheless, the simple capacity to start and end the game at will and to select the games to be played gave the player a new level of control over the content of the medium. This capacity was broadly comparable with the ways in which the video-cassette recorder (VCR) was changing the domestic experience of television during the same period (Wasser 2002).

The capacity to 'programme' and 'schedule' our own media content marked a significant change in the relationship between mass media and its audiences. For the most part, however, the spread of computers into our daily lives during the 1980s was firmly located in the workplace and its attendant informational processes (like spreadsheets and word processing). These developments were rarely, if ever, considered within the ambit of media studies. The development of network technologies that made email a feature of daily life in the modern office did, however, draw the attention of scholars in the more empirical domain of mass-communications research, as did the increasing volumes of interaction taking place via UseNet and other text-based systems (Baym 1999). Nonetheless, the formulation of a healthy subdiscipline dealing with 'computer-mediated communication' still remained outside the ambit of mainstream media studies. It did so primarily because media of communication (such as telephony) were considered apart from media of entertainment (such as television). In communication media, the technical and semantic components of exchange between individuals via a mass system formed the object of interest. In that respect, the actual 'meaning' of those exchanges was of less concern. In the domain of entertainment, however, with its close links to popular culture and emotive engagement, the study of content and its social significance enjoyed primacy.

Because computer-based media systems did not initially serve as a delivery platform for mass culture, and because their usage was seen as being largely functional rather than expressive, they did not impinge upon the wider debate surrounding media power and active audiences until the take-off of the public Internet in the early 1990s. From that moment onwards, it quickly became apparent that this 'new media' would overturn the founding logics upon which the sociology of media audiences was founded. This 'paradigm shift' became evident because for the first time more or less anyone with access to an Internet connection could publish media content that had the potential to reach a mass audience. The existing stranglehold of media specialists and corporate concerns over other media forms was not readily transferrable to the new medium. In that respect, it has been critically important that no one owns the Internet, and that anyone who wishes to can create content. As a consequence, the authorship of digital media content has become a prerogative of all users. At the same time, the orientation of the PC interface to a single user, when combined with the capacity to personally select the content that will be accessed, necessarily inferred that our established understanding of 'mass' media would have to be reconsidered. Further, the co-location of entertainment media (in the tradition of performance) with communications media (providing conversational functionality) promised to undermine the existing distinctions between these two forms of media use. Indeed, looking back from our present time, there is little trace of this longstanding division between interpersonal communication and spectatorship. We tend to do both things in the same locations, via the same devices and, often as not, at the same time.

Box 4.1 What is an audience?

- An audience is a collective social body formed around an act of performance
- An audience takes on particular structural forms in relation to the media around which it is formed (thus, the 'reading public' has a different nature from the 'theatre crowd')
- An audience may be co-present within the same social space (as in cinema) or it may be dispersed across different locations (as in radio)
- An audience may be co-present within the same space of time (as in broadcast media) or it may be dispersed across different timeslots (as in playback media)
- An audience can emerge from an existing social group engaging with the mass media (teenagers in Iowa) or it can be comprised of individuals who share no other commonality beyond their media use (*Twilight* fans)
- An audience only 'exists' during the moment of reception, although the common experience of reception can be seen to persist after the event

---

Web Surfers

Given the establishment of the 'active' audience as the predominant model for understanding media reception, the rapid growth of Internet users into the world's largest media 'audience' appeared to represent the most concrete and radical example of audience power over the media apparatus. What was immediately problematic, however, was that this audience engaged with the medium at an individual level. Further, this new audience was not co-present within any particular location in the way that cinema and even television audiences were generally taken to be. Nor could a common experience of the medium be easily defined upon the basis of the content that was being accessed, because individual control over the selection and sequence of their 'web surfing' habits meant that each user could engage with a unique field of content. Thus, the corollary to the digitally enhanced triumph of the 'active' audience was the apparent disembodiment, fragmentation and even dispersal of the very idea of the audience as it had previously existed. As such, it was reasonable to ask whether we could consider a large-scale collection of Internet users to be an 'audience' at all. As more and more people turned their hand to publishing Internet content, and various platforms were developed to make interactive web design widely accessible, the distinction between media producers and the audience was seen to be collapsing. This led to the present popularity of Alvin Toffler's notion of the 'prosumer' and Axel Bruns's more recent formulation of the 'produser' as metaphors for new forms of engagement where the audience is also the primary producer of content (Toffler 1980; Bruns 2008). It is critically important that both of these concepts address the audience member in singular terms, signifying that our basic understanding of the audience has been transferred from an imagined social body to an individual frame of reference.

In the past decade, the rise of social media and 'user-driven' platforms has begun to blur yet another set of distinctions, this time between audiences and the content itself. For all these reasons, any clear definition of the digital audience has proved elusive.

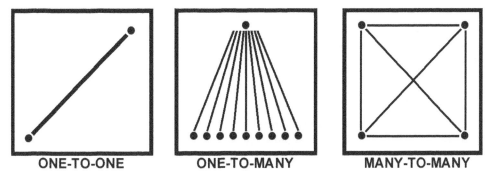

Figure 4.1 *Media systems by diffusion structure*

In attempting to resolve the analytical problem of online reception, scholars in media studies turned initially to the concept of the 'user' as developed in computer science and deployed in studies of CMC. What they nonetheless preserved from their earlier work was the notion of the active audience as the basis for emphasizing the power of media consumers (Van Dijk 2009: 42–6). In making the shift to 'new media', this concept inevitably became separated from its origins in the critique of media monopolies and audiovisual manipulation. Indeed, in the early years of the public Internet, there was no central source of content upon which to rest an oppositional criticism. Instead, the active audience concept was dovetailed neatly with the functional interactivity of digital media content. As a consequence of this reorientation, audience activity has become understood primarily as a matter of writing rather than reading, and of doing rather than thinking. Thus, the 'meaning' of the digital media is increasingly seen to exist not so much within the content of those platforms, but within the activity of media users.

In order to illustrate these seismic shifts in the conceptual terrain, media analysts deployed a functional terminology that distinguishes between the interaction patterns arising from the affordances of different media technologies. Broadcast media like television and radio were defined as 'one-to-many' media, where a single message is sent from a single source to a wide number of recipients. Personal communications technologies like telephones are defined as 'one-to-one' media, allowing two participants to utilize a channel of private communication. Networked media, such as the Internet, were classified as 'many-to-many' media, since they allow any number of communicators to communicate with all or any of the other participants. Even these distinctions proved difficult to maintain, however, since the rapid growth in 'multimedia' capacity on computer platforms (from the late 1990s) indicated that structural distinctions between audiences for different media technologies would become obsolete in the new millennium. The personal computer (in a range of shapes and sizes) became the primary means of engagement with all forms of image, text and sound, enabling all the various configurations of connectivity (from one-to-one to many-to-many). As the prevailing technology of social communication, a customizable many-to-many medium necessarily precipitated yet another reorientation of the idea of the audience (Napoli 2010). Consequently, media scholars have now almost entirely discarded the historical analogy between the media audience and a crowd of onlookers gathered in a performance space (Gauntlett 2007a; Nightingale 2011). In its place, studies of digital audiences have consistently sought to establish a new analogy with a more complex metaphor that has been central to parallel debates in sociology: the concept of community.

Creating Communities

The notion of community is central to the practice of sociology for fairly obvious reasons. Without this concept we would have no obvious scale of reference positioned between the family unit and the nation-state. More than this, however, much of the foundational work in early sociology was inspired by a profound sense of crisis surrounding the status of community. The rapid growth in urbanization during the Industrial Revolutions that swept across Britain, Europe and America during the eighteenth and nineteenth centuries led many to believe that a world of closely integrated 'traditional' communities centred upon the agricultural system were being swept aside by a new way of life. This modern existence was urban, mobile and anonymous, and it separated individuals from the enduring bonds of kinship and place that had previously characterized social life. For early sociologists, like Émile Durkheim, this loss of traditional structures raised the spectre of 'anomie' (normlessness) and social breakdown. For Durkheim, the earlier foundation of social life in familial, spiritual and physical proximity had imposed a 'mechanical solidarity'. The impact of modernity, however, was to increase functional interdependence across a broader social domain, whilst also giving rise to a more impersonal, individualized social experience that was largely dependent upon self-regulation and 'organic solidarity' (1893). For Karl Marx, too, the isolation of the individual within the oppressive regimes of the urban factory was leading to the intense 'alienation' of human beings within industrial society (1927). Classical sociology therefore adopted a largely retrogressive concept of community that became powerfully associated with small-scale groups, centred upon intimacy and locality and broadly equated with the loss of a romanticized pastoral lifestyle (Tonnies 1957).

Correspondingly, in the late nineteenth century, modern anthropologists sought to record, preserve and recover this vanishing world amongst the 'tribal' societies of the 'primitive' world. Here, again, the concept of community was closely linked to kinship and belief systems, with the important addition of a strong emphasis on the particularities of ethnicity and race. Elsewhere, under the influence of Marx, the communities formed within industrial societies were increasingly seen as being determined by the ordering of the economic system and the fraternal structures of social class (1867). Much of the work conducted on community in the industrialized world during the twentieth century focused upon social dislocation and corrective 'community-building' within large urban populations. In this respect, the work of the American sociologists of the Chicago School during the 1920s marks an important watershed in a modern conceptualization of community. In documenting community structures within this large American city, Robert Park made the observation that urban communities appeared to be defined by their functional patterns of interaction every bit as much as by the immediate environment. Furthermore, Park argued that urban communities were being formed and maintained largely through social communication, and operated in new ways that were being facilitated through media technologies (1923, 1929). Local newspapers provided their readerships an overview of goings-on in the community. Telephones allowed for the maintenance of enduring relationships across distance. By these means, effective communities were formed and maintained within a wider social environment that was characterized by mobility and the simultaneous presence of other communities (Lindner 1996).

Park did not abandon the importance of location to the community concept, but he expanded the definition to encompass another broader notion of community as something constructed primarily through social interaction. This idea of community as a set of conscious actions and mediated relationships was to gain ground in the 1960s, as mass-media systems became pervasive and the primacy of tradition (lost or otherwise) was widely challenged. A counterpoint to the ideal of the modern, dispersed and mediated community existed simultaneously in the varied pursuit of 'alternative' communities that were founded upon a broad rejection of the impersonal order of the modern world, and of urbanism in general. There are various early examples of this tendency: the agricultural communism of the Israeli Kibbutz movement, the showpiece villages of the English home counties or the self-contained rural Christian communities found across North America. These experiments with self-selecting rural communities were subsequently revived by various counter-cultural groups that took to the backwoods of California or the wet, windy hillsides of Wales in the early 1970s. In all these contexts, there was an emphasis on the communal mode of subsistence and the normative conditioning of a shared set of political beliefs by which the community would be regulated. Back in the mainstream, the expansion of television was playing an important role in the steady evolution of suburban communities from architectural to social formations. In the years that followed, desegregation in North America and immigration in Europe began to make ethnicity a central concern in the identification and analysis of community structures (heralding the era of 'multiculturalism'). Thus, across a large number of social contexts, researchers sought to examine the formal properties of various manifestations of community through the mapping of existing social groups.

Communities of Practice

Throughout the 1970s, the community concept saw a broad weakening of its associations with occupation and social class in favour of a stronger association with personal identity and lifestyle choices. Patterns of sexuality and the taste cultures derived from new forms of popular culture came to be seen as constituting distinct forms of community (Hebdige 1979; Levay and Nonas 1995). In these interpretative approaches, communities were reconsidered in the form of 'active' self-selecting social constructions (much like the new model of the media audience that emerged during the same period). The 'classic' normative model of the community as an inherited, tight-knit, homogeneous and interdependent unit (essentially an extended family) was also challenged by the work of Mark Granovetter (1973). Granovetter noted that social relationships could be usefully distinguished between close relationships ('strong ties') and more circumstantial, selective relationships ('weak ties'). In comparing the different ways in which these patterns of association provided the interface between the individual and the wider social structure, Granovetter observed that a large portion of social action was conducted through 'weak ties'. He also noted that individuals with less 'strong ties' tended to maintain more 'weak ties', giving them greater access to public life, employment and an overall advantage in social mobility (1974).

Granovetter's work contributed to the extensive development of 'social network analysis' during the 1970s. This methodological practice of mapping social relationships in graphical form was influenced by the 'British School' of anthropology that had previously approached the question of community through the systematic description of the bonds between individuals (both within and across social groups). As such, the question of community was encountered here in functional, rather than conceptual terms (see Cavanagh 2007: 27–37). This methodological approach to the mapping of social relationships proved to be a good fit with the similarly functional outlook of the Chicago School of sociology and the Toronto School of mass communications research in North America. Furthermore, the growing importance of information technologies for conducting empirical social research during the 1970s provided both practical and intellectual inputs to the formalization of social network analysis as an influential set of approaches towards community in the late twentieth century. Scholars such as Barry Wellman advocated detailed mapping exercises in which information regarding social connections is collected and rendered into diagrammatic form (Wellman 1979; Wellman and Berkowitz 1988). Consequently, community members are defined as 'nodes' in a dense network of interrelations that provide a graphical account of the 'ties' within social groups. Wellman became a longstanding champion of the computer analysis of social structures. Wellman has also advocated a new conceptual approach to community expressed through the notion of 'networked individualism' (Wellman et al. 2003). Here, the individual is defined less by their categorical position within overarching social structures, and more by their own unique network of associations with other people. Another related formulation of community that enjoyed widespread interest was Etienne Wenger's notion of 'communities of practice', which emphasizes the collaborative bonds between professional groups (1999). By this model, self-selecting communities seeking mutual advantage provide another distinctive model for community formation. Here, a largely impersonal affinity serves concrete purposes and engenders coordinated actions. Once again, it is interpersonal communication that provides the functional connection between individual experience and social structure. This is because, in a mass society, the proliferation of weak social connections is necessarily pursued via various media systems that extend the scale and scope of those relationships.

At the turn of the millennium, the convergence of the methodological study of interpersonal connections ('social network analysis') and the theoretical elaboration of collaborative self-interest ('communities of practice') served to demarcate another milestone in the incremental reorientation of the community concept. As in the contemporary work of Manuel Castells, the focus of community shifts decisively towards informational connectivity rather than physical proximity, and towards diffuse social communication ('weak ties') rather than close kinships and shared experiences ('strong ties') (1996). An important countervailing argument was nonetheless put forward by Robert Putnam who argued that American society was actually witnessing a crisis of community brought about by the decline in social formations organized on the basis of strong ties (1995). According to Putnam, the 'social capital' created through interaction can be distinguished between 'bonding capital' (within social groups) and 'bridging capital' (across social groups). The two resources are nonetheless mutually reinforcing.

Thus, rather than increasing social mobility and social cohesion, Putnam argued that a decline in strong ties had actually led to a corresponding decline in weak ties and widespread social fragmentation. This concern, of course, takes us back to the classic arguments of Émile Durkheim.

Even from this brief account, it is immediately evident that whilst the concept of community has evolved more or less constantly alongside sociological enquiry, it continues to be strongly associated both with vanishing ways of life and with utopian propositions for future societies (Segal 2012). In that sense, the particular ways in which the concept of community is described in each and every case provides a litmus test for the politics of a wide range of sociological approaches. In certain usages, the concept is equated with an immutable biological and cultural inheritance. In other readings, it is evidenced by volunteerism and self-expression. Furthermore, depending upon the context into which it is introduced, a community could be defined by physical proximity (the village) or by social class (the business community), by ethnicity (the Hispanic community) or by occupation (as in academia). Equally, it might be founded upon sectarian lines (by religion) or upon lifestyle choices and mutual interest (as in subcultures). What remains consistent about the various uses of the term is that it is invariably deployed in a positive light, a point noted many years ago by Raymond Williams (1961). Everyone is for community and nobody is against it, even though (and perhaps precisely because) it can encompass so many different and often opposing things.

Virtual Communities

Given our present concern, it is equally significant that media systems have come to be seen as playing a key role in the organization of modern communities (from television at the national level to newspapers in the locality). Nonetheless, prior to the growth of the public Internet in the 1990s, the use of media by pre-existing communities ('community media') did not necessarily extend to our present view of media audiences as constituting fully-fledged communities in their own right (Jankowski and Prehn 2001). One critical intervention in the convergence of the audience concept with community formation came from an unexpected quarter. Benedict Anderson, an historian and anthropologist of South East Asia, set out to interrogate how the rise of nationalism in the former colonial world had come to establish such a strong foundation in the minds of these newly formed citizens. Fundamentally, Anderson's conclusion was that communal bonds in the modern world are largely imagined into being (1991). His influential concept of 'imagined communities' drew upon fellow historian Eric Hobsbawm's notion of the 'invention of tradition' being intrinsic to the formation of modern myths (Hobsbawm and Ranger 1992). Anderson also drew upon Hegel's famous analogy of the modern newspaper as the secular form of daily prayer (Pinkard 2000: 242). Anderson claimed that the experience of participating in the new audiences created by the emergence of mass media encouraged individuals to imagine themselves as part of larger and more abstracted social formations. In doing so, they were moved to imagine a community of anonymous, comparable others in whom they invested a lasting fraternal bond.

This notion of a community created imaginatively around the shared experience of mediation and performance was widely used during the 1990s by anthropologists and media scholars for describing ethnic minority audiences (for example, Appadurai

1996). It was also applicable for sociologists seeking to understand the emotional bonds between strangers in modern communities, since it emphasized the importance of communication in facilitating abstract and emotive social bonds. In the emerging domain of 'new media' studies, the notion of a disembodied yet emotionally connected polity proved readily compatible with the radical proposition of rich 'online' communities forged through anonymous digital interactivity. The coming of the 'virtual community' was popularized by Howard Rheingold in his book *The Virtual Community: Homesteading on the Electronic Frontier* (1993). Rheingold's arguments were based upon a long-term familiarity with the early text-based forums conducted via the Internet during the 1980s and early 1990s. At that time, there was no graphical capacity, no World Wide Web or web browsers. There was nonetheless already an extensive series of Internet-enabled message boards and other topical forums for mutual discussion between computer users. Much of this interaction was based upon the UseNet system, which had gone from being a technical forum to become an extensive domain of social communication encompassing a vast array of subject matter (from *Star Trek* to sex, and with more or less everything in between).

People in virtual communities use words on screens to exchange pleasantries and argue, engage in intellectual discourse, conduct commerce, exchange knowledge, share emotional support, make plans, brainstorm, gossip, feud, fall in love, find friends and lose them, play games, flirt, create a little high art and a lot of idle talk. People in virtual communities do just about everything that people do in real life, but we leave our bodies behind. You can't kiss anybody and nobody can punch you on the nose, but a lot can happen within those boundaries. To the millions who have been drawn into it, the richness and vitality of computer-linked cultures is attractive, even addictive . . . The cutting edge of scientific discourse is migrating to virtual communities . . . At the same time, activists and educational reformers are using the same medium as a political tool. You can use virtual communities to find a date, sell a lawnmower, publish a novel, conduct a meeting. Some people use virtual communities as a form of psychotherapy . . . Most people who have not yet used these new media remain unaware of how profoundly the social, political and scientific experiments underway today via computer networks could change all of our lives in the near future.

Howard Rheingold (1993) *The Virtual Community: Homesteading on the Electronic Frontier*, New York and Reading: Addison Wesley, pp. 3–4

By comparison with today, Rheingold was writing at a time (the early 1990s) when the number of Internet users was still relatively low, and the standard of technical expertise amongst them was disproportionately high (as was the level of education and material wealth). Rheingold had enjoyed a long-running and extensive engagement with a Bay Area counter-cultural forum, the WELL, and this experience informed his utopian model of a self-selecting and technologically enabled 'alternative' community. For Rheingold, this virtual community was characterized by its volunteeristic ethos and the strong attachments forged between its members. The text-based personas presented by the members of the WELL were notable for the spirit of public engagement that motivated their participation. They were also notable for the displays of personal intimacy that arose (somewhat paradoxically) in response to the depersonalized nature of the digital interface. For Rheingold, this made the dynamics of an 'online' community entirely different from the dynamics of an 'offline' community. The nature of membership in the virtual community was also highly distinctive. In the case of the WELL, the forum brought together a group of people with particular investments in computer technology, public participation and personal revelation. The simple fact that this 'online' community existed only in a virtual form precipitated novel modes of interaction and affinity. Thus, for Rheingold, a virtual community was a liberating and mutually supportive enterprise relatively free of the structural constraints that determine communities in the 'real' world.

Rheingold's work was subsequently followed by Nancy K. Baym's studies of online forums devoted to the discussion of popular television soap operas (1995, 1999). Baym also found that the nature of communication between members of these forums was characterized by a mutual kindness that offered emotional support to its members in a host of ways. Thus, for Baym, the online exchanges between soap fans also came to constitute a particular pattern of social interaction and emotional connection that was amenable to the notion of a meaningful online community. Baym's work found resonant connections with the work of feminist scholars in media and cultural studies who had also been seeking to 'recover' the social potentials of cultural forms that had been doubly denigrated on the basis of their popular aesthetics and female audience (Ang 1991; Radway 1991). The growing emphasis on the empowerment of media consumers through their active engagement in discussions around the narratives and star personas of popular forms was also an outcome of the wider shift in media studies towards the 'active audience'. By the 1990s, this shift in emphasis had seen the 'power' of media texts being largely jettisoned in favour of a 'popular democracy' centred upon 'fan cultures' (Jenkins 1992). The rapid expansion of the public Internet during the 1990s reinforced this paradigm by providing the practical means for extending the accessibility, range and scope of fan cultures in the public arena. In the early years of 'free content', fan clubs and their amateur publications suddenly came to enjoy a major presence in the public domain of popular culture, and open participation in these new online forums saw 'community' status being automatically conferred upon these new interactive audience formations.

Naturally, the notion of the online community also proved to be of immediate interest across the broad field of sociology. For Barry Wellman, the coming of the Internet provided compelling evidence of social networks as a tangible expression of contemporary social life (Wellman 1999). Not only did the Internet inevitably produce the most extensive record of social connections seen to date, but it did so as a by-product of an organic, real-time, functional process (Wellman and Hampton 1999). That is, these social networks were living organisms rather than graphical records. Consequently, the Internet medium proved to be a critical factor in the metamorphosis of social network analysis from being an empirical methodology to becoming a predominant theorization of social life in its own right (Rainie and Wellman 2012). In his ongoing quest to recover the status of community organizations in American culture, Robert Putnam was also to become an Internet enthusiast. Despite having identified television as a major contributor to reduced public participation, Putnam subsequently pointed towards the Internet as a vital resource for rebuilding civic groups and social capital in American society (2000). Whilst Rheingold had been keen to demarcate the utopian proposition of the virtual community from the prospects of community in the physical world, both Wellman and Putnam were keen to connect the two domains in their elaborations of social networks and social capital. In the former case, the Internet was an enabling technology and a natural expression of the long-term shift from 'mechanical solidarity' to 'communities of practice'. In the latter case, the Internet represented an important device for redressing the ills caused by that very process.

Audience to Community

To a significant extent, the convergence between the conceptual evolution of the media audience and the modern community was the result of a technological intervention. The digital media, and the Internet in particular, brought about an all-encompassing merger of the media of social communication and the media of mass entertainment. At another level, their convergence was made possible by a parallel transition from approaches largely derived from the primacy of social structure to approaches largely derived from the primacy of individual agency. In media studies, it was top-down ownership of the media and the predominant meanings within media content that saw the audience relegated to a 'passive' category of compliance or resistance. In sociology, it was the primacy of kinship, belief systems and economic relations that saw individuals consigned to pre-existing communities largely from birth. Over the course of the past forty years, these prevailing wisdoms have been displaced in favour of a more fluid, individuated and active formulation of citizenship in both disciplines. As a consequence, the media audience has been recast as an active participant in the creation of social meaning, even to the extent that the audience is now positioned as the driving force in the production of culture. In sociology, community membership has increasingly come to be seen as a matter of conscious choice that is available across a number of different registers. Individuals can engage with (or disengage from) many different formations of community in the course of their daily lives. As a consequence, our understanding of community has also become a far more 'active' category.

In the public domain, the term 'community' came to serve, more or less by default, as the plural of 'users' in the expanding popular language of digital culture. Accordingly, a successful website does not merely build a 'user-base' or 'audience' but seeks instead to create and maintain a 'community'. The reconfiguration of the Internet as the main site of commercial culture in the twenty-first century saw this utopian terminology being carried forward into applications that are a long way from the not-for-profit civic citizenry of Rheingold's WELL or the conceptual ambitions of sociologists. The pervasive commercialization of the electronic frontier has witnessed an unreflexive categorization of innumerable consumer demographics as 'communities' (usually on the basis of an online interface and the inclusion of a bulletin board). With the advent of online shopping and the evolution of the Internet into a major delivery system for mainstream media culture, the audience-as-community combination has subsequently been overlaid with the ideal types and communal preferences of market research and product development (Arvidsson 2005). For Allison Cavanagh, this proliferation of the term across the digital domain represents not only a categorical imprecision, but also a 'severe attenuation' of the concept in terms of its original meaning (2007: 106). In empirical terms, the uncertain status of digital 'community' has to be assessed in terms of the actual quantity and quality of interactions between users in specific cases (Van Dijk 2009: 44). In that respect, the sheer scale of the digital domain today presents us with a further problem. Even in highly collaborative interactive domains we have yet to account for how the early conception of online community can be usefully applied to applications with millions of participants (such as *World of Warcraft* or *YouTube*) (Baym 2010: 72–98).

How should we understand a single-purpose community whose membership outstrips the population of many countries, let alone a single medium whose audience outstrips the membership of any nation-state? Which configurations of strong and weak ties produce the optimum coherence within online communities, without leading to a mosaic of relatively closed groups? Which forms of online interaction develop social capital, and which forms diminish it? All these questions have yet to be answered, but it is clear at least that, for now, there is no obvious substitute for concept of community itself. Revisiting his own formulation in light of the meteoric expansion of the Internet medium, Howard Rheingold defended his utopian proposition of disembodied community, while also conceding that the arrival of a larger and more heterogeneous audience had produced an overall decline in the predominance and quality of the positive engagements that had inspired his original account (2000). The Internet has simply become too large and too varied in its usages to assume any single model of online community will prevail. Nonetheless, what remains a consistent feature of the medium is the way in which membership of an online community is not experienced collectively but rather through the interface of each individual with a multivocal interactive space. Consequently, a single community or audience structure that we might see from a 'bird's eye view' (as it were) does not necessarily correspond with the individualized viewpoints from which participants in those formations experience their 'membership'. Bearing this in mind, it is those personal imaginative experiences of digital society that we will now begin to explore in depth.

Think and Discuss

1. Key Terms
Can you describe in simple language what is meant by the following terms found in this chapter?

- Many-to-many media
- Organic solidarity
- Active audiences
- Strong and weak ties
- Communities of practice

2. Critical Questions
Try answering the following questions, drawing upon your own understanding, experience and knowledge.

1. What examples of your own media use would you associate with participating in a community?
2. How important is interactivity with other participants in your consumption of popular culture?
3. What proportion of your interaction online is devoted to the maintenance of strong or weak social ties?
4. At what scale would you locate the operation of a meaningful online community?
5. Can you provide two examples illustrating how digital technologies are contributing to the maintenance of traditional communities?

Further Reading

Baym, Nancy K. (1999) *Tune In, Log On: Soaps, Fandom and Online Community*, London and Thousand Oaks, CA: Sage.

Cavanagh, Allison (2007) *Sociology in the Age of the Internet*, Buckingham: Open University Press.

Jankowski, Nicholas W. and Prehn, Ole (2001) *Community Media in the Information Age*, New York: Hampton Press.

Napoli, Philip (2010) *Audience Evolution: New Technologies and the Transformation of Media Audiences*, New York and Chichester: Columbia University Press.

Putnam, Robert (2000) *Bowling Alone: The Collapse and Revival of American Community*, New York: Simon and Schuster.

Rainie, Lee and Wellman, Barry (2012) *Networked: The New Social Operating System*, Cambridge, MA: MIT Press.

Rheingold, Howard (2000) *The Virtual Community: Homesteading on the Electronic Frontier: Revised Edition*, Cambridge, MA: MIT Press.

Segal, Howard P. (2012) *Utopias: A Brief History From Ancient Writings to Virtual Communities*, Malden, MA: Wiley-Blackwell.

Tonnies, Ferdinand (2011) *Community and Society*, New York: Dover Publications.

Wenger, Etienne (1999) *Communities of Practice: Learning, Meaning and Identity*, Cambridge: Cambridge University Press.

Go Online

Bowling Alone (Robert Putnam) – http://bowlingalone.com/
Better Together (Robert Putnam) – http://www.bettertogether.org/
Journal of Computer-Mediated Communication – http://jcmc.indiana.edu/
Online Fandom – http://www.onlinefandom.com/
Howard Rheingold – http://rheingold.com/
Theory.org (David Gauntlett) – http://www.theory.org.uk/
Barry Wellman at NetLab – http://homes.chass.utoronto.ca/~wellman/
Etienne Wenger: Communities of Practice – http://www.ewenger.com/theory/

Part II

Digital Individuals

CHAPTER 5

Pleasing Bodies

The early computer games asked us to identify with a crude electronic icon and its activity within a basic two-dimensional space ('this is you, and . . .'). Since those days, the steady development of network protocols has transformed the desktop computer from a single-user medium to a vast social domain, where individuals engage in extensive virtual interactions with other computer users via complex intuitive models of mathematical space. Nonetheless, what remains equally profound about our personal encounters with the digital media in both these examples is this primary demand that we identify with a graphical metaphor and develop a subjectivity that is located outside of our material, corporeal self. To put that more simply, we must loosen our association with embodied presence in order to operate electronically as an icon. This is no simple matter, however, and it initially presents itself as something of a subjective absurdity, whether we were attempting to identify with a pixel-shooting triangle in the seventies, a blue-haired hedgehog in the eighties, a disembodied gun barrel in the nineties or a finely rendered sexualized avatar in the early twenty-first century. Even as we seek to engage in transferring our sense of self out-of-body and into the space of the screen, the intensely personal nature of the individual computer terminal, and the interactivity inherent to its function, mobilizes a profound sense of intimacy in human–machine relations.

The central paradox, then, is that our engagement with digital technologies is an out-of-body experience (as a subjective engagement) that nonetheless remains closely responsive to the physical actions of the body (in its functional operation). This makes the subjective distance between digital technology and its users radically different from the paradigm of spectatorship established by earlier media technologies (that is, watch without touching). In a large part, this is because the *physicality* of the digital medium (that is, the biological interaction of users with the technology) is markedly different. The digital experience must therefore be understood as an intimate affair, a form of mass communication that is radically individualized in both its function and appearance. In order to comprehend the full significance of this mass individuation in practice, however, we must revisit the fundamental notion of the individual. In the first instance, we must supersede, or at the very least upgrade, our intensely embodied ideal of the human subject at a philosophical level. As a matter of sociological practice, we must retrace those steps in order to reposition the user from being a general behavioural category to becoming comprehensible as an embodied identity and a situated social agent.

Micro-relations on the Net

Given the technical complexity of computer-mediated communication (CMC), it is no surprise that early approaches to understanding online communications were largely framed in technologically determined ways. That is, these studies took the functional affordances of the medium as a starting point, asking what forms of interaction could be undertaken and how effective online communication was in achieving its goals (e.g., Price 1975). In considering the range of visual and aural signals that could be deployed by a computer interface operating through a remote connection, CMC applications were assessed in terms of the relative 'richness' of the information exchange (Daft and Lengel 1984). A video conference, for example, was considered relatively rich in that it could communicate spoken communications along with facial and bodily gestures in real (synchronous) time. By contrast, the interrupted (asynchronous) exchange of text-only communications via email was regarded as a 'lean' or lesser medium for personal interaction, where much of the contextual content of the communicative exchange was not available to the receiver.

Despite a marked focus on technological possibility as a frame for understanding CMC, almost all early studies contrasted online interactions with an idealized embodied 'face-to-face' human encounter (e.g., Hiltz and Turoff 1978). By this model, CMC researchers understood interpersonal communication to include a range of sensory exchanges that were socially determined, including the use of verbal and textual language alongside a range of facial expressions, bodily gestures and spatial arrangements that embodied the fullest expression of social actions (Bales 1950; Blumer 1969). For this reason, early experiments with CMC platforms were designed to assess the quality of computer-mediated communications under the prior assumption that many of the essential qualities of everyday face-to-face interactions were absent. The lack of an embodied human presence was seen as an inherent drawback of digital mediation, with some applications better placed than others to convey an impression of the 'social presence' of partners in communication (Short, Williams and Christie 1976).

As Nancy Baym has noted, the initial concerns of research into personal online communication were mostly task-focused, being oriented around the work environment, and sought to apply measures of the efficiency of CMC in laboratory exercises where teamwork was undertaken or simulated by groups of remote users connected by text-based interaction (2006: 36). In general, the lack of social cues common to embodied communication and the weak sense of social presence in text exchanges appeared to suggest that collective discussion would be more difficult to coordinate effectively and the efficiency of decision-making would be impaired. Furthermore, 'because social identity cues would not be apparent, interactants would gain greater anonymity. Their gender, race, rank, physical appearance, and other features of public identity are not readily evident. As a result, people would be "de-personalized," losing their sense of self and other' (Baym 2010: 54). As such, it was anticipated that the social norms guiding group interaction had the potential to break down online, primarily due to the loss of visual cues that defined the social hierarchy. 'With the cues to hierarchy (e.g., age, attire, seating arrangement) missing, participation would become more evenly distributed amongst group members . . . For those seeking speedy task resolution, the plurality of voices could mean tasks take longer to accomplish' (Baym 2010: 55).

A further concern arising from early studies of online communication in institutional settings was an apparent loss of social inhibition that caused participants to conduct communications seen as being overly aggressive and inappropriate to social communication. In the first instance, the loss of visual cues caused misunderstandings of the content and intentions of messages, which sometimes led to conflict within online groups. Simultaneously, the apparent loss of social hierarchy reduced social inhibitions, encouraging some participants to challenge other group members. In addition, the lack of social presence appeared to produce a cocooning effect, similar to the automobile, where participants felt emboldened to perform aggressive acts that they would not normally countenance, due to the apparent protection of a technological barrier between participants. These were all factors seen as contributing to the phenomenon of 'flaming' where participants in online discussion would behave aggressively towards other group members by means of abusive, mocking or explicit remarks intended to insult, offend and intimidate (Walther 1992).

Despite the negative framing of online communications in many of these approaches, some researchers saw far more positive things happening in online communication as it expanded in usage throughout the 1980s and 1990s. Participants in online forums were seen to compensate for the lack of social cues by expressing themselves in new ways, such as the early use of emoticons to provide a graphical representation of the mood of the writer (Rezabek and Cochenour 1998). To counter any misconception of their messages, online communicators became more skilled in expressing themselves in ways that were variously more conversational, clear and conciliatory. Arguably, these gradual developments in the idiom of online communication furnished more socially supportive, inclusive and socially minded interactions than the task-based experiments of earlier applications. As the Internet developed into a public medium, the broader context for assessing online interaction underwent radical changes in its terms of reference. Indeed, many researchers came to believe that the loss of visual physical cues and bodily proximity actually made the medium a good deal more pro-social than the majority of everyday human experience (Turkle 1996).

During its first decade (1993–2003) as a graphical medium, as images augmented textual interaction, the Internet rapidly became a pervasive technology of contemporary life for people living in the most economically advanced societies. At that time, utopian accounts of the 'new media' posited a future free of bodily constraints and material discrimination (Poster 1995). The disembodied anonymity of online communication offered the promise of an inclusive 'virtual' society composed of computer-enabled interactions and characterized by newfound freedoms in identity-shifting, self-realization and creative fantasy. Nonetheless, the nature of disembodied communication explored by early studies of CMC continued to have salience for our interpersonal usage of the medium, since: 'After millennia as creatures who engage in social interaction face to face, the ability to communicate across distance at very high speeds disrupts understandings that are burned deep in our collective conscience . . . How can we be present and also absent? What is a self if it is not in a body?' (Baym 2010: 3).

Sigmund Freud, the Body and the Self

It is a fundamental premise of human thought that the self is located in the body and that we define ourselves in relation to that body in the first instance. In modern Western philosophy, following René Descartes, we have generally come to recognize a mind–body dualism where the body and the mind are considered to be distinct from each other, being a material machine-like body and an immaterial conscious mind. These two entities constituting the individual self are nonetheless joined to each other in a mutually interactive fashion. The mind is aware and directs the body, but the needs of the body also influence the intellectual operation of the mind. Since the nineteenth century, the writings of Sigmund Freud have also popularized the notion that the bodily imperatives of the individual are a primary component of social behaviour, as the individual becomes conscious of their own embodiment and subsequently explores and experiences the social world through the bodies of other people (Isbister 1985).

Freud's theories of human psychology have been important and influential in sociology since, in essence, Freud sought to explain how a human being, in the course of his or her individual cognitive development, comes to be incorporated within the structures of social and cultural relations that organize social life. According to Freud, this process of socialization takes place alongside the gradual separation of the infant from its mother, when the formulation of a distinct sense of self takes place (in the form of the ego). The intense experience of a desire for sensory gratification (the pleasure principle) that is natural to human beings, and satisfied initially by the mother, becomes increasingly repressed by the intervention of the social order that prescribes the acceptable adult forms and focus of libidinal interest (the reality principle). This intervention between the infant and their immediate source of gratification, the mother, typically takes the form of the father. This provides the basis for Freud's famous postulation of the Oedipus complex.

From this perspective, the desire for bodily gratification is the most pressing impulse for social behaviour (of which the sexual is the most urgent, and hence the most heavily regulated). This impulse, being fundamental to our embodied state of existence, does not disappear as a result of its external and internalized repression. Instead, much of this instinct is relegated to the realm of the 'unconscious' where it continues to exert subliminal influence over our behaviour. As such, beneath the patina of our conscious, regulated and recognized experience of society (and of ourselves) lies the denied, unconscious, transgressive realm of our unfulfilled desires for sensory gratification. The nature of the unconscious mind, according to Freud, is most discernible in the form of our dreams, where the repressed yearnings of the self reveal themselves in various narrative forms. Dreams, for Freud, represent the symbolic fulfilment of unconscious wishes. Accordingly, some of the most wide-ranging and influential theoretical approaches for understanding why people engage with media, and what happens to them when they do, have emerged from the application of Freud's psychoanalytical techniques to the arena of visual language.

The reasons for this linkage are fairly straightforward. Freudian approaches to media postulate a well-defined relationship between mind and body, allowing the intellectual content of communication and its embodied experience to be considered as a whole (or *gestalt*). As such, psychoanalysis provides a plausible explanation for the profound emotional impact arising from visual communication, where exposure to symbolic content has been seen to elicit physical responses amongst audiences. Further, given the dominant themes of conflict and desire that characterize visual culture, a psychoanalytic approach provides a thematic rationale for the visceral pleasures of popular entertainment while simultaneously foregrounding the critical importance of the gendering of bodies. In that sense, our experience of visual media not only involves the conjoined stimulus of the mind and body as an individual but, through the use of coded symbolic representation, it also mobilizes our powerful attachment to the bodies of others. As such, the Freudian concern with desire in a narrative form draws our attention to the symbolic content of visual media as indicative of a collective sexualized fantasy.

The Birth of Cyberspace

If we position the dramatic content of media as symptomatic of human desires (be they intellectual, corporeal, primal or sensuous), then it makes sense for us to consider the fictional representation of disembodied communications in popular culture. It becomes significant, therefore, that the notion of inhabiting a 'virtual' world where disembodied individuals interact via sensorial 'inputs' generated by computer technologies emerged first in the popular form of science fiction. A very specific description of 'cyberspace' first appears in William Gibson's novel *Neuromancer* (1984), where the term was used to describe an immaterial, digital world inhabited by characters who have 'jacked in' to a universal computer network and who, effectively separated from their material bodies, undertake actions and interactions within this electronic domain. Gibson's book follows on conceptually from Steven Lisberger's 1982 film *Tron*, where the protagonists are able to enter the diegetic world of an early computer game, and Gibson's cyberspace in turn becomes reproduced in *The Matrix* (1999) and other products of mainstream American culture that correspond with the sci-fi genre.

Gibson's 'cyberspace' is also a significant term, since it stems from an older term – 'cybernetics' – which was coined to describe the control systems by which both biological life and man-made machines receive their direction. Developed during the 1940s, when the advanced mechanization of human societies and the new field of electronics was encouraging the re-evaluation of human intelligence, the idea of cybernetics brought together the instrumental goal of developing an artificial thinking machine with a new understanding of mankind itself as a being of this kind (Wiener 1962). At its heart, the basis of cybernetics rests upon a perceived parallel between the mechanical and electrical networks by which the function of things is directed (e.g., the human brain in neuroscience, the reproduction of cells in genetics and the integrated circuit in electronics) (see Von Neumann 1958). Subsequently, the term 'cyborg' was employed by Clynes and Kline to describe a human-machine hybrid being, a biological-mechanical combine that would be suited to survival in outer space (1960). The cyborg was thus imagined in the technology contest of the Cold War as a technologically enhanced 'superman' (Licklider 1960).

The combination of sentient life with mechanized function, and the possible extension of human capability by artificial means had been a prevalent theme in fictional works since the late nineteenth century. A fascination with more powerful bodies was frequently juxtaposed with 'grotesque automation' as a violation of the natural order. As it emerged over the course of the twentieth century, the genre of 'science fiction' was (and is) symbolically marked by mankind's increasing dependence on, and fear of, technology. In that context, cyborgs instantly became stock-of-the-trade villains in popular science fiction (i.e., in the BBCs *Doctor Who* in 1962) and our fascination/revulsion with the mechanical augmentation of the human body continues to find expression in numerous works of popular culture. In the 1980s and 1990s, it was Arnold Schwarzenegger in the form of the *Terminator* films that epitomized our fascination with the mechanized body.

These various works of science fiction, and the scientific agendas that they fictionalized, exerted considerable influence over the ambitions of computer scientists and other researchers involved in the development of digital technologies. Thus, 'cyberspace', as a term that became popular in discussing the potentials of the new media during the 1980s and 1990s, was marked by a legacy that signified the merging of the biological and the mechanical. The visual representation of this hybridization provided a ready indication of the extent to which electronic technology was already associated with the fetish of the body. Despite its prior association with the grotesque, feminist scholar Donna Haraway famously used the term 'cyborg' to describe the new bodily relationships being made possible by personal computing. Harraway's lyrical work heralded the arrival of a genre of 'cyberfeminism' – where the social constraints of femininity previously imposed upon the biology of women would become negated by new forms of social relations that operated at the meeting point between the technologically enhanced body and the anonymous operation of the disembodied self.

There are several consequences to taking seriously the imagery of cyborgs as other than our enemies. Our bodies, ourselves; bodies are maps of power and identity. Cyborgs are no exception. A cyborg body is not innocent; it was not born in a garden; it does not seek unitary identity and so generate antagonistic dualisms without end (or until the world ends); it takes irony for granted. One is too few, and two is only one possibility. Intense pleasure in skill, machine skill, ceases to be a sin, but an aspect of embodiment. The machine is not an it to be animated, worshipped, and dominated. The machine is us, our processes, an aspect of our embodiment. We can be responsible for machines; they do not dominate or threaten us. We are responsible for boundaries. We are they.

Cyborg imagery can suggest a way out of the maze of dualisms in which we have explained our bodies and our tools to ourselves. This is a dream not of a common language, but a powerful infidel heteroglossia. It is an imagination of a feminist speaking in tongues to strike fear into the circuits of the super-savers of the new right. It means both building and destroying machines, identities, categories, relationships, space stories. Though both are bound in the spiral dance, I would rather be a cyborg than a goddess.

Donna Haraway (1991), *Simians, Cyborgs and Women*, New York: Routledge, pp. 180–1

Virtual Reality

Gibson's notion of cyberspace inverted the penetration of the human body by electronic machinery with the possibility of human intelligence entering electronic spaces composed of sensorial stimuli. This idea of information technologies allowing the conscious mind to operate independently of the material body within an immersive media environment was also popularized by the appropriation of 'virtual reality' (VR) technologies. The first crude VR apparatus was developed in 1968 with a visual-only capability for applications such as flight training. These technologies were gradually enhanced in order to service 'defence' needs (as in headset control interfaces for the pilots of supersonic combat aircraft). Sensory simulators combining image and sound were also used for medical research and training. In popular culture, however, the future of virtual reality was imagined as a fully realistic simulation of an 'unreal' world. From the 1970s onwards, and in particular during the late 1980s and early 1990s, the arrival of 'immersive' virtual environments was widely shown as being imminent in popular culture (e.g., the 'holo-deck' in *Star Trek*). Californian technologist Jaron Lanier started VPL Systems in 1985 to develop and commercialize virtual reality systems using visual (headsets), aural (headphones) and tactile (sensor gloves) interfaces. Despite a high degree of public interest, the sensory 'reality' made possible by these technologies remained very limited and it has gradually become clear that virtual reality in this particular form has not proved to be as successful as the foundational idea of virtual reality itself.

There is plenty of evidence that the continuing appeal of a waking dream world remains strong. The technological pursuit of the 'virtual' as a controllable, interactive and out-of-body fantasy rendered by digital simulation is indicative of a widespread desire to go beyond the possibilities and norms of everyday existence as defined by the limitations of our physical bodies (Juul 2005). Without the trappings of VR technologies such as helmets and goggles, the creation of digital environments for fantasy and role play has long been a central pursuit of the computer gaming industry. Early Multi-User Dungeon (or MUD) games allowed a number of players to adopt the roles of wizards, warriors and the like, and to act out those roles in environments created by the game. These 'role-playing game' (RPG) environments have steadily grown in sophistication, from text-based environments, to two-dimensional graphical animations and to three-dimensional modelling. In recent years, the growth of MMORPGs (Massive Multiplayer Online Role-Playing Games) has led to the creation of large-scale virtual worlds where millions of players interact with each other through conventional mouse, keyboard and voice interfaces. Many of these games also allow for the wide-ranging personalization of the game environment in response to the commands of game players.

In the distinctive out-of-body experience of online gaming, the body once again takes centre stage in a symbolic form. Each player represents themselves through a recognizable anthropomorphic character acting under their direction. These are called 'avatars' (drawing somewhat immodestly upon the terminology of Hinduism – where an avatar is an earthly form taken by a divine being). Overwhelmingly, the avatars chosen or designed by game players are bodily representations which massively emphasize the gender traits symbolically marked as desirable (e.g., voluptuous females and muscular males). These super-bodies also display a marked flamboyance of costume (bold colours, tight-to-the-body styles, high boots, masks and capes) and body adornment (dramatic make-up patterns, tattoos, strapping and prominent personal weaponry). The avatar, then, expresses divinity mainly in the form of fetish. This would appear to reflect not only the historically prevalent obsession with the ideal human body, but also the wider impact of the saturation of society with images of human perfection in an era of personalized consumption and mass advertising. In part, we might justify the general schemata of game avatars in the context of the environments and roles in which they operate (sword and sorcery, superheroes, etc.). Typically, game designs offer very limited choices of body shapes to players, since these are themed fantasies and not naturally occurring social environments.

However, the popularity of Second Life – a 'game' in which players are able to play out the immensely detailed everyday lives of their characters – is perhaps the most telling example of the ongoing quest for immersive out-of-body experiences (Enslinn and Muse 2011). As a collaborative disembodied fantasy based upon everyday life, the body images deployed in Second Life are consciously created by game players, and are therefore subject to the demands of players in important ways. In this context, it seems likely that consistent demands for more realistic modes of bodily representation could, and would, be responded to. However, the bodily forms assumed in Second Life are markedly homogeneous in their youthful perfection. Avatars taking the form of elderly, physically fragile or 'overweight' bodies are almost never used. Indeed, if we survey the nature of the human body on view in cyberspace in more general terms (recognizing that depictions of the human body in some form comprise the majority of available digital information), then we quickly come to the realization that the human body in cyberspace has inexorably taken on a highly sexualized and exaggerated form. It is logical to assume then, on the basis of empirical evidence, that this display of body fetishism is likely to be an important part of the appeal of the online world for most users.

Box 5.1 Digital liberation

From one set of perspectives, the capacity for disembodied social relations articulated through the new media is potentially liberating, because:

- It allows people to escape the physical limitations placed upon their own bodies in the material world
- It allows people to supersede the social constraints that are widely enforced by the embodied discourses of race, gender, age and so on
- It allows the full expression of our inner selves in an environment where we face no physical harm as a result of those expressions

Therefore, the opportunities offered for switching identity roles (shape-changing) and exploring new forms of self-identity and expression allow us to become multidimensional beings, something more than our physical selves.

Jacques Lacan and the Ideal Self

Extending Freud's psychoanalytic theories within the post-war tradition of French structuralism, Jacques Lacan claimed that the interplay of conscious and unconscious desire is made evident in the form of language (Lacan 1953; Wilden 1968). For Lacan, it was language that takes on the role of the father, and enforces the reality principle (and hence the social order) through its internalization by the individual. Lacan believed that the given form of language determines what are acceptable and unacceptable desires within its own inherent symbolic order. Thus, as we begin to learn language, we move away from our natural instinct towards immediate physical gratification and instead enter the adult realm of language, and hence the social world, where gratification becomes largely symbolic in nature. As such, language shapes our personal experience of desire, which is subsequently manifested socially in the form of texts and images. Lacan nonetheless maintains the central place of the body in Freudian psychoanalysis, linking it to the notion of the body as a symbolic device in its own right.

Prior to the development of language skills, Lacan sees the infant as incapable of distinguishing between itself and its object of desire (the mother). Lacan goes on to identify a subsequent 'mirror stage' where the infant begins to comprehend the distinction between self and (m)other. At first, the child mistakes the body image it sees in a mirror for another self (an as-yet-unrealized complete self). Afterwards when the mirror image of the self is perceived consciously as a reflection of the physical self, it continues to function unconsciously as an idealized other self. This externalized ego provides the focus for a narcissistic identification with a body image. As such, it is useful to think of the parallels between Lacan's account of the ideal self as a symbolic body and our identification with the digital avatar. Arguably, the capacity to not only see, but also personally direct, the symbolic body of the avatar demonstrates the strongest psychological link between the ego of the viewer and their idealized self that we have seen to date in the visual media. In this respect, two of the most fundamental aspects of the bodily pleasures obtained from digital media can be related, respectively, to the *pleasure of looking* and the *pleasure of transference*.

Box 5.2 Visual pleasure and the virtual body

Voyeurism: The pleasure of looking relates to the gratification that is derived from gazing upon what is symbolically marked as pleasurable. The act of looking is unidirectional, and therefore represents an action of subjective power from which personal pleasure is derived. The most common experience of voyeurism is the capacity to observe the physicality and the bodily intimacy of others, for example, the pleasure derived from viewing the body of a film star, the virtual body of Lara Croft or from pornographic imagery.

Identification: This is a form of pleasure derived from the temporary transference of the self-identification of the viewer to the body being shown on the screen. The sensory detachment of the conscious mind from our physical body allows us to imagine ourselves as occupying the more pleasurable body depicted in symbolic form, taking on its potency and sharing its sensory experience. This transference of self to a superior symbolic body can be closely related to Lacan's theorization of the mirror stage and the unconscious desire for an idealized self that is symbolically whole. This is another way of understanding the pleasure that people derive from identifying with the bodily image and capacities of their digital avatar.

Cybersex and Electronic Pornography

Whilst early research on online communication struggled to accommodate the absence of the body and its symbolic contribution to social communication, the advent of the graphical Internet in the early 1990s unleashed an informational flood of body images. As the interaction of human beings and computer interfaces produced a fundamental destabilization of bodily norms and constraints in game environments, it should come as no surprise that the wider Internet became, right from its inception, a highly sexualized domain. From the early mass distribution of pornographic images on UseNet newsgroups to contemporary on-demand video streaming, the pursuit of pornographic pleasures (and their attendant profits) has always been one of the major uses of the Internet medium. The popularization of the Internet demonstrated the enormous potential for growth in the consumption of pornography via the digital medium. In large part, this was to do with the private and individualized nature of reception via the personal computer.

The intimacy of the one-to-one relationship between computer and user that had already been felt so keenly by early adopters of the medium tended to generate the same sense of technological cocooning that had previously encouraged flaming in professional forums. Emboldened by a perceived distance from the physicality of the pornographic subject, the private context of domestic viewing also lowered many of the social inhibitions that circumscribed the consumption of pornography. The advent of Internet search engines also made it possible for viewers to seek out sexually explicit material directly without the mediation of a physical human supplier. The viewer of online pornography was thus able to avoid the embarrassing social encounter that this inevitably entails, further mitigating the social stigma surrounding masturbation in most cultures. During the late 1990s, 25 per cent of Internet searches were for sexually explicit images, making pornographic content a major driver for the uptake of the new medium. Pornographic content still represents some 12 per cent of web content and about 20 per cent of all traffic (Search Engine Watch 2011).

UseNet groups soon became inoperable due to their targeting by opportunistic advertising. Consequently, pornographic content rapidly migrated to dedicated websites offering access to low-resolution images of nudity and sexual acts. Building initially upon the visual conventions established by magazine pornography, these 'adult' websites quickly extended and reconfigured the presentation of sexual imagery as the semantic organization of the pornographic exchange was translated (or remediated) into the digital medium. In the process, folders of pornographic images were carefully indexed and arranged around a common set of typologies that offered a menu of sexual acts and body types, either within a single website or across an interlinked system of websites (known as 'webring'). The sequential image sequences of the magazine format gave way to a hyperlinked catalogue arrangement of sexual imagery, where bodies are 'galleried' by race, age, shape and costume. As such, race, far from disappearing as a structure of power, was recast within an exaggerated matrix of exploitation (Nakamura 2007). With the simultaneous medium shift from analogue video to digital interactive services and DVD playback as a mode of delivery, the revenues of pornographic producers soon exceeded the takings of both the music and mainstream film industries. Combining a low cost of production, premium pricing and what appeared to be particularly compulsive patterns of demand, it was evident that massive profits were being made in the arena of sexual entertainment (Cronin and Davenport 2001; Lane 2001).

As a consequence of this expansion in the market, competitive pressures have arisen from a sudden oversupply of pornographic content. With a far greater volume of pornographic material in circulation, this appears to be resulting in increasingly explicit and 'hardcore' representations of sex becoming the norm. Nudity, evidently, is no longer enough to arouse sufficient interest amongst a smorgasbord of sexual content, and so commercial sexual images and performances have entered a new era of experimentation. The supply of pornographic images has been augmented by other variants of so-called 'cybersex' that combine the pictorial capacity of the medium with its interactive capabilities. 'Contact' magazines for individuals seeking like-minded sexual partners were upgraded in the electronic format, using personal profiles, email and anonymous chat to bringing together individuals with particular sexual objectives (e.g., adultfriendfinder.com). Phone sex services also moved swiftly to make use of online chat technologies and the advent of the webcam facilitated the arrival of online peep shows. Anonymous communication also favoured the proliferation of cybersex community forums where sexual information and opinion could be shared. Taking one example, Lynne Pettinger has recently studied the use of online customer reviews in the prostitution business (Pettinger 2011).

More broadly, it has been the personalized mode of consumption that has finally made the mass media suitable for explicit sexual entertainment and exploitation at such a broad scale. Nonetheless, the basic premise of pornography remains the pursuit of a perfect visual representation of sexual satisfaction. In the process, the bodies associated with pornography have evolved from the 'natural' bodies of traditional still photography to the hyper-athletic, cosmetically and surgically enhanced bodies that seem to define this new era of pornography. Nonetheless, pornography continues to articulate a symbolic desire whose appeal cannot be seemingly separated from the transgressive positioning of its production and consumption. At the same time, various forms of virtual electronic sex have, without a doubt, already become part of everyday life for millions of people in digital society. The sociology of sex has yet to fully accommodate the scale and import of 'cybersex' activities, but it has become clear that the generation born since the 1990s has grown up with access to an arena of sexual imagery that exceeds the experience of preceding generations by a large margin. This seems likely to impact upon their sexual expectations and attitudes.

In the last few years, technical advances in digital video and animation have heralded what we could call the era of 'Porn 2.0'. User-driven web portals – where sex videos are shared amongst users – are undermining the market for commercial porn websites as well as hitting DVD sales in the pornographic 'mainstream'. In that respect, this industry is undergoing a similar crisis to other traditional content providers in the networked media environment. In other arenas, the development of sophisticated three-dimensional modelling software, such as DAZ 3D, has seen an explosion in sexually explicit animations that use digital avatars in simulated video clips and as participants in interactive sexual representations. The crossover between the explicit realism of pornography and the bodily fetish of the avatar has already been prefigured extensively through the development of sexually themed computer games, as well as sexually explicit modifications to mainstream games, suggesting that there is sufficient cause to be attentive to 'the impact that including, or engaging in sexual encounters will have upon the pleasures and experiences associated with the act of *playing* digital games and the narratives themselves' (Schott 2005: 18). It is already notable that a considerable proportion of interaction between users in online games such as Second Life has a sexually explicit dimension.

Box 5.3 Digital degeneration

From a permissive viewpoint, the advent of cybersex applications underwrites the agenda for personal liberation operating through the discourse of the virtual body. Users are free to pursue their own sexual expression online, remaining safe from censure, disease and violence. The libido is freed from the constraints imposed by the material body and by the wider social order. From a countervailing set of perspectives, however, sexual activity in cyberspace can also be seen negatively as:

- A graphical expression of oppressive social norms defining beauty, power and sexuality
- A violation of divine laws that govern sexual modesty
- Evidence of widespread insecurity about our 'real' bodies
- An expression of an urgent desire to comply with (impossible) social expectations about sexual performance
- Responding to a profound alienation from human intimacy
- A final symbolic retreat from the pursuit of interpersonal relations in a material form

---

The Digital Body as a Gestural Device

In accordance with other domains of bodily representation enacted through digital media, the sexed function of the pornographic actor increasingly appears as a caricature of digital and surgical exaggeration. This body is deployed symbolically as the ultimate site of gratification, rendered explicit for remote consumption without any affective intimacy, and marked as a cipher for sensory excess. In that sense, the sexual politics of the digital body provide a visual account of the power relationships enacted between sexed bodies, expressing corporeal desires with overtones that are as much disturbing as liberating. Correspondingly, the use of virtual environments for the pursuit of bodily gratification can be seen to reinforce the primacy of the biological order within social communication. In this respect, the broader phenomenon of cybersex further highlights the new electronic dualism of subjective disembodiment being articulated through the fetish of the body image. The critical question is whether: 'By pursuing a purely realist aesthetic, in common with pornography, will we reach a point where digital bodies will be able to directly hack into the central nervous system to actualize their virtual affects for pleasure?' (Schott 2005: 18)

Given the early recognition that remote communication destabilizes existing norms of social communication due to the loss of proximate consequences and the (mis)perception of technological cocooning, it should come as little surprise that the popularization of the digital medium has witnessed upheavals in the sexual mores of societies across the globe. From a Freudian perspective, where the social world is constructed around sexual inhibitions, this is a logical outcome of a reconfiguration of social power. As such, the various phenomena of digital sexuality could be easily anticipated through a psychoanalytical approach to social conditioning and to the graphical representation of the human body. This line of thinking was, of course, prefigured via the social revolutions in Europe and North America during the 1960s. The so-called 'counter-culture' of the baby-boom generation had already established a precedent for the flattening of social hierarchies, the pursuit of sensory expansion and the social expression of the self through a sexually liberated body. 'The cyborg', as Donna Haraway reminded us, 'is a bad girl' (1991). In that sense, it is of passing interest that the widespread celebration of the virtual body was coterminous with the passing of that generation into late middle age. It is more broadly significant, however, that the avatar was conceived as a forever-young (and exhibitionist) body.

While Haraway chose to position the shape-changing possibilities of bodily impersonation as liberating, allowing those marginalized by age, gender or race to leap into new subjective positions, other critics pointed to the symbolic symptoms of economic, racial, gendered power that continued to structure interpersonal relations on both sides of the screen (Balsamo 1997; Nakamura 2007). In another dimension, we could see the very notion of cyberspace as an alternative site of existence to be an unrealistic exaggeration of the capacity of the medium. Certainly, the attendant emphasis placed upon the binary opposition of online and offline worlds failed to recognize the necessary symbiosis of material and virtual lives implied by the cognitive and corporeal needs of the human subject. Nonetheless, our obvious ambition to supersede this Cartesian dualism of mind–body by technological means certainly proved to be a powerful factor in the making of the electronic domain. In electing to immerse our consciousness within a new immaterial body, the symbolic fetish of the body (its language function) has become paramount, shaping a new electronic dualism that consequently transcends and reaffirms the embodiment of the self in explicit relation to other iconic bodies.

Clearly, in order to understand the import of this newfound subjectivity, we need to approach interpersonal communication online as something much more than a functional instance of information exchange within hierarchical groups. Instead, we must situate embodiment, potency and presence as being constituted by broader social practices that act upon us in a number of ways: as conduits for language, as technological-sensory interfaces, as transmitters of ideology, as sites of debate and as sources of pleasure. Much of the time, we may only be unconsciously aware of the influence of those social forces, and arguably we need to be much more cognitive of the fact that the human body is inherently a social possession. It is this social, rather than individual, nature of embodiment that has been made graphically evident in such effective fashion by the phenomena arising from the meeting of digital technologies, sensory extension and the intrinsically organic manifestations of human behaviour.

Think and Discuss

1. Key Terms
Can you describe in simple language what is meant by the following terms found in this chapter?

- Voyeurism
- Avatar
- Virtual reality
- Dualism
- Social presence

2. Critical Questions
Try answering the following questions, drawing upon your own understanding, experience and knowledge.

1. If the body forms a essential component of face-to-face communication, what are the implications for disembodied social interaction via media?
2. Do interactive technologies effectively separate sensory consciousness from the parameters of the physical body ?
3. Why does Donna Haraway see the figure of the 'cyborg' as offering new possibilities for personal liberation?
4. How does the expression of sexuality manifested on the Internet to date relate to the accounts of human sexuality offered by Freud and Lacan?
5. Anne Balsamo argues that the virtual realities that we have created are actually extending the scope of gendered embodiment. Taking the example of Second Life, what is your assessment of that argument?

Further Reading

Balsamo, Anne (1997) *Technologies of the Gendered Body: Reading Cyborg Women,* Durham, NC, and London: Duke University Press.

Baym, Nancy (2010) *Personal Connections in the Digital Age*, Cambridge: Polity.

Ben-Ze'ev, Aaron (2004) *Love Online: Emotions on the Internet*, Cambridge: Cambridge University Press.

Cronin, Blaise and Davenport, Elisabeth (2001) 'E-Rogenous Zones: Positioning Pornography in the Digital Economy', *The Information Society*, 17(1): 33–48.

Featherstone, Mike and Burrows, Roger (eds) (1996) *Cyberspace, Cyberbodies, Cyberpunk: Cultures Of Technological Embodiment,* London: Sage.

Haraway, Donna (1991) *Simians, Cyborgs and Women*, New York: Routledge.

Hayles, Katharine (1999) *How We Became Posthuman: Virtual Bodies in Cybernetics, Literature and Informatics*, Chicago, IL: University of Chicago Press.

Lane III, Frederik (2001) *Obscene Profits: The Entrepreneurs of Pornography in the Cyber Age*, London: Routledge.

Turkle, S. (1996) *Life on the Screen: Identity in the Age of the Internet*, New York: Simon and Schuster.

Go Online

Second Life – www.secondlife.com/
Jacques Lacan – www.lacan.com/
World of Warcraft – www.battle.net/wow/
DAZ 3D – http://www.daz3d.com/
Digital Body Enhancement – http://demo.fb.se/e/girlpower/retouch/retouch/index.html

CHAPTER 6

Reality Checks

The 1990s, the decade of the public Internet, started (as most decades do) with a war. The role of the media in this war was highly significant (as, of course, it always is). What was seen as markedly different in the Kuwait War of 1990–1 was the altered status, or putative absence, of something previously known as 'reality', a touchstone to which media accounts of warfare had always been assumed to refer. New media technologies, new military technologies, new command-and-control systems and new media management doctrines all coalesced around a visual spectacle of warfare that was quite unlike anything those away from the battlefield had ever seen before. Whilst television journalism in Vietnam had brought the 'reality' of war home to millions of spectators on photographic film during the 1960s and 1970s, the conflict in the Persian Gulf acquired a very different look. The mediation of this desert war mobilized a digital resolution that brought something of an 'unreal' quality to the gaze of viewers accustomed to equating truth with grainy images. For this reason, the war in Kuwait became known as the first 'video-game war', starting a long process of cohabitation between computer gaming and bloodshed in the Middle East.

At this point in history, images of war became accessible, instantaneous, 24/7, and 'live' in a manner that was previously unimaginable. The procession of computerized animations of battlefield situations and camera feeds from the noses of falling bombs – all of which brought us closer than ever before to the technologies of war (if not to their victims) – made it effectively impossible to distinguish between the war itself and the media spectacle through which we participated in its conduct. Watching the images that defined this war in the public imagination, Jean Baudrillard famously concluded that the Kuwait War was a virtual event, since for all intents and purposes, the war that we saw didn't actually happen at all – except in the media (1995). Baudrillard's statement, on the face of it, appeared to be a preposterous claim (it is a matter of record that hundreds of thousands of people died). However, the real focus of Baudrillard's remarks was the apparent (and, for him, irreconcilable) disconnect between the electronic media and the depiction of reality, a tearing apart that was as much psychological and philosophical as it was technical in nature.

Hyper-realism

The pre-digital mass media largely displayed what we could call an 'indexical' link to things that were widely understood by its audience as being somehow 'real'. In the nineteenth century, the photochemical image captured 'everyday' realities (and time itself) in the form of the frozen image of light on paper. Even the twentieth-century fantasies of cinema had to be staged in, and assembled from, slices of reality. In the digital era, however, the linkage between media representations and reality suddenly seemed to undergo an irrevocable shift. The computer-manipulated images that now surround us are no longer intuitively understood as having any intrinsic basis in reality. They could be entirely built up from the abstractions of computer code, or have been modified pixel by pixel to alter almost any aspect of what is being depicted. At one level, the staging, 'touching up' and framing of images are mundane processes of visual production. At another level, however, our newfound capacity to electronically airbrush the complexions of magazine models and produce flawless good looks is an indication of the extent to which we have come to expect almost any image to become something 'better' than real. We can see this clearly in the domain of cybersex and, as Baudrillard pointed out, we can also see this exaggerated aesthetic emerging in the images of war as they become increasingly stylized by the look and feel of the video game.

The aesthetic that prevails in the era of digital imaging software becomes emblematic of an enhanced and modified iconography. It renders a visual language couched in phrases of impossible symbolic perfection. Like the contours of the digital body, the visual narratives of the contemporary electronic media seek to exceed, enhance and replace the reality that they supposedly represent. In doing so, they pursue the most emphatic symbolic use of the image (its iconicity) at the expense of any compulsion to remain faithful to the subject of the image (its indexicality). This shift towards a hyperbolic language-world becomes increasingly naturalized in our thinking, at the expense of any prior assumption that something more than an arbitrary connection exists between the image of something and the substance of that thing. This disconnection overturns the primacy that was given to the real in the earlier photographic mass media, as immortalized by the phrase 'the camera never lies'.

The 'realist aesthetic' was critically important to modernist thinking because it implied that there was an observable material reality that could be recorded objectively. Such a claim was in accordance with both the 'scientific' sociology of positivism and the materialism of the Marxist school. The *observable* existence of a material reality, independent of human spiritual or political beliefs, provided a new foundation for objective truth and scientific evidence. Attempts to 'capture' this reality via media technologies nonetheless represented a significant challenge, since the technical processes of mediation invariably required numerous human interventions in order to appear 'naturalistic' to the human eye. Modern realism consequently took on two major forms, a 'documentary' tradition that favoured direct modes of 'recording' with minimal intervention, and a 'Hollywood realism' that sought to give various genres of visual storytelling a more 'natural' appearance. In practice, the two forms were often combined and blended into each other in order to construct the visual language of the modern. As such, the authoritative claims of the realistic aesthetic were necessarily subject to several layers of mediation. Nonetheless, despite a broad recognition of photographic artifice, much of the symbolic power of the image in the twentieth century was derived from its foundational claims upon a real subject.

In the emergent idiom of the digital image, the reality of the image source becomes effectively inscrutable. As Arild Fetveit points out: 'The development of computer programs for manipulation and generation of images has made it, at times, very hard to see whether we are looking at ordinary photographical images or images that have been digitally altered . . . Thus the evidential power of composite and digitally manipulated images is practically lost' (1999: 795). No primary material referent is needed, and the mutability of a digital record means that no definitive version of an image can be seen to exist. Consequently, it is not the origin of the image, but the aesthetic perfection of the subject that becomes predominant. In place of 'indexicality', we get 'simulation', as the digital image enacts social and linguistic gestures that supersede material proof. In place of 'representation', we get 'remediation'. The 'look' and 'feel' of the photographic medium is reprocessed through digital algorithms, the imprint of the older medium providing a touchstone for a 'photo-real' aesthetic that has become an everyday phrase, albeit one that is rarely interrogated in any depth.

Photo-realism

'Photo-realism' was a leading ambition of digital software and hardware designers at the turn of the millennium. In the 1990s, the processing power of affordable computers, the limitations of visual display technologies, the scarcity of Internet bandwidth and the sensitivity of CCD sensors all served to ensure that the digital image remained visibly inferior in terms of 'image resolution' that could be achieved. Images capable of matching the 'quality' of photographic images required very large bitmap files and very expensive equipment. Even then, the capacity to print high-resolution images was ill-served by the dominant 'inkjet' technologies. Despite the perceived shortfall in resolution that made the need for 'photo-realism' so apparent, there was an explosion in the popularity of digital imaging technologies. Software such as Adobe's Photoshop was widely taken up by amateur photographers and art students. The newfound capacity to manipulate photographic images, and exceed the inherent limitations of the original medium in countless ways, saw the advent of a more compositional and experimental approach to photography.

This 'painterly' mode of visual language was a shot in the arm for surrealists, combining photographic realism with the expressive potential of painting and drawing. However, the artistic exuberance of early experimentation was always subordinate to the pursuit of higher image resolutions and their commercialization. On the back of massive investments by technology developers, the suite of applications that constitute the digital imaging process were able to surpass the resolution of the photographic image during the first decade of the twenty-first century. Photo-realism was achieved comparatively quickly, and ceased to be a selling point of next-generation imaging equipment. The term itself, however, has remained in the public imagination, imbued with wider associations with symbolic perfection. The greatest significance of photo-realism is the ease with which colours can be corrected, visual blemishes removed, shadows altered, legs lengthened, chests enlarged and plumes of smoke added to reportage.

As a matter of habit, the new status of images substitutes the physical index for what Baudrillard and other thinkers (such as Italian semiotician Umberto Eco) referred to as the 'hyper-real' (Baudrillard 1994; Eco 1986). The hyper-real operates as a symbolic exaggeration that produces something more suggestive of meaning than the faithful depiction of the real object. It is the unprecedented saturation of these 'larger-than-life' images in the conduct of everyday affairs that led Baudrillard to claim that our fundamental experience of major events in the world had been obliterated by the power of their 'hyper-real' representation (1995). Our everyday encounter with hyper-reality is deeply embedded in the process of communication. That is because, practically speaking, very little of what we know about our world comes from first-hand sensory experience. As a result, our social imagination is largely framed in reference to various forms of representation (images, words, sounds) operating through what Stuart Hall called the 'circuit of communication' (1980). In this 'social constructivist' view, the process of mediation involves the production of a symbolic account of the world, as opposed to containing objective 'truthful' representations of anything in that world.

Pursued to a more global level, this is a loss concerning our sense of contact with reality through audio-visual representations. Within a McLuhanesque understanding, media are 'extensions of man', prosthetic devices that extend our perceptive apparatus. From this perspective, the loss of indexicality could be interpreted as a powerful refiguration of these extensions, implicating our perceptive apparatus. In this refiguration, representations based upon the iconic/indexical are being replaced by representations sustaining the iconic, but losing the causal connection to reality. Thus, to the extent that indexicality is lost, we might not only lose evidential power, we might come to feel a sense of losing touch with reality, like being stranded in the world of the simulacrum.

Arild Fetveit (1999), 'Reality TV in the Digital Era: A Paradox In Visual Culture?', *Media, Culture & Society*, 21(6): 797

Jean Baudrillard and the Order of Simulation

The term 'simulacrum' (meaning an artificial reproduction) is ancient in origin. According to Baudrillard, images are always simulacra because they are always pictures of things, not the things themselves. Despite being inherently artificial and unreal, images are nonetheless imbued with real meaning. The force of those meanings is not limited by what is literally depicted within the image, so much as what is being signified or suggested at a deeper level. This language-function of images invariably operates by association and/or juxtaposition with other images. Images as a means of communication can be seen to constitute a symbolic language that exists over and above the actual objects they represent. For example, the visual aesthetic of beauty has far greater symbolic power than any individual body image of a single human being. The body is required to conform to the social meanings given to body images and thereby submit to what we might, following the French school of semiology, call the power of the sign.

In the contemporary electronic media, Baudrillard argued that images function well beyond their descriptive role in denoting some form of 'reality principle' through which meanings are underwritten. Instead, digital images, as they multiply in everyday practice, take on an exaggerated iconic nature that is far more like a word than a painting. Working not singly, but always in combination, these iconic images begin to create new meanings of their own, that is, images composed with reference to images. Visual statements subsequently refer to long chains of other images before they provide any indexical link to a real person or object. As a consequence, the meaning of anything and everything becomes firmly located within this larger 'signifying order', which Baudrillard characterizes as a massive cumulative fabrication. By this logic, we live in an era of visual simulation on a grand scale. Within such a context, images can only be judged by the efficacy, or the depth, of the simulation itself (that is, the virtuosity of their performance). Since, following McLuhan, Baudrillard also believed that we have come to live our lives largely as a second-hand sensory experience, he claimed that the multiplication of image-worlds has resulted in a splintering of objective reality that can be best understood in relation to the 'order of simulation'.

Box 6.1 The order of simulation

In a world increasingly defined, to all intents and purposes, by its mediation, Baudrillard distinguished between three different scales of 'simulation', each step up in scale signifying a further progression away from the notion of objective physical reality:

First-order simulation – a consciously artificial representation of the real, intended to be read as such (e.g., a chemical photograph of my house)

Second-order simulation – where the symbolic representation of the real is given a reality of its own (e.g., a map of France is a powerful symbol of social identity)

Third-order simulation – where the dominant mode of representation has no necessary relationship to (or need for) a source of reality (e.g., any image produced through the abstract calculations of computers)

Stratified Realities

If we accept Baudrillard's diagnosis of a modern society reeling from the saturation of media images, we might still seek a practical means of understanding the likely impact of this upon the 'real' world of social interactions. As such, the order of simulation can be applied to the subjective experience of mediated hyper-reality in everyday life as well as to the purely 'virtual' realities of 'online' worlds. That doesn't make it a simple matter in either case. A photograph of my baby can be read as a first-order simulation, but were it placed on the cover of a mothering magazine (as a symbolic referent to infants in general), then it would become a second-order simulation. If, in the process, the image was altered digitally to become more pleasing, then it is on the verge of becoming a third-order simulation. This is where mass communication and digital imaging both work to drive the hyper-reality effect. Conversely, the 'virtual' status of immersive media environments is primarily claimed on the basis that those representations have no indexical value, and thus no basis in (or need for) the first order of simulation. Visually, they appear to function at the level of second-order simulation in terms of the graphical references that make up the interface of the virtual worlds (bodies, objects, places, spatial movements).

More broadly, taking the digital media as a technology of representation, we could argue that technically, since its content only exists at the level of binary digital code, these are all third-order simulations. From this perspective, all digital 'realities' are purely symbolic. As a means of compensation, the longstanding pursuit of the 'photo-real' aesthetic across all applications of digital imaging reveals an inherent longing for 'texture' – that is, a desire to garb the world of pure simulation with the 'surface' conditions recorded by earlier media technologies. In that respect, hyper-real visualizations emerging from both 'real' and 'virtual' domains render digital fantasies that mimic the same aesthetics. The new photo-realism of digital imaging consequently imitates, hollows out and collapses the realist aesthetic that was once considered so essential to modern life. In its absence, reality is stratified via several layers of mimicry.

Box 6.2 Orders of reality

Physical reality – this is the subjective experience of life that privileges the material world that we can touch, that we can assess empirically and to which we are bound biologically
Hyper reality – this is the subjective experience of life that gives meaning to the world, located in the symbolic order of language; this is the dominant arena of social communication
Virtual reality – this is the subjective experience of life existing purely through the sensory experiences that frame the viewer within a fictional domain, whether alone or with others

Dangerous Realisms or Threatening Fantasies?

The pursuit of the highest possible degrees of image resolution has not been confined to the static image. It has been a practical concern for the movie business in making the switch to digital production, and a selling point for the remediation of motion pictures. Much more significantly, it has been the computer gaming industry that has driven the development of advanced graphical capabilities in everyday digital devices. From the very basic two-dimensional simulations of the earliest computer games to the immersive game environments of the present, the possibility of 'photo-realistic gaming' has been a consistent feature of product development and advertising. Given that computer games constitute a purely simulated environment, the photo-realism deployed by the gaming industry eschews any indexical referent. Rather, the incredible 'realism' of computer gaming is taken as a relative measure of the graphical sophistication of the virtual environment in which the game takes place. In the last decade, the commercial and aesthetic cohabitation of digital cinema animation and computer gaming has increasingly come to define the boundaries of contemporary photo-realism.

The increasing resolution of the graphical interface has been accompanied by rising concerns about the 'realistic' nature of representation seen in popular gaming titles. Whilst the 'shooting up' of geometric objects and crude pixel graphics in the 1970s did not raise serious concerns about the 'violent' content of computer games, the advent of photo-realistic games has since provoked concerns about the potential harms stemming from graphic depictions of violence (and more occasionally sexual acts) in computer games. At the heart of this criticism is the notion that the more 'lifelike' a given representation becomes, the more power it has to influence the outlook and behaviour of the viewer. As such, photo-realistic game content becomes associated with a propensity to commit violent acts, due to a perceived cognitive spillover between simulated and physical realities. In this way, the ghost of the realist aesthetic has come to haunt the computer gaming industry (Anderson et al. 2007).

In 2007, 'popular' psychologist Tanya Byron cooperated with the UK government in a major campaign to assess the dangers that video games present to children. It was subsequently recommended that an age-based restriction by the British Board of Film Classification be extended to include all electronic games and gaming devices (Byron 2008). The BBFC is required to classify all video games on the basis of the suitability of their content for minors. This classification regime was conceived in thematic terms. That is, the problem of computer games was seen to be primarily a representational one, stemming not from how difficult, infuriating or manipulative any game design is, but rather the degree to which the game presents violent or sexualized content considered to be too 'realistic', and therefore graphically 'explicit'. However, only 2 per cent of games released in the UK have since been '18' rated, which suggests either that games are generally mild in content or that the BBFC regime compares them to norms seen in film and television, where violence has long been tolerated in the context of entertainment.

A marked emphasis on child safety may well seem incongruous when the average age of a UK gamer is twenty-eight. Despite the professed comparison with other mediums such as film and television, it is also clear that the player of computer games is conceived in quite different ways from the TV viewer or the cinema spectator. This is due to a number of factors, including the interactive nature of game-playing, the intensity of engagement required to play the game, the consistent targeting of older male children as primary consumers and the generally one-on-one interface for most games. For all these reasons, game players are not understood as a mass audience in the same way that audiences for broadcast media are, even if their numbers are comparable. Similarly, gaming is not seen as a social activity in the way that going to the cinema is. As a consequence, the game player has commonly been infantilized and associated with anti-social tendencies stemming from their 'withdrawal' from reality into compulsive use of the media. Whilst a number of studies (e.g., Durkin and Barber 2002; Gee 2003) have sought to emphasize the acquisition of problem-solving and pro-social skills through games, it is fair to say that the game player has primarily been approached as a social problem by researchers.

Box 6.3 Common sociological concerns with computer games

- The psychological and cognitive conditions that structure game play
- The behavioural effects following exposure to computer games
- The nature of the symbolic representations that determine the 'meaning' of computer games
- The relationship between the game world and the formation and expression of personal identity amongst game players

---

Games as Media

It is worth noting that the computer game, patented in 1948, is almost as old as the electronic computer itself. Many of the early computer games were offshoots of programs that were using computers to calculate missile trajectories. Others, such as 'flight simulators' for pilot training were slightly less sinister in nature. For the most part, the enjoyment of these games was initially restricted to the highly educated technicians who operated the massively expensive government-owned computing machineries. A handful of games were nonetheless adapted for commercial coin-operated machines by the beginning of the 1970s. Electronic chess and chequers were also reasonably successful as novelty domestic games, but computerized versions of these existing game practices were quickly superseded by the appearance of new kinds of games that only computers and rasterized graphics displays made possible. By the end of the decade, the fairground model of the gaming arcade had become a significant pastime for the entertainment of children. Most critically, it was the advent of the personal computer in the 1970s, and the popular enthusiasm to own these new machines, that provided the impetus for the lucrative computer entertainment industry we recognize today (see Wolf 2007).

One of the major factors to be overcome was that those who had traditionally been involved in the world of entertainment (in movies, TV, music or making toys) were not generally literate in the new information technology. At the same time, the computer technicians and programmers of the Cold War had little knowledge of what the masses required by way of fun. Nonetheless, despite all the conceptual difficulties this must have posed for those seeking to create content for the new medium, the rise of the computer game was spectacular in its speed and reach. In the initial phase of commercial development, the personal computer was not yet connected by telephony and game content was primarily designed as an intensive one-on-one application. This individuation, along with the inherent interactivity of the medium, made it strikingly different from the older broadcast media in technical as well as conceptual terms. Consequently, the computer game represented a critical shift from modes of entertainment focused on fixed, linear, dramatic narratives towards a media experience constituted by interactivity, ongoing response and narrative fluidity. It also marked a sea change in the media environment, ushering in a paradigm that favours individual rather than shared use.

There are a number of factors to consider when we think about the computer game as a contemporary media form. Certainly, the military origins of the format are significant, but the central premise of hand–eye coordination and spatial recognition exercises also make it worth remembering that the computer game is as much the descendant of mechanical pinball as it is of strategic missile applications. Equally, there were other antecedents to the simulated environments of the virtual game, not least in the allegorical combat of the medieval chess board. With the advent of electronics, the widespread integration of sport via television had already instigated a social setting where this highly symbolic form of leisure had become a mediated experience for most of its audience. The TV game show had already flourished on the popular demand for competitive, reward-driven rituals as a form of entertainment. Games and gaming, then, as an ancient form of social practice, had steadily become more and more mediated in modern society, and the computer game can be seen as a logical development within this context.

Computer games, in their design origins and in their contemporary formats, are inherently problem-based. 'Winning' a game always entails the resolution of defined logical and spatial problems within a simulated game environment. Play is undertaken by means of coordinated mental and physical responses expressed through strategic thinking, hand–eye coordination and intensive stimulus–response exchanges between the computer and its user(s). Advanced games are commonly described as 'challenging', 'difficult' or even 'impossible', not a common selling point in other entertainment media. By convention, games are designed to get more difficult as play progresses, and thus 'success' in most games is defined in terms of how effectively the player is able to master the problematic of the game before being overwhelmed by increasing game speeds, more precise spatial deployments or less favourable computer-player game ratios. In order to both maximize their appeal and perpetuate the interest of players, most games contain parameters that can be set to skew variables within the problem more or less in the player's favour.

Box 6.4 The game algorithm

Wolf and Perron describe the major functions of a game algorithm under four headings:
Representation is the manner in which the game interface shows the 'world' in which the game takes place, both visually and conceptually.

Rules are the logical precepts by which goals are established, possible actions and reactions determined and by which victory or defeat is measured.

Responses include the actions and reactions taken by the algorithm in responses to the changing situations within the game, as determined by the integral game logic, programmed events and player inputs.

Randomness is the capacity of the game to vary game events in an 'unpredictable' fashion. Since randomness is computationally impossible, the algorithm constructs a large enough shuffle of variables to appear 'random' within the limits of human cognition.

Mark Wolf and Bernard Perron (2003), *The Video Game Theory Reader*, New York and London: Routledge, pp. 15–17

Player activity is facilitated, as well as delimited, by the parameters of the game interface and the game algorithm. The game interface connects human actions with game objects. It is composed of a series of devices that structure the relationship between the game and its player. In the physical domain, these include joysticks, the electronic mouse, light guns, microphones, headphones, D pads and motion-sensitive controllers. Within the graphical dimensions of the game, elements of the game interface might include pictorial habitats, scrollbars, function icons, object icons and message screens. The game algorithm is the computer program that controls the operation of the game interface, determines the symbolic forms of audiovisual representation and applies the rules and parameters of the game itself. It is significant to note that computer games are traditionally abandoned once their players have mastered the challenge of the game problem and/or exhausted the available variations in the game. In the opposite direction, because of the combinative influences of interactive and problematic engagements with the game, failure to master a game tends to result in feelings or adjectives of failure or rejection ('I'm rubbish at this game', 'I hate this game . . .', etc.).

Games as Narrative

While the mutable, rather than static, operation of narrative in computer games escapes many traditional understandings of storytelling, the critical importance of visual representation indicates that the themes and settings are an essential element of the gaming experience. All computer games feature a narrative component, whether this is presented through formal game 'stories' that structure play or more implicitly through the visualization of game settings, icons and avatars (see Kucklich 2006). These could all be considered to be symbolic devices that constitute meanings. Thus, while we can approach game mechanics from a functional perspective (referred to as ludology), it is equally valid to approach games as a narrative media (and thus subject to narratology). Taking this view, we could posit the appeal of games as arising from the fashion in which they grant symbolic rewards within a heroic narrative structure. Taking account of the psychological interaction between game and player, we might also conclude that computer game narratives are designed to manipulate latent urges for certain forms of symbolic reward, and for emotional and physical stimulation.

In what form, then, are game narratives expressed? A simple content analysis readily indicates the prevalence of military and combat themes, along with simulations of what are also stereotypically assumed to be male obsessions: racing cars and TV sports. The major exceptions to this rule are maze games and platform games which emphasize movement and avatar-orientation. These games have been successfully adapted to a wide number of subject themes, depending on the audience they are marketed to (from *Pac Man* and *Donkey Kong* to *Sonic the Hedgehog* and *Dora the Explorer*). Strategy games, much like digital board games, tend to operate on personal computers rather than gaming consoles, and generally target older male players who vicariously direct battlefield situations. *The Sims*, as a strategic approach to everyday life, was a major thematic innovation in the genre, broadening the cross-gender appeal of desktop-based games and heralding the immersive 'reality show' of Second Life in this decade.

It can be argued that computer game narratives display a strong gender bias in their choices of themes. They typically deploy modes of human representation that are heavily marked with the male determination of what Judith Butler has called the 'heterosexual matrix' (1990). The consistent reward of aggressive tendencies and actions is also a marked feature of a large proportion of game titles. Over time, combat games have seen a steady shift from the mechanized combat of *Space Invaders* to more anthropomorphic, point-of-view experiences of violence, exemplified by the 'first-person shooter' games of the past decade. The text-based role-playing games of the late 1970s, which involved the progression of players through heavily structured narratives with outcomes varied by player interaction, have taken on sophisticated graphical forms as well as incorporating platform and combat gaming into their game worlds. In recent years, we have become increasingly familiar with games that draw together different genres in this fashion, such as *Tomb Raider* (platform/maze game with combat) or *City of Heroes* (point-of-view role-playing with combat).

Box 6.5 Computer game genres

- **Space and aerial combat** (*SpaceWar!, Space Invaders, Asteroids, Star Wars*)
- **Terrestrial mechanized combat** (*Tank, Battlezone, Desert Strike*)
- **Physical hand-to-hand combat** (*Streetfighter, Mortal Kombat, Tekken*)
- **Urban infantry combat** (*Doom, Call of Duty, Medal of Honour*)
- **Driving simulators** (*Nightdriver, Pole Position, Grand Theft Auto*)
- **Remediation of traditional games** (*Chess, Checkers, Solitaire, Backgammon*)
- **Virtual sports** (*Pong, Football, Cricket, Golf*)
- **Role playing** (*Dungeon, Myst, Final Fantasy, City of Heroes, World of Warcraft, Second Life, Red Dead Redemption*)
- **Governance and strategy** (*Civilisation, Rome, Age of Empires, the Sims, Sim City*)
- **Mazes and platform games** (*Pac Man, Donkey Kong, Mario, Sonic the Hedgehog, Echo the Dolphin*)

The violent themes seen in a large proportion of computer games build upon historically established practices of using toys to indoctrinate children in the socially sanctioned use of violence. Indeed, the prevalence of such themes across a broad range of entertainment media from text to film indicates that this agenda is by no means confined to computer games, or to the young. As such, it is not surprising that the computer game format has frequently adopted this narrative form. What is more significant is the interactive function of such games, which are designed for entertainment but also used to provide virtual battle training for military personnel. Given their origins, computer simulations have been used extensively to augment the flight-time of combat pilots for several decades, reaching back to the early years of electronic technologies. More recently, immersive digital environments simulating street-to-street urban combat in the first-person shooter format have been developed for military training.

In the past decade, both the US and UK have made extensive use of battlefield simulators to prepare their ground troops for service in the Middle Eastern theatre. An application such as *Virtual Battle Space 2* (UK) is intended to provide troops with a realistic simulation of urban conflict in a simulated Middle Eastern setting, with the aim of preparing soldiers for the 'real thing' (Bohemia Interactive 2011). The US military have also been involved in the development of software training vehicles such as *America's Army*, which has subsequently been released as a commercially available immersive combat game. As Michael Zyda has noted, this software proved of some use in military training, but it was widely seen as making a far greater contribution as a recruitment tool that persuaded young males to consider joining the armed forces (2005). The clear similarity between these military gaming applications and the predominant commercial gaming titles, such as *Call of Duty* and *Medal of Honour*, naturally returns us to the questions posed by Baudrillard about the extent to which the symbolic violence of computer gaming has become infused, confused even, with the intense mediation of modern warfare.

When textual detail is exhibited in virtual combat, as for example, enemies stumble backwards having sustained a shot to the shoulder or are felled by a shot to the leg, it also serves to reconfirm the players' embodied presence as they witness the impact and accuracy of their aim . . . by witnessing carnivalesque deaths that are more protracted, it is plausible to argue that the status of the enemy in games like *F.E.A.R.* is raised . . . observations of *Call of Duty 4: Modern Warfare* (Infinity Ward) revealed how it not only employed confirmatory visual signifiers of player actions, such as blood spraying and staining, but that such textual detail could be experienced in a detached fashion during players' use of long-range sniper rifles. Even so, sensory immersion is ruptured by reassertion of the 'gameness' of the game in the instant where existents [virtual enemies] disappear from the screen. Kingsepp (2003; 2007), when discussing *Medal of Honor*, makes the same observation, describing the event as 'postmodern death' – similar to Baudrillard's (1991) notion of a 'clean' war, owing to its highly sanitized media representation of death.

Gareth Schott (2009), '"I'm OK": How Young People Articulate "Violence" in Videogames', *Refractory: A Journal of Entertainment Media*, 16 (November) at: http://refractory.unimelb.edu.au/2009/11/18/

Intertextuality

Intertextuality is a term that directs our attention to the fact that all narratives, visualizations, texts or, indeed, statements are made with reference to other things that have been expressed elsewhere. Thus, the contemporary game narrative is fashioned with an awareness of all the games that have preceded it, as well as the dominant narratives within the culture of the society in which the game is produced and subsequently played. Accordingly, we can use this term to emphasize the fact that all media representations are intertextual because they inevitably refer to a wider symbolic world beyond any particular text, and typically to specific texts (either explicitly or implicitly). For example, modern movies are descended from both the dramatic play and the novel, and thus display those influences. Movies also reference a wider film culture, in that one western makes sense in relation to other westerns. Since storytelling is also a social practice, the western film both reflects and perpetuates the historicist mythology of the US frontier.

The multiplication of media narratives reaching a mass audience gradually builds up a common terminology. Media products soak up references from popular culture and public debate. The meanings framed by each mediation of the social world consequently spill over into public life, where conversations and ideas are relayed through common expressions familiarized by the media. For example, while the movie *Star Wars* could be read as an allegorical fiction of the United States in its imperial era, terms which reference the film (like 'Star Wars' and 'Evil Empire') subsequently became official rhetoric in US foreign policy. Thus, we could argue that intertextuality also threatens the barrier between the 'real' world and the order of simulation. From another viewpoint, however, we could argue that the breadth and depth of popular culture offers an expansive symbolism that speaks both allegorically to the real and subjectively to individual experience. For Barry Atkins, the intertextuality between the game world and the wider social sphere actually allows us to cross the line between reality and representation without disrupting our capacity to distinguish between the two (2003).

> This is emphatically not life, but is half-life, a representational approximation of 'life' fully aware of its limitations (as an attempt at mimesis) rather than something that represents a fractional attainment of 'life' that implies eventual realisation of its potential for simulation in a confusion between text and real. Should it ever go too far . . . toward the absolute simulation of life [the computer game] would fail as a readable text. It is the recognition of limits, as well as its attempts to push those limits, that is the major achievement of this as readable fiction . . . game fiction negotiates the competing demands of the need for the unseen hand of the games' authors to retain narratorial control of what is possible (that risks alerting the player to the fact [that] suspension of disbelief, or immersion, is an act of will) and the desire to hand over narratorial control to the reader (that runs the risk of forcing the game into unplayability).
>
> Barry Atkins (2003), *More Than A Game: The Computer Game as a Fictional Form*, Manchester: University of Manchester Press, p. 75

The intrinsic capacity of computer games to combine digital video, still images, vector graphics, text and sounds within the game environment erases the earlier distinctions between different branches of the mass media. This creates an intertextuality of another kind, making computer games the quintessential 'multimedia' product. As earlier media forms are remediated via the digital environment and deployed in new forms, their narrative aesthetics get remediated too. Thus, *Red Dead Redemption* is a game that not only recontextualizes the realist aesthetics of modernist photography, it is also a game that rests and builds upon the well-established narrative conventions of popular American cinema. The meeting point of 'Hollywood realism' and computer gaming finds expression in many ways. It is apparent in their common narrative intertextuality and in the conscious incorporation of game aesthetics within contemporary feature films. The widespread popularity of computer game characters and the importance of ancillary products for the film industry has also encouraged movie and game tie-ins that deploy a star persona and/or narrative theme across both formats (such as *Star Wars* or *Tomb Raider*). On a smaller scale, game players have experimented with the format of 'machinima', where screen capture is used to record segments of game action for editing into video narratives (Lowood and Nitsche 2011). As media formats blend into each other, narratives interact with our social experience in an increasing range of settings. The question is how we manage the intertextuality of television news, *Saving Jessica Lynch* and *America's Army*.

Postmodern Death

The broad school of thought referred to as 'postmodernism' has its origins in the 1930s, with many of its central tenets being laid down during the late 1960s (Husserl 1936; Debord 1967; Derrida 1973; Foucault 1969). Nonetheless, it was during the 1980s and 1990s that postmodernism reached its apogee in terms of its 'cultural capital' and influence in the social sciences and humanities (Jameson 1991; Lyotard 1984). Many of the central claims of postmodernism revolved around the perceived collapse of the 'grand ideas' of scientific truth, universal history and technological progress that defined the worldview of modernism in the nineteenth century. Critically, the reliance of modernist thinking on the idea of material reality (and its aesthetic exposition of realism) were abandoned by postmodern theory in favour of an emphasis on the artificial, contingent and constructed nature of reality. Reality became an intensely subjective affair, not so much 'represented' as 'performed' through the realms of language and discourse. In this view, the consciousness of a 'normative' human subject was replaced by the fluid interaction of individualized subjectivities, identities and viewpoints. Thus, for postmodern sociologists, the point of critical focus naturally becomes the shifting metaphors that underwrite the 'performativity' that supplants objective truth in a postmodern society (Lash 1990).

The philosophical shift from a modern to postmodern view remains controversial and has by no means found universal acceptance. Nonetheless, it is highly significant that this intellectual movement was coterminous with the technological transition from analogue to digital media. The advent of digital media replaced a media of record (photography) with a media of simulation (digital imaging). As we have seen, this entailed a paradigm shift from a realist aesthetic to its digital simulation in the form of photo-realism. It is far from coincidental, therefore, that the rise of postmodernism as a way of understanding society was contemporary with the advent of the digital era. Indeed, the 'new worlds' of digital simulation provided much of the evidence drawn upon by the key theorists associated with postmodernism (e.g., Baudrillard 1994; Virilio 2002). The emergence of the hyper-real, the increasing velocity of social interaction and the inexorable mediation of human subjectivity through the digital medium were all seen as providing compelling evidence of the death of the 'real' in contemporary social experience. The computer game, as a 'pure' simulation emerging from the computational union of mathematics and language, provided the most obvious example of a social world without a material origin.

The intense subjective connection established between game players and their avatars certainly appears to provide accessible evidence of a human capacity, indeed propensity, for impersonation and the external transference of our social identities. Beyond this, postmodern logic directs us towards the uniquely 'immersive' nature of the game experience, suggesting both an 'out-of-body' social experience and a subjective integration with a symbolic narrative. That is, we become disconnected from our material reality and lose ourselves in the sensory environment and narrative structures of the game world. The intensely compelling nature of visual language, the stimulus–response operation of computers and the problem-solving rationale of gaming all contribute to what Sherry Turkle once called the 'holding power' of the computer game (2005). As a consequence, the single-minded, time-consuming and apparently addictive nature of gaming as a pastime encourages us to wonder whether players are indeed losing touch with reality and wilfully immersing themselves in a virtual world of symbolic rewards. This sense of unease becomes more acute as the 'photo-realism' of game environments threatens to achieve a parity with first-hand sensory experience.

By comparison, the steady spread of digital enhancement throughout our visual language represents a far more insidious threat to the 'reality principle' in modern thought. From an excessive faith in visual evidence ('the camera never lies'), we have moved rapidly into an intense scepticism where nothing is taken for what it appears to be ('anything can be faked'). At the same time, the aesthetic perfection of photo-realism does increasingly appear to stand over reality as we struggle to contend with the larger-than-life images that now surround us in everyday life. As our exposure to media content reaches unprecedented levels, the sheer saturation of images provides further support for Baudrillard's claim that our fundamental experience of world events is being obliterated by the intensity of their hyper-real representation (1995). In recent years, it has become apparent that the hyper-real and the virtual have begun to look more and more alike. Whether we concur with Baudrillard's exaggerated claims or not, it is easy to see why our assumptions about reality have come into question. The present confusion is evidenced clearly enough by prevailing attitudes to computer games, which are regarded as dangerous, both for luring people away from reality and for being too realistic.

Think and Discuss

1. Key Terms
Can you describe in simple language what is meant by the following terms found in this chapter?

- Hyper-reality
- Photo-realism
- Simulation
- Ludology
- Intertextuality

2. Critical Questions
Try answering the following questions, drawing upon your own understanding, experience and knowledge.

1. How do the terms 'iconicity' and 'indexicality' describe different functions of photographic images?
2. Can you provide a contemporary example for each of the three 'orders of simulation' described by Baudrillard?
3. Various government agencies have determined that young people are particularly vulnerable to the forms of representation used in computer games. What is the basis of this argument?
4. Should the violent and militaristic themes of computer games raise greater concerns than similar themes in other media formats?
5. Does the remediation of the realistic aesthetic by digital technologies provide sufficient evidence to suggest the 'death of the real'?

Further Reading

Anderson, Craig, Gentile, David and Buckley, Katharine. (2007) *Violent Videogame Effects on Adolescents and Children: Theory, Research and Public Policy*, Oxford: Oxford University Press.

Atkins, Barry (2003) *More Than A Game: The Computer Game as a Fictional Form*, Manchester: University of Manchester Press.

Baudrillard, Jean (1994) *Simulacra and Simulation*, Ann Arbor, MI: University of Michigan Press.

Baudrillard, Jean (1995) *The Gulf War Did Not Take Place*, Bloomington, IN: Indiana University Press.

Bolter, Jay David and Grusin, Richard (2001) *Remediation: Understanding New Media*, London and Cambridge, MA: MIT Press.

Carr, Diane, Buckingham, David, Burn, Andrew and Schott, Gareth (2006) *Computer Games: Text, Narrative and Play*, Cambridge: Polity.

Juul, Jasper (2005) *Half-Real: Video Games Between Real Rules and Fictional Worlds*, Cambridge, MA: MIT Press.

Rutter, Jason and Bryce, Jo (eds) (2006) *Understanding Digital Games*, London: Sage.

Wolf, Mark (2007) *The Videogame Explosion: A History from Pong to Playstation and Beyond*, Westport, CT: Greenwood Press.

Wolf, Mark and Perron, Bernard (2003) *The Video Game Theory Reader*, London and New York: Routledge.

Go Online

Games Studies: International Journal of Computer Game Research – http://www.gamesstudies.org/
British Board of Film Classification Advice for Parents – http://www.pbbfc.co.uk/videogames.asp
International Game Developers Association – www.igda.org/

CHAPTER 7

My Personal Public

Thus far, we have considered the individual experience of digital society in a somewhat introspective light. We have looked at psychoanalytic theories of self, language and body, and we have considered a postmodern perspective on subjectivity, aesthetics and social reality. Arguably, these were the dominant strands of thought within the humanities as the Internet was becoming a feature of everyday life during the 1990s. As a consequence, perhaps, the functional and micro-social dimensions of digital communication in this medium were neglected, initially at least, in favour of a broader reconceptualization of the self. It was the identity of the hypothetical subject, not the social actions of actual subjects, which formed the major target of inquiry. That is not to say that these approaches did not favour sociological applications, or that they had only abstract intentions. Rather, the aim of those approaches, for thinkers like Mark Poster and Donna Haraway, was to seize the moment of newness when communicative norms were being disrupted by the new media, and to put in place a paradigm which expressed the rebirth of the virtual self in equation with a goal of social liberation. Of course, not all theoretical accounts of the digital were utopian, with certain thinkers (notably Jean Baudrillard (1994) and David Lyon (1994)) responding with more pessimistic readings of the emerging digital society.

This debate in the theoretical domain during the 1990s was paralleled by a wave of anxieties in the public sphere regarding various negative social impacts of the public Internet. Accordingly, the social sciences were prompted to respond via practical studies that assessed the relative risks and benefits of going online. In the process, there were many practical challenges to be considered in an applied sociology of digital media. Some of these, such as the anonymous nature of communication in the first phase of the Internet, represented a radical departure from established norms. Other factors seen previously in other media forms also appeared to be exacerbated by the digital switchover, not least, the increasing quantities of media content to which we are exposed and the increasing mediation of everyday interpersonal interactions via digital technologies. Of course, both the philosophical and practical concerns of social inquiry come together in the lack of social presence, given the relative invisibility of interactants communicating online. In that sense, the phenonema that we have considered so far through psychoanalysis and postmodernism were also a major concern for a more functional 'interactionist' approach to social communication.

Herbert Blumer and the Self as a Social Object

Symbolic interactionism is a significant tradition within sociology, stemming from the philosophical pragmatism of George Herbert Mead (1934) and significantly extended through the work of Herbert Blumer (1969). The interactionist tradition stems from the premise that social reality is created (and re-created) through human experience, from which meanings are derived. Consequently, our capacity to interpret the significance of human activity suggests a guiding rationality behind our individual participation in society. This, in turn, denotes the independence of the social subject and a capacity for significant action. At the same time, the agency of individuals is *necessarily* expressed through their interaction with others, making the empowerment of the self a social process. Indeed, like Freud and Lacan, Blumer understood the self as a social construct emerging out of the socialization process that we undergo in childhood. Blumer, however, was less interested in the internal symbolic struggles of the individual unconscious and much more interested in concrete symbolic exchanges between individuals. This directed his work towards the empirical and observable world of everyday human encounters.

In common with the semiotic basis of French structuralism, symbolic interactionism sees the expression of a thing as not simply a description of the thing, but primarily as the association of meaning with a thing. However, the attribution of meaning arises not from the language system but from social interaction, because meaning is determined by what we call something or what we do with it. The symbolic usage of any object is therefore an action that someone undertakes. In order for the meaning of that action to be understood, it must be recognizable and intelligible to others. Symbolic interactionism therefore implies the creation of a common language that goes beyond written or spoken words, including the bodily gestures and physical actions of interactants as well as their symbolic usage of social objects (both figurative or physical usage). Social action takes place not simply between self and object, but primarily through symbolic exchanges, or interactions, between people.

The interest of symbolic interactionism goes beyond formal processes and rituals of communication, since it recognizes that throughout our lives we are watching other people in order to observe their actions. In doing so, we associate them with meaning and thus turn them into social objects in their own right. Since our sense of self exists relative to those others, this entails an empathetic capacity for understanding how others regard us, and thus an understanding of our own self as a social object. This requires us to augment the innate individual 'I' (instigator of our actions) with the ability to take on the imagined roles of external others observing us, both in the form of actual people and the more generalized perspectives of social types and groups. This imaginary 'looking back' at the self produces another aspect of the persona, the public image we refer to as 'me'.

The Internet as a Social World

Since the take-off of the public Internet in the early 1990s, scholars of all disciplines have been attentive to the potential impact of widespread digital communication upon social life. From the particular perspectives of symbolic interactionism, the removal of established conventions and procedures for embodied social actions implied the need for new semantic arrangements. In order to operate successfully, these new arrangements for conferring meaning upon actions first needed to become universally understood and collectively enforced. In many respects, the North American tradition of media sociology was well placed to record the evolution of this new signifying system. The United States led the world in designing and implementing commercial computer systems, and the influence of symbolic interactionism remained strongest in American universities. As we have seen, the study of 'computer-mediated communication' in this vein had already sought to investigate how networked interaction through computer interfaces transformed the rituals of communication in corporate, educational and other public settings.

The lack of bodily presence appeared to reduce social intimidation, and the capacity to dominate in meetings passed from the biggest, loudest, oldest or highest-ranking participants to those better able to use the new medium. In synchronous communication, typing skills became a major advantage. In asynchronous communication, the capacity to write succinctly and unambiguously became more important than seating position or the tonal qualities of real speech. At this stage of analysis, however, the direction of the research agenda consistently neglected the investigation of personal communications in favour of a small-scale model of public communication. That is, studies in CMC tended to favour defined scenarios of communication rather than the more open and free-form context of private conversation. Similarly, group communications that were task-oriented appeared to provide more readily quantifiable data than one-to-one interactions between individuals. Until the late 1990s, these approaches also made sense because it was in places of work, study, trade and governance that the majority of computer-mediated communication was taking place. Thus, prior to the World Wide Web protocols, interaction studies typically chose to emphasize the affordances of new media in terms of the conduct of public as opposed to private social experiences (see Baym 2006).

The rapid growth in the popularity of the World Wide Web after 1993 dramatically transformed not only the scale, but also the tenor of digital interaction. The global reach of the Internet represented an obvious challenge for successful social communication due to the wide range of human cultures and language systems that it sought to mediate. At the same time, even within established social formations and areas of activity, a new set of symbolically coded social rituals were required to account for the implications of greater social distance, loss of visual cues and the anonymity of interactants. Emoticons, avatars, acronyms, abbreviations and various forms of web jargon – all of these innovations constituted social objects that could be deployed by social actors in the conduct of online communication. In various ways, they augment or adapt the conventions of disembodied communication inherent to the written word. They do so in order to account for the more rapid pace of real-time publication, the mutability of digital text, the limitations of screen-reading devices and the novel interactivity between participants. The introduction of images, most potent of all social objects, utterly transformed the sensory experience of the Internet, infusing interpersonal communication with the visceral impact of visual allegory. The subsequent introduction of video conferencing also brought the ritual aesthetics of television into the domain of personal interaction.

As such, there is plenty of observable evidence that web-based interactions between human beings are being expressed through a new gestural language, albeit one that remains directed at an anthropomorphic subject. As we have seen, the symbolic domain of the Internet continues, in many respects, to be a body language. It is also significant that much of the linguistic evolution of the Internet did not take place in the formal settings of business emails, institutional webcasts or virtual meetings. In a large part, the conventions of digital interaction emerged organically through millions of informal social interactions. Some of these were between individuals in professional settings, but just as many were between friends, lovers and relatives living everyday lives, or between strangers exploring new social domains on the World Wide Web. Whilst all these activities shared the same medium of communication – and may well have been taking place in proximity to each other moment by moment – it is equally significant that the distinction between public and private speech was maintained in most commentaries on the Internet. In the former case, new potentials for public speech were linked to political participation (as exemplified by newsgroups, blogs and bulletin boards). In the latter, the realm of private communication was framed by the conceptualization of a disembodied social experience conducted semi-anonymously in virtual realities of various kinds (exemplified by MUDs and MOOs). This division between the public and private domains of speech, and between political and personal imaginaries, represents one of the most fundamental dialectics of the modern world.

Erving Goffman and Self-presentation

From a symbolic interactionist viewpoint, the public–private binary denotes a series of mutually understood social conventions which determine the most appropriate gestures for social interaction. The distinction between public and private also has practical implications for maintaining an appropriate relationship between the 'I' and the 'Me'. The more public an act of communication is, the more firmly it is directed towards generalizable others as opposed to individuals with whom we have unique social bonds. As a consequence, public speech becomes more firmly determined by societal norms that require a coherent presentation of 'me' that corresponds with generalizable norms. Setting is similarly important. While I might speak more informally, and personably, to a postgraduate student in a small seminar, I will present a much more stereotypical version of the academic 'me' in a large public lecture. This shift in register between different social situations provides the major focus of Erving Goffman's influential work on self-presentation (1959). Goffman employed the metaphor of the public theatre to describe the presentation of the self in everyday life. According to Goffman's distinctive 'dramaturgical' approach, we continuously adopt different roles to suit different social contexts during the conduct of our social lives. Goffman claimed that, since every human being is a social actor, it follows that each persona that we project on stage is carefully prepared backstage. The major implication of this view is that there is a 'backstage' self that directs our social performance on the 'front stage'. This implies a private realm where public performances are prepared. Public performances, as a consequence, can take on many different guises depending upon the social context.

Goffman's notion of self-performance is different from the postmodern view (where the self exists only as performance) because he maintains that there is a real backstage self directing that performance. However, like Butler's notion of gender performity, Goffman concluded that particular social interactions inevitably impose certain roles upon the individual. Accordingly, every social setting comes with predetermined parts that we are invited to play, and the 'backstage' self directs the 'front-stage' self to perform the role best suited to a given situation. In doing so, we work hard (through our appearance, manner and script) to present a version of our selves that fits the expectations of the role. We do this, not simply because making the right impression confers a social advantage, but because it is necessary for us to perform successfully if social interaction is to take place at all. As such, our social encounters inevitably entail a degree of literacy in established social rituals that, in turn, informs the conscious management of how the self is being presented. In this sense, our social experience is comprised of a series of contextually sensitive and self-reflexive performances between social actors, each of them engaged in a strategic presentation of the self that Goffman referred to as 'impression management'. Without role-taking and impression management, the 'interaction order' would break down because the nature of our performances could not be easily understood by our fellow actors.

Online Dating

In the online domain, the proliferation of online dating sites provides us with a conducive environment in which we can observe impression management in operation. As Adam Arvidsson has noted, the origins of online dating lie in the use of newspaper classified advertisements by migrants and other dispersed people looking for marriage partners (2006). Marriage invitations emerged as a feature of media use precisely as urbanization and human mobility accelerated at the end of the nineteenth century. Nonetheless, until the 1970s, Arvidsson describes this as a 'marginal' process in human coupling (2006: 878). For a mass readership, printed advertisements seeking potential spouses or sexual partners coalesced around certain conventions of wording in the presentation of a 'personal profile' and a matching profile for a desirable mate. These brief sketches of an individual's chief characteristics (as a potential partner) could be quickly assessed by readers scanning through the columns of text. This crystallization of individual self-presentation was explicitly intended for consideration against any number of other self-presentations constructed in the same format. The remediation of classified personals via the Internet medium in the mid-1990s signalled a major shift into the 'mainstream' of marital arrangements.

The niche sexual practices that previously made use of classifieds for 'swinging' following the sexual revolution of the 1960s were early adopters of the Internet medium, but this domain was kept firmly separate from the new Internet services focusing on those seeking love online. Match.com in the United States was the early market leader in online dating, conceived simultaneously with the launch of the World Wide Web and focused on long-term pair-bonding. Adult Friendfinder, launched in 1996, was oriented towards people looking for sexual partners rather than spouses or companions. Both of these domains have subscription bases in the millions and constitute a significant commercial economy in human matchmaking. Subscribers are able to construct a personal profile using a predetermined format, and to browse through the profiles of other site 'members'. By providing a subscription payment, members are able to send messages to other members, engage in online chat and organize dates. In mainstream dating, subscribers publish a categorical self-presentation that covers physical appearance and established markers of social positioning such as education, profession and religion. Personal consumption of legal narcotics (cigarettes and alcohol) is also a required category. Beyond this most 'basic' demographic data, subscribers are also asked to provide more 'private' information such as astrological signs, pets, hobbies and whimsical responses to (hypothetical) romantic situations.

Match.com does have a strong and coherent format. Browsing through the site one is struck by the apparent similarity of profiles. There appears to be a fairly generally accepted normative model for self-presentation on the site. Interestingly this model differs substantially from what has been observed in earlier studies of mainstream, offline dating media . . . It is true that, sometimes, men tend to stress their financial standing or market value, presenting themselves as 'single, sane, solvent' (WM, 30), but this is neither a frequent or very dominant trait. Similarly, some women stress their physical appearance or sexual readiness, presenting themselves as a 'fun-loving up for it all sex-kitten' (WF, 19), but again, this is rare . . . Rather, the dominant element of the vast majority of the profiles surveyed here was what one would call an 'experiential ethic' of self-discovery, an orientation towards touching, revealing or sharing one's true self through open-hearted and intimate communication with others, or through an active or experientially rich life conduct.

Adam Arvidsson (2006), 'Quality Singles: Internet Dating and the Work of Fantasy', *New Media and Society*, 8(4): 671–90

The ready adoption of this generic format for human intimacy is highly suggestive of the operation of normative gender structures that determine the most valued attributes of the sexed subject. Although most dating sites accommodate different sexual preferences, there has been a marked tendency for non-heterosexual pairings to migrate to specialized niche dating sites, and for the mainstream to organize the dating format around traditional gender roles. Because romance is marked as a terrain coterminous with 'feminine' perspectives, the female presentation of a sociable, caring and romantic persona is relatively unremarkable. An emphasis on the 'fun-loving' and outgoing side of female subscribers appears as the major marker of the 'modern woman', with a large proportion of single mothers particularly keen to emphasize a capacity for a full social life. The male formula is more notable since dating continues to be a domain in which men are sanctioned (indeed required) to present particular 'emotional' traits that are elsewhere seen as unsuitable in the public performance of masculine identity. Wholesome hobbies and 'sensitive' yearnings are seen as reliable markers of a 'well-rounded' male in the private domain.

In order to compensate for the sterility of a form-based personality profile, dating subscribers are commonly given a free text area where they can offer a unique self-description. This more individuated act of self-presentation is a somewhat fraught process since there is a simultaneous compulsion to present the most attractive self without being transparently boastful or deceitful. Similarly, the 'absent presence' of bodily attraction requires subscribers to rate themselves against the ideals of the mediated body image. This inevitably entails the cautious admission of a physical lack, which compounds the lingering social stigma that only the unattractive, middle-aged, divorced and otherwise desperate will resort to dating services. In order to counter the sense of insecurity that arises from a candid public admission of one's social worth in the highly competitive mating arena, dating websites often present elaborate advice instructing subscribers how to accommodate their deficiencies (such as age, weight, dependent children) and present themselves suitably to potential dating partners.

In order to overcome the inherent difficulties of gendered relations, the online dating environment is framed in terms of a common search for 'love', positioned as an intangible emotional bond of an enduring nature. There is an explicit disavowal of the transaction between sex and social security. For the purposes of dating, therefore, the social construction of gender must be positioned in a double-blind against the property relations and sexual mores that bind human affections into wider social structures. Thus, online dating is emphatically not about sexual needs, reproduction or financial advantage, but rather about seeking a romantic companion or a 'soul mate'. Accordingly, an emphasis on 'finding love' and a putative (more or less astrological) compatibility between persons replaces the instrumental with the serendipitous and spiritual, even though the very nature of systematically selecting partners from a data-base clashes somewhat with the quaint ideal of love as a chance meeting or random event. We must recognize, of course, that the occurrence of love by random destiny is a very rare and fleeting thing, as cultures that follow practices of arranged marriage are always quick to point out.

The systematic nature of dating profiles and the peculiar nature of personal testimo-nies in the dating arena provide a clear instance of impression management at work. A backstage self consciously plans how to present the most suitable face for the social setting, taking on the role of a potential marriage partner. The face that is subsequently presented on the front stage is tailored to established social conventions about love and individual expression, while simultaneously paying attention to the pragmatics of pair-bonding (in a suitably low-key fashion). The online dating self is thus a highly particular version of the self, and one that is understood in this context by both the presenter and the audience as being quite different from the self-presentation of that person in other social settings. Equally, the relative 'lean-ness' of information in online dating, when compared to live social encounters, requires the readers of dating profiles to extract as much information as they can, based upon what is being presented as well as what is not. Thus, the self designed in the backstage is augmented by further clues 'given away' inadvertently on the front stage. It is the combination of the social performance and the critical reception of that role by the audience that constitutes the presentation of the self as a romantic proposition.

The Rise of Social Networking

The elaborate presentation of personal profiles in dating sites can be productively related to Erving Goffman's work on the dramatic performance of the self, precisely because this is a context in which the roles being performed are well defined within a single social setting. It is far more challenging to account for the more open-ended and multipurpose self-presentations that have emerged with the rise of 'social network sites' (SNS) over the past decade. By augmenting the architecture of self-publishing (or 'blogging') applications with extensive media-sharing functions, group mail, instant messaging and novelty 'apps' of various kinds, portals such as Myspace and Facebook have placed electronic public diaries at the heart of contemporary social life. The inte-gration of vanity publishing and media sharing with new tools for selectively manag-ing connections to other users has witnessed the emergence of millions of small-scale social networks operating in cyberspace. Although commonly presented as a 'bolt for the blue', SNS represents a new configuration of network sociability, rather than an entirely new phenomenon. Online social networks have existed in various forms since the earliest days of computer networking in the 1960s. Indeed, from the outset, the social atmosphere of the Internet has been one of its most notable features, despite the common perception that participation in virtual communication infers an anti-social withdrawal from proximate, material social relations.

What is most distinctive about contemporary SNS, however, is their capacity to integrate online social networks with those formed in the physical context of everyday life. This is a development that heralds a new register between biological and digital social relations. A portal like Facebook, for example, is predicated upon its inherent personalization. Facebook requires its users to construct a personal profile and then to connect that self-presentation to the personal pages of other Facebook users that they know. This forms an electronic version of the user's existing social configuration and this, of course, makes it radically different from the purely virtual communities of online games or the meet-and-greet culture of online dating. Updates to personal pages are instantly notified to other members of the network, allowing Facebook to function as a live collective journal. As a constantly rolling event, Facebook pages are primarily used for informal chat, quirky self-declarations and the mundane organization and augmentation of everyday social activities. The more active users compensate for less active members of the network in maintaining a dynamic field of content that retains the interest of network members. The infrastructure of the Internet medium allows users to combine everyday interaction with those close at hand with a long-distance reach to those who are far away. In an age of increasing mobility, the utility of Facebook for maintaining and restoring sundered relationships is quite considerable.

Relational maintenance and the technological augmentation of active and latent social bonds is the primary function of SNS. Since each member of an SNS network has their own customized network of relationships, the format provides for the linkage of vast numbers of people across the world. Like all social applications of the Internet, the value of an SNS portal increases proportionately with its membership. As such, the content produced by the popularity of Facebook, with 800 million users in 2011, constitutes a vast social field and quite possibly the largest single store of personal information in human history. The popularity of picture-sharing across these personalized networks, for example, has made Facebook the primary forum for the storage and exchange of digital images via the Internet. As such, Facebook usefully combines a number of pre-existing Internet formats (including dating sites, email, blogs and file-sharing), but its main attraction is the capacity to order and manage a personalized network in a public forum with restricted access. Although larger and more public networks also coexist in Facebook, the target audience for the vast majority of Facebookers tends to be people they already know.

We define social network sites as web-based services that allow individuals to (1) construct a public or semi-public profile within a bounded system, (2) articulate a list of other users with whom they share a connection, and (3) view and traverse their list of connections and those made by others within the system . . . What makes social network sites unique is not that they allow individuals to meet strangers, but rather that they enable users to articulate and make visible their social networks. This can result in connections between individuals that would not otherwise be made, but that is often not the goal, and these meetings are frequently between 'latent ties' . . . who share some offline connection. On many of the large SNSs, participants are not necessarily 'networking' or looking to meet new people; instead, they are primarily communicating with people who are already a part of their extended social network.

danah boyd and Nicole Ellison (2007) 'Social Network Sites: Definition, History and Scholarship', *Journal of Computer-Mediated Communication*, 13: 210–30

In social networking, the phrasing of text messages, the choice of pictorial content, hyperlinks and (in portals like Myspace) the graphic design of personal pages all collectively serve the purposes of self-presentation. However, what is most significant about the SNS framing of the self is the public display of friendships and other social connections as a constitutive feature of self-presentation. Here, the founding inspiration of the college yearbook and the distinctive popularity contests of American youth culture inform a mode of self-presentation that is far less concerned with the inner qualities of the private individual and much more with the public presentation of social assets. As such, there is an inherent bias towards a self-presentation that emphasizes regular social activity and connectivity. In taking up this particular role, the things that we choose to share about ourselves, and the way that we present this information via SNS, are undertaken in the context of presenting ourselves as the centre of a social network. Whilst this public narcissism is certainly redolent of the generic celebrity culture of the mainstream American media, the intimacy and informality associated with peer friendships also make Facebook performances highly distinctive in nature (Marshall 2006).

As in online dating, social actors within an SNS setting generally seek to emphasize the traits associated with success in this arena, and downplay traits associated with other social contexts. The problem posed for the backstage self in this regard is that the nature of our social interactions necessarily spans a range of individuals with whom we have quite different relationships. The role we perform for our college friends may not be suitable for senior or junior family members. Equally, the typical 'youthful' self-presentation (by people of all ages) as a fun-loving, party-hard and iconoclastic personality is often incompatible with the more diligent, serious and responsible roles that we act out for our professors, employers or students. Facebook has enormous ramifications for social interaction because it marks a critical shift in interpersonal communication via the Internet as anonymous profiles suitable for a single context are supplanted by a singular presentation seeking to present the 'authentic' self across a range of contexts. This is necessarily a much more difficult undertaking, with the complexity of this performance being compounded by the live, instantaneous and public nature of user contributions. An inappropriate performance that may have produced acute social embarrassment in a traditional social encounter becomes a permanent and public record when it occurs through social networking technologies. As such, we have already seen numerous instances of people losing not only public credibility but also employment, visa permits and marriage partners due to inappropriate admissions in SNS forums like Facebook and Twitter (see Trepte and Reinecke 2011).

SNS portals thus provide a powerful illustration of how the adoption of the Internet medium across a broad range of social interactions (and the co-location of Internet terminals in professional and domestic settings) has significantly eroded the distinction between private and public. Our personal networks speak to us at our desk as much as our colleagues petition us at home. The public and private self have steadily shifted into a simultaneous performance. Thus, while SNS also reveals the operation of the backstage and front-stage self (as publisher and profile), it also provides an indication of a collapsing distinction between personal and social identity. The 'social identity' presented in public becomes mingled with the 'personal identity' established through deeper social bonds forged between individuals over time. In the context of SNS, private individuals seeking to serve both audiences simultaneously must take as much care of their self-presentation as public figures. The water is muddied further, of course, by commercial institutions, social movements and public figures using SNS as a way to 'personalize' their public image and confer greater intimacy upon the messages they are seeking to transmit. This is the point of convergence between the 'impression management' of private life and the institutionalized domain of 'public relations'.

> The problem is that increasingly, in the context of SNS moving into the cultural mainstream, the 'everyday sense' of friend can often be the SNS Friend. So what we are missing here is a sense of the recursive nature of these processes as SNS become mundane and as the version of friendship they offer begins to remediate and shape understandings of friendship more generally. So we cannot think of friendship on SNS as entirely different and disconnected from our actual friends and notions of friendship, particularly as young people grow up and are informed by the connections they make on SNS.
>
> David Beer (2008) 'Social Network(ing) Sites . . . Revisiting The Story So Far: A Response to danah boyd and Nicole Ellison', *Journal of Computer-Mediated Communication*, 13: 516–29.

Another significant barrier that is rapidly being eroded by the culture of SNS is the earlier dialectic between offline and online worlds as a structuring principle for social interaction. As a consequence, David Beer is critical of approaches which continue to 'separate online and offline living', or which infer that: '"Friends" on SNSs are not the same as "friends" in the everyday sense', because: 'everyday life is defined and organized by a mixture of these two things, with users having "friends" offline and "Friends" online' (2008: 520). Thus, the social world of SNS is not consciously virtual, but is instead premised on a social presence that is hyper-real in form whilst retaining strong physical referents and remaining mundane in its expression.

Sharing as a Social Strategy

The rapid rise of SNS provides a microcosmic reflection of Manuel Castells's proclamation of a new world where power is vested in social networks (1996). Connectivity is everything in this new world. To be inside a network is to inhabit a communication-rich vantage point where social interactions are densely multiplied. In turn, Castells's reconceptualization of broader social relations in the form of networks was itself predicated upon the available evidence of new social networks being formed in online spaces during the 1990s. In the public domain, the rise of 'networking' courses and their attendant literature represented a broader recognition of the importance of personal associations in the functioning of contemporary organizations. Thus, arguably, the very phrase 'networking' is a symptom of the widespread acceptance of nepotism in professional life. The phenomenon of Facebook, however, draws our attention firmly to the importance (and the politics) of 'social capital' operating in the realm of private life. The influential French sociologist Pierre Bourdieu defined social capital as the personal advantages derived from various forms of non-financial resources embedded in social relations (1993). The importance of 'who you know' and how those relationships are formed and managed provides the critical linkage between interpersonal associations and social structure (Wenger 1999).

Although many symbolic interactionists would reject the idea of social structure (seeing individual social actions as being freely undertaken), the systematic pursuit of digital connectivity as a store of social capital infers an awareness that goes beyond the sum of each individual interaction. As we have already seen, what is most significant about SNS profiles is the very public display of our social connections in the form of the 'friends' list. This list encourages visiting friends to 'check out' other friends that they don't know, but it also presents as an aggregate measure of popularity, and is therefore an overt display of social capital. The Facebook portal is designed in such a way as to prompt us to expand our social network, trawling our email accounts for friends that we might have forgotten and regularly suggesting potential new friends through common association. There is incipient pressure, therefore, to increase our store of social capital. No doubt, for the image conscious, it is also important to have the right kind of friends.

Box 7.1 Social benefits of SNS

- Social networking sites allow participants to continue lifelong associations that may otherwise lapse due to time constraints, relocation or physical distance
- By giving us the opportunity to share our social experience, online social networks provide a supportive structure that reduces the impact of social alienation
- Social networking allows for a fuller expression of personal identity, bringing out social potentials traditionally repressed in the public domain
- Social networking sites allow us to personalize our web experience and give us control over the online world

---

For Bourdieu, writing in another era, the capacity to possess and deploy social capital was heavily dependent upon social class, which he saw as being perpetuated by our upbringing in particular cultural idioms (1993). Accordingly, Bourdieu saw social status as being reproduced through particular cultural literacies which found expression in public displays of 'good taste'. Certainly, close references to a public-taste culture constitute a large part of the personal profiles created by many people. Indeed, much like a dating forum, the medium encourages us to present in this particular way. Musical taste, favourite films and television shows, admired celebrities, adored pets and popular causes are all proffered as indicators of the self. Interestingly, with the heavy demographic bias towards the under thirty-fives, the display of 'class-specific' tastes is a fairly marginal factor in SNS. Rather, it is the display of an overtly popular taste culture, and a consumer literacy of considerable depth and complexity, that characterizes the cultural capital of the Facebook self. Nonetheless, liking the right things remains important, and similarity in consumption patterns (whether generic or narrow in their scope) is taken implicitly to suggest affinity between individuals. Product placement thus enters the personal domain decisively as the names and faces of contemporary mass-media franchises are placed side by side with the most flattering pictures of the self and the cutest pictures of our children.

Sharing our tastes in SNS is a logical extension of online fan cultures as a dominant mode of personal expression in a 'consumer society'. Sharing our address book, however, is predicated upon new and novel understandings of social connectivity fostered by email and mobile phones. Taken together, the two social actions constitute a significant degree of self-disclosure in the public domain. Nor is this the full extent of the demands for self-declaration that are placed upon the SNS user. The 'status update' feature exhorts us to regularly inform the members of our networks of our present activity. Thus, both emphatic and trivial actions that we undertake in our everyday lives become 'news items' that we share with our network via a personalized 'news feed' in which we are the central subject. This becomes a delicate matter, since those who have little to notify their associates about soon appear dead in the water socially. Those who notify their friends of a hundred trivial thoughts everyday rapidly become a nuisance to their 'subscribers', manifesting as a volume of vacuous self-oriented spam in the mailbox of close friends, long-suffering relatives and passing acquaintances alike. In the other direction, the default privacy settings of SNS encourage the sharing of conversations between network members across the entire network. This means that we are continually eavesdropping on conversations between acquaintances of which we would previously have been unaware.

Taken in total, then, SNS constitutes a major site of self-disclosure, requiring a considerable degree of time investment in monitoring and maintaining the symbolic interactions within our personal network. By its nature, SNS requires us to share ourselves in public and, without our newfound willingness to self-disclose in such an open forum, these applications would not maintain any lasting appeal for their users. The question, of course, is to what extent this degree of sharing is beneficial or detrimental to the individual. As with all Internet applications that have achieved popular participation, social networking sites have been assessed by sociologists in terms of the risks that they represent to the individuals who take part in them (Livingstone 2008). Given that Facebook has been highly popular with teenagers, a group traditionally associated with vulnerability, there has been considerable attention paid to the potentially risky behaviours that young people may be engaging in through 'oversharing' on SNS. Sonia Livingstone is keen to remind us that the timeless notion of teenagers as being 'at risk' in this way has to be understood in the context of the deliberate risk-seeking that characterizes that period of life (2008). However, given the permanency of digital records, we may still need to question the capacity of SNS users to adequately assess the risks associated with transgressive self-presentations and with excessive self-disclosure at this stage in their lives. As a generation that is growing up in public, many young SNS users may fail to appreciate the exponential spread of connectivity through social networks or believe (wrongly) that their profiles are private rather than public forums.

Box 7.2 Negative impacts of SNS

- Online social networks are time-consuming and can be seen as discouraging the formation of new social relationships in the material world
- Social networking can develop into a performance of popularity that has little to do with significant personal association
- Social networking exposes our private lives to public scrutiny and has the potential to cause us harm as a result
- Social networking sites encourage the formation of closed groups that detract from participation in wider public discussion

Network Activity as Symbolic Interaction

As much as online dating provides a textbook case of Goffman's theory of dramaturgy, the complexities of SNS provide an expansive empirical test for Blumer's model of social interactionism. The expression of individuals via shared thoughts and actions, product tagging and public connectivity clearly serves to demonstrate how the self is constructed as a social object. The expression of the self as a social actor in SNS also necessarily deploys our associates as social objects. By moving through SNS profiles, we can witness the dual function of acting and watching others act, considering in turn our own conscious self-presentation and assessing the self-presentations of people that we know to varying extents. The myriad exchanges within SNS networks are providing us with a permanent empirical account of innumerable symbolic exchanges that have been consciously planned and 'published' in the social arena. This is a social domain that is at once self-recording and self-regulating. This, of itself, provides support for the notion of a guiding rationality behind social action. This inverts the postmodern reading of online communication, suggesting that rather than dissociating from the self and from reality, millions of social actors are using SNS to interlace digital media within a wider domain of symbolic interaction that is premised upon the guiding hands of concrete selves. It makes sense, then, to assume that our engagement with SNS platforms constitutes a much more explicit engagement with the self as a social actor.

For Blumer, however, individual social interactions were the only sociological reality. In that sense, the social capital on display in Facebook is primarily a by-product of symbolic interaction between individuals. Nonetheless, the strong shaping of self-presentation by the Facebook formula, and the emergence of definite patterns of self-presentation amongst SNS users, appears to support James Coleman's assertion that, taken in aggregate, the macrological effect of social capital is the production of a social structure (1994). Social capital is also a necessary precondition for participation in SNS interaction since, at the very least, we need a network to put on show. We must also cultivate a conscious relationship between the 'I' that conducts our interactions via any number of SNS platforms and the public 'me' that finds expression in the socially connected profiles that we create. Both of these facets of the self are able to cross back and forth between online and offline interactions, and appear to do so in a manner that is acutely self-reflexive. Social interaction can therefore perhaps be best understood as a process of becoming. People take note of the Facebook self, compare it to other social objects and work to improve it through various strategic deployments of image, language and social capital. Thus, the 'I' directs the 'me', but over time the empathic assessment of the 'me' begins to influence the behaviour of the 'I'. As such, you can reasonably expect participation in SNS platforms to transform your sense of self over time.

Think and Discuss

1. Key Terms
Can you describe in simple language what is meant by the following terms found in this chapter?

- Social action
- Self-presentation
- Social capital
- Oversharing
- Impression management

2. Critical Questions
Try answering the following questions, drawing upon your own understanding, experience and knowledge.

1. To what extent does an online dating profile or an SNS page constitute a rational presentation of the self?
2. Are you confident that you can assess the identity of another person through an online profile?
3. In what ways do digital platforms free us or restrict us in assuming different roles on the social stage?
4. Have you ever witnessed problems with excessive self-disclosure in online encounters?
5. Is the symbolic modelling of our relationships in SNS likely to impact upon the ways we understand social interaction?

Further Reading

Arvidsson, Adam (2005) *Brands: Meaning and Value in Media Culture*, London and New York: Routledge.

Baym, Nancy (2010) *Personal Connections in the Digital Age*, Cambridge: Polity.

Blumer, Herbert (1969) *Symbolic Interactionism: Perspective and Method*, Berkeley, CA: University of California Press.

Field, John (2008) *Social Capital*, London and New York: Routledge.

Goffman, Erving (1959) *The Presentation of Self in Everyday Life*, Garden City, NY: Doubleday.

Miller, Daniel (2011) *Tales from Facebook*, Cambridge: Polity.

Papacharissi, Z. (ed.) (2010a) *The Networked Self: Identity, Community and Culture on Social Network Sites*, London and New York: Routledge.

Trepte, Sabine and Reinecke, Leonard (eds) (2011) *Privacy Online: Perspectives on Privacy and Self-Disclosure in the Social Web*, Berlin: Springer.

Whitty, Monica, Baker, Andrea and Inman, James (eds) (2007) *Online Matchmaking*, Houndmills: Palgrave Macmillan.

Go Online

Match – www.match.com
E Harmony – www.eharmony.com
Shaadi – www.shaadi.com
Facebook – www.facebook.com
My Space – www.myspace.com
Twitter – www.twitter.com

CHAPTER 8

Going Mobile

It was the advent of the personal computer that fundamentally individuated our usage of information technology. In the early 1990s, the rise of the World Wide Web facilitated a new sense of sociability based upon a hyper-real individualism. The heyday of the desktop paradigm during the 1980s and 1990s was nonetheless accompanied by the parallel rise of mobile devices, as various technical barriers to smaller portable devices were overcome by the vast industrial machinery of global electronics. As far back as the 1970s, the notion of a portable tablet device for computing applications was envisioned by the likes of Microsoft chairman Bill Gates (1995). For many years, however, the 'laptop' was a scaled-down and more expensive variant of the personal computer, earmarked for executives and basic office applications. By the early 2000s, however, new display technologies, faster microchips, more efficient batteries and bigger hard drives made powerful laptops widely available at a low cost. Very quickly, the laptop device became the primary computer for the upcoming generation, something that you could take with you wherever you went. This critical switch in the relationship between user and terminal was prefigured by the steady rise of miniature electronic devices from the early 1980s onwards, from handheld digital games and personal stereos to the definitive portable device: the mobile phone.

The mobile phone sold itself in massive numbers on the basis of communicative convenience and personalization, reaching 4 billion subscribers by 2008 (Ling and Donner 2009: 3–8). In the same decade, the format of the personal stereo was revamped for the digital age in the form of the Apple iPod. This stylish, handheld device allowed individuals to carry a vast store of digital music with them, and it propelled the Apple Corporation to the forefront of consumer electronics. The iconic status of these two devices has encapsulated the pursuit of technological 'convergence', where the capabilities of audiovisual playback, photography, telephony and Internet have been packed into a bewildering array of multimedia products (Jenkins 2006). Consequently, personal media devices have become powerful symbols of contemporary society, representing the central promise of hi-tech consumerism. These devices allow us to integrate our bodily space with a custom-built social world, every bit as deeply as the personal computer combined work spaces with domestic ones. The intensely ergonomic design of personal media devices, shaped for close integration with the human body, provides the contemporary realization of the 1950s fantasy of a cyborg existence. Their ready acceptance as a bare necessity of modern life can be taken to infer the incompleteness of individuals living without such technological augmentation in our present society.

Mobile Privatization in Everyday Life

Although personal media devices are very much the technology of the moment, they were anticipated for half a century, and consistently drew the attention of scholars throughout their development trajectory. Much of this work was done in the cultural studies tradition, which brings together sociological and 'literary' perspectives on culture. Defined by this subject matter, cultural studies has incorporated a diverse range of theoretical perspectives in different settings, from Marxism to liberal pluralism, structuralism, postmodernism, postcolonialism and futurism (Turner 2002, 2011). In the early decades of electronic media, the shift towards an intense individuation of mass-produced electronics began with the shift of media technologies from the public arena into the living rooms of the 1950s and 1960s. Raymond Williams, a defining figure in British cultural studies, posited the emergence of a 'mobile privatization' (1974). Williams saw this as an emergent way of life that constituted an individuation of social experience through technological mediation. It was at once dependent upon the gains made by mass politics, while being inimical to the cultural environment of mass politics. In his later work, with the personal computer and personal stereo making their presence felt, Williams returned to this theme, arguing that mass-produced technologies were empowering individuals with greater social and sensory mobility while simultaneously disassociating them from the wider society (1988).

> There is then a unique modern condition, which I define [as] 'mobile privatization'. It is an ugly phrase for an unprecedented condition. What it means is that at most active social levels people are increasingly living as private small-family units, or, disrupting even that, as private and deliberately self-enclosed individuals, while at the same time there is a quite unprecedented mobility of such restricted privacies . . . You may live in a shell of this kind in which you and your relatives, your lovers, your friends, your children – this small-unit entity is the only really significant social identity. It is not living in a cut-off way, not in a shell that is just stuck. It is a shell which you can take with you, which you can fly with to places that previous generations could never imagine visiting.
>
> Raymond Williams (1974), *Television Technology and Cultural Form*, London: Fontana, p. 26, and Raymond Williams (1988) *Resources of Hope*, London: Verso, p. 171

Williams's foundational work in cultural studies (which drew heavily on historical, humanist and materialist perspectives) was by this time making way for the social constructivism pioneered during the late 1970s by Stuart Hall and his colleagues at the Birmingham Centre for Contemporary Cultural Studies (Hall et al. 1980). This approach was focused upon individual experience, qualitative in its logic and combined textual analysis with ethnographic methodology. In that sense, this form of cultural studies positioned itself against quantitative methods and inverted mainstream sociology's preoccupation with large-scale social structures. In the early 1980s, the sudden and massive popularity of Sony's portable cassette device, the 'Walkman', prompted Hall and others to undertake an in-depth study of the device. They positioned the Walkman within a multidimensional model (the 'circuit of culture') that analysed its representation (in advertising and popular culture) along with the many ways in which its use contributed to individual identities. They also paid attention to the broader political economy of production, consumption and regulation that made the technology available on such a wide scale. They sought to emphasize how the rich symbolic meanings conferred upon the technology informed, and were informed by, the unique social experiences that emerged from its usage. As such, the Walkman was treated as a social object, rather than simply as a technology with functional affordances (in this case, playing audio-cassettes). Accordingly, the research team investigated the interaction of personal stereo devices with the experiences of everyday life, making particular reference to the programming of the aural environment at an individual level.

> What makes the Sony Walkman a part of our culture . . . is not only the 'work' that has gone into constructing it meaningfully, but the social practices with which it has become associated. We do various things with the Walkman. We make use of it in certain ways and thus give it significance, meaning and value in cultural life. There are a whole set of wider practices associated with it which define what is culturally distinctive about the Walkman: like listening while travelling in a crowded train . . . Also, more metaphorically, the very 'modern practice' of being in two places at once, or doing two different things at once: being in a typically crowded, noisy, urban space while also being tuned in, through your headphones, to a very different imaginary space of soundscape in your head which develops in conjunction with the music you are listening to.
>
> Stuart Hall, Paul Du Guy, Linda Janes and Hugh Mackay (1983), *Doing Cultural Studies: The Story of the Sony Walkman*, Milton Keynes: Open University Press, p. 17

Listening to music was a practice previously confined to specific settings such as performance venues, and subsequently made reproducible in the home and workplace using record players and radio. The spatial fixity of listening to music, and the social nature of its consumption, was consequently transformed in critical ways by the new-found capacity of individuals to carry an interchangeable musical soundtrack around with them as they moved through different social spaces. Music, which had primarily been a communal experience, was now being individuated and privatized. A process that began with modern recording technologies, commercialization and domestic playback machines was now reaching its conclusion in the single-user device. At the same time that the aural experience was being individualized, it was also going mobile, due to a parallel process that began with cheap transistors, printed circuit boards and miniaturization, paving the way for the belt-clip machine and stereo headset. The immediate impact of mobile music in cars and on Walkmans was that individuals quickly became accustomed to 'soundtracking' their own lives with their chosen music. The broader sociological significance of such practices was the manner in which a sensory privatization altered our experience of public space and our perception of social proximity. Urban life became more insular and our mundane daily interactions started to sound more like our own personal hit parade. The Walkman became an iconic device because it appeared to encapsulate broader transitions in social life. It signified the evolution from a uniform industrial mass culture to a more diversified cultural economy. It reflected the maturity of post-war commercial pop culture. It symbolized significant investment in the promise of hi-tech gadgets, and it flagged the triumph of consumerism as the defining form of social relations.

Shuffle Play

Designed to operate in tandem with the Apple Personal Computer, the iPod remade the Walkman phenomenon for the twenty-first century. The Walkman had previously gone through an interstitial phase using compact disc technology, but the switch from cassettes to CDs had offered no additional functionality to the personal stereo, with the precise nature of compact disc making those machines prone to 'jumps' in playback. The iPod used the new miniature hard drives developed for laptop computing to make the big leap from a cartridge-style device to one with its own internal memory. Thus, the iPod offered a large storage capacity for digital music in the compressed MP3 format that became popular with network file-sharing during the late 1990s. Following its launch in 2001, the iPod went on to sell over 300 million units by 2011, leading to a large number of copycat devices and battles over the patents for the operating software. The iPod's success was based on its capacity to extend the proven popularity of personal 'music on the move' with large capacity digital storage that could house an entire collection of music. This miniaturized jukebox was presented with a graphical operating interface and the visually distinctive styling pioneered by Apple during the 1990s as a means of differentiating their computer hardware from the cheaper and more commonplace IBM PCs. The iPod massively extended the functionality of the personal stereo while simultaneously presenting itself as a status device with upmarket brand value and all its attendant cultural capital (Bull 2007). It was cheap enough to sell, and expensive enough to earn respect. It was also proprietary, requiring an Apple personal computer to 'upload' music into the device.

Because music has a powerful emotive charge, the privatization of the sound environment by personal stereo has important behavioural implications because it necessarily changes the way that we inhabit and experience social space. Thus, at one level, we could locate the sociological significance of the iPod in terms of an increased sensory distance between individuals (a 'cocooning' effect). At another level, we also need to take account of the remaking of everyday life through the interaction of public spaces with moods and concepts associated with different pieces of music (a 'soundtracking' effect). Because music is also a major art form, the privatization of the sound environment raises aesthetic concerns (it alters the nature of the audience, and thus the musical form). The longer formats of popular music that became popular with the long-playing record quickly receded in favour of shorter pieces to fit into shorter periods of time, generally requiring less concentration while on the move. The dominance of the static 'album' format was steadily undermined by consumers changing habits. In the first instance, cassette technology was used to produce customized programming (the 'compilation tape') and, more recently, hard drives and sophisticated data-management techniques have been employed to play music in innumerable dynamic combinations. Finally, because lyrics make popular music a communicative practice, the privatization of the sound environment takes on deeper cultural significance, where musical expression is powerfully associated with the production of social meanings. Taking all of this into account, the capacity to fine-tune our control of the sound environment through the interface of the iPod can be seen as conferring a disproportionate sense of individual empowerment.

The creation of a personalised soundworld through iPod use creates a form of accompanied solitude for its users in which they feel empowered, in control and self-sufficient as they travel through the spaces of the city. The disjunction between the interior world of control and the external one of contingency and conflict becomes suspended as the user develops strategies for managing their movement mediated by music. The mobile and contingent nature of the journey is experienced precisely as its opposite precisely by creating and managing their own soundworld. The iPod, in effect, warms up the spaces of mobile habitation for its users. The increasing ability and desire of users to make the 'public' spaces of the city mimic their desire for accompanied solitude also has other potentially ambiguous results . . . Users tend to negate public spaces through their prioritisation of their own technologically mediated private realm.

Michael Bull (2005), 'No Dead Air: the iPod and the Culture of Mobile Listening', *Leisure Studies*, 24(4): 353

The iPod marked an important watershed in consumer electronics, as miniaturization progressed steadily and the mobile device displaced the comparatively 'big rig' of the desktop computer. From a purely technological perspective, the iPod was simply a by-product of that larger quest to combine the personal computer with the mobile phone. From a financial perspective, however, it encapsulated the eclipse of technological wizardry by a proven form of usage, clever marketing and close attention to consumer appeal. From an academic perspective, the iPod became important to contemporary cultural studies for many of the same reasons that the Walkman drew the interest of a previous generation of scholars: it was focused on the individual, it mediated everyday social encounters and it combined aesthetic expression with the technology and ideology of the day. In that sense, the significance of the iPod could be equated with the project of cultural studies itself. In recent years, the convergence of cultural studies scholarship with the rise of individuated media devices and the principle of ubiquitous (everywhere) computing promoted by technology companies provides a useful indication of this broader ecology of digital technologies (Agar 2004; Burgess and Green 2009; Goggin 2006; Jenkins 2006). Across a longer period, the unfolding trajectory of popular music, from public broadcast to domestic playback to personal playlist, exemplifies Williams's prediction of the ways in which mobile privatization would change the nature of our social participation, and transform our sense of place in the world.

The Irresistible Intruder

The story of the personal stereo, in both analogue and digital formats, went hand-in-hand with the rise of the mobile phone. In that sense, the accompanied solitude of mobile music provided an emotional counterpoint to a hyperactive social proximity achieved via mobile communications. As with the iPod and the Internet, the mobile phone was a story of technological convergence that was long in the making. Without any doubt, the advent of the telephone in the late nineteenth century signalled the arrival of one of the most characteristic media technologies of modern life. Telephony was a key component in the rise of both nuclear family units and the contemporary forms of official bureaucracies and industrial organizations. The telephone extended the function of social networks over large distances, as well as serving to break down the barriers between the domestic and public spheres. McLuhan called it the 'irresistible intruder in time and space' (1964: 271). This was also an enabling technology that allowed us to organize our professional and social schedules more efficiently. In doing so, the telephone paved the way for a digital society by demonstrating the potentials of mass communications that were personal in their operation. At the global scale, it was the combination of the telephone with the personal computer that gave rise to the Internet. Telephone lines allowed static computers to talk to each other and, in a reverse pairing, digital information exchanges subsequently allowed telephones to become reliable mobile devices that could go almost anywhere.

Once you have a telephone, you only need to take a couple of steps backwards to realize that a mobile telephone would be a good idea. As such, attempts to construct a reliable mobile telephone technology were under way from the early years of the twentieth century. For many decades, mobile communications devices took the cumbersome form of two-way radio systems (such as the walkie-talkie) that were incompatible with the wired technology of the telephone network. The first mobile phones that could connect to regular telephone systems were developed in the USSR in the late 1950s. It was in the 1960s that the infrastructure of hexagonal cell-phone transmitter-receivers was developed in the United States (Gow and Smith 2006). This allowed users to make roaming conversations as long as they remained within the area covered by a single cell. In 1970, a protocol was developed for continuous transmission as a user moved from the area of one cell into another. This made it possible for the first roaming cell-phone networks to be trialled in a small number of cities. The allocation of a broadcast frequency came in the early 1980s, which allowed the commercialization of the technology. The earliest cell-phone systems were restricted to urban areas and were generally too large to carry, being designed as a fixture in cars (called the carphone). It was Motorola who first managed to commercialize a handheld model of the mobile phone (the DynaTAC).

In the 1980s, mobile telephony was considered a cutting-edge technology and mobile phones became status symbols due to an expensive purchase price and the high costs of making calls on a wireless network. The entry of mobile phones into public consciousness was characterized by comedy skits of obnoxious characters who shouted vacuous comments into handsets during train journeys and in cafes and bars. The mobile phone thus replaced the Walkman as the technology that appeared to symbolize a new individualistic and inconsiderate order of social behaviour. Needless to say, none of these associations reduced the desire to own these conspicuous technological accessories. The second generation of mobile phones (hence 2G) that followed during the 1990s marked the critical shift from analogue to digital transmission of signals. The rapid advances in miniaturizing circuitry that had come with the laptop computer, along with improvements in battery technologies, meant that 2G mobile phones were a lot smaller than the older brick phones, could be used for longer periods without recharging and could be fitted into the palm of your hand. The rapid growth in demand for these new devices saw mobile phone ownership steadily reaching downwards into the masses of ordinary people. Most important of all, the following decade saw the steady extension of mobile networks in developing countries where the infrastructure for fixed-line telephony was lacking (Castells et al. 2007; Goggin 2010).

The digitization of mobile telephony allowed new forms of usage to come into being, with text messaging and downloadable content such as ring tones becoming popular in the last years of the twentieth century. The proliferation of personal media devices, including mobile phones, iPods, GPS and 'palmtop' computers in the 2000s made multi-function devices an obvious goal for manufacturers competing for market share. Their stated objective was to develop a mobile phone that could offer full Internet capability, and to serve this end a new generation (3G) of phones were developed with greater bandwidth capabilities intended for multimedia content. As such, mobile phones have been rapidly augmented with extra features. Digital games lacked broad appeal for consumers, but the inclusion of a low-format digital camera was a very popular feature (Goggin 2006: 143–61). Using protocols developed for the Internet, images could now be sent along with text messages, giving the mobile phone much of the functionality of email. Following the popularity of the iPod, audio playback capacity was added to various mobile phone models, and the two devices have since been merged in the form of the iPhone. In this way, the mobile phone, by now the most prevalent technology in everyday life, was recast as what Henry Jenkins describes as the 'Swiss army knife' of digital society (2006).

Phones as Media

The mobile phone is also a useful case study for McLuhan's proposition of media as being sensory extensions rather than vehicles for content (1964). This is a media device that extends our capacities for both speaking and hearing and, in doing so, the mobile phone provides geographical reach and temporal constancy to our social behaviour. Unlike other media forms such as the Internet or TV, the standalone mobile phone was supplied (almost) without content, and all the material that transmitted via the medium was provided by the users themselves. As such, the mobile phone was not primarily an entertainment device by any commonly understood definition of the term. Rather, it was an enabling device for sociability and personal logistics. Nonetheless, mobile phones have increasingly combined enabling and entertainment functions in recent years, reflecting the format of the Internet where email is co-located with access to audiovisual content. In this new combinant form, phone functions are integrated with established leisure technologies like photography and music playback. Thus, the digital mobile is also breaking down the distinction between entertainment and interpersonal communication. As the dominant social mediums of contemporary society, the interrelated development of the mobile phone and the Internet have increasingly informed each other, with attempts to successfully combine the appeal of both becoming a consistent agenda for the electronics industry.

The confluence of the two mediums is no frivolous matter, since the telephone is such a fundamental technology of modern life. Its co-evolution with information technology inevitably implies large-scale reorderings of social relations. At its heart, the most distinctive feature of telephony is its capacity to overcome the obstacle of distance that previously structured human communications. For millennia, long-distance communication was hindered both by physical barriers and by the sheer time it took to transfer messages in a physical form. We therefore lived much of our lives oriented towards those in our physical proximity, living in what Anthony Giddens called the 'co-present' (1990). In our everyday social experience time and space operate as a single dimension, with human activity being instinctively measured in relative terms between these two components and the mobility of the physical self. For this reason, one of the most significant outcomes of mass communication was the 'stretching' of social interaction, where the negation of distance constraints exerted a powerful effect on our perception of time and space. The advent of instantaneous two-way communication on a mass scale via the telephone radically disrupted the rhythms of social life that had been constructed around co-presence. The 'disembedded' availability of social actors via technology supplanted their physical presence in the conduct of human affairs. This resulted in a new order of what Giddens called 'presence-availability', with our social interactions becoming far less local in orientation, without being any less sociable (1990). Indeed, instantaneous communication allowed far greater volumes of communication to take place, creating a densely interactive social world.

In telephony, we can see this as a process unfolding in three phases of spatial deployment. Initially, the telephone overlaid official communications with an institutionalized global structure grounded in militarism, capitalism and imperialism (Standage 1998). Subsequently, the widespread availability of domestic telephony created a vast network of home-to-home connections that stitched the domestic sphere into formal social communication. In the past three decades, the mobile phone revolution has displaced the practice of 'going to the phone' (and essentially speaking to places) with a new form of connectivity centred on the individual regardless of their precise location. This is what Ling and Donner have referred to as 'individual addressability' (2009: 136–9). Because there is an implicit expectation that the body-mounted device will always be in close proximity to its owner, an attendant 'effect' of mobile phone technology is a new configuration of distance that implies constant connectivity regardless of the movements of individuals within their own individualized time-space continuum. In that sense, the earlier negation of large-scale physical distances is powerfully extended through the negation of the everyday movements of individuals around fixed points and times. Thus, the portability of the mobile phone inverts 'disembedded' social proximity between homes and offices back upon the human body and, in doing so, adds a radical expectation of constancy to social communication.

Nicola Green has proposed that we seek to understand the impact of 'mobile time' on our social behaviours in terms of three different sets of 'rhythms' that govern our interaction with these devices (2002: 285–90). The first set of rhythms emerges from the interaction of the user with the device itself, in terms of the occurrence and duration of usage. Thus, the individual patterns of use habituated by each user-device pairing gives rise to a personalized rhythm of mobile time as we integrate talking or texting into our daily routine. The second set of rhythms arises from the interaction of our mobile usage with the wider orders of social interaction. Here the time-honoured rituals of family networks, coordinated patterns of sociability and the temporal ordering of working life all become interlaced with the everyday life of each user. Finally, Green locates a further set of rhythms that arise from institutionalized structures. Here, the affordances designed into each device (such as the extent of coverage or the interface with other digital media) and the commercial conditions of usage (costs and contracts) all serve to shape wider patterns of usage and our experience of mobile time. We can see some similarities between this scaling of mobile time and the 'circuit of culture' that Hall et al. applied to the Walkman. The fundamental difference is that Green's interest is overwhelmingly functional, having little concern in this instance with the symbolic value of the mobile device.

Functional Applications in Mobile Time

Much of what could be said about our personal rhythms of mobile time can be productively related to our previous discussion of the Walkman and the iPod. We introduce new private mobility into unlikely spaces and, in order to do so, we inevitably reorganize our social behaviours, withdrawing from co-present forms of social participation into our own mediated sensory environment. In the case of the mobile phone, however, we must simultaneously open up both convenient and inconvenient moments to planned and unplanned social interaction, conceding sensory control to greater demands for 'presence-availability'. At the scale of institutional rhythms, a detailed investigation of mobile time must account for broad social structures and complex digital economies that belong elsewhere in this book. My focus in the remainder of this chapter will therefore be upon the second set of mobile rhythms, those exploring the interaction of mobile temporalities at the immediate scale of what Green also refers to as 'everyday life'. Even in confining the social life of mobile phones to the domain of personal interaction, we can readily identify numerous patterns of social behaviours that have arisen or been modified by the functional mediation of mobile telephony.

One of the more obvious examples is the changing dynamics of speech patterns within the ritualized structures of communication. This has proved to be a dynamic process, progressing from the characteristic short and loud interactions of the early mobile phones ('I'm on the train . . . what? . . . you're breaking up') to the interrupted but continuous mumble of long-duration conversations with invisible partners that we experience as we walk down the street today. We must also take note of the advent of text messaging and the rapid evolution of its associated language of abbreviations. In this merging of electronic mail with the mobile phone, new literacies in rapid short-hand have become widespread, transforming our everyday usage of text as a form of communication (Goggin 2006: 65–88). We cannot ignore the fact that many, if not most, people are writing more text in this form than they ever will in the formal written language of print. All of these incremental developments in the linguistic form of mobile communication have been shaped to some extent by the affordances of the technology. For many years, expensive calls, battery power and coverage problems all promoted short talk and staccato rhythms. Similarly, the ergonomic difficulties of sending and reading text on miniature devices, or of simply conducting a conversation whilst moving through busy streets, have favoured new forms of shorthand (Baron 2008). As a consequence, mobile time has always been compressed time.

The rise of a new textual code, in the form of the short message system (SMS), allowed cheaper, more plentiful communication to take place. Breaking with the conventional use of telephony, SMS messages can be composed without the pressures for an instant response. This is a useful example of convergent media forms, where the recently learned practices of email communication were imported into the previously live format of the telephone. The shift towards phone-based textual communication also multiplied the available channels within mobile time. SMS allows several conversations to occur simultaneously, replacing the one-to-one logic of the phone call, and its attentive mannerisms, with the many-to-many sociability of email. The pleasures of co-coordinating rapid, but not live, responses allows for backstage coordination. The prompting of our inbox also makes text messaging compulsive in much the same manner as email systems. A further crossover between mobile phones and the wider domain of digital media arises from the adoption of the filing and sorting mechanisms originally developed for the everyday use of personal computing in the workplace. The organization (and individualized customization) of our contacts into electronic address books held within our mobile phones transforms our perception of the social networks that we inhabit. This 'social map' confers a new order of simulation upon our personal affairs, and it subsequently structures our affairs in a process markedly similar to the way that the sorting software of iPods transforms our usage of music.

The immediate impact of these social maps was a further increase in the efficiency of communication. Much as spellchecking software replaced everyday feats of linguistic memorization, phone numbers no longer need to be memorized and large numbers of contacts can be kept with you at all times without the need for cumbersome diaries. More critically, the computerization of our personal contacts constitutes a formal, yet fluid, reorganization of our personal relationships. As such, the address book formalizes the status of the mobile phone as the mediating technology at the heart of our social networks (since, by definition, you cannot include someone without a phone, however much you like them, or include someone whose number is withheld from you). In 'filling up' our address books we imprint an electronic record of our social lives within the device in precisely the same way that our email address book at work preserves a record of our professional activities. The portability of this social map has some downsides, as the loss of our mobile phone delivers up detailed information of our personal networks to anyone who retrieves the device (making us responsible for, and to, the privacy of others). At the same time, the skills that we developed in maintaining and managing our social networks via mobile phones paved the way for the rise of social network sites via the Internet, where the form of the personal computer and the mobile phone converged once more. As a consequence, there is more than simply speed and efficiency at stake, because in many different ways we have come to understand our social positioning via the functional metaphor of the address book.

Constant Proximity

One of the most powerful rhythms of everyday life is set by the regulated meeting and parting of individuals. From the daily separating and reuniting of couples to the regularized assembly of familial orders, friendship networks or bureaucratic functionaries, we can see how the rhythms of everyday life are organized around the appropriate proximity of individuals at any given time. The most obvious intervention of the mobile phone is to replace some of these congregations with virtual gatherings, although it is less efficient for this purpose than Internet-based audiovisual formats (such as Skype). In fact, the most powerful intervention of the mobile phone in this order of things lies in its ability to disrupt and reorder the learned protocols and patterns of meeting and parting. Due to their instantaneity and the prevalence of their ownership, mobile phones allow those separated by daily social obligations to remain in virtual contact at all times. As a consequence, mobile phone use has given rise to an increasing tendency to organize social lives on-the-fly, rather than relying upon pre-agreed times and locations for meetings and actions. Accordingly, everyday social organization becomes a more fluid process, subject to constant revision and amendment whilst its constituent actors remain in motion. This greatly decreases the inconvenience of unanticipated absence and unanticipated events, making our use of time more 'efficient'. Conversely, however, it also means that increasing amounts of time have to be devoted to the increasing volume of communications that now dictate the course of daily events.

Effectively, the personalization of the telephone means that we now live our lives in constant proximity to communication. We can receive messages, in one way or another, whether we are at the desk, in the bath or (via SMS) even while we are asleep. The tenor of distantiated communication consequently changes as things 'not worth writing a letter about' become the staple of mobile communication. Of course, for some, the mobile phone may be a lifeline to love or even to a world outside confinement. For most of us, however, the mobile becomes a coordinating device that carries mundane synchronization across time and space. Shoppers in supermarkets are guided by partners at home to replace particular groceries, teenagers request transportation and we routinely phone people a few yards from their doorstep to notify them of our imminent arrival. As such, we don't primarily use mobile phones to conduct singular exchanges, but rather to maintain perpetually ongoing conversations within our social network. In doing so, we quickly become accustomed to what James Katz and Mark Aakhus refer to as 'perpetual contact' (2002). This sense of living within a close network of family, friends and colleagues who are only the touch of a button away produces a communal awareness that serves to mitigate a social world where dislocation and migration have become commonplace.

Because of the possibility, as well as the fact, of perpetual contact, we begin to form the impression that we live in constant proximity to our loved ones and not, after all, in the company of strangers on city streets. This continuous access to intimacy, sociability and reassurance provides a powerful sense of ontological security. That is, it reassures us of our place in the world and it makes us feel safe. So much so that many young women choose to hold a mobile phone rather than a mace spray when they enter dark alleyways and car parks (Ling and Donner 2009: 97). The adoption of the mobile phone as a safety umbrella leads to powerful moments of disorientation when phones become lost or dysfunctional. The owner of the missing mobile phone, and members of their social network, become gripped with anxiety about the loss of connection, equating this with personal danger, disappearance or tragedy ('nomophobia'). At one time, being 'away from the phone' was taken to mean you were 'out'. Now it is readily assumed that you must be in hospital, incarcerated or dead. At the very least, a loss of communication is somewhat suspicious ('Why was your phone off?'). Similarly, the mobile phone becomes a disciplinary device by which our professional lives are extended across space, with executives, self-employed tradesmen and salaried employees all increasingly required to 'stay in touch' with instructions, transactions and queries both within working hours and without. A failure to take and to make such calls regularly is not generally treated with favour.

We incorporate the advantages and demands of constant proximity into our daily lives by keeping our phone close to us and interspersing all our activities with regular 'hands-free' moments as we maintain a multitude of continuous conversations. As this behaviour becomes normative, the mobile phone intervenes further in the rhythms of everyday life because we also use it to impose constant proximity upon other people. The gifting of mobile phones to children in order to monitor their whereabouts at all times, and the use of mobile connectivity to keep track of the activities of a partner, are both common examples of a mutual surveillance predicated upon the demands of constant proximity. The replacement of trust with the broad assumption of long-distance supervisory powers within our personal relationships can be seen as an outcome of the utility offered by mobile phones to uncover evidence of delinquency, infidelity or deception by employees and family members. In that respect, it is notable that providers of mobile phone services have emphasized not only the capacity to dial for help at any time or place, but also the capacity to regularly check up on the well-being of loved ones, using their mobile phones. The motivations for this new set of expectations emerge from stretched social relations and from the 'cultivation of fear' that characterizes mediated societies (Gerbner and Gross 1976). Mobile privatization in this more insistent form is offered as a remedy for a frightened society in which individuals seek to protect themselves with private car ownership and media connectivity.

Convenient Distance

The new spatiality oriented around the mobile phone can be seen as being explicit in nature because it reaches us regardless of our present engagement in back-stage and front-stage social encounters. As a consequence, the rhythms of everyday life become permanently public in their operation, with the private sphere continuously available to the intrusion of public affairs. Constant proximity compels everyday private conversations to spill over into the conduct of professional lives and vice versa. Nonetheless, the one-to-one nature of telephony also bears a legacy of private intimacy that compels us to negotiate new ways of being private in public. In corridors and meeting rooms, we hunch our shoulders and mumble into phones in order to mitigate the disruption that constant proximity creates when it clashes with the demands of co-present activities. In lifts and trains, we pretend not to notice that we are being compelled to listen to one half of a private conversation, and we expect others to do the same. Having any appearance of attentiveness typically produces a scowl and a functionally superfluous turning away from the offender, a gesture that seeks to assert the segregation of a portion of the public area into a personal domain. In other settings, such as cinemas and lecture theatres, the taking of a private phone call produces quiet disapproval from onlookers (or rather onlisteners). It is rare, however, for the self-centred imposition of mobile privatization to receive any vocal challenge, since this would itself involve the negation of a social distance that has already become the norm in public participation.

Accordingly, in considering the interaction of mobile phones with the rhythms of everyday social life, we might argue that the advent of constant proximity is necessarily counterposed by a paradoxical assumption of convenient distance. This is manifested in a range of small gestures, including the positioning of the body, the hand and the orientation of the gaze. It is also evidenced in more functional terms via the asynchronous (not at the same time) nature of digital textual communication. In our everyday interactions, SMS appears to provide for a degree of hostile behaviour to be conducted at a safe distance. The text message fulfils the old function of the written letter in facilitating terminations of arrangements or accusations of cowardly or shameful acts. The digital 'dear john' has become a staple of teenage dating, where we can easily 'dump' a romantic partner without having to witness the consequences. The ready identification of incoming voice callers on digital mobiles also empowers us to selectively reject unwanted contacts. In some cases this is intentionally callous or rude, but more often those communications may simply be coming at an 'inconvenient' time. In other cases, those callers may be repeat offenders seeking to impose an unwanted degree of constant proximity upon us ('stalking' by phone) and we may even be compelled to change our phone and go through the (also inconvenient) process of re-establishing the contacts that we do want to have. Thus, selectively accepting and rejecting communication becomes an important defensive deployment of the convenient distance that the mobile phone also brings to our social behaviours.

The fact that mobile phone communications take up an increasing proportion of our social interaction has the obvious implication that there is great deal of everyday social interaction that is not face-to-face. It does not necessarily follow that face-to-face interaction is reduced in absolute terms, but the growth in personal communication is predominantly through distant communication. In the public domain, one of the perceived advantages of convenient distance is the negation of the social rules that govern proximate social behaviour. As such, rude and aggressive behaviours that might constitute risk to participants in face-to-face interactions become safer for distant communicators to undertake. For example, the relocation of customer service offices to call centres not only saves money, but also demonstrates the advantages of telephony for circumventing dangerous instances of hostility when things go wrong. Digital phone management systems also mitigate the demands of constant proximity on service providers in the public and private sector by automating responses and making complaints a lengthy and arduous process for customers to undertake. Constant proximity and convenient distance via the telephone also work in combination with other technological forms of mobile privatization. That is why large numbers of people are happy to risk killing other people when they use mobile phones and drive.

Are You a Gadget?

Since the mobile phone formally records social networks, facilitates social activities and enables mutual surveillance, it is understandable that access to mobile phone services is increasingly considered as a prerequisite for social participation. However, the centrality of the mobile phone to contemporary life inevitably raises questions concerning the extent to which people are becoming device dependent in their social interactions. The popularity of personal media devices more broadly and their fostering of a new sensibility (where we carry our 'life' with us in a pocket) has taken 'mobile privatization' to a new level, where it becomes less a matter of choice and more of an imposed state of affairs. Equally, mobile devices represent a further step towards the annihilation of circadian time-space by the sunless clocks and perpetual present of digital time. As Paul Virilio and Robert Hassan have noted, digital media devices of all kinds work incessantly to speed up human activity, with sheer velocity being a goal in its own right (Virilio 2002; Hassan 2008). As a consequence, personal media devices are both cause and effect of increasingly busy and complex lives organized around interpersonal communication. To reveal the full extent of their impact upon everyday life, an account of the social shaping of mobile time must also take note of the symbolic value that is conferred upon these devices. In that respect, Gerard Goggin's use of a cultural studies approach to cell phones has sought to interrogate the commercial representation of mobile phones as well as the many forms of cultural expression that have emerged from their everyday use in different societies (2006, 2010). James Katz and Satomi Sugiyama have also explored the ways in which the conspicuous possession of mobile devices is commonly intended to make statements about personal identity, fashion and social status (2006). It has always been important to have the right kind of phone, and to regularly upgrade to the latest device.

As the individual and their technological displays are promoted as the primary site for extracting economic and social value, personal media devices have to be understood as a significant coinage of cultural capital. Of course, they also operate as an enabling device for everyday commercial exchanges as much as personal ones. As such, the stylish devices on offer today furnish us with a portable customizable media experience that empowers us in numerous small ways, but these are also gadgets that consciously embody a fetishist ideal of a digital lifestyle. In that respect, we appear to have come full circle. The notion of an out-of-body experience taking us into cyberspace gives way in favour of a commercial ergonomics that digitally augments private mobility, whilst simultaneously embedding us further into established social relations. Certainly, when compared to the scholarly intentions of cultural studies, the projection of 'ubiquitous' computing clearly has quite different designs upon everyday life. In the present phase, this design agenda takes concrete form in the pairing of the World Wide Web and the personal media device, which eschews the postmodern ideals of the 'electronic frontier' and gives physical form to the faux individuation of mass consumption. These devices now represent a central pillar of the digital economy, a global agglomeration of technology concerns whose collective aim is nothing less than the continuous transformation of human affairs. It is upon this terrain that we will extend our journey into digital society.

Think and Discuss

1. Key Terms
Can you describe in simple language what is meant by the following terms found in this chapter?

- Mobile privatization
- Soundtracking
- Presence-availability
- Convenient distance
- Individual addressability

2. Critical Questions
Try answering the following questions, drawing upon your own understanding, experience and knowledge.

1. To what extent should we understand 'mobile privatization' as a technological and sensory 'effect' of personal media devices?
2. How do you manage your own use of 'soundtracking' in everyday spaces, and do those strategies create a sense of empowerment?
3. 'Perpetual contact' emerges as the lived experience of connectivity. Does this bring us closer in the manner suggested by the notion of 'constant proximity'?
4. Do personal media devices reflect a more selfish, individualistic society or do they encourage new forms of social connectivity?
5. To what extent do you think that participation in everyday social life is becoming 'device dependent'?

Further Reading

Baron, Naomi (2008) *Always On: Language in an Online and Mobile World*, New York: Oxford University Press.
Bull, Michael (2007) *Sound Moves: iPod Culture and Urban Experience*, London and New York: Routledge.
Giddens, Anthony (1990) *The Social Consequences of Modernity*, Cambridge: Polity.
Goggin, Gerard (2006) *Cell Phone Culture: Mobile Technology In Everyday Life*, New York: Routledge.
Goggin, Gerard (2010) *Global Mobile*, London and New York: Routledge.
Hall, Stuart, Du Guy, Paul et al. (1983) *Doing Cultural Studies: The Story of the Sony Walkman*, Milton Keynes: Open University Press.
Katz, James and Aakhus, Mark (2002) *Perpetual Contact: Mobile Communication, Private Talk, Public Performance,* Cambridge: Cambridge University Press.
Ling, Rich and Donner, Jonathon (2009) *Mobile Communication*, Cambridge: Polity.
Turner, Graeme (2002) *British Cultural Studies: An Introduction*, London and New York: Routledge.

Go Online

Apple Store – www.store.apple.com
Blackberry – www.blackberry.com
Nokia – www.nokia.com
Samsung – www.samsung.com
Vodafone – www.vodafone.co.uk

Part III

Digital Economies

CHAPTER 9

The Road to Serverdom

Our everyday encounters with digital technologies naturally allow us to explore the domain of personal interaction in digital society. Our personal encounters with digital formats also form the basis for projecting our own experiences into a wider social field, and thereby interrogating the subjective positioning of the social imagination. Nonetheless, because those interactions and imaginings are inevitably interlaced within wider social structures, we also need to consider the role of digital technologies within society at a broad scale. In many ways, this bigger picture directs us towards the operation of digital economies, not least because digital media technologies are mass-produced commodities, but also because they are the enabling technologies that shape the day-to-day functions of global commerce. Accordingly, we are compelled to situate digital technologies within the economic process. In the following chapters, I will seek to illustrate the economic rationale of information technologies, the contested nature of the digital commodity and the emerging social relations of both production and consumption that revolve around digital technologies, commodities and markets. Extensive as this approach may seem, you should see this as just the tip of the iceberg, given the breadth and complexity of the numerous digital economies that encompass hardware and software, distribution and interaction, culture and communication. To begin, I will return to the broad notions of 'information society' and 'network society' that were introduced in the first chapter of this book. At that point, I noted the significance of the fact that both of these attempts to theorize the social structure took the form of a political economy. In this chapter, I will seek to expand upon the implications of this for the present form of digital society.

Political Economy and Ideology

To understand the economic rationale by which our everyday encounters with digital technologies are organized, we have to understand the systems of value which inform the everyday relationships between producers and consumers and between buyers and sellers. For this task, we inevitably turn to the traditions of political economy as the most extensive account of such matters in the modern world. The formal study of political economy (the finances of states) has its origins in the eighteenth century, and takes the economic conditions under which we live as its central focus. As with sociology, the ambit of political economy was divided in the late nineteenth century between those who wanted to provide an empirical, scientific account of commercial systems and those who continued to define economic relationships within a set of moral and philosophical questions. Accordingly, the twentieth century witnessed the emergence of a positivist tradition of 'economics', which, having become a social science discipline in its own right, primarily involves the functional modelling of economic systems.

By contrast, an interpretative political economy has remained a major constituent of contemporary sociology. While there are many fruitful and necessary engagements between economics and political economy, and variable approaches to each, we might generalize by saying that modern economics tends to focus on the functional efficiency of economic exchanges (the maths), while political economy seeks to interrogate the social values that shape those exchanges (the meaning).

In that sense, one of the prevailing concerns of political economy is the necessary impact of ideology upon economic relations. Again, as with sociology, the term 'ideology' originated in the nineteenth century and was originally posited as a 'science of ideas'. However, following the enormous influence of the seminal political economist, Karl Marx, ideology came to be understood as a governing logic that structures a set of ideas about society. Thus, ideology is often employed as a term for describing a particular set of 'political' ideas that constitute a distinctive view of the world. Operationally, ideology can be usefully understood as a set of spoken or unspoken rules that makes society possible (internalized by individuals in the form of 'common sense'). From the critical perspectives associated with 'Marxism', however, ideology is also described as an 'oppressive' system of psycho-social control (Althusser 1971; Marx and Engels 1938). This negative connotation also extends to other viewpoints, where the term 'ideology' is commonly applied to ideas that we don't like (especially those that challenge our own 'common sense'). Not all political ideologies are economic in their logic (for example, 'Nazism' or so-called 'Islamism'), but many of the most important ideologies of the modern world (capitalism, communism, socialism) are explicitly economic in form. Within the domain of political economy, as within sociology itself, we can thus identify many differing ideological positions. Nonetheless, broadly speaking, political economy perspectives all tend to place their emphasis upon the 'economic base' of a society. That is, the organization of the economic system is seen to underpin the values of the wider society.

The Magic of Markets

In the last thirty years, the favoured model of political economy has been the Chicago School associated with the 'monetarist' economics of Milton Friedman (1962) and the ideological critiques of socialism by Friedrich von Hayek (1944). Broadly speaking, these neoclassical approaches reject the nationalist state-management of capitalism pursued from the 1940s to 1970s under the influence of British economist John Maynard Keynes (1936). Seeing state-spending as an economic distortion producing inflation and requiring excessive regulation, neoclassical economics extols the virtues of a 'free-market' capitalism from the era before widespread state intervention in the economy (that is, prior to the twentieth century). Monetarist (or 'supply-side') economic models work in tandem with a neoliberal political economy that argues for minimal state intervention in society, open borders for trade and the freedom of individuals to engage in the pursuit of wealth. Comparable with the rational functionalism of Robert Merton in sociology, both neoliberal political economy and neoclassical economics emphasize the rational nature of individuals and the functional efficiency of exchanges. As such, economic matters must be assessed in terms of their efficiency and overall utility, without the distorting influence of political institutions or value-based judgements about equality. Ultimately, a free market is posited as the best guarantor of individual freedoms and, by implication, the market should regulate governments, rather than the other way around.

Box 9.1 Neoliberal political economy

- Is underpinned by the notion that society is comprised of rational individuals who make decisions based upon their own interests
- Argues that the pursuit of self-interest inevitably involves social interactions at the level of exchange, primarily commercial exchange
- Assumes that each individual will pay a reasonable amount for a desired good or service and that this determines the value, or price, of particular exchanges
- Claims that the cumulative effect of large numbers of individuals pursuing rational self-interest through exchange is a social order that functions efficiently according to the 'rules of the market'
- Embraces the computerization of both commercial trade and economic management, seeing computers as the ultimate expression of rational logic and efficiency

---

The online auction site, eBay, provides a useful illustration of the neoliberal model in action. The eBay platform provides an open market through which individuals can buy and sell goods. Because eBay is open to entry by all, there is an effectively limitless field of competition. This eliminates various market barriers caused by distance, communication costs and infrastructure constraints. This levelling of the playing field prevents any single player from exerting a monopoly over particular goods or services. As such, eBay is a 'free market' that allows individuals and small traders to compete effectively with larger companies. The price for goods is not fixed by the producers or by state regulation, but is instead set collectively on the basis of what individual buyers are willing to pay. Those seeking unreasonable recompense for their wares will not find a buyer, since all buyers will make a rational assessment of the exchange value of each and every purchase. Consequently, sellers will not expend their energies trying to sell wares that are over-valued, or consume resources to produce items for which there is no demand. Thus, the market mechanism provides the most effective means of allocating resources to actual needs and wants. Those who provide competitively priced goods that people want, and do so transparently and honestly, will make money. Those trying to fix prices, sell shoddy or defective goods or defraud buyers will be quickly identified by the 'reputation' system that supports transactions and subsequently shunned within the marketplace. In that sense, eBay is a self-regulating mechanism for distributing goods by matching genuine buyers and sellers. It does not rely on the central management of those transactions, but relies instead upon the commonly accepted rules of the market and the reasonable self-interest of all its users.

From the perspective of political economy in general, market relations are the primary logic that governs the form of society. For this reason, the social relations modelled by neoliberalism can be seen as an ideological expression of the guiding principle of logical self-interest as the most fundamental human trait. These ideas became popular in response to the previous dominance of Keynesian economic models that saw the market as being periodically irrational and destructive. Following the rise of European fascism during the Great Depression of the 1930s, Keynesian policies were adopted in order to deter the market failures and widespread social unrest that tended to follow the collapse of speculative bubbles driven by irrational greed. Social democratic polities therefore gave the state a significant role in investment and taxation intended to mitigate recessions and reduce the 'boom-and-bust' cycles of capitalism. In the heyday of Keynesianism, governments also regulated their economies at the international level in order to maintain employment and protect important businesses from the vagaries of global trade. Under the growing influence of neoliberalism, this doctrine of 'protectionism' was steadily abandoned after the 1970s in favour of a single global free market regulated by the spirit of competition alone, heralded as the era of 'globalization' (Held and McGrew 2007).

Hardware Conflicts

Both Keynesian and neoclassical economics were, of course, formulated in response to the much more radical political economy of Karl Marx. Marx saw the market not as an efficiency mechanism for creating prosperity and freedom, but instead as an oppressive regime by which the rich enslaved the poor, harvested the fruits of their labour and speculated upon their fortunes. He noted that the competitive nature of this process fuelled exploitation to such an extent that capitalism was prone to periodic crises, which further impoverished the lives of ordinary people. The historical trend of this process was towards ever increasing inequality between rich and poor, implying the self-destruction of capitalism over the longer term. Thus, Marx called for the end of capitalism and for the socialization of the economy. In its more extreme variants, a Marxist ideology underpinned the authoritarian communism that replaced the market entirely with state ownership in Russia and China during a large part of the twentieth century. In other instances, the Marxist critique of capitalism was accepted to the extent that even liberal governments invariably sought to regulate the market and, via this 'double movement' of free trade and protective legislation, mitigate the destructive effects of the profit cycle on the social environment and monetary system (Polanyi 1957).

At its heart, the 'historical materialism' of Marx saw the changing forms of society as being determined by the 'economic base' (in its technological and institutional forms). That is, the technologies upon which we depend (the means of production) and the institutional forms of the social system (the forces of production) serve to determine the social organization of economic activity (the relations of production). Those relations of production, in turn, structure the broader social and cultural environment (that is, society itself). If we relate this to the ideal of the information society, then digital technologies could be seen as the primary means of production. The forces of production would be the technology corporations, venture capitalists, software companies, telecommunications providers and their regulators. The relations of production are consequently expressed in the differential between the profits of the technical elite and the everyday exploitation of workers through quotidian tasks of information processing. In the context of industrial society, Marx argued that the monopolization of the economic system by an elite inevitably gives rise to a 'class society' where people's lives are determined by their place in the economic system (as owners or workers), and where their interests inevitably come into conflict. This led to Marx's theory of 'class struggle', and the notion that the mass of workers would eventually stage a revolution and seize control of the means of production. The elite supposedly sought to prevent this by dispersing their own ideological viewpoint throughout the social system.

Box 9.2 Neo-Marxist political economy

- Is underpinned by the notion that individuals are not free, since their role in society is determined by the interests of dominant social groups (the elite)
- Argues that the 'means of production' are monopolized by the elite in order to appropriate the value of the commodities produced by workers (as profit)
- Claims that the competitive pursuit of profit under capitalism (accumulation) exacerbates inequality, leading to the formation of a 'class society'
- Assumes that 'class conflict' is an inevitable characteristic of capitalist economies, because workers are systematically exploited (in the boom) and periodically impoverished (in the bust)
- Embraces technological development and scientific economic management, in the hope that the capitalist system can be superseded by a more equal distribution of wealth and a fairer society

To apply an 'orthodox' Marxism to digital society in very crude terms, we might argue that workers sitting at computer terminals across the world will grow tired of working ever longer hours to make technology corporations rich and will one day rise up to take control of computing resources for their own needs. Technology corporations would therefore seek to prevent this by infusing the social environment with their own commercial and competitive ethos. In reality, this is rather a simplistic view of society and an 'information revolution' of this kind seems highly improbable. As such, contemporary Marxists continue with the structural analysis of economic relations and the problem of inequality, but they have in general dispensed with the 'inevitability' of revolution and the classical Marxist notion of capitalism as a passing phase in social development ('stagism'). There are, accordingly, a wide range of neo-Marxist critiques of contemporary capitalism in circulation today that build upon Marx's extensive modelling of capitalism and maintain the critical tone of his work (Harvey 2005). Neo-Marxists tend to emphasize the monopolistic extraction of value from digital commodities and to characterize the economics of the information age as a struggle over knowledge (see Hassan 2008). In the formulation of these positions, the legacy of German sociologist Max Weber (1947) and his more nuanced understanding of class relations (or 'stratification') is at least as important as Marx's famous critique of capitalism.

Weber described social classes as being formed not simply through economic divisions, but also by broader beliefs and cultural practices (1978). In that respect, there are many more class formations in a democratic society than simply workers and capitalists. Similarly, in the twentieth century, American sociologist Erik Olin Wright has developed a much more elaborate theory of stratification that seeks to account for the expansion of the middle classes and the growth in social mobility that sees some workers become more empowered than others within the economic process (1985). The theory of social class therefore remains an intrinsic feature of modern sociology and political economy, and its investigation and expression tends to represent the oppositional pole between a functional sociology (predicated on individualism and consensus) and a critical sociology (predicated upon inequality and exploitation). In practice, however, despite their opposing ideological positions, it would be simplistic to suggest the absolute dominance of either perspective. There have been numerous attempts to accommodate, reconcile or synthesize these competing understandings of society in theory (Giddens 1984; Habermas 1984). At the level of policy, even the most neoliberal economies of the day (US, UK, Japan) continue to pursue various forms of government regulation and social welfare schemes intended to mitigate market excesses. Similarly, the neo-Marxist and Keynesian-liberal critics of the information age are not promoting wholesale public management or state ownership of information technologies. Rather, the primary concern is with identifying and rectifying the structural inequalities, inefficiencies and tendencies towards monopoly that are intrinsic to the capitalist system, and that are subsequently reproduced via digital applications (Dyer-Witheford 1999; Schiller 2000). Naturally, this democratic conversation produces points of debate and conflict, but there are also many instances of agreement and compromise.

American Futurism and Post-industrial Society

One of the central tenets of political economy in the Western world over the past three decades has been the inevitability of a shift away from physical manufacturing as the central plank of the economy in favour of an economy where information management is the main source of activity. As a consequence, the industrial 'materialism' of Marx is seen as being replaced by a 'knowledge economy' driven by computer technologies (Drucker 1969). In this framing, the nature of economic and political power becomes dependent upon the ability to manipulate digital information and to communicate globally using new media technologies. This makes an 'information age' very different from previous epochs where control of material resources and productive capacity was the dominant concern. Alvin Toffler, in his book *Future Shock*, was an early advocate of the notion that technological change had already brought a new age into being (1970). According to Toffler, one of the immediate consequences of electronic technology was the sensory experience of 'information overload', but beyond this he subsequently went on to argue that the era of industrial society had passed with the coming of information technologies (1980). By this logic, American society was seen as having passed through a series of 'waves' whereby technological advances reworked economic and social organization. With mechanization, the first wave (agricultural society) had given way to a second wave (industrial society) and, from the 1970s onwards, computerization was ushering in a third wave of technological and social progress (post-industrial society).

In making this argument, Toffler combined the 'stagism' and economic determinism of classical Marxism with the functionalism of modern liberalism. This synthesis was mobilized primarily upon their common investment in scientific progress and a strong technological determinism. Nonetheless, for Toffler, arguments about class structures or classical capitalism belonged to the industrial epoch, and are therefore largely arguments about the past. Toffler's stated position as a 'futurist' was to move on to predicting the course of the third wave, which he saw as being overwhelmingly determined by the development of computers. In this respect, Toffler's book drew heavily upon an earlier work by Harvard sociologist Daniel Bell, *The Coming of Post-Industrial Society: A Venture in Social Forecasting* (1973). Bell had previously noted (during the 1960s) that there had been a steady decrease in labour-intensive manufacturing as a proportion of the American economy over the course of the twentieth century. In the US, employment in 'services' had grown six times faster than employment in manufacturing in the decades after the Second World War. Consequently, Bell believed that these trends would accelerate and he sought to extrapolate the wider significance of this process in economic and social life.

A post-industrial society is based on services. Hence, it is a game between persons. What counts is not raw muscle power, or energy, but information. The central person is the professional, for he is equipped, by his education and training to provide the kinds of skill which are increasingly demanded in the post-industrial society. If an industrial society is defined by the quantity of goods as marking a standard of living, the post-industrial society is defined by the quality of life as measured by the services and amenities – health, education, recreation, and the arts – which are now deemed desirable and possible for everyone . . . the growth of technical requirements and professional skills makes education, and access to higher education, the condition of entry into the post-industrial society itself.

Daniel Bell (1973) *The Coming of Post-Industrial Society: A Venture in Social Forecasting*, New York: Basic Books, p. 127

Bell predicted the emergence of a 'post-industrial society' where white-collar work predominates over blue-collar work, and where political consensus is maintained by the educated middle classes, rather than by political elites or unionized working classes. The increasing flexibility of more highly skilled labour would see individuals taking on different jobs over the course of their lives. This newfound mobility was predicted to mitigate the alienation of the workplace and therefore remove the rigidity of class conflict seen in the industrial era. Bell's ideas were taken up by Toffler and others as an intellectual framework to support policy shifts towards an economy driven by finance, services and information technologies. In the context of the industrial crisis of the early 1970s, the 'services sector' therefore began expanding even more rapidly as an overall proportion of employment, with over half of all American workers engaged in the services sectors by the mid-1980s. The services sector is a very broad category that includes healthcare, education, retail, banking, real estate, catering, interior decorating, hospitality and tourism, entertainment, childcare, legal services and more. As such, we should perhaps understand this sector not as a set of comparable practices, but instead as everything that is not farming, mining, building or manufacturing (so-called 'primary' and 'secondary' industries).

A similar pattern of 'de-industrialization' was repeated across the so-called 'developed world', balanced by the rapid industrialization of certain 'developing' economies. Employment in primary production and manufacturing thus dropped sharply in Canada, France, Germany, Italy, Japan, the UK and the US between 1979 and 1993. Critics of this process saw de-industrialization as responsible for the advent of permanent structural unemployment in the developed world, but advocates noted that there were actually more jobs overall as a result of parallel growth in the expanding services sector. For Toffler, the benefits of the de-industrialization process were also reflected in the growth of self-employment and he predicted a dispersal of work back into the home via the 'electronic cottage' (1980: 210, 214). This IT-enabled return to a medieval 'putting-out' economy (where craftsmen worked at home and sent their goods to market) would constitute a de-massification of the industrial workforce and further ameliorate the conditions which Marx saw as fostering alienation (thereby making socialism obsolete).

The coming of post-industrial society since the 1970s has constituted both a symptom of, and an ideological platform for, the computerization of advanced economies. This process occurred, in general terms, over a series of distinct phases in the last decades of the twentieth century. In the first phase, computerization extended the deployment of electronics in the production process. Computers enabled manufacturing robots to become increasingly sophisticated in terms of the operations that they could accomplish. The investment in computerized production techniques therefore reduced the numbers of employees needed for manufacturing. This lowered labour costs for employers and resulted in cheaper mass-produced goods for consumers. In numerous areas of the economy from ship-building to printing, computer applications were developed to carry out high-precision tasks that had previously been the preserve of a skilled labouring class. Elsewhere, many unskilled repetitive tasks could be even more effectively automated using computer technologies. In this respect, information technologies further extended the processes of automation that had defined the industrial age. Naturally, this also meant that a range of jobs and skills quickly became obsolete, creating unemployment and thereby reducing the political influence of organized labour.

The Rise of the Machines

The use of computers in automating industrial processes was in many ways a logical extension of long-term historical trends towards machination. What was more radical about the rise of the post-industrial paradigm in the second phase was the widespread deployment of the personal computer as the primary device for creating and manipulating knowledge, for managing and storing data and for handling personal and organizational communications. The advent of digital applications like spreadsheets, databases, email, Internet and word processing rapidly transformed the ways in which government and commercial organizations operated. The production and processing of information resources became faster, cheaper and more sophisticated. Both internal and external organizational communications were enhanced in speed, reach and volume. Virtual meetings and remote collaboration increasingly became a feature of executive operations, whilst email steadily supplanted the telephone as the major technology for internal communications amongst the various departments of large organizations. The standardized nature of major office applications (such as Microsoft Word) streamlined secretarial and bureaucratic tasks and made digital exchanges of documents a straightforward process. The limitations of scale and efficiency inherent to a paper-based system of organization were quickly overcome by the 'PC revolution', unleashing a massively expanded architecture of information exchange (Steffens 1994). This enabled commercial organizations to become larger and more spatially dispersed in their operations without sacrificing the speed or efficiency of their administration.

An equally significant effect of placing information processing at the centre of economic activity was a new instrumental attitude to knowledge. Knowledge became seen as a primary commercial resource, rather than being an exploratory endeavour or a facilitating process for physical production (Mosco and Wasko 1988). Accordingly, information was subjected to price valuation on an unprecedented scale. With the development of the World Wide Web, the third phase of computerization revolutionized the services industries that Bell had described as central to the new economy. The free exchange of information on such a broad scale radically changed the context in which knowledge professionals (such as doctors, lawyers, academics, civil servants, engineers and architects) conducted their affairs. Previously, 'expert' knowledge was acquired though jealously guarded professional bodies such as universities and trades unions. Once apprentices had gained entry to these institutions and completed their training, they were accustomed to expect that the possession of these specialisms would provide a guarantee of lifelong employment in these roles. Personal distributed computing, however, allowed vast bodies of information to become separated from the human bodies that had been their repositories. Information became available in quantities never before seen, and to a much larger audience. In response, the information professions sought to guard it more jealously. Companies, now in the business of relocating their factories elsewhere in the world, came to believe that that it was no longer physical infrastructure, but rather technological innovation and brand loyalty that underpinned their economic future. For both of these reasons, patent applications rocketed and intellectual property legislation was strengthened throughout the world. Information was now seen as the major lever of wealth creation, the defining commodity of the era.

A large part of the 'information society' paradigm was initially constituted by the implementation of computerized processes and the commoditization of information. It is equally important, however, that the political economy of the post-industrial society extended well beyond the pursuit of market efficiency and the resolution of industrial conflict. Its advocates were keen to emphasize the leisurely nature of the coming society. Just as Fordism had redistributed the benefits of industrial capitalism via cheap consumer goods, the post-industrial society was expected to yield a bounty of entertainment and information services to individual citizens. More or less everyone would come to possess greater wealth not only in material terms, but also in terms of a far higher proportion of 'free' time and intellectual stimulation. In that respect, the projections of Bell and Toffler chimed with the futurism of Yoneji Masuda, who saw the information society as a post-industrial milieu where efficiency gains resulted in a greater emphasis on 'time-value' and personal fulfilment. Masuda's approach is similarly stagist, seeking to project a world where class interests are replaced with self-realization, where collective organization is replaced by an individualistic 'participatory democracy' and where the welfare state gives way to citizens' movements (1980). During the 1990s, Microsoft chairman Bill Gates (the reigning champion of corporate information technology) explicitly endorsed the confluence of neoliberal political economy and futurism in his book *The Road Ahead* (1995). By this stage, Gates believed that the computerization of the global financial system advocated by Milton Friedman was more or less complete, and that the World Wide Web was about to bring the same seamless efficiency of the free market to each and every individual through an Aladdin's cave of Internet shopping, price comparison websites, desktop trading and targeted advertising. For Gates, the era of 'Friction-Free Capitalism' had finally arrived (ibid.: 180–207).

The Network Economy

The euphoria of the 1990s stands in such obvious contrast to the mood of 2012. The advent of the public Internet saw vast volumes of capital flooding into information technology companies, driving the so-called 'dot.com' boom. The world's first online stock exchange, the NASDAQ, surged in value throughout the decade. Thus, information technology had already become far more than an efficiency mechanism for the market and the workplace. The combination of consumer electronics, software applications and (increasingly) entertainment and services products was already a major component of the American economy (and hence the global economy). The neoliberal doctrine was firmly established in the major institutions of the global economy (such as the IMF and World Bank), with Keynesianism being put into retirement. Trade unions were undermined both by automation and the new availability of cheap labour in the developing world. With the sudden collapse of communist economies at the beginning of the decade, the rapid expansion of the market system and the public Internet made globalization a reality. There really was a sense amongst technologists and entrepreneurs that the sky was now the limit, with even that barrier likely to be overcome before much longer (Thussu and Sarikakis 2006). As an astute businessman, Bill Gates noted that the technology economy was over-heating, and predicated a correction before the value of the Internet came to be fully realized over the longer term (1995: 259–83). He was right, of course, and the deflation of the stock-market bubble in 2000 (the so-called 'dot.com crash') produced a very minor recession (by contemporary standards) at the turn of the century.

It was amidst the high tide of dot-com enthusiasm, however, that Manuel Castells sat down to write his three-volume epic on the 'network society' (1996, 1997, 1998). Although Castells built upon the work of the information society theorists, he was cast in quite a different mould. Castells was born in fascist Spain in 1942 and grew up in Barcelona, becoming active in protests against the Franco regime as a student. As a consequence, he relocated to Paris to continue his studies and (like his colleague Jean Baudrillard) subsequently took part in the leftist 1968 protest movement that threatened the government of Charles De Gaulle. Having been expelled from the Nanterre campus as a result, Castells eventually relocated in 1979 to Berkeley, where he became professor in sociology and urban planning. This appointment was based upon the widespread recognition of his 1972 book, *The Urban Question: A Marxist Approach* (1977), which emerged out of his doctoral research under the famous French urban sociologist and Marxist, Alain Touraine. In his later work, however, Castells's interest in urban sociology and social movements was transformed by his intellectual embrace of a new political economy based upon information society theory and the architecture of computing. Thus in the context of 1990s, and the 'end of history' popularized by Francis Fukuyama (1992), the three-volume *The Information Age* was intended as a post-Marxist exposition of the new era. Widely regarded as the most extensive and sophisticated political economy of information technology, *The Information Age* posited a 'global network economy' that fundamentally restructures economic and social relations across the entire planet.

The emergence of a new technological paradigm organized around new, more powerful, and more flexible information technologies makes it possible for information itself to become the product of the production process. To be more precise; the products of new information technology industries are information-producing devices or information processing itself. New information technologies, by transforming the processes of information processing, act upon all domains of human activity, and make it possible to establish endless connections between different domains, as well as between different elements and agents of such activities. A networked, deeply interdependent economy emerges that becomes increasingly able to apply its process in technology, knowledge, and management to technology, knowledge, and management themselves.

Manuel Castells (1996), *The Information Age: Economy, Society and Culture, Vol. I: The Rise of the Network Society*, Cambridge, MA, and Oxford: Blackwell, p. 67

At the outset, Castells makes a sustained attempt to illustrate how social life becomes redefined by the decline of industrial capitalism and the rise of 'informational capitalism'. Previously, we have noted the correlation in Castells's work between the network metaphor in computing and sociological methodologies for mapping social relations (see Cavanagh 2007). As a political economy, however, it is the structural fusion of global financial markets and Internet technologies that provides the defining features of Castells's theory. He further diverges from the earlier information society theories in that his description also provides an account of stratification in the network society, taking note of both the destructive force of electronic capitalism and the conflicts which arise from its operation. Thus, we could arguably call Castells's political economy 'neo-Marxist' rather than 'post-Marxist'. Nonetheless, in his account of the network society, Castells largely concurs with the triumph of markets over socialism, the ascent of global free trade over national governments and the switch from trade unionism to social movements formulated around specific social issues. As such, it is undeniably important that Castells's work on 'informational capitalism' and 'network society' became highly influential in the setting of public communications policy worldwide during the 1990s and 2000s. It was widely embraced by academic, financial, technical, governmental and civil society institutions as a model for understanding the phenomenon of globalization.

The Means of Information

Castells argues that the network society is replacing older forms of social structure, notably municipal and industrial polities, due to newly de-centred, individualized and globalized architectures of social communication. On a far grander scale, however, he describes a 'global network society' furnished by the computerization of global finance and the logistical integration of distant economies. This supra-national formation simultaneously overwrites the old order of nation-states with a new partitioning of informational power. Thus, the architecture of the Internet produces a 'space of flows' that is 'concentrating the directional, productive, and managerial functions of all power over the planet; the control of the media; the real politics of power; and the symbolic capacity to create and diffuse messages' (1996: 403). In a digitized world of this kind, the most densely connected locations ('nodes') represent concentrations of information and 'Megacities articulate the global economy, link up the informational networks, and concentrate the world's power' (ibid.: 404). The reason for this concentration of productive capacity in select urban centres is the necessity of a critical mass of technological expertise. Silicon Valley, then, is a (if not the) primary hub of the global network society, operating in connective exchange with the global entertainment hub in nearby Hollywood, the financial hubs of New York and London, and the concentrations of electronics manufacturing in Tokyo, Taipei and Seoul.

In response to the power emanating from the hotspots in the global network, other nations rush to engineer similar concentrations of information technology expertise, giving rise to a global phenomenon where 'in Bangalore, Mumbai, Seoul or Campinas, engineers and scientists concentrate in high-technology hubs, connected to the "Silicon Valleys" of the world' (Castells 1999: 3). For Castells, this strategy of 'clustering' the infrastructure and institutions that support information processing, along with the highly skilled workforce required to perform those operations, becomes a prerequisite to participation in the new global economy, where 'there is little chance for a country, or region, to develop . . . without its incorporation into the technological system of the information age' (ibid.). Not all locations in the physical world can successfully combine the necessary telecommunications infrastructure, IT expertise and venture capital in a favourable configuration. The space of flows is thus highly selective at the global scale. It remakes older geographies by 'turning off' hinterlands, connecting some city districts into global flows while bypassing others. Castells's global network society is not a utopian 'global village' but instead expresses a network of power with narrow, instrumental purposes. Consequently, a network of information-rich 'global cities' come to direct information flows that bypass much of the world, leaving other towns, cities, regions and communities in a new kind of darkness.

This rather bleak vision has inspired a series of policy initiatives to mitigate the selective focus of the network society by redistributing informational resources (for example, laptops for Africa). Simultaneously, governments, entrepreneurs and municipal authorities directed further investments towards information technology concentrations (what we might call the 'Bangalore effect'). Naturally, the global information technology concerns that direct the space of flows have proved amenable to this extensive combination of private and public investment in their products. Simultaneously, the increased uptake of information technology in the developing world has further accelerated the relocation of older industrial processes into those parts of the world, a greater density of communications and information processing in low-cost markets being a prerequisite for the logistics of dispersed global operations. As such, it is important to remain aware that the pursuit of a post-industrial economy only became possible in a situation where physical goods could be obtained cheaply from elsewhere. The industrial economy did not disappear, but was instead relocated to parts of the world where markets were growing faster and labour was cheaper. Problems like labour unrest and pollution were taken elsewhere, leaving developed countries 'time-free' to concentrate on higher-value knowledge industries. Thus, the 'offshoring' of industrial production (primarily to Asia) was widely celebrated during the 1990s by the leading exponents of a post-industrial economy (Friedman 2005).

Is Digital Society a Class Society?

According to Castells, a new division of labour came into existence with the information age. The visible distinction between owners and workers was obscured by financialization and the diffusion of power amongst different entrepreneurial and managerial groups spread across the network. Amongst workers in the post-industrial economies, the distinction between blue-collar (industrial, working-class) and white-collar (clerical, middle-class) workers no longer held true. On a global scale, the emergent relations of production became stratified between: 'the producers of *high value*, based on informational labour; the producers of *high volume*, based on lower-cost labour, the producers of raw materials, based on natural endowment; and the redundant producers; reduced to devalued labour' (1996: 147). This recasting of the 'international division of labour' within the global economy attempted to describe a world no longer divided between industrial and pre-industrial societies but instead between post-industrial, industrial and resource-producing countries. By this formulation, the most advanced developing countries were taking on the burden of industrial production as the developed countries metamorphosed into technologically rich post-industrial societies. Newly industrialized countries would continue to depend upon the post-industrial countries that control global markets, while pre-industrial resource-producing societies would inevitably occupy the lowest rung in the system.

Aside from the international division of labour, Castells also put forward the argument that the nature of the network society gave rise to three major occupational categories that, in turn, served to distinguish social groups and social status. At the top are the 'networkers', the information-rich, highly skilled and mobile professionals who inhabit the space of flows and who direct economic activity. Networkers are autonomous, self-programmable, ambitious creatives. In the middle strata are the 'flextimers', a new kind of worker who occupies the labour stations of the network society. These workers lack the mobility of networkers, but nonetheless move with the rhythms of the global network economy through increasingly transient ICT-based occupations. They are required to offer generalized, flexible skills in response to the changing demands of the network. Flextimers suffer from underemployment, workplace surveillance and heightened insecurity. The world of flextiming, according to Castells, is a world of generic interchangeable labour that favours the female worker and the compliant worker (these being commonly equated in the male-dominated domain of executive management). At the bottom of the class order are the jobless, permanently swollen by the now-redundant masses of physical and skilled labour whose bargaining power (always slight) has now entirely disappeared with international competition and automation. The lower and middle strata of the male-dominated worlds of traditional work consequently become 'legions of discarded, devalued people who form the growing planet of the irrelevant' (1998: 341).

Given the enormous disparities described in the relations of production, it becomes logical to question the extent to which informational capitalism engenders social conflict. Castells addresses this question by emphasizing both the intangible nature of informational commodities and the overwhelming power of the network structure. In practical terms, since the nature of wealth now takes a digital form, its possession becomes much more difficult to discern. In addition, the convergence of pension schemes, insurance policies, personal loans and institutional finance within an increasingly complex financial system effectively draws the whole of society into venture capitalism. At one level, this bore the promise of a 'stakeholder society' in which everyone stood to gain from the wealth generated in the market. On the other hand, it embedded financial capitalism (and risk) in ways that made opposition to its operation appear fruitless and self-defeating. Furthermore, since information flows also represent the major channels for social communication and cultural expression, Castells highlights the ubiquitous mediating power of the global communication networks that now straddle the world. The media industries, previously constrained by national governments, had transformed themselves through new media technologies (and global finance) into supra-national forces of autonomous political power. In this context, access to global media 'airtime' becomes a prerequisite for holding power or achieving social change (and this is true for all players, including governments, insurgents and civil society movements). Thus, paradoxically, any resistance to the network society must be expressed through the network itself. That is because, in order to be effective, all modes of resistance must themselves take on the form of global networks. Resistance to the network society does not provide an alternative, but rather becomes a component of the network society. This is evident whether we are looking (as Castells does) at religious fundamentalists, gay rights activists, environmentalists or radical political groups. It also leaves us with the glorious irony of the global anti-globalization movement.

The Systemic Crash

Another feature of Castells's description that is absent in the projections of 'friction-free capitalism' is the increasing regularity and severity of financial crises. Castells noted that the incredible speed and scale of computerized global capitalism was capable of spreading a market crash in one part of the world very rapidly into other parts of the system. Similarly, the increasing volumes of capital flows were becoming so large that when they switched direction to a new source of profits, entire economies and nations could be left in ruins. This happened in South America during the early 1990s, and it happened on a much larger scale in the Asian Currency Crisis of 1997–8. Thus, the disruptive power of a de-regulated global market was already becoming apparent at the end of the twentieth century. The problem of scale is usefully indicated by the growth in the volume of international trade in currencies over the first decade of the twenty-first century (a tenfold increase). The problem of speed is usefully indicated by an algorithm on the computer of a single trader that managed to instigate an automated light-speed panic amongst 'quant trading' programs and knock 10 per cent off the value of the US stock exchange in fifteen minutes during 2010 (BBC 1 October 2010). In that sense, the amplification of events in a global computerized market system cannot be readily forecast by those who operate it. Consequently, trading concerns have turned to mathematicians and computer programmers who have initiated automated trading systems that their day-to-day operators cannot comprehend. In turn, those overseeing the global financial system (in banks and in government) have also become unable to understand the complexity of the automated and integrated markets that they have created (Ford 2009).

This, then, lies at the heart of the present crisis of 'undue complexity'. Most people could see that what allowed developed economies to continue consuming more without producing more was a toxic mixture of equity spending backed by asset bubbles in their property markets. Although a correction was anticipated, what was not foreseen was that a massive automated sell-off in mortgage-backed securities would start a global market collapse. Once this happened, it was also impossible for those at the head of the world's banks to calculate the extent of their exposure to the losses now spreading through the system. As a consequence, the entire global financial infrastructure came within hours of complete collapse following the onset of the 'subprime crisis' at the end of 2007 (Stiglitz 2010). The market could not rebalance or correct itself and the governments of the day could not allow the global economy to come to a calamitous halt ('game over'). As a consequence, national governments were forced to prop up the global banking system with taxpayers' money. In order to preserve a system suddenly perceived to be too complex to regulate and 'too big to fail', governments across the world were forced to socialize previously unimaginable losses by printing vast sums of money and injecting an enormous coordinated Keynesian stimulus into the global economy. In that sense, the global financial crisis showed us the very worst and best of globalization during the space of a few days.

Since then, however, the post-industrial world has entered a sustained period of recession in which the failure to resolve the systemic causes of the problem has prompted a 'race to the bottom' reminiscent of the Great Depression in the 1930s. Effectively, our system has overloaded itself and crashed, and a technician is standing at our shoulder asking if we have remembered to back up our life's work (in this case, by turning informational capital into gold).

Consequently, we are witnessing an acute crisis in both economics and political economy. The advocates of free markets and computerization are nonetheless promising us that the bug can be fixed and the system rebooted before too long (Gorham and Singh 2009). Monetarists are decrying the distortions of easy credit and stimulus spending and asking us to endure 'austerity' and keep our faith in the great project. Others are dusting off Keynesian-era textbooks and drawing up long lists of regulatory fixes for the banking sector. The economists and politicians who built the global network society are simultaneously vilified and asked to save us. Marx's *Capital* is starting to appear on bookshelves again, although the Marxist school has yet to offer any easy solution to the problem (see Harvey 2010). Bill Gates is recently retired and donating a large proportion of his wealth to charity. We are thus caught between a generation of leaders invested in a revolutionary system that has crashed spectacularly, and a new piece of software that is not yet written. For political economy, this is the equivalent of Thomas Kuhn's famous 'paradigm shift' (1962). Perhaps the most promising avenue presently available can be found in the notion of 'sustainability', which has sought to frame the debate in terms of reducing the environmental and social degradation of unrestrained and highly abstract capitalism (Jackson 2011). This is an idea that has increasingly found favour with both politicians and business leaders, including those at the helm of information technology.

Think and Discuss

1. Key Terms
Can you describe in simple language what is meant by the following terms found in this chapter?

- Political economy
- Neoliberalism
- Relations of production
- Post-industrial society
- Stratification

2. Critical Questions
Try answering the following questions, drawing upon your own understanding, experience and knowledge.

1. What proportion of your usage of digital media is structured by commercial exchanges?
2. To what extent do the products of major IT companies (Apple, Microsoft, Google et al.) shape your use of digital media? What are the benefits/drawbacks of their market dominance?
3. In what ways do the market efficiencies delivered by computerization contribute to your everyday quality of life?
4. Is Castells's model of digital stratification a reasonable characterization of the economic opportunities that exist for different groups of people?
5. To what extent do information technologies reflect (or project) the influence of a particular political economy?

Further Reading

Bell, Daniel (1973) *The Coming of Post-Industrial Society: A Venture in Social Forecasting*, New York: Basic Books.

Castells, Manuel (1996, 1997, 1998) *The Information Age: Economy, Society and Culture, Vols. I, II and III*, Cambridge, MA, and Oxford: Blackwell

Hayek, Friedrich August von (1944) *The Road to Serfdom*, New York: Routledge.

Gates, Bill (1996) *The Road Ahead*, London and New York: Penguin.

Gorham, Michael and Singh, Nidhi (2009) *Electronic Exchanges: The Global Transformation from Pits to Bits*, Berlington: Elsevier.

Harvey, David (2005) *A Brief History of Neoliberalism*, Oxford: Oxford University Press.

Hassan, Robert (2008) *The Information Society*, Cambridge: Polity.

Schiller, Daniel (2000) *Digital Capitalism*, Cambridge, MA: MIT Press.

Stiglitz, Joseph (2010) *Freefall: Free Markets and the Sinking of the Global Economy*, London: Penguin.

Toffler, Alvin (1980) *The Third Wave*, New York: Bantam Books.

Go Online

Manuel Castells – http://www.manuelcastells.info/en/

Milton Friedman – http://www.colorado.edu/studentgroups/libertarians/issues/friedman-soc-resp-business.html

http://www.nybooks.com/articles/archives/2007/feb/15/who-was-milton-friedman/?pagination=false

http://www.nobelprize.org/nobel_prizes/economics/laureates/1976/friedman-autobio.html

David Harvey – http://davidharvey.org/

Friedrich August von Hayek – http://hayekcenter.org/

Alvin and Heidi Toffler – http://www.alvintoffler.net/

CHAPTER 10

Digital Property

Beyond their capacity to streamline the operation of business processes, digital technologies are important commodities in their own right. Computer hardware and software industries are major contributors to commercial activity. Nonetheless, the undeniably important business of consumer electronics does not prompt fundamental questioning of the operation of digital economies to the same extent that the content of digital communication does. 'Content' is a contemporary (and somewhat ugly) phrase that encapsulates the equalization of all forms of knowledge, interaction and expression within a single state. Unlike the guiding logics of computing, there is nothing inherently sacred or profane in mathematical terms about the data that a computer processes. This gives rise to a very critical feature of the digital age, where the reducibility of all forms of communication to binary code obscures the previously important differences between holy texts, industrial designs, pornographic images and family movies. As with ideas, conversations and artistic works are given a digital form and consequently become subject to the process of 'informationalization' identified by Manuel Castells, a process which also positions them unequivocally as commodities within an 'informational economy' (1996).

Digital Commodities

We can define commodities as being goods or services brought to the market for profit. All commodities have some form of usage that determines their value, as well as a set of market mechanisms that determine their price. Anything that is traded or exchanged can be seen as a commodity, including labour (and thus both people and time are commodities). The distinction between goods and services rests upon the nature of the commodity being exchanged. A physical commodity such as a table, a sack of coal or a plate of food constitutes a good. It is a material thing that becomes yours through the process of payment. By contrast, an 'intangible' commodity such as a haircut, dance performance or a medical consultation constitutes a service that you purchase without coming into the ownership of any material item. Some services do provide access to a material resource (such as housing), but the transaction provides 'time-based access' (or rent) rather than transferring ownership of the physical resource. Rent, as such, is the purchase of time rather than the commodity itself, and can therefore also be seen as a services transaction.

Digital commodities can be broadly divided into three categories. First of all, computers and peripherals are electronic goods available for purchase. Second, subscriptions to communication services (such as Internet and mobile phones) are 'access' services sold as time-based commodities. Third, 'media content' in the form of data accessed by users for reading, viewing, or listening to, constitutes an intangible informational commodity. The same can be said for the software that provides particular functional applications of computing. Unlike hardware sales, media access and content are always 'intangible' commodities (you cannot touch them). Thus, data is not a 'good' in the material sense. Furthermore, the 'consumption' of informational commodities does not end their existence (as with food or energy). As a consequence, almost all informational commodities are rented in some way and this positions them within a 'services' economy. At a fundamental level, this conceptualization of the digital commodity is built into many digital systems at the level of software and interface design. Of course, due to the nature of the technology, the purchase of digital goods (hardware) inevitably implies a further transaction for the intangible services that each device will be used for (software and content). In this matter, the technologies themselves can be seen as being value neutral since, in technical terms, information services and media content could be provided free, sold outright or rented. As a consequence, in each and every aspect the 'social life' of informational commodities has been powerfully marked by debates over the legal and philosophical nature of commercial exchange (see Ess 2009).

Hard and Soft Value

In order to understand the ways in which the digital commodity is framed in contemporary society, we need to understand something of the technical and moral questions that digital technologies bring into being. At the most fundamental level, the presentation of software and media content in the form of commodities requires us to consider how their value is conceived by the parties concerned (Bolin 2011). 'Value' is a term that we hear a lot in the commercial world, but it is rare that we see the term 'value' being defined. Value is not a given, however, and the ways that we define it have an immediate bearing upon the rules of commercial exchange. The conventions of political economy give us the most fundamental definition, which is that the value of a commodity is the absolute difference between the costs of inputs (raw materials, processing, labour and distribution) and the price commanded by outputs (what the commodity is worth in the market). Neither of these values are static, which means that the value of a commodity inevitably fluctuates (a fundamental feature of modern capitalism). As electronic components become faster and more efficient (following Moore's law), and manufacturers launch competitive products, both input and output values tend to go down over the life of a computing device. If the market price of a product drops faster than the cost of inputs, then manufacturers are encouraged to launch new models that extend functionality and re-create the device's appeal. This tends to happen on a three-year cycle in information technology, a fast-moving field by any standard.

This 'manufacturing' approach to value does not seek to explain the rules of supply and demand or how a similar product comes to be given a higher price than another (insomuch as the most expensive things to produce do not always gain the highest multiplier in price). Thus, to understand the demand for commodities at market, we also have to take account of 'use-value' (or utility). This is what can actually be done with a commodity. The use-value of Microsoft Windows, for example, is that it allows you to use your computer without having to program every function you wish to carry out. Most of us cannot do much without an operating system, and thus software of this kind has a high use-value insomuch as it becomes a prerequisite for running other software applications. The 'exchange-value' of a commodity, by contrast, is its worth in relative terms. In this context, exchange-value is highly dependent upon the spending power of consumers, upon the social capital of a brand and upon the symbolic power of the commodity (via the social relations that it infers). As such, the exchange-value of an Apple laptop can be expressed in monetary terms, but it nonetheless encompasses all the symbolic value associated with the company, with individualism, one-upmanship and with digital gadgets in general. Exchange-value, then, is very complicated in operation, although it also tends to be pushed down by high levels of competition, decreasing novelty and market saturation.

An equally fundamental feature of any commodity is that it must be privately owned. The ownership of a commodity must be enforceable to prevent it being taken without payment, and this implies a comprehensive system of commercial law along with the means to impose penalties for transgression. Across the board, the private ownership of digital technologies is not as clear-cut as we may at first assume. The vast majority of their initial development was undertaken by military and civilian institutions in the public sector, and paid for by social taxation rather than by private investment. The Internet, for example, was almost wholly paid for by the public purse, even as the major telecommunications networks that it serves have since passed into private hands. Typically, technological innovations are commercialized via the registering of patents (essentially monopoly rights) and their subsequent application in product designs. In the development of modern computing, the sheer scale of the technological apparatus required necessitated a massive international effort far beyond the ambit of even the largest company. For this reason, an international community of scientists and technicians shared much of their work with others working in the field. However, as the era of personal computing got off the ground and full-blooded commercialization was imminent, much of this collegial spirit began to dissipate.

Open and Closed Systems

The Apple computer was a patented design that ran patented software. In responding to competition from small companies like Apple and Commodore, Don Estridge of computer giant IBM (which had previously worked in a similar way) decided to take a risk by building an 'open-architecture' system (the IBM PC). The IBM PC could be built from generic components, was open to third-party expansion products and would run software programs designed by other companies and individuals. This made the IBM PC cheaper to produce and much more adaptable than its competitors. It was this innovation that saw the IBM PC (and its many legally permitted imitations) become the predominant machine in personal computing for twenty years. Famously, this approach also extended to the commissioning of operating system software from a small company named Microsoft. IBM did not demand the ownership of the operating system (Windows) once it had been developed and, as it rapidly became the standard OS for the PC, Microsoft (who did insist on the ownership and control of the software) rapidly became the largest and richest software company in the world (Campbell-Kelly 2003). Thus, the 1980s saw a new ethos of proprietary software where a licence had to be purchased for usage, and where the 'source code' was protected legally from alteration, extension or re-use. This development prompted something of a backlash from the programming community. In 1985, Richard Stallman, a programmer from the MIT Artificial Intelligence lab, attacked the increasing use of copyright restrictions in computer software and formulated the key principles of the 'free software movement' (Williams 2006).

Box 10.1 The principles of Free and Open Source Software (FOSS)

- The freedom to run the program for any purpose (freedom 0)
- The freedom to study how the program works, and adapt it for your needs (freedom 1).Access to the source code is a precondition for this
- The freedom to redistribute copies so you can help your neighbour (freedom 2)
- The freedom to improve the program, and release your improvements to the public, so that the whole community benefits (freedom 3). Access to the source code is a precondition for this

---

The free software movement does not propose that all software should be given away for free. Instead, what it proposes is that the programming that constitutes the software should be available for scrutiny and modification by users. That is, the user should be free to use the software in any number of ways, and not have this freedom curtailed by restrictions placed upon and within the software itself. In that sense, the free software movement sees programming as a linguistic resource, like the English language, that belongs in the public domain. From this perspective, the development of proprietary or restricted code software is a violation of a commonly held resource, comparable to a 'digital enclosure'. Advocates of 'open-source' software, where the source code is shared, point to the open peer-review process as a superior vehicle for software development. Collectively, the Free and Open Source Software movements have developed several pieces of important software, very much in the spirit of the hacker culture of the 1970s that wanted to put computing technology in the hands of the people rather than see it monopolized by corporations. Building upon Stallman's programming work, Linus Torvalds developed the kernel for an alternative open-source operating system called LINUX in 1991. LINUX is now used on a large proportion of the world's servers and super-computers and has also been adapted for desktop and mobile devices (Williams 2006).

Tim Berners-Lee made the source code for the first World Wide Web browser freely available as open-source software. The subsequent development of the public Internet was, however, marked by the early dominance of the commercial Netscape Navigator browser which, in turn, gave way to the Internet Explorer browser that Microsoft gave away 'free' with every copy of their Windows 95 operating system. It was alleged at the time that Microsoft were using their dominance over the operating system to favour their own applications and block competitors. Whilst these allegations had been made previously about Microsoft's incredibly successful Office applications, the 'bundling' of Internet Explorer with Windows led to anti-trust cases in the US and EU, along with a public backlash that Gary Rivlin characterized as 'the plot to get Bill Gates' (Rivlin 1999). In spite of this, Internet Explorer became the most widely used web browser, with around 90 per cent market share, although it has been increasingly challenged in recent years by the Mozilla Firefox browser, another highly successful open-source project. At the heart of the conflict between the big software companies and the FOSS movement is a fundamental disagreement about the role of software. By seeking rents from the use of their products, commercial software companies claim ownership over particular configurations of code. The registering of patents over software products seeks to prevent other developers from benefiting from the advances that they represent. Patents, by their very nature, are intended to institute monopolies over particular applications.

In order to enforce this monopoly, it becomes necessary to 'protect' the source code and thereby restrict the use-value of software in order to maximize its exchange-value. The FOSS movement opposes this dynamic because it imposes a technical barrier to further innovation (Berry 2008). For the global community of hackers and computer enthusiasts, it became a matter of pride to 'liberate' software by 'cracking' proprietary controls embedded within software products (Jordan 2008). This ongoing contest between the hackers and commercial developers has spurred on the development of ever more complex security procedures within everyday software. In this respect, we have to pay attention to the ways in which digital commodities are fundamentally different from material commodities. Software is a collection of information, not a physical object. The information contained in software can be altered or replicated without removing or damaging the original commodity itself. In that sense, the ownership of a digital commodity is radically different from the ownership of a car. If someone else steals your car, that restricts your own usage. It someone else finds new uses for your source code, that does not necessarily restrict your own usage. What it does do, however, is undermine your commercial advantage in the market for consumer software. As a consequence, commercial software companies point to the considerable investments that they make in each and every one of their products. The cost of employing large teams of programmers, designers and marketers to produce a piece of software is relatively high, and if this investment is not protected by patent, then the incentives that drive software development are removed. A community of volunteer software developers cannot provide the strong product development focus that commercial companies can, and their overarching ethos tends to lead to piecemeal development and products that are relatively insecure due to their open architecture. Thus, arguments made for proprietary software claim that it is more secure, more reliable and comes with the guarantee of technical support for all levels of user.

A further fundamental feature of software as a commodity is the need for interoperability and common standards. Personal distributed computing relies upon the easy exchange of information across different machines and this requires a wide range of standards for communication, operating platforms and data formats. For the IBM PC, the Windows platform provided a desktop standard for other software applications. Products like Microsoft Office provided common file formats that ensured data could be read on any number of different machines. However, because these were commercial products sold under licence, their adoption as a standard inevitably led to a de facto monopoly for Microsoft over the PC platform. Apple, of course, has always enjoyed an even stronger monopoly over its own platform (since its control extends to the hardware itself). Once in place, these monopoly positions inevitably restrict competition from other developers, since the adoption of alternative software will immediately introduce problems of compatibility with computers running the predominant software, and thereby considerably reduce the utility (use-value) of the personal computer. As such, it can be argued that when the market share of a company reaches a certain point their monopoly not only hampers software development, but also distorts the free market for software and inhibits consumer choice. Equally, this monopoly position can be used to drive changes in the computer environment through regular updates which require all customers to repurchase licences to maintain compatibility. This favours an economy of rent-seeking over a market led by innovation and competition, but it also ensures stability in the software environment and allows new features to be introduced rapidly and on a large scale.

Property Rights and Intellectual Estates

What is most ironic about the debates surrounding the dominance of Microsoft during the 1980s and 1990s is that it was the combination of the open architecture of the IBM PC and relative ease of 'cracking' Microsoft products that drove the popularity of the platform. In that sense, the widespread illegal replication and usage of Microsoft products was a significant factor in their implementation as a global software standard. Initially, much of this piracy was tolerated in the drive to increase market share, but over time the major software corporations (overwhelmingly based in the US) began a concerted drive to clamp down on the piracy of their products, particularly in the developing world (Johns 2011). By this stage, the revenues being 'lost' to piracy were calculated in billions of dollars and the software industry began to align itself with the traditional media industries who were themselves suffering from a crisis of piracy due to the proliferation of digital formats and the coming of the public Internet. As Manuel Castells and Jean Baudrillard noted in the 1990s, the vast realms of identity and expression were being remediated through digital technologies, with the consequence that all expressions of cultural practice took on the form of code (1997, 1994). The libraries of artistic works held by the commercial 'cultural industries' were being rapidly transferred into digital formats, both by the companies that owned them and by the consumers themselves. This process soon produced a commercial crisis, precisely because digital commodities are inherently reproducible without loss of the original or loss of quality.

In practice, this means that all forms of digital media content (including both software and artistic works) can be shared without loss to the originator of the transaction. This simultaneously removes both the technical obstacles and possessive inhibitors that previously prevented individuals from freely distributing the content in their possession amongst other users. As such, it is important to recognize the ways in which media 'content' industries like television and popular music were implicated in the unfolding of major changes in social attitudes that underpinned the rise of digital society. Whilst the 'old media' of the industrial era were seen primarily as providing entertainment for the industrial workforce, their profitability had become absolutely central to the functioning of post-industrial economies by the 1980s. The United States, in particular, came to rely heavily on the revenues generated by software, movies, music and computer games. The role of entertainment as a mainstay of mass consumption also saw creative works taking on a more central role in public culture throughout the developed world. Initially, all of these industries relied to some extent upon their control of the physical means of reproduction. The basis of the record industry lay in its monopoly over recording facilities and industrial pressing plants for vinyl records. The Hollywood studios relied upon their ownership of the industrial machinery of film production, which was subsequently extended to financial and legal control over the distribution and exhibition of the films that they produced. This Hollywood model was subsequently adopted by most of the other cultural industries, as well as by the emerging software industry.

The increasing value and longevity of creative works were made possible by modern storage mediums and, over time, the commercial focus of the culture industries moved inexorably towards maintaining the value of their 'back catalogue'. This contributed to important changes in copyright law (particularly in the US copyright Act of 1976) that brought the interests of the cultural industries into alignment with the new scientific economy of the post-war years, where technical innovations were given greater emphasis as the major source of wealth creation at the expense of physical plant and productive capacity. Modern copyright law began to take shape in the nineteenth century, although just a small proportion of creative works were subject to this regime until the last decades of the twentieth century (Johns 2011). At its heart, copyright law restricts the practice of making copies of an existing work without making recompense to the originator of the work. It therefore constitutes an explicit recognition of the intellectual labour that goes into expression and innovation. It formalizes in law the entitlement of a creative originator to be recompensed for their intellectual labour, in order that such efforts be encouraged by sufficient reward. This mechanism supported the development of a professional creative class, and saw the end of an intellectual sphere dominated by individuals of independent means. It is equally important that copyright gave rise to a form of intellectual property that was transferrable from the originator to their agents. Intellectual creation consequently becomes productive in a commodity form, and underwrites claims for economic entitlements in both the implementation of ideas and the making of expressive statements (Haynes 2005).

Copyright and patent legislation allows for a sophisticated industrial economy of mass production and distribution to acquire intellectual property rights upon a commission or contract basis. This formalization of informational labour within a larger industrial and legal structure paved the way for a wage economy of informational labour that seeks to parallel the world of physical labour in its economic logic. Originally, there was a simultaneous recognition of the need to balance the recompense of originators with the social benefits arising from the public diffusion of ideas. Therefore, in the Berne Convention of 1886, copyright was granted (on application) to the originators and their agents for a set period of time before the 'copyrighted' works passed into the public domain. Even within the period of copyright, the 'fair use' of the work in commentary and further intellectual development was permitted. With the rise of the post-industrial paradigm in the 1970s, however, the new copyright regimes set in motion by the 'content' industries were intended to massively extend the scope and duration of copyright privileges. The right to recompense in the early years of an innovation was transformed into a longer-term monopoly over unique works (the lifetime of the author plus 100 years). As such, copyright brought an enduring intangible commodity into being, an economic legacy that would inevitably give rise to an estate that outlived its originator.

A regime of this sort reflected the new centrality of knowledge production in the informational economy, but it was also a response to the increasingly widespread public availability of technologies for reproducing information. Previously, copyright disputes were largely conducted between rights-holders and the manufacturers of counterfeited products. The advent of technological replication by the general public, however, saw the focus of copyright actions being brought to bear upon the replication of works by consumers. This crucial shift in the intent of copyright law was originally formulated in response to electronic cassette technologies (both audio and video) and photocopiers in the 1960s and 1970s (Lessig 2002). Not long afterwards, it underwent a step-change with the advent of the personal computer. At its heart, information technology is inherently a medium of record, in that every action produces a new 'recording' of the original information. As such, every time a piece of information is processed by a computer, a new copy of that information is produced. This consequently brings each and every use of a computer device within the ambit of copyright law and the pursuit of intellectual property rights. Today, the extension of copyright privileges is applied automatically to all forms of informational production. That is, copyright is no longer focused upon encouraging scientific invention or works of artistic genius, but instead becomes applicable to policing the mundane replication of information and, indeed, even to personal communication. This is a textbook case of commodization.

Box 10.2 Key arguments for copyright regimes

- That the production of 'software' entails significant investments in research and development and, without patent and copyright privileges, technical innovation is effectively discouraged
- That the free exchange of digital commodities such as music, movies and photographs will destroy the industries that undertake the production of 'content' as their primary business
- That the production of all digital commodities requires specialized creative skills and, if financial rewards are not available, the creative professions will cease to exist
- That the widespread practices of reworking, adapting and remixing the work of others is intellectual theft, particularly where it allows people to profit from the efforts of others without recompense or acknowledgement
- That the entities who manage media content (such as publishers and executive producers) play an important role in sourcing new talent and separating the truly innovative creators from the hobbyists and imitators, thereby ensuring a high level of quality for consumers
- That, consequently, the enforcement of copyright mechanisms is the only means of ensuring the future of technical innovation and creative expression

---

Music to Burn

Although we tend to see the Internet as a communications technology, it becomes critically important to recognize that in a digital society where media forms have been reduced to code, it becomes possible to transmit all these 'files' of code via the Internet. This makes the Internet not just a communication system but also a distribution system. This potential of the World Wide Web was not lost upon the industries that relied upon the manufacturing of physical media for their income. It was to prove incredibly difficult, however, to adapt their business model to the rapidly changing technological conditions. In this respect, the fortunes of the popular music industry provide a fruitful example of the challenges posed for traditional content providers in the digital era. The music industry was, of course, itself a modern, industrial innovation. The invention of the phonograph in 1878 heralded a transformation in the ways in which music was produced, enjoyed and exploited commercially. It was in the 1910s that music-recording technologies became subject to a process of industrialization, with the mass production of gramophone equipment designed to play recordings within domestic spaces. The selling point of the phonograph was not only the realistic quality of sound it could capture, but also the capacity to change between records and move from one piece of music to another.

The advent of radio mass broadcasting during the 1920s gave further impetus to the commercial potentials of recorded music. The radio differed from the phonograph in that the listener could not select the material, or replay it at whim, but they could access an impossibly vast selection of compositions through the radio – which they could never hope to purchase through gramophone technology. Given that the gramophone companies were not prepared to allow radio 'shows' to purchase recordings and share them with millions for free, new arrangements were made for 'royalties' from records played on air to be paid to the record companies. Music became good business in the post-war decades for a number of reasons. The musical talent was self-sustaining and could be recruited at low cost. The recordings themselves were cheap enough to guarantee a mass market, and an increasingly young population meant a growing market. However, the organized exploitation of music in this mass market relied upon the recording companies maintaining a monopoly over expensive analogue recording facilities as well as over the manufacture and distribution of the recordings themselves. Accordingly, the advent of digital technologies disrupted the music industry from the 1980s onwards. Music changed, since digitization changed the range of available sounds (with electronic keyboards and synthesizers becoming widely available). Digitization changed the way that music was recorded as old expensive analogue studios were refitted with digital systems. With the rapid spread of personal computers, software for mastering and mixing music became accessible to both amateur and professional musicians. The recording monopoly was thus broken by digital audio workstation (DAW) software but, perhaps most importantly, digitization changed the ways in which music was stored and distributed.

In the initial phase, two major technology corporations, Sony and Phillips, were behind the development of the compact disc. Designed to hold an hour of music in a high-quality digital form, the CD was intended to replace the vinyl record and bring a new era of long-lasting high-quality audio playback. The CD format was launched commercially in 1982 with a target audience of affluent classical music fans. Over the next decade, more and more music was released on compact disc, with sales overtaking vinyl records by the end of the 1990s. The CD was marketed as an indestructible recording, free from the deterioration of vinyl records and magnetic tapes used previously. Once set up, CD plants actually allowed for cheaper production than the old vinyl technology, and with CDs selling for three times the price, the profits margins grew. Although album sales declined steadily throughout the 1980s, the switch to a new format meant that consumers began to replace entire collections of music. The transfer of older releases to CD became a lucrative business. What wasn't anticipated by the music industry was the adoption of the compact disc as a storage medium by the personal computer industry. With computer programs growing in size and complexity, the large storage capacity of the compact disc made it a natural choice for incorporation within the generation of Pentium personal computers that emerged in the mid-1990s. As a storage medium for digital data, however, it was necessary to adapt the CD format to be written with data rather than pressed in a plant.

Engineers came up with the solution of changing the storage layer of small holes read by the laser for a storage layer where a reflective layer was 'burned' with data to produce the same optical effect for a reading laser. By this mechanism, a dozen years after its inception, the compact disc became copyable. This had obvious implications for the music industry. As a new generation of multimedia personal computers with both sound and compact disc 'writing' capability became available after 1995, consumers began to make copies of compact discs. Anyone with a personal computer could now make an unlimited number of copies of any audio CD. Unlike the old analogue formats, digital audio did not degrade during replication, so there was no loss of quality and copying was considerably faster than 'real time'. Given that the inflation of retail prices that followed the switch to CDs was a major complaint amongst consumers, the illegal copying of compact discs through CD-burning quickly became prevalent. Thus, the monopoly over replication was broken. By the mid-1990s, the advent of the Internet had the potential to undermine the industry's sole remaining control, that is, over distribution. In the first instance, traditional distribution hierarchies were disturbed as new online, Internet 'shops' began to undercut high-street retailers, with 'e-commerce' companies such as CDNow and Amazon beginning to sell millions of compact discs via post at wholesale prices. The resulting contraction in the high-street retail market for music was highly apparent by the early 2000s.

Share and Share Alike

Hot on the heels of the by-mail Internet retailers was a more radical use of Internet technology. Here, individual computer owners began using their Internet connections to share music files with others via the Internet. The only limitation was the size and number of files to be sent and the networks of association between users. These limitations were quickly overcome by the introduction of peer-to-peer (P2P) software, which allowed users to browse through the available files on countless other computers connected to the Internet. Using the new compressed MP3 format, they could both upload and download many files simultaneously, and thus exchange whole collections of music without charge across the Internet. The sudden uptake of P2P platforms provoked an instant response from the recording industry. Software companies were lobbied to provide built-in restrictions preventing unlimited file copying in audio software, websites offering MP3s were sued and individual 'downloaders' were very publicly prosecuted (albeit in small numbers). All of these actions stemmed from a natural desire to protect the copyrights held by the industry over original recordings, which constituted their remaining economic resource.

[T]he trend in the music industry has been toward the monopolistic intermediation of the musical product. The music industry has over time developed the means by which it mediates the movement of music as physical goods . . . New technologies of communication lead to disintermediation (essentially removal of routinized business practices involving middlepersons) and, in some cases, to a redefinition of the nature of a product, insofar as what had once been a physical item (a record, for instance) is now a digitized one (e.g. a downloadable file).

Steve Jones (2002) 'Music that Moves: Popular Music, Distribution and Network Technologies', *Cultural Studies*, 16(2): 213–32

Technical disintermediation via digital technologies inevitably brings the role of commercial intermediaries into question. Some musical artists (such as Metallica), horrified by their own lost royalties, came out in support of the recording companies and campaigned for music fans to respect their intellectual property rights. Other artists (such as Marillion) elected to use the Internet themselves to direct-market their music, and free themselves from the monopoly of the recording companies which kept the lions' share of revenues. Many new artists also experimented with P2P technology in order to publicize their work without signing to any recording company. Within the space of a couple of years, this was an industry in upheaval. Nonetheless, the possibilities for legitimate digital distribution also presented obvious benefits for the industry (they had their own middlemen to get rid of). In the initial uptake of Internet distribution, however, there was a very real threat to the survival of the recording companies if illegal file copying and sharing could not be contained. Consequently, the most prominent case of copyright action in 2001 was the action by the Recording Industry Association of America (RIAA) against the popular P2P platform, Napster. This software – developed in 1999 – had signed up 27 million users by 2001, all sharing photographs and videos, but mostly music, over the net. The RIAA took out a massive lawsuit for copyright infringement, had the service frozen by July 2001 and liquidated by 2002. Napster argued that it was merely providing a file-sharing service to users and had no control over the information being exchanged, being similar in status to an Internet Service provider (ISP). The US courts, however, ruled in favour of the recording industry. This victory proved short-lived, as new P2P platforms came on the scene (such as Grokster and Bit Torrent). These platforms allowed 'file-sharers' to exchange data without any intermediary server where copyright infringement could be ruled to have taken place, and thus presented no central operation that could be subject to lawsuits.

The file-sharing controversy during the 2000s demonstrated that the days of music as a physical product, where the purchaser had use rights but not copyrights, were over. Digitization appears to have forever separated music from any physical medium, and the existence of common code standards for audio playback made sound infinitely transferable between computers. At the beginning of the decade, the situation in the music industry (along with similar problems with film and television and the ongoing distribution of 'cracked' softwares) provoked even more stringent copyright legislation in North America and the EU. It became a serious criminal (as opposed to civil) offence to share music files or to download copyrighted material without payment (whether for profit or personal use). Similar penalties were applied to users who 'remix' music, who make personal compilation CDs or who use images 'fished' from the Internet in their own web pages or presentations. Over the past decade, the mass infringement of rights (held by what were now being referred to as the 'copyright industries') has been highly illegal but effectively unpreventable. The sheer number of downloaders and the cocooning effect of the personal computer made downloading practices appear to be easy and low-risk crimes. A whole generation of Internet users was reluctant to relinquish this new culture of abundance in intangible goods and expressed their growing sense of entitlement in a similar language to the libertarian arguments made by the Free Software movement. That is, it was argued that culture was a commonly held resource that people should be free to consume and adapt as they saw fit.

In European countries such as Sweden and Germany, political parties were formed on the basis of the 'right' to commit piracy in the cultural domain. Even though the illegality of piracy appears to have been widely recognized by the younger population, the majority seemingly refused to consider it to constitute a 'real crime' in a moral sense (Ess 2009). Along with other industries threatened by this free flow of creative content (such as book publishers and Hollywood studios), the recording industry has worked to regain control over its product by including a new regime or 'digital rights management' (DRM). This has taken the form of scrambling technologies on CDs, new proprietary sound formats (for example, .AIFF) for media players, and persuading software providers to provide built-in permanent records of how media player software is used in order to record (and thus deter) illegal reproduction of copyrighted material (for example, in Windows Media Player). The music industry has also followed a twin track of legal suits alongside the launch of 'legal download' retail services. In the former case, successful revenue-sharing settlements with downloading services such as Grokster and Kazaa have been established in recent years. In the latter case, the popularity of Apple's iPod was a huge benefit for the music industry because it required an Apple computer to load files into the device, and its proprietary format meant that only files acquired from Apple's royalty-paying iTunes service could be played. Music files could not be transferred from the iPod to other devices, so the capacity to share content was restricted by technical as well as legal means. DRM regimes therefore mark an important shift from controlling the structures of distribution to controlling the ways in which music (in a dematerialized form) is used by consumers after sale.

Box 10.3 Arguments for a free-use culture

- That media content such as music, poetry or research is an important cultural resource that belongs in the public realm (or 'commons')
- That the personal use of media content does not represent commercial gain and should not be subject to market control
- That all creative works are based upon access to earlier forms, and their imitation, extension and revision is central to the creation of culture
- That a large proportion of creative innovations do not have a commercial motive, and the exploitation of their legacy for financial gain constitutes a public theft (or 'enclosure')
- Most creators develop their craft at their own expense and the contracting of commercial rights over their works by third parties is simply a form of rent-seeking
- That both creators and consumers have traditionally been ripped off by intermediaries, whose unfair monopoly over the process of exchange is being disintermediated by digital technology
- That the extension of new privileges over the ways we use the products that we purchase (via DRM) is an infringement of established consumer rights
- An equitable balance between creators, commercial intermediaries and consumers cannot be achieved by purely technical means

---

The Crown of Creation

By its very nature, the Internet was bound to have major implications for the music industry, since its economic position was originally founded upon a technological monopoly over recording, replication and distribution. Digitization 'disintermediated' music and made all of those monopolies redundant. Today, however, the same technology that 'liberated' music is now proving eminently useful for constraining and commodifying it in new (and perhaps unforeseen) ways. Indeed, there has been a rapid increase in proprietary controls over all intangible commodities during the past decade, augmented by technically imposed restrictions that push the envelope of the most stringent copyright legislation. Consequently, a technology (the Internet) which was sold on freely available content is now becoming one in which content is vigorously controlled both before and after sale. That is, the books, images, video clips and academic works that became freely available during the 1990s are now increasingly contained within a pay-per-view model of the kind used in cable television. This is proving to be the most readily effective means of ensuring that the principle of recompense for originators can be imposed upon digital commodities. At the same time, the increasingly sophisticated forms of control over the use of digital products works to undo the new flexibility over the use of media forms that digitization originally brought about. Certainly, all of these strategies appear to be unpopular with consumers, and both piracy and content-restriction are seeing per unit sales for media 'content' continue to fall across the board.

There are also growing concerns that the emergence of DRM technologies on the Internet and elsewhere are undermining the principle of the free exchange of information upon which the early Internet culture was based. Opponents to the new DRM regime continue to argue for the importance of the 'fair use' of copyright materials not just by creators but also by consumers (Lessig 2005b). An important strategy in this regard has been the increasing adoption of the 'creative commons' copyright licenses developed by Richard Stallman. These reiterations of copyright allow originators to retain ownership of their works while granting a broad range of re-use rights to consumers. These licences are now used extensively by open-source software developers and media artists (Guertin 2012; Williams 2006). Critics, however, see these mechanisms as utopian propositions that cannot provide any realistic alternative for those who make their living through works of the mind (Epstein 2005). The 'free culture' dispute therefore reflects the contested nature of popular culture in contemporary society. Your position within this debate hinges upon whether you see culture and creativity as inherently social enterprises that belong to the public realm (that is, as a 'common good') or whether you see creative genius as an individual possession that requires legal protection (that is, as a commercial commodity). This is, of course, not simply a legal but also a fundamental moral question with enormous economic ramifications in an information society. It is also a pressing practical matter in the day-to-day operation of digital economies.

The ongoing debates over software, music and other digital commodities provide an important illustration of the new dilemmas posed by informationalization. They also highlight the inherent contradictions within a creative and research environment that is simultaneously collective and commercially competitive (Boldrin and Levine 2008). Another, and perhaps equally pressing, question to consider is whether the digital coding of such a wide range of creative practices inevitably reduces all forms of human contributions to digital society to the level of 'content'. What impact is this likely to have upon how we conceive of the philosophical aesthetics of culture and innovation? Music is now measured in megabytes, not in melody. Innovation is associated with the manufacture of commercial patents, not the realization of profound revelation. Similarly, interoperability, interactivity and the mutability of information are all absolutely central to the founding logics of networked computing. Yet, by the mechanisms of commercial privilege, the ongoing monetization of information can only be enforced by restricting these qualities. Thus, we inevitably see the use-value of digital commodities being subjected to technical restrictions. At a more functional level, then, the rapidly changing legal environment powerfully illustrates the critical differences between the use-value and exchange-value of digital commodities. As a consequence, access to all forms of 'content' is increasingly structured by 'price points' in the formalization of an information market. Against this backdrop, what more or less everyone does agree upon is that the digitization of intellectual outputs marks an irrevocable shift from an older trade in specific material reproductions of human expression to a new commercial, legal and technical nexus through which a universal digital commodity is brought into being.

Think and Discuss

1. Key Terms
Can you describe in simple language what is meant by the following terms found in this chapter?

- Copyright
- Use value
- Disintermediation
- Open source
- Digital rights management

2. Critical Questions
Try answering the following questions, drawing upon your own understanding, experience and knowledge.

1. To what extent is your own everyday usage of digital content restricted by legal and technical means?
2. In what contexts can 'file-sharing' be considered as a hindrance or driver of innovation?
3. To what extent does the extension of patent protection and copyright seek to update older forms of commercial monopoly?
4. Does digitization inevitably imply the disintermediation of creative products? If so, what are the implications of this trend?
5. Can we distinguish between forms of digital content that should be freely available and digital commodities that should be owned exclusively?

Further Reading

Boldrin, Michele and Levine, David (2008) *Against Intellectual Property*, Cambridge: Cambridge University Press.
Bolin, Goran (2011) *Value and the Media*, Farnham: Ashgate.
Campbell-Kelly, Martin (2003) *From Airline Reservations to Sonic the Hedgehog: A History of the Software Industry*, Cambridge, MA: MIT Press.
Ess, Charles (2009) *Digital Media Ethics*, Cambridge: Polity.
Guertin, Carolyn (2012) *Digital Prohibition: Piracy and Authorship in New Media Art*, London and New York: Continuum.
Haynes, Richard (2005) *Media Rights and Intellectual Property*, Edinburgh: Edinburgh University Press.
Johns, Andrew (2011) *Piracy: The Intellectual Property Wars from Gutenberg to Gates*, Chicago, IL: Chicago University Press.
Lessig, Lawrence (2005a) *Free Culture: The Nature and Future of Creativity*, New York: Penguin.
Stallman, Richard and Gay, Joshua (2009) *Free Software, Free Society: Selected Essays of Richard M. Stallman*, CreateSpace, available at: https://www.createspace.com
Wikstrom, Patrick (2006) *The Music Industry: Music in the Cloud*, Cambridge: Polity.

Go Online

Digital Millennium Act – http://www.copyright.gov/legislation/dmca.pdf
Grokster – http://www.grokster.com/
Motion Picture Association of America – http://www.mpaa.org/
The Pirate Bay – http://thepiratebay.org/
Recording Industry Association of America – http://www.riaa.com/
World Intellectual Property Organisation – http://www.wipo.int/

CHAPTER 11

Consuming Power

The present usage of digital technology reflects the predominant economic philosophies of our time. To a significant extent, this is illustrated by the ways in which digital commodities are being formed and contested within the intersection of market forces and legal instruments. In this chapter, however, we will direct our attention towards the equally significant ways in which the field of consumption is being reordered around the exchange of digital commodities. While traditional approaches to political economy tend to focus on the productive capacity of the economy, it is critically important that the fine-grained dynamics of mass consumption have become absolutely central to the health and day-to-day operation of advanced economies across the globe. This long-term trend has been reflected in the massive expansion of the advertising industries over the past thirty years, along with the rise of new formal commercial disciplines in areas such as marketing and public relations. Similarly, the pursuit of a services economy is underpinned by a model of social transactions where the provision of basic utilities, personal communications, government services, mass entertainment and education all increasingly fall into line with a shopping economy based upon brand values and free choice.

Henry Jenkins and Convergence

As with the analysis of new media content, a large portion of the sociology of media consumption has been undertaken within the domain of cultural studies. Throughout the era of distributed computing from the late 1970s to the present, this school of thought has itself undergone a significant period of evolution. Much of this change has operated in tandem with the advent of 'new media' forms and the 'globalization' of the discipline itself. With its origins in the politics of the British 'new left' of the 1950s and 1960s, British cultural studies had always sought to emphasize the worth of a common culture in the face of cultural elitism. This particular context made the scholars of British cultural studies acutely attentive to the role of class in the cultural domain. Consequently, culture was consistently promoted as being something ordinary and available to everyone, not something to be rarefied and monopolized by dominant social groups (Hoggart 1957; Williams 1961). Popular culture was also seen, on occasion, as being a useful site of resistance against the established social order (Hebdige 1979). Thus, the account provided by cultural studies sought to emphasize the progressive potential of new media technologies and their 'content' in the hands of the common citizen (Hall et al. 1983). The maturity of cultural studies as an accumulation of sociological approaches to mass media and popular culture was marked by the internationalization of the field during the 1980s and 1990s (Turner 2011).

In adapting British innovations for social inquiry in the United States, a new form of cultural studies emerged that was less concerned with working-class politics and more concerned with the democratic potentials of individualism and the 'grassroots'. In that context, the approaches of cultural studies to popular culture proved a better fit than the structural critiques of the Frankfurt School (Adorno 1991). In the United States, the idea that individual freedom is the guarantor of a free society underpins a particular model of liberal pluralism, one that positions freedom of expression and the exercise of free choice as being synonymous with American culture. This culture is generally held to be in common, and not monopolized by different social classes. This is not to say that American society is perceived uncritically as an individualist utopia. Indeed, the American counter-culture of the 1960s employed these populist notions of freedom as an antagonistic check on what was perceived to be an increasingly coercive political establishment. The role of popular culture in political protest during that era subsequently informed the worldview of many people in the information technology field, as well as those in the entertainment business. Thus, the hackers of Silicon Valley and their academic counterparts in American cultural studies were very much concerned with putting communication power in the hands of the people. With that in mind, they saw 'mobile privatization' much more favourably than British scholars, and wanted more of it.

At present, one of the most influential figures in American cultural studies is Henry Jenkins. For Jenkins, the digital media effectively empower individuals by giving them independent access to everything (2006). The ongoing personalization of media devices extends the reach of consumer choice to all fields of life. This, in turn, leads to ever more sophisticated consumers who direct technology corporations, via the mechanisms of the market, to commercialize media technologies that allow people to do ever more things for themselves. This virtuous circle now allows consumers to challenge the information monopoly of traditional professionals (for example, in medicine or education) and also to displace the old cultural elites and their monopoly over popular culture. In this context, the 'cultural elite' is not the ruling class, but instead signifies professional musicians, artists, film producers and critics. These 'expert' producers of culture are sidelined as the fans of popular culture access technologies that allow them to produce the 'content' for themselves. This rise of 'fandom' as a guiding force in cultural production underpins Jenkins's notion of a grassroots 'participatory culture', where volunteerism replaces professionalism and 'remixes', 'mashups' and 'fan-fictions' replace professional authors and the rarefied canons of modernism. This, then, is the cultural arm of Yoneji Masuda's 'participatory democracy' (1980).

The amateurization of production is just one aspect of Jenkins's larger model of a phenomenon of 'convergence', where old distinctions, barriers and hierarchies are broken down by a combination of technology, democracy and personal expression. In that sense, Jenkins's usage of the term 'convergence' denotes the coming together of things, and the merging of domains that were previously understood as distinct entities. As such, 'convergence' can be seen as a valid term for describing the integration of various technological, economic, cultural and political processes. Jenkins identifies an overarching trend towards increasing convergence not just within, but also between, all of these domains. The term 'convergence' therefore implies that we need to develop a more joined-up understanding of social life, as traditional distinctions between production and consumption, private and public, culture and technology, local and global are overtaken by new ways of doing things. At one level, the metaphor of convergence is supported by a recognizable pattern of technological development seen in the Internet, in SmartPhones and across information technology more broadly. However, the capacity of digital technology to bring about convergence in hardware systems did not of itself create an era of convergence. Of equal importance were parallel processes of convergence in the economic and cultural (and, consequently, political) landscape.

Media convergence is more than simply a technological shift. Convergence alters the relationship between existing technologies, industries, markets, genres and audiences. Convergence refers to a process, but not an endpoint. Thanks to the proliferation of channels and the portability of new computing and telecommunication technologies, we are entering an era where media will be everywhere and we will use all kinds of media in relation to each other . . . Fuelling this technological convergence is a shift in patterns of media ownership. Whereas old Hollywood focused on cinema the new media conglomerates have controlling interests across the entire entertainment industry . . . In turn, media convergence impacts the way we consume media…Convergence is taking place within the same appliances . . . within the same company . . . within the brain of the consumer . . . and within the same fandom.

Henry Jenkins (2004), 'The Cultural Logic of Media Convergence', *International Journal of Cultural Studies*, 7(1): 34

Economic Convergence

In order to accommodate the new possibilities for integrated high-technology products, the specialist consumer electronics companies of the 'old media' era had to expand their operations to include new areas of activity. Notably, this involved an expansion from hardware manufacturing to integrated software and content production. Within the traditional media businesses, the largest companies (with well-defined interests in television, cinema or recorded music) also began to reinvent themselves for the digital media era by embarking on a series of acquisitions and mergers from the 1980s onwards. Companies that had previously prospered within a single 'platform' of media content expanded their interests to encompass a much broader range of content. The guiding logic of convergence in this form was the development of a systematic capacity to integrate the production and delivery of media content through all the various media platforms (and spin-off products). Each part of this larger business model supported the other, and media products could be created with a multimedia market in mind. That is, movies were made with the intention of creating brands that could be applied across a range of other products such as computer games, music and children's toys. Similarly, the competing interests of film theatres, home video and cable TV could be reconciled through the formalization of defined 'windows' for the release of a product at different stages in its commercial life.

This expansion of interests by the major producers of hardware, software and content was largely achieved through acquisitions and growth, and this increase in scale therefore represented a considerable logistical challenge at an organizational level. In addition, many established media companies were already relatively large organizations and the particularity of their markets and products also made them culturally different (Sony's acquisition of Columbia Tri-Star Pictures via soft drinks company Coca Cola being a case in point). Initially, at least, there was also a series of legal barriers to

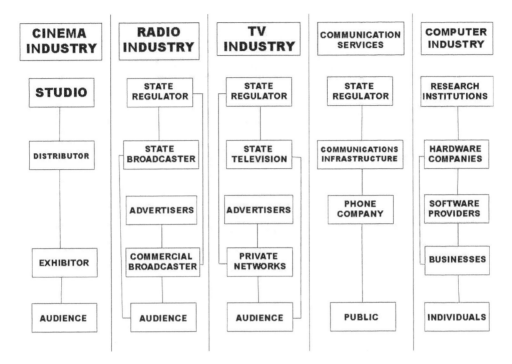

Figure 11.1 *The 'old media' industries*

economic convergence, since existing anti-competition laws and mass-media regulations were intentionally designed to discourage cross-media ownership. Dominance in
a single media market was regarded suspiciously as a commercial monopoly, but even
this was typically considered as less of a problem than an integrated presence across
all forms of media. This 'horizontal integration' of media outlets was widely regarded
as giving media providers too broad an influence in public debate. It was in the liberal-
izing economies of the United States, Australia and the UK that these regulations were
initially relaxed over the course of the 1980s and 1990s, thereby allowing TV companies
to acquire publishers, and movie studios to become owners of software companies.
From this point onwards, the process of convergence between the media industries saw
the rapid consolidation of very large media companies with interests across all areas
of media production and consumption. This process of consolidation took place on an
international stage, with expanding 'media empires' providing the definitive example
of globalization during the 1990s.

Global media corporations drove convergence in a number of ways: the integration
of television, radio and cinema with Internet content, the provision of telephone, cable
and data services in a single package, the tie-in of software titles with hardware systems.
Through massive financial consolidation of holdings and investments, the media industries of old became the information industry of the present. The rise of multinational
media corporations like Sony, AOL-TimeWarner, Microsoft and NewsCorp became
possible in a large part because of the relaxation of national regulations in a world
system that was increasingly committed to free trade. At the same time, information

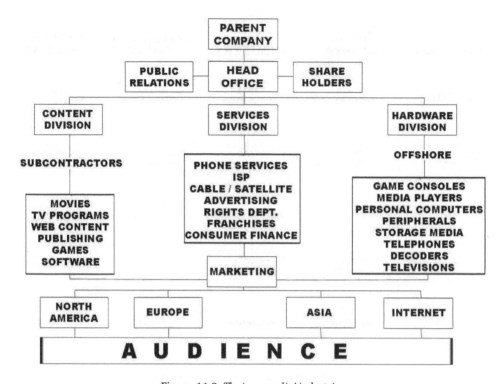

Figure 11.2 *The 'new media' industries*

technologies were themselves absolutely crucial for operating massive global businesses of this kind. An affordable data-processing standard, cheap access to global
communications and the organizational capacity of information technology were
both the product and the process of the media multinationals. Information technology
allowed companies to be run efficiently over huge distances, and thus, arguably, the
digital media made twenty-first-century globalization possible. Networked communications on a global scale effectively enabled the phenomenon of outsourcing industrial
production and managing factories remotely (Farrell 2007). It also allowed businesses
to recruit informational labour from developing countries located offshore. Satellite
television and the Internet provided the information 'pipes' for the globalization of the
advertising industry. The convergence of multimedia businesses and global markets
consequently gave these companies significant leverage over international trade and
national governments. It is no accident, then, that the era of multimedia has also been
the era of the multinational corporation.

Cultural Convergence

The growing size and power of multinational media companies meant that they needed
to generate vast profits in order to maintain their ambitions for growth. As a consequence, they were fervently keen to enter new markets. The use of satellites to make
transnational television a reality, and the connection of ever larger portions of the

world's population to the Internet, were major technical vehicles for these ambitions. Once they had implemented a delivery mechanism in a new market, they could then sell media content (movies, TV, computer games and programs) to the local population, and then subsequently sell the eyeballs of the local population to advertisers with equally global ambitions. Naturally, the presence of information technology was itself a major intervention in many societies, but the social setting (or 'resident condition') of the content or software being delivered also carried powerful cultural connotations. The rapid growth in the global media system that resulted from both technological and economic convergence was frequently associated with spreading the cultural imprint of Western culture and consumerism around the world (the two aspects often seen by critics and sympathizers alike as being the same thing). A growing familiarity everywhere with transnational television shows, the World Wide Web and the flaunting of global fashions has been seen by conservatives worldwide as symptoms of the obliteration of local cultures in the face of a pervasive global monoculture driven by capitalism and American populism. As such, the third aspect of the global media revolution can be described as a form of cultural convergence.

Not all readings of cultural convergence are so negative, however. For some, the mobility of culture, through the movements of people and of media products, are seen to exemplify a new multicultural reality where all parts of the world are in constant contact (Appadurai 1996). Roland Robertson challenged the 'monoculture' thesis, arguing that people generally encounter foreign culture on their own terms and in their own social domain, and subsequently rework it from an indigenous perspective, producing a hybrid product that interlaces the global with the local, thus leading to 'glocalization' (1994). Essentially, this is an argument about the adaptability of culture and the tendency of consumers to appropriate popular culture in a way that makes sense within their own social and cultural environment. It encapsulates a classic 'cultural studies' position of the 1970s, an outlook which also underpins Henry Jenkins's account of our everyday experience of living in a consumer society. In this context, the value of commercial brands is traded freely across a wide range of goods and services. Brand value becomes a cipher of social status more significant than any particular set of goods (Arvidsson 2005). More and more of our income is spent on the consumption of intangible brands and services such as mobile phones, broadband and cable TV. As such, cultural consumption moves from the peripheral realm of 'off-duty' entertainment into the heart of economic activity. For Jenkins, the consequences of this shift are not the obliteration of cultural diversity by a monolithic commercial machinery, but rather the empowerment of ordinary consumers with the cultural domain.

Appropriating brands and media icons within their own social environment, media consumers come to appropriate, rework and reshape culture from a grassroots perspective. Through their collective innovations, individuals throughout society liberate cultural authority from the monopolistic inclinations of the mainstream media. The very products in which multinational media corporations have invested so heavily become reconfigured as raw material for the expression of highly individualized identities that are frequently ironic, oppositional and subversive in their intent. The freedom to re-create and innovate, argued for so forcefully by Lawrence Lessig and others, defies the strictures of intellectual property laws on a grand scale as consumers become increasingly adept at operating the technologies of cultural production (Lessig 2009). As bandwidth capacity has increased over the past decade, the Internet has come to provide the perfect system of decentred distribution for making this mass-individuation a workable reality. Similarly, the ready availability of consumer software for reworking images, sounds and video underpins a giant machinery of perpetual 'post-production' with an almost infinite capacity for the appropriation and re-use of digital commodities. It is these processes of convergence, where the traditional divisions between producers and consumers of culture are breaking down, that Henry Jenkins wants to emphasize the most. In this he is not alone. Thinkers from Walter Benjamin to Marshall McLuhan to Alvin Toffler have all made arguments for an era in which the masses would no longer be mere consumers of ideas and products handed down to them, but would instead become active producers of culture in their own right (Benjamin 1972; McLuhan and Fiore 1968; Toffler 1980). For Jenkins, this is the ultimate democratization of culture, which he seeks to encapsulate in Alvin Toffler's notion of the 'prosumer', a new form of citizen who is simultaneously both producer and consumer of our contemporary culture.

Box 11.1 Definition of the prosumer

It might be worth asking yourself what the category of being a 'prosumer' entails, and whether you belong within it:

- **Media content production** – do you take digital photographs, write for the Internet, make movies, record your own music?
- **Cultural practice** – do you participate in fan organizations, role-playing games, celebrity gossip, TV/online polls?
- **Amateur professionalism** – do you now do things for yourself that people used to pay others for? That is, do you make your own birthday cards and calendars, fix your own computer or car, make your own clothes, etc.?
- **Skilled consumption** – do you keep up with the latest technological and cultural developments in certain areas of consumption? Do you know all about the latest developments in music software, camera hardware or mobile phone apps?
- **Economic activity** – do you trade on the Internet? Have you sold material things (like your old CDs, old clothes, your house, your car) or your services (like essay writing, fashion advice, hypnotism)?

If you answer yes to any of these questions, then you are a prosumer.

At its heart, the evidence that Jenkins presents for the rise of 'fandom' as the steering force in contemporary culture is an argument about consumer power. From this perspective, the new efficiencies in the exchange of creative works enabled by digital media are creating a society of volunteer artists and commentators. This proliferation of authorship amongst ordinary people creates a radically pluralistic media environment and makes freedom of expression not so much a personal freedom as a very public one. In many respects, we can see this polyphony as the expression of liberal pluralism in its purest form. This, therefore, is the great contradiction of convergence. On the one hand, Internet technologies, software standards and consumer electronics have created a singular media apparatus of unprecedented power, an apparatus that is increasingly dominated by a handful of corporate giants. On the other hand, this same apparatus has also introduced hundreds of millions of new voices into the cultural domain. The inherent interactivity of digital media consequently provides the ultimate means for realizing the dream of an active audience displacing the 'mass society' model of top-down transmission and passive consumers. As this power shift becomes embraced commercially, the new centrality of prosumers to the digital economy is exemplified by the amateur video-sharing site YouTube and the participatory culture that it facilitates (Burgess and Green 2009).

There have, of course, been plenty of other comparable platforms coming on stream in recent years, like the peer-to-peer audio-sharing site Soundcloud and the various other sites that showcase mashups and remixes (such as mashuptown.com). The popularity of these exchange portals for amateur content underpins the present reformulation of the Internet via the notion of 'Web 2.0', where the digital distribution of mass-produced products (legal or otherwise) is predicted to give way in favour of the networked exchange of user-produced content. It is important to remember, therefore, that this culture of free expression is also a commercial market.

Chris Anderson on the Long Tail

Outside of cultural studies, a similarly utopian line to user-produced content has been pursued by Yochai Benkler, professor of entrepreneurial legal studies at Harvard University. For Benkler, too, it is the power of enthusiasts and amateur content that will become the major source of wealth creation in the digital economy. Echoing Adam Smith's famous text, the *Wealth of Nations* (the central point of reference in liberal economics), Benkler posits the enormous benefits of a growing culture of 'social production' intermediated by the Internet as the most efficient exchange mechanism of our time. For Benkler, digital technologies are finally delivering the liberal dream of a free and open market between individuals. In that context also, the consumers of digital culture become synonymous with producers (that is, the same). In the process of convergence, their restless creativity becomes the primary commodity that constitutes what Benkler calls the 'wealth of networks' (2006). Writing for a similar audience in the marketing and business community, Chris Anderson makes the further point that it is not simply the empowerment of fan cultures and the growth in authorship that is transforming the cultural industries. For Anderson, the fundamental changes in the nature of shopping brought about by Internet retail are equally important in defining the contemporary cultural environment (2006).

Anderson's thesis is that we are moving from a Fordist cultural economy of mainstream products designed for mass appeal (like blockbuster movies and best-selling books) towards a broader cultural repertoire of more distinctive works. This is made possible by digital reproduction technologies and the capacity of Internet retailers to hold an almost inexhaustible inventory of works. Anderson's prediction, therefore, is that the commercial significance of blockbusters will diminish as consumers redirect their attention towards a vast array of niche products. Anderson illustrates this argument via a diagrammatic representation of the 'long tail'. The statistical basis of this is the major portion of market share in cultural works dominated by a handful of mass-produced products (around 80 per cent). The remaining field of consumption (around 20 per cent) is distributed across a declining curve of sales for a vast number of lesser-known books, films and creative works. As amateur authorship becomes increasingly common, and modern recording mediums prolong the life of older works, the 'long tail' of the 20 per cent becomes further stretched. For the consumer, this means a far

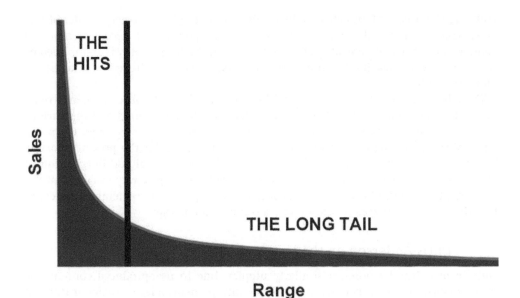

Figure 11.3 *The 'long tail'*

greater choice in the range of available culture. Previously, however, this expanded rep-ertoire was almost impossible to access because traditional retailers had limited space for physical stock and their business was restricted to customers in their immediate locale. This 'tyranny of geography' made both stocking and selling any significant part of the long tail an onerous and largely unprofitable exercise. Consequently, the cultural industries focused their attention on producing and selling the most broadly popular forms, effectively the 'lowest common denominator' in cultural taste across the general population. Thus, the planning and marketing of culture, along with the point-of-sale infrastructure, was oriented to mass-produced hits.

Throughout its history, modern popular culture has been formalized through mecha-nisms such as the hit parade and box office rankings. In a commercial environment of this kind, the 'top' 200 CDs account for 90 per cent of sales, the 'top' thirty films accrue 86 per cent of box office profits per year. Other titles struggle to find an audience due to the inherent physical limitations in screen capacity and shelf space at the level of retail. Many of these marginalized titles are simply failed attempts at similar products, and thus expendable. However, a more serious consequence is that more innovative or distinctive cultural productions are also marginalized, narrowing what Pierre Bourdieu has called the 'cultural field' (1993). Classical arts, for example, are restricted by the more limited infrastructure for exhibition, media sales and performance. They cannot compete with the big popular hits amongst the general population, and their core audience is only present in sufficient concentration within major cities. This is what explains the enormous differential in the cultural repertoire of metropolises like London, Paris and New York compared to Bedford, Lille or Des Moines, Iowa. Similarly, niche and subcultural forms of popular culture are confined to marginal publics in other social strata. Thus, they also tend to become the preserve of a small hardcore audience of specialist consumers (a typical 'minority media'). These self-contained 'alternative' sectors are usually well known by the community of cultural producers, and they tend to indirectly inform the stylistic development of more mainstream products, but their direct availability to the general public, and to 'light users', remains restricted (McPhee 1963).

Internet retail, however, changes all of this. Anderson offers the example of Amazon. com, one of the first and foremost Internet retailers. Amazon is able to offer an unprecedented range of goods because it does not hold the vast majority of its offerings in a warehouse. Amazon does stock large volumes of major products ready for immediate shipping, but most of what it offers is sourced from a vast network of secondary suppliers and, indeed, directly from the producers themselves. There is no need to organize and present this universal catalogue in any physical store, and products are instead organized by a combination of descriptive 'meta-tags' (essentially key words identifying relevant genres), product association (links to titles with similar tags) and consumer data (what a customer has bought before or other customers have combined in their purchases). This combination of Internet search mechanisms and consumer profiling produces a hypertextual version of shopping. A trail of links guides consumers to products they may not be aware of, or wouldn't find, in a mainstream store. According to Anderson, these are mechanisms that are beginning to reveal both the hidden wealth of cultural production and the economic value of the long tail. His conclusion is that, with the removal of the distribution bottleneck, niche products inevitably flourish. It is notable, in that regard, that 25 per cent of Amazon's book sales come from outside its top 100,000 titles.

In eliminating storage, staffing and property expenses, Amazon was able to offer physical products at a lower cost, and it quickly became a serious threat to traditional bookstores tied up in bricks and mortar. With the growing availability of digitized works via download, we may soon see a situation where the distribution costs are also eliminated. For consumers, shopping becomes easier because everything can be readily located by electronic search algorithms. Shopping also becomes more 'efficient' as information trails lead consumers to products that they do not even know about when they enter 'the store'. Since Amazon also remembers the previous purchases of all customers, it begins to form an overall impression of their tastes, allowing it to offer the most suitable 'recommendations' for additional or alternative purchases. In that sense, Amazon is not only a 'disintermediation' of distribution overheads, but is also an incomparably well-informed sales assistant. This breadth of knowledge favours the long tail, as does the capacity to offer a title and source it (or even produce it) only as and when an order is actually placed. This retail variant of Japan's famous 'just-in-time' industrial production strategy assumes that everything has an audience of some size. Since there is no significant cost in listing any product, a virtual store of this kind can offer unlimited 'stock', or at least anything that can be posted or downloaded. That is why iTunes can offer a million pieces of music for sale, regardless of whether any of them is purchased more than once a year.

Peer-to-Peer Selling

The eBay site, a contemporary of Amazon that was also founded in the dot.com boom of the 1990s, provides an even more radical example of the disintermediation and amateurization of everyday commercial transactions. Here, individuals place online auctions of goods and services which are indexed and organized by category. Other users can then place bids for those items, with the highest bidder at the end of a specified time becoming the purchaser. This mode of 'peer-to-peer selling' between individuals has grown rapidly in popularity, and the commissions collected by eBay make it an $8 billion dollar business. In the eBay market a vast array of new and second-hand goods from around the world change hands, ranging from sea shells to houses, and from cars to pre-loved children's toys. In that sense, the eBay environment combines the informal trade in second-hand goods with the efficiencies of Internet retail models. As a result, massive amounts of 'garage sale' goods are placed online and exchanged around the world. This is a marketplace that operates essentially on trust, in that the bidder takes the chance that the object may be damaged, misrepresented or never turn up following payment. In the vast majority of cases, however, this does not happen. A mechanism for building trust in anonymous transactions is provided via the capacity of buyers to comment on the services of a seller and rank their performance. This ranking becomes critically important for serious traders and they will go to some lengths to protect their eBay 'reputation' as a commercial resource.

For traditional dealers in collectibles, rarities and antiques, eBay is a favoured commercial medium (Hillis, Petit and Epley 2006). In 2000, this form of trade accounted for 80 per cent of total eBay revenues, although it has subsequently declined proportionately as other forms of trading have increased in volume (Bunnel and Luecke 2000). Parents around the world are saving vast sums by trading barely used toys and clothes, and established outlets for second-hand trade in collectibles and durables are rapidly disappearing in favour of this virtual shopfront. More problematically, eBay has also been a major site for the trade in counterfeited and stolen goods, because it is relatively easy to set up a false trading identity, and the two partners in the exchange do not need to meet. A large proportion of eBay trade is international (as much as a third) and this serves to make the eBay payment service, Paypal, a major international exchange bank. In recent years, the development of numerous algorithms for seeking out and automatically bidding on eBay listings has seen the robot economics of the mainstream international finance industry increasingly applied to the mundane transactions of everyday life. The rapid rise, and sheer scale, of the eBay marketplace has also prompted governments to make sustained efforts to regulate and tax the transactions taking place (with varying success). Amongst all of this, the extended afterlife of an expanding range of products can also be seen as an extension of Anderson's long tail. In that respect, the eBay economy also threatens the profits of 'blockbuster' products in almost any category, either directly or by diverting disposable income into second-hand purchases.

Aladdin's Cave

A prosumer economy injects unprecedented competition into the marketplace, creating a situation where you can make an album over the weekend and have it listed right away along with the projects of all the major recording studios and the world's best musicians (both living and dead). Despite a far lesser investment at all levels, your work becomes equally accessible to consumers. Consequently, the rise of the prosumer implies an ongoing culture of abundance within the marketplace. As more and more consumers become producers, consumer choice becomes massively extended and our capacity to sift through the available goods and services is powerfully enhanced. As Bill Gates predicted, the inevitable effect of Internet exchange is the looming obsolescence of the many middlemen who previously mediated between producers and consumers (1995). The optimistic conflation of prosumers also appears to suggest that, in the creative industries at least, this process of 'disintermediation' will eventually make most traditional producers of culture redundant. The obvious danger of this trend is the effective loss of quality-control regimes and the sheer abundance of material that such an open field will create. Thus, potentially at least, we are facing a situation of information overload in the market for popular culture, a problem that will only be remedied by ever more sophisticated technologies of information management and strategies for standing out in a morass culture.

Chris Anderson's celebration of the long tail as an interaction between a broadening-taste culture and an aggregation of dispersed consumers for niche products also has some caveats. It may well be a matter of indifference for Amazon, as a retailer, whether they sell 5 million units of one album, or one copy of 5 million books. For the producers of those works, however, a single sale is unlikely to generate anything passing for a living or, indeed, to return the investment made in producing the work in the first place. In that sense, Anderson, Jenkins and Benkler all lean heavily on the assumption that people will be prepared to produce cultural works for less than nothing. This flies in the face of the liberal economics that they expound, because it is profoundly irrational. This is not to say that people are not doing it every day. Nonetheless, we could assume that many of these 'do-it-yourself' producers of niche content are hoping to generate a high enough profile online to break out of the long tail and obtain some significant commercial or social reward. In that sense, the objectives of peer-to-peer creativity are as much a matter of self-promotion as they are of exchange efficiencies.

It also pays to be sceptical. Anita Elberse (2008) attempted to assess the validity of Anderson's long-tail theory by looking at the music industry (2008). Taking the example of the online music service Rhapsody, Elberse found that over a three-month period in 2007, of 32 million plays, the top 1 per cent of titles accounted for 32 per cent of plays and the top 10 per cent of titles 78 per cent of plays. This suggested a fairly static long-tail curve, rather than any major shift in favour of niche products. Overall, online music is already suffering from a crisis of overproduction. Will Page and Andrew Bud found that 10 million of 13 million digital music tracks available online failed to find a single buyer. In the online 'singles' format, 80 per cent of revenue came from 'just' 52,000 tracks. Of the 1.23 million albums available online, 85 per cent do not sell a single copy (MCPS-PRS Alliance, 2008). As such, it is probably much more significant overall that Internet retail (or 'e-commerce') naturally changes the behavioural habits by which we browse, assess and obtain goods. As e-commerce becomes increasingly normative in digital societies, the social practice of shopping is irrevocably transformed. We buy different things, and we do so in different ways and for different reasons. Whether they are niche or mainstream formats is, at best, a side issue.

From a sociological point of view, there are more important intellectual developments taking place within this wide-ranging discussion of consumer empowerment. As we have already noted, it provides the meeting point for various strands of liberalism, from the market efficiencies of neoliberal economics to the self-expression of the counter-culture. The adherence of a significant cohort within contemporary cultural studies to this standpoint is also an important evolutionary dimension. A discipline that began with humanist critiques of popular culture as an ideological system of control shifts in favour of a new utopia where shoppers take over the mall. As such, there are also signs of an important convergence between the oppositional cultural studies tradition and the functional sociology that underpins modern marketing. In marketing, too, we see a maturing intellectual evolution – in this case, moving from a product-focused approach centred on 'techniques of persuasion' for the purpose of profit to a consumer-focused approach centred on 'creating value' for the buyer by making consumption more emotionally rewarding. In this way, contemporary marketing logic 'recognizes that in a consumer democracy money votes are cast daily', and marketing therefore 'asserts the democratic character of a market transaction over other means of social interaction: the market is seen as giving power to people by ensuring the right to voluntarily choose what they want' (Lee 2005). All in all, there are a number of distinctive political undercurrents that inform these formulations of consumer power. As Stuart Hall (a pivotal figure in British cultural studies during the 1970s) once said, he did not 'give a damn' about popular culture beyond its potential in achieving social change (1981). Henry Jenkins, too, has a great project to be carried forward by an army of fan(atic) prosumers, that is, a democratic balance in the public sphere based upon plural self-expression and the collectivization of marginal voices.

> Our media future could depend on the kind of uneasy truce that gets brokered between commercial media and collective intelligence. Imagine a world where there are two kinds of media power: one comes through media concentration, where any message gains authority simply by being broadcast on network television; the other comes through collective intelligence, where a message gains visibility only if it is deemed relevant to a loose network of diverse publics. Broadcasting will place issues on the national agenda and define core values. Grassroots media will reframe those issues for different publics and ensure that everyone has a chance to be heard. Innovation will occur on the fringes; consolidation in the mainstream.
>
> Henry Jenkins (2004), 'The Cultural Logic of Media Convergence', *International Journal of Cultural Studies*, 7(1): 34

Another important intellectual convergence, therefore, is the alignment of fan studies with social movement theory, cleverly dovetailing popular culture and popular politics. In this sense, Jenkins and Anderson both place their faith in a progressive future firmly in the hands of the 'grassroots'. In doing so, their respective arguments about culture and consumption converge with Manuel Castells's prescient description of the politics of the network society (1997). Nonetheless, we may be unwise to equate virtue uncritically with the common citizen. The 'grassroots' is swiftly becoming an intellectual formation that is being placed above criticism, a critical shift seen in sociology since the passing of the Frankfurt School. Arguably, this is giving rise to a world where traditional political and social institutions are eschewed, and where politicians of both left and right decry 'elitism' in any form. 'Big business', 'big money' and 'big government' are all bad. 'Big culture' is, apparently, going the same way. To argue otherwise smacks of elitism and privilege. Nonetheless, there are many substantive critiques of the cultural politics of consumer power. Cornell Sandvoss, for example, inverts Jenkins's version of cultural studies to argue that fan cultures are not a threat to, but rather a manufacture of, the dominant cultural industry (2005). Sandvoss sees little to support Jenkins's utopian conclusions about the sociological import of mashups and remixes. Elsewhere, Andrew Keen has loudly predicted that the user-produced content of 'Web 2.0' will deliver a world of cultural mediocrity and intellectual pap (2008). For Joseph Heath and Andrew Potter, the rhetorical 'rebellion' of consumer power is simply the inevitable outcome of a vainglorious transition from 'counterculture to consumer culture' (2006).

The Sociology of Shopping

It is far from a settled question, therefore, whether volunteerist fans are simply dupes with toys or the greatest innovators of the twenty-first century. Similarly, we are yet to see whether the 'long tail' and 'peer-to-peer selling' will extend cultural diversity by disintermediating professional artists and retailers alike. To be fair, the long tail is an argument about shopping behaviours. It is not really about aesthetics. What has already become abundantly clear in this regard, however, is that the opening up of cultural production reveals the inconvenient truth that humanity possesses more talent than the market actually needs (in almost any field of activity). This may prove to be the larger question for a culture committed to empowerment through self-expression. In that respect, it is worth noting that YouTube, Amazon and eBay are all more or less indifferent to the quality of the commodities that are being brought to market through their platforms (as long as they are legal). Similarly, their ethos of service is focused on quick and efficient transactions, with the prosumers themselves left to police the degree of 'satisfaction' that they are accessing in this way. There is some chance, then, that algorithmic efficiency and cultural innovation may not prove as natural a pairing as all that.

Further, as Jenny Shaw has pointed out, a large portion of shopping behaviours involve ritualistic pleasures and emotional reward (2010). Marketing professionals have long known that these forms of pleasure are as necessary and vital as supply-side efficiencies. However, the sensual, symbolic and environmental pleasures of online shopping have yet to see substantial coverage in the leading models of e-commerce. Accordingly, shopping online reconfigures our understanding of the value of social objects. It also removes the embodied encounter from the commercial transaction, and the immediate consequence of this is a hollowing out of the social spaces where those transactions have traditionally taken place. The effects of this can already be seen in almost any urban commercial centre. Certainly, sales expertise is automated and less partial, product information is readily available and delivery mechanisms are steamlined, but, at the same time, the social rituals of purchase and the environments in which shopping take place become disembedded from the material fabric of society. You can window shop online, but it is harder to enjoy it. You could 'run into' friends and neighbours or fall in love while doing it, but none of the existing formats make that likely. Another obvious sticking point in the proclaimed utopia of peer-to-peer exchange is that while we may be comfortable becoming both producer and consumer, the impacts of disintermediation inevitably make it harder to become an employee in order to pay for the privilege. In the information society, we are all 'middle-persons' of one sort or another.

At the same time, most of us would not give up our newfound access to the vast range of goods that can now be delivered to our doorstep after expending little more than five minutes of our lunch break tracking them down. Similarly, our capacity to fine-tune bargains through price-comparison sites and to drive down the price of everything that we want to have is already a deeply ingrained pattern of behaviour. This is an activity in which we rarely pause to consider the economic and environmental implications of unending 'cheap-ness' and convenience. However, connecting the 'front-end' of choice to the 'back-end' of e-commerce is precisely what we must do if we want to understand the effects of consumer power adequately enough to either pronounce or debunk an era of prosuming liberation. Whatever our conclusions are in that regard, there is no escaping the fact that shopping is now a round-the-clock pattern of social actions. As such, shopping has become an issue of critical importance for sociology, something long foreseen by foundational sociologists such as Georg Simmel (see Frisby and Featherstone 1997). For each and every one of us, the rise of e-commerce also marks a more explicit engagement with a networked economy that is global in its operations. At the point of sale, it requires a considerable degree of literacy to 'do consumption' properly and thus, whether we are selling ourselves or not, it becomes a form of work.

Think and Discuss

1. Key Terms
Can you describe in simple language what is meant by the following terms found in this chapter?

- Convergence
- Prosumers
- The long tail
- Consumer-focused marketing
- Horizontal integration

2. Critical Questions
Try answering the following questions, drawing upon your own understanding, experience and knowledge.

1. How much of your own personal shopping takes place through an online platform? Can you distinguish between the kinds of exchanges that belong 'online' or 'offline'?
2. How would you characterize your own behaviours and motivations as a 'prosumer'?
3. In reflecting on your recent online purchases, can you see any evidence of your cultural tastes being diversified by the 'long-tail' effect?
4. To what extent do critiques of fan cultures reveal a residual elitism amongst the cultural professions?
5. What is the likely nature and extent of consumer power in any digital application of capitalism?

Further Reading

Anderson, Chris (2006) *The Long Tail: How Endless Choice is Creating Unlimited Demand*, New York: Random House.

Benckler, Yochai (2006) *The Wealth of Networks: How Social Production Transforms Markets and Freedom*, New Haven, CT: Yale University Press.

Burgess, Jean and Green, Joshua (2009) *YouTube: Online Video and Participatory Cultures*, Cambridge: Polity.

Heath, Joseph and Potter, Andrew (2006) *The Rebel Sell: How the Counterculture Became Consumer Culture*, Chichester: Capstone.

Hillis, Ken, Petit, Michael and Epley, Nathan Scott (2006) *Everyday eBay: Culture, Collecting and Desire*, New York and London: Routledge.

Jenkins, Henry (2006) *Convergence Culture: When Old and New Media Collide*, New York: New York University Press.

Keen, Andrew (2008) *The Cult of the Amateur: How Today's Internet is Killing Our Culture and Assaulting Our Economy*, London and Boston, MA: Nicholas Brealey.

Sandvoss, Cornel (2005) *Fans: The Mirror of Consumption*, Cambridge: Polity.

Shaw, Jenny (2010) *Shopping: Social and Cultural Perspectives*, Cambridge: Polity.

Turner, Graeme (2011) *What's Become of Cultural Studies?*, London: Sage.

Go Online

Amazon – http://www.amazon.com
Chris Anderson – http://www.longtail.com/about.html
eBay – http://www.ebay.com, http://www.ebay.co.uk, http://www.ebay.com.au
Henry Jenkins– http://henryjenkins.org/
Mashup Town – http://mashuptown.com/
Soundcloud – http://www.soundcloud.com/
YouTube – http://www.youtube.com/

CHAPTER 12

Information at Work

For many years, one of the most critical and prolific areas of sociological enquiry was in the domain of labour, at both industrial and managerial levels (for example, Glucksmann 1982; Willis 1978; Whyte 1963). Since the 1980s, however, the post-industrial model has seen the former fall by the wayside, and the latter swept up in the new specialist domain of management studies. As office-based and IT-based work has become normative at all levels of the labour market, far less attention has been paid to the role of information technologies at work than we might expect. Instead, there has been a consistent bias towards the recreational use of information technology and to studying economies of consumption. Nonetheless, most of us have been only too keenly aware of the rapidly changing work environment across all fields of activity. Academics, not least, have been umbilically attached to workstations and many upcoming scholars will scarcely touch a book (at least, by the standards of the previous generation). Office-workers and administrators undergo a constant regime of retraining with every operating system upgrade that is 'rolled out' into the organizations that they serve. Manual workers see their daily labour routines shaped, recorded and (frequently) interrupted by the algorithms of 'the system' that provides an impersonal guidance over the regime of production. Skilled workers everywhere, from printers to performing artists, have to contend with a constantly moving field of technologies that variously extends, augments or replaces the practices by which they seek to make a living. As such, the new capacities and flexibilities that we have come to value so much in the personal domain are frequently matters of anxiety, perplexity and concern in the professional arena. For this reason at least, the present shortfall in the sociology of work is one of the most crucial areas to be addressed in any assessment of a digital society (Edgell 2006; Pettinger, Parry, Taylor and Glucksmann 2006; Watson 2008).

Knowledge Workers

The idea of a 'knowledge worker' has been around since the 1960s (Englebart 1963). In the nascent information technology field, this phrase denoted an individual playing a scientific and technical role in the management of information. The term became more broadly applicable to the changing conceptualization of labour throughout society via its adoption by influential exponents of the post-industrial economy. For Peter Drucker, the model of a 'knowledge worker' sought to differentiate between the manual labour of the working classes and the cerebral, intellectual work of white-collar workers and managers (Drucker 1969). Redefining 'knowledge' as work directed the notional source of value away from labour power and material production. Instead, the creation of wealth would entail the acquisition, application and production of information. Thus, in many respects, the overarching purpose of the elevation of the knowledge worker at this early stage was to emphasize the economic value of managerial tasks deemed necessary, but intrinsically 'unproductive', under the Marxist paradigm. From the perspective of today, when corporate executives are given plaudits for almost every economic success and 'management roles' proliferate at all levels of work, it is difficult to imagine this recent past when management was seen as a mid-ranking domain of pedestrian competence. Nonetheless, it is precisely when we consider the paramount status of the 'executive' in contemporary society that the significance of the tilt from labour to knowledge becomes fully apparent. In a broader economic context, the meteoric rise of an expanded management culture was also a consequence of the progressive growth in the complexity of commercial organizations. In many ways, it was also a necessary response to the widespread economic reorganization that took place following the industrial crisis of the early 1970s (Scase 1989).

As the 'informationalization' of the work environment gathered pace during the 1980s, the recasting of more mundane clerical tasks through digital technologies created ever larger numbers of employees whose roles fell between organizational management and traditional labour. This growing army of what Castells called 'flextimers' provided the semi-skilled equivalent of the more specialist 'networker' (1996). Flextimers rely on possessing broad generic information-handling skills that enable them to take on short-term roles in a wide-ranging and fast-moving labour market standardized by computer systems. Networkers, by contrast, are the creators and shapers of new knowledge commodities, from artworks to patents to market research. In an economy dominated by digital commodities, the basic unit of production is the knowledge worker at both levels. We can define the knowledge worker as someone who uses their intellectual and technical capacity to transform raw data into commercially significant knowledge that can be applied to either product or process. Consequently, in an era of global economic competition led by knowledge work, it is human capital in the form of aptitude, education and communication skills that underpins 'employability' and guarantees participation in the workforce (Hind and Moss 2005).

Melting into Air

In a global economy increasingly dominated by the pursuit of intellectual property, proponents of the knowledge-economy model tend to see certain kinds of creative, managerial, free-market friendly, entrepreneurial knowledge as being the ideas that constitute intellectual capital and create wealth (McKercher and Mosco 2007). The Internet, in particular, has been widely seen as further enhancing the capacity and advantages of these particular skills, by enabling information handling, distributing creative applications and improving the efficiency of the 'knowledge networks' that underpin informational capitalism (Hildreth and Kimble 2004; Johnson 2009). By the 1990s, several commentators came to the conclusion that knowledge work was on the verge of replacing the world of physical work entirely. Thinkers like Danny Quah and Diane Coyle characterized this new world of electronic labour as a 'weightless economy' (Coyle 1999; Quah 1999). Unlike the 'heavy' industries of old, wealth would be generated through activities where innovation and creativity were far more important than industrial skills such as dexterity and stamina. On the demand side, the products that we had come to value most highly and pay most to consume would be largely virtual and intangible. As such, our working lives were being rapidly reorganized around producing and consuming information of this kind, rather than manufacturing physical products. The freelance journalist Charles Leadbeater proclaimed that Britain had become a society where software programmers, web designers, pop performers and advertising executives had become the new labour elite (2000). These were the people seen to be 'adding value' to knowledge, and making knowledge work a profitable exercise. From here on, we would spend our money on data services, invest in virtual banks and compete with each other on the basis of creative thinking and digital communication.

In a post-industrial society of this kind, we would no longer sell our bodies to the factory but instead find ourselves 'living on thin air' (Leadbeater 2000). Thus, we can see how the maturing model of the knowledge worker continued to emphasize the social and economic importance of traditional white-collar professions, while also incorporating a range of the new professions that arose with digital technologies. These major changes to the ways in which we understand the nature of work have inevitably been reflected in a changing work environment for most of us. Some groups have benefited, while others have lost out. It has been argued that the labour market underwent a process of 'feminization' during the 1990s, when the male-dominated, hierarchical world of industrial production was surpassed by a cleaner, computerized open-plan workspace for information work (McDowell 2003, 2009). This new environment, and the new commodity form, favoured the advancement of women because they were (somewhat uncritically) seen as being 'better at communication'. Certainly, the era of 'thin air' explicitly favoured the educated worker over the manual worker (Drucker 1993). Flagship companies of the day, like Google, claimed that the secret of success in this new economy was to encourage innovation, rather than obedience, amongst staff. As part of this strategy, the traditional markers of hierarchy were to be removed from the workplace, and a more informal 'open shirt' environment would consequently reduce workplace tensions and engender a higher net output of 'creativity' (Levy 2011).

Creative Industries

We can define creativity in any number of ways, but in general the word carries a particular set of associations covering intellectual, aesthetic and material actions. To create is to bring something into existence. This might be mundane (cheese on toast) or it might be sublime (the Sistine Chapel). Typically, however, we associate creativity with productive acts that are either singular, original or of great aesthetic merit. This is why creativity is so strongly associated with fine arts. In a world increasingly dominated by scientific discovery, however, we have also come to associate creativity with invention and innovation in the natural and applied sciences. For many people, creativity in either realm also continues to be associated with divine provenance and the actions of God. Creativity thus covers a broad range of the most valued and sanctified expressions of human thought. Its adoption as the centrepiece of a new philosophy of work, however, has given rise to a new set of associations that revolve instead around the notion of productivity. A new definition of 'creative industries' emerged from the United Kingdom following the establishment of a Creative Industries Task Force (DCMS) in 1998. This was an initiative inspired by the then Prime Minister Tony Blair's endorsement of Charles Leadbeater's vision of a 'thin air' economy. The CITF defined the creative industries broadly as 'those industries which have their origin in individual creativity, skill and talent and which have a potential for wealth and job creation through the generation and exploitation of intellectual property' (CITF 1998: 4).

Box 12.1 Identified subsectors of the creative industries

advertising
architecture
arts and antiques
computer games
crafts and folk art
designer fashion
film
graphic design
journalism
software design
music
performing arts
publishing
television
radio

At: *http://unctad.org/en/docs/ditc20082cer_en.pdf*

The commercialization of creative skills via media technologies has been taking place over several centuries, but its explicit pairing with the word 'industries' is a more recent phenomenon. The fundamental meaning of industry is work (*industria*), and in the previous 'industrial era' this overwhelmingly meant the processing, manufacturing and commodification of physical goods. In the context of informational capitalism, however, a new form of industry entails the production, management and dissemination of information in a commodity form. Where the creative industries model diverged from this functional 'information economy' of recording and processing data was through its emphasis upon unique human inputs and its association with the expressive domain of the arts. This highly effective rebranding of both the traditional arts and the newer fields of commercial art and design was thus intended to emphasize their growing importance in a new global marketplace for ideas, entertainment and communication. Under this paradigm, the developed countries saw their future in a formal wedding of human innovation and hi-tech processes, supported by various forms of intellectual, expressive and creative labour to be undertaken by a university-educated workforce (see Flew 2011). The creative industries were identified as one of the key areas for future economic growth, along with 'bio-technology', financial services and computer science.

The creative industries are among the most dynamic emerging sectors in world trade. Over the period 2000–2005, trade in creative goods and services increased at an unprecedented average annual rate of 8.7 per cent. World exports of creative products were valued at $424.4 billion in 2005 as compared to $227.5 billion in 1996, according to preliminary UNCTAD figures. Creative services in particular enjoyed rapid export growth – 8.8 per cent annually between 1996 and 2005. This positive trend occurred in all regions and groups of countries and is expected to continue into the next decade, assuming that the global demand for creative goods and services continues to rise.

Creative Economy Report 2008, Geneva: United Nations Conference on Trade and Development

The attention of the British to the economic worth of the 'artistic' fields was part of a much broader global re-evaluation of the sources of wealth and the professions that were likely to add the most 'value' in a post-industrial economy (Caves 2002; Hartley 2005; Howkins 2002). In the United States, Richard Florida presented a similar set of arguments, suggesting that we were entering a new age that he called 'the age of creativity'. This new age was to be defined not so much by artistic developments in aesthetic terms, but by the commercial realization of the potentials of creativity as an economic resource. According to Florida: 'Today's economy is fundamentally a Creative Economy. I certainly agree with those who say that the advanced nations are shifting to information-based, knowledge-driven economies' (Florida 2002: 29). Creativity would be 'the key driver. In my formulation, "knowledge" and "information" are the tools and materials of creativity' (ibid.). As a consequence, Florida claimed that we were witnessing the 'rise of the creative class' through the enabling infrastructure of digital technologies. Hard evidence was readily available for the growth of media content and information services industries, areas that had the most obvious need for creative inputs from artists of various kinds.

In a context where creativity 'needs to be the core competency of a nation', the digital media apparatus naturally expands the market for expressive content in new commodity forms (ibid.). In addition to the direct contribution of 'creative professions' to economic growth, the particular skills sets and technical competencies that underpin the digital arts have been increasingly seen as being more broadly applicable. In a highly competitive white-collar economy, innovation becomes of at least equal importance to the 'efficiencies' pursued in previous applications of digital technologies. Thus, at the beginning of the millennium, it was assumed that there was going to be a high level of demand for people who could combine technical skills with intellectual dexterity and a more imaginative approach to social communication. For those able to fulfil these demanding criteria for flexible, commercial and competitive applications of creativity, there would be a wide range of roles in the new economy. The established creative professions were already becoming more economically astute, and expanding (Jeffcutt and Pratt 2009). The 'proper' jobs of old were becoming more varied and intellectually challenging. They therefore presented far more interesting career options for ambitious creatives. In a work environment of this kind, employment itself was being personalized in tandem with the commodities that this new economy produced. Old hierarchies were giving way to young tech-savvy 'brainstormers' for whom each working day would hold the promise of personal achievement and fulfilment.

The Networkers

The changing expectations of employers and employees alike have not been confined to the rebranding of the cultural industries. There have been far-reaching reorientations in the culture of work across the length and breadth of the economic system. The work cultures that have emerged within the digital economy are, in general terms, more personal, informal and atomized than the collective formations that emerged out of the less flexible professions of old. In addition to being smaller, the rapidly changing roles undertaken by most workers weaken their investment in a static occupational identity or permanent location. For this reason, it has been increasingly common to consider working identities as taking the form of fluid subcultures rather than concrete social classes. The closest we come to a class order of digital labour is in Manuel Castells's stratified account of the network society. Nonetheless, here too, there is a tendency to emphasize the cultural environment that comes to define particular levels of employment. At the top of the pecking order, Castells identifies that the 'networkers' have developed their own characteristic cultural environment within the space of flows that they inhabit. Consequently, a patchwork of urban enclaves across the globe have been transformed into generic, globalized spaces of anonymous, temporary residence to serve the needs of networkers engaged in constant motion across the earth's surface. This is a bourgeois habitat of anonymous modernism specifically designed to facilitate the cultural expression of informationalism and networking as a set of practices that make up a distinct way of life.

> [T]he regular use of spa installations (even when travelling), and the practice of jogging, the mandatory diet of grilled salmon and green salad, with udon and sashimi providing a Japanese functional equivalent; the 'pale chamois' wall color intended to create the cosy atmosphere of the inner space; the ubiquitous laptop computer; the combination of business suits and sportswear; the unisex dressing style and so on . . . a culture of the ephemeral, a culture of each strategic decision, a patchwork of experiences and interests, rather than a charter of rights and obligations. It is a multifaceted virtual culture.
>
> Manuel Castells (1996), *The Information Age: Economy, Society and Culture, Vol. I: The Rise of the Network Society*, Cambridge, MA, and Oxford: Blackwell, p. 417

The spaces created for the networkers who direct the technological, intellectual and financial operation of the network society are thus infused with signifiers that emphasize both the spatial indifference and the splendid isolation of a decision-making class. This is a social space with its own rules and rituals and, much like the creative class and the Apple brand, this group also comes with its own conspicuous gadgets, dress codes and customized softwares. This subculture is studied diligently by management students who aspire to master the professional performance of innovation, mobility and economic literacy that surrounds the making of commercial deals. 'Executivism', then, has in itself become a whole way of life that requires a detailed anthropological understanding of the daily mores of managerial privilege (Seldman and Seldman 2008). Nonetheless, in its engagement with the digital economy, the world of 'the suits' is compelled to converge with the much more ad hoc culture of the technological elites who are shaping the digital infrastructure of global business. Although they are also networkers of comparable standing under Castells's formulation, the 'computer boys' represent a subculture that is far more diverse and arcane in its operations (Ensmenger 2010).

As a consequence, the 'Internet culture' described by Castells identifies a number of different subcultures that contribute collectively to the direction of the online environment. These are: the 'techno-meritocratic culture', the 'hacker culture', 'virtual communitarians' and 'entrepreneurs'. For Castells, these are the four major interest groups that determine the culture of the Internet. These four groups are not digital classes per se, but rather competing collectives that embrace particular functional, ideological and cultural subjectivities in relation to their specific occupational roles. As such, these groupings differentiate a body of managerial operations within the domain of the Internet, each guided by an identifiable ethos and corresponding broadly with a distinct professional group. They are all networkers within his larger model of stratification, and despite their ideological differences, they therefore constitute an elite within network society. In that sense, it is telling that Castells describes Internet culture as being defined by this managerial class and not by the cultures of consumption arising amongst the general public.

Flexible Lives

So far, the story has been a largely positive one. Creativity and self-expression are playing a much greater role in the workplace, new professions in digital media have come into being, and the merging of a technical and financial elite is giving rise to a more meritocratic management culture within the digital economy. The prevailing wisdom was that, at this level at least, the world of work was becoming more interesting and therefore more fulfilling for employees. However, the corollary to these new opportunities for networkers was the loss of security that went with more static professional roles and the increasing demands being made upon employees both within the workplace and beyond. Most of the new roles that came into being with the digital economy required a considerable degree of self-investment, and this inevitably leads to a work culture that requires a large proportion of work being undertaken in 'off-duty' time. For those further down the food chain of the network society, however, the rise of 'flexible' labour patterns came to denote an even broader range of expectations that were placed upon more junior employees (Handy 1994). In practice, flexibility means short-term contracts and part-time work. Flexibility means working outside conventional hours. Flexibility means regular switches in professional roles, with more or less constant retraining in new technical and bureaucratic processes. Flexibility, once again, also means taking work home with you. In that sense, computerization has not only changed our official places of work, it has also powerfully altered the relationship between the domestic sphere and the world of work (Carnoy 2000).

Box 12.2 Internet cultures and managerial roles

- **The Techno-meritocratic culture** – represented by the information elite, the 'no-collar' workers who build and manage the network. Unlike elite groups in industrial society, the technocratic elite is 'meritocratic' in that it recognizes technical skills above all else, and is thus open to the best thinkers
- **The hacker culture** – represented by those who possess the technical expertise of the previous group, but who employ those skills within an open spirit of 'free' informationalism. Hackers remove log jams in development raised by vested interests and provide management for a community of shared idealism
- **Virtual communitarians** – these are the 'content managers' who create communal spaces on the Internet, using technical and social engineering skills to provide the Internet with spaces that empower users to publish their content on the web. This group manages the digital platforms that enable online social interaction
- **Entrepreneurs** – these are the professional groups of creative capitalists that exploit the existence of the Internet for commercial gain. The 'culture' of Internet entrepreneurs is also marked by workaholism and relative informality, but the predominant ethos is competitive and technical merit is favoured less than financial acumen

See Manuel Castells (2002), *The Internet Galaxy: Reflections on the Internet, Business and Society*, Oxford: Oxford University Press, pp. 36–63

In a wider social and economic context where commuting has become a major drain on the time of employees, and where increasing numbers of households rely on multiple incomes, the flexibility of 'working from home' did prove to be highly attractive to many. Initially, working in the home office was seen as a privilege of employees at the managerial level. For other staff to leave the highly disciplined conventions of the workplace was regarded as problematic by most employers. However, it was also apparent that there were significant savings to be made on premises and running costs if workers were prepared to turn part of their home into a place of work. Alvin Toffler's idea of the 'electronic cottage' was championed by some as the workplace of the future, where independent, highly motivated employees would work remotely from their own residences (1980). Over the past decade, the electronic cottage has started to become a reality for a sizeable number of people choosing to become self-employed and run their own businesses from home. For most people, however, the advent of home computing and 'teleworking' really facilitated the addition of homework to their normal working day. Standard applications like email allow business communications to carry on throughout the evenings and weekends, and consequently deadlines for information work are no longer constrained by the working day. For employers, this means greater efficiency without extra costs. For many workers, it means longer working hours without extra pay, since information work tends to be salaried and measured in terms of outputs rather than hours worked.

In this sense, the distinction that Castells makes between networkers and flextimers may not hold true across the present generational divide. In a recent ethnographic study, Melissa Gregg looked in depth at the lives of young professionals in the Australian city of Brisbane (2011). Gregg found that the present regime of short-term contracts and strategic networking that characterizes career pathways in marketing, broadcasting and information technology was shaping a convergent work–life pattern that left employees exhausted and emotionally drained. In this context, digital technologies drove the constant proximity of the workplace, a 'presence bleed' which employees quickly came to resent (ibid.: 2–3). This 'on-call' culture has rapidly been naturalized as an expectation of knowledge workers, even as a commitment to long-term employment and investment in staff is withdrawn by employers seeking flexibility on their own terms (ibid.: 153–65). At the same time, digital technologies are critical tools for the professional networking and impression management that becomes essential for managing these mobile careers. Less instrumentally, the compulsive nature of socio-professional connectivity through digital platforms (such as Facebook and Twitter) also begins to form an emotional security blanket through which these workers seek to negotiate the lived experience of 'precarity' and executive ambition (ibid.: 154). This new 'intimacy' of professional work operates in two directions, as emotional investments are increasingly required in professional 'friendships' and the domestic interiors of the home (and family units of all kinds) are reconfigured around the presence of the home office (ibid.: 121–52). Thus, the widespread casualization of the professional classes of tomorrow is played out in sensory environments that are quite different from Castells's accounts of business hotels, gyms and airport VIP lounges. This, then, is the backstage workshop of contemporary network culture, a very human sphere of insecurity, compromise and perpetual contact. In many respects, the insistent 'intimacy' of this form of work represents an affectual colonization of the life-world in a digital form (see Habermas 1987; Schutz 1972; Weber 1949).

Job security is no longer obtained as a result of social networking. Rather, networking is an addi-tional form of labor that is required to demonstrate ongoing employability. The crucial difference is that the stability of a permanent job is no longer an end result of the practice. The practice is itself the job . . . In information jobs, the content of the project is less important than the general fact of activity . . . In this [study] workers without something in the pipeline were the first to suffer during the downturn. But those who survived also suffered costs in the quests to maintain multiple 'projects' . . . Legitimate feelings of instability and overload were dealt with by 'professional devel-opment' courses designed to ease the anxiety arising from constant churn. They were later met with requests to accept reduced hours or unpaid leave. Such gestures placed the onus on employees to develop the emotional and psychological capacity to withstand positions and workloads with no definite beginning or end.

Melissa Gregg (2011), *Work's Intimacy*, Cambridge: Polity, pp. 13–14

Lifelong Learning

The skilling of information work is by nature very different from the world of industrial work. Industrial processes tend to require large plant investments, and the attendant skills of employees change slowly and are often highly specific to their own industry or, indeed, to their own section or department. By contrast, information processes, standardized through the spread of common operating systems and software, tend to rely on technologies common to the knowledge sector as a whole (personal computers, telecoms systems, etc.). Hardware and software systems evolve far more rapidly than engineering machinery, which makes the evolution of the production process much quicker than in older industries. At the same time, the skills required to process data are much more general. Designing or operating a database or website requires the same skills regardless of the nature of the business. This means that employees throughout the knowledge economy tend to have skills in common. Such skills can be readily transferred from one occupation to another and, as a consequence, these workers are relatively easy for employers to replace. For most people, it is their level of attainment in these key, transferable skills (rather than specialized ones) that makes them employ-able. The result of all this is much greater mobility in employment across the board, with the 'jobs-for-life' ethos of old being replaced by 'portfolio careers' where our work-ing lives are characterized by a procession of different jobs, and much more short-term employment (Hopson and Ledger 2009; Inkson 2007).

An inevitable result of greater mobility within the workforce, whether that be upwards, downwards or sideways, is that the accumulation of long-term skills is regu-larly interrupted and new domains have to be mastered in order to retain sufficient employability. Unlike creativity, skills are not so much personal attributes as forms of acquired knowledge that require training. A notable feature, therefore, of a knowl-edge economy is that it demands much greater investment in the reskilling of staff. However, the cost of 'lifelong learning' has largely been divested by employers in most professional fields. Instead, the expense of acquiring skills has been passed down to the employees themselves, and the provision of the actual training has largely been under-taken by the university system (Jarvis 2010). This has produced a very noticeable change in the role of public education, not least, since the university system in most societies has only catered to a very small section of the population for much of its history. For the first half of the last century, no more than 5 per cent of the UK workforce received a university education. In the British case, the 'privilege' of a university education was overwhelmingly restricted to the upper and upper-middle classes, with only a tiny number of exceptionally gifted individuals allowed entry through scholarships. This meant that the university system effectively policed the social boundaries between the managerial and working classes. Many people in the present generation may also not be aware that universities have excluded women for much of their history.

Staying, for the sake of convenience, with the British example, the implementation of Keynesianism and the welfare state in the 1950s, the rising prosperity and aspirations of the lower-middle class that followed, and the growing importance of scientific 'white heat' to economic planning were all factors that drove the first expansion of higher education in the 1960s. By the 1970s, it was the larger crop of graduates from a much wider social spectrum that provided the skills that supported the initial growth of the knowledge economy model. At the same time, the simultaneous decline in heavy manufacturing industries from the late 1970s onwards created mass unemployment amongst those without a university education. In this context, successive governments sought to further expand participation in higher education in order to maintain the overall employability of the workforce. During the 1980s and 1990s, mature students retraining for new jobs and young adults undertaking degrees in the face of growing youth unemployment drove up university enrolments. This second wave of expansion was a necessary step for helping the workforce to adapt to changing economic conditions, but it was also becoming prohibitively expensive. To offset the cost of vocational education, academics were encouraged to redirect their research towards commercial goals, students were required to subsidize their training through the introduction of university fees and universities began to compete for international students as another source of revenue. In the process, education became a major knowledge industry in its own right (Richmond 2011).

In the United States, of course, students and their families have had to bear the full cost of university education for a long time. Here too, however, the number of students has increased and the costs of study have risen steadily (Tuchman 2009). With the simultaneous identification of higher education as a prerequisite for meaningful employment in a knowledge economy, these increasing costs begin to take on the flavour of a tax on jobs. Given their crucial role in the development of computer technologies, it is ironic that one of the major drains on the finances of universities has been the cost of commercial software licences and computer hardware. This expenditure became necessary in order to support the computerization of learning and the massive demand for computer-based courses of all kinds. At another level entirely, competing internationally in the world of hi-tech research has become a major role for universities in the wider knowledge economy, and this cost also has to be borne by someone (Branscomb 1999). There have, accordingly, been both gains and losses in the industrialization of education. Those who found themselves out of work, or made obsolete by automation, have been able to retrain and pursue new careers. Access to higher education has steadily increased, as have the ranges of courses available, and this has produced the best-educated workforces in history. For the first time, women outnumber men in university admissions in the Western world. Nonetheless, today's graduates must also contend with the increasing levels of competitions for jobs in all fields. To remain competitive, a higher degree is becoming a necessary additional investment, and years of unpaid 'internships' or low-paid 'career development' are likely to follow (Perlin 2011). Thus, the cost of paying for more and more education, along with the years spent undertaking it, is becoming a major contribution to a 'shrinking middle' that will have to wait longer for lower returns in their careers (Ornstein 2007).

The Digital Dole

Elsewhere, for those for whom higher education has not been a realistic prospect, the old industrial convention of buying labour time continues. In this domain, digital technologies allow for highly efficient monitoring of the workforce (Andrejevic 2007b). This is present in most workplaces in some form, from retail and logistics to manufacturing and transport (via GPS). In the office environment, employees undertaking routine and repetitive information work are increasingly placed under electronic surveillance, which allows for an extremely fine-grained management of the efficiency of employees. In the other direction, the temptation to do some online shopping or message friends on Facebook has led to the phenomenon of 'cyber-slacking', where employees surf recreationally on company time. Across the board, however, it is undeniably the case that the computer workstation has become the primary work environment for ever larger numbers of people, from artists and accountants to engineers and antique dealers. From a few metres' distance, it would be hard to tell the difference between their endeavours. In the process, many of the old industrial injuries of the past are being replaced by repetitive-strain injury (RSI) complaints, eye-strain and obesity. It is questionable, therefore, whether work has become more rewarding or fulfilling for most people, but there is no doubt that the work environments of the digital economy are quieter, cleaner and more homogeneous than the factories of the recent past.

In that respect, an inevitable consequence of promoting knowledge work over physical labour is the decline in fortunes of those who are least equipped to operate in this new working environment. For those with little education or information-processing skills, and for those whose specialist skills have become redundant with automation and the downsizing of the industrial economy, the era of knowledge and creativity has presented a major challenge to their well-being. The necessary adjustments are by no means a simple matter. Exciting new digital applications become basic skills in just a few years. The level of basic training required to remain competitive in a job market of this kind already goes far beyond the standard provision of school education to the less-privileged sections of society. Those unable to keep up will increasingly find themselves unemployed or underemployed, unless they can capitalize on the decline in 'traditional skills' amongst the creative generation (because software cannot yet unblock your plumbing). As such, it is pertinent to note that the era of the knowledge economy has been an era in which unemployment has remained persistently high in developed societies. At either end of the 'shrinking middle', the under-twenty-fives and over-fifties are increasingly likely to find themselves out of work. This poses serious social problems for governments seeking to guide the transition between the old economy and the new. In the worst cases, particularly areas where the local economy was overwhelmingly industrial, whole communities have descended into poverty and welfare dependency. This costs welfare states a lot of money in lost tax revenues, benefit payments and policing.

In the short term, this is a problem that requires major interventions by social policy in order to mitigate the human cost of a changing work culture. In the longer term, it will take more than compulsory higher education to resolve the underlying problem of structural unemployment (Werding 2006). On a more positive note, the growth in the overall availability of computers and Internet access, along with the provision of unprecedented quantities of information through 'open information' resources make it possible for the unemployed of today to take a hand in their own education and reskilling. Contrary to the popular image of older workers unable to contend with new technologies, the availability of 'free' time has seen notable growth of computer skills amongst older workers and 'silver surfers'. For the young, the centrality of digital technologies to the worlds of entertainment and popular culture confers a significant degree of literacy in information technologies that can be usefully transferred into work opportunities should they arise. With free time on their hands, the participatory cultures celebrated by Henry Jenkins and others are well-staffed by intelligent and capable people whose energies would otherwise be directed towards the needs of the workplace (2006). Recessions, in that sense, are always fertile ground for popular culture. This does something, at least, to mitigate the sense of social isolation and worthlessness that has traditionally been associated with being out of work.

Offshoring and Outsourcing

At the present time, there has been a marked tendency to ask 'where have all the jobs gone?', and then to point to the rapid economic growth under way in China and India. The inclination of commentators, particularly in the United States, to link the two developments is a result of the organizational trends of 'offshoring' and 'outsourcing' during the 1990s and 2000s (Farrell 2007; Oshri, Kotlarsky and Willcocks 2009). As investment streams slowed with the end of the first dot.com boom in the United States in 2000, cutting costs became an increasingly important feature of the information technology economy. Following the previous shift of hardware manufacturing to Far East economies such as Taiwan and Korea, many of the leading players in the software sector also moved to take advantage of cheaper labour and lower operating costs by setting set up their own 'offshore' subsidiaries, notably in India (Carmel and Tija 2005; Lacity and Rottman 2008). As this offshoring phenomenon gathered pace, the relocation of programming and software work was augmented by a similar desire of large companies across a wide range of fields from banking, insurance, utilities and retail to cut their own labour costs dramatically. They did this to a significant extent by taking advantage of Internet communication and outsourcing the bulk of their quotidian data-processing and customer-service work to call centres in India and other locations, where labour was cheap and plentiful and telecommunications were sufficiently reliable (Dossani and Kenney 2007; Kobayashi-Hillary 2005; Nadeem 2011; Narayan 2011). The rationale for these strategies was that the developing world would remain oriented towards generic labour supply and low-end services, providing 'cyber-coolies' who would simultaneously lower labour costs and free up their Western counterparts for more innovative and profitable knowledge-based occupations.

This somewhat racist and ill-informed view of Asia's human capacity failed to take sufficient note of the wider significance of relocating manpower within the global IT economy. The investment of the Indian government in technical institutes over several decades began to pay off handsomely as well-trained Indian software engineers were increasingly able to compete for the best IT jobs in the developed countries. Not long after, companies such as Infosys and Wipro in India also began providing more highly skilled information services to international clients at comparatively low cost. Thus, by the 2000s, it was not only the mundane jobs of the information economy that were following industrial jobs eastwards. For the first time, middle-class occupations in the West were also under threat, and permissive attitudes to outsourcing began to change accordingly. In the context of recession since 2007, the neoliberal orthodoxy of the win-win advantages of a competitive global labour market and a 'new international division of labour' are becoming highly contentious (Taylor 2008). In that respect, many of the new jobs created by the information revolution have proved to be even more vulner-able to international competition than the industrial jobs that they were intended to replace. With the hardware of the digital economy being made in East Asia and programmed and (increasingly) operated in South Asia, difficult questions necessarily arise for the information industries in the West. Nonetheless, the 'loss' of information-technology jobs can be overstated. The IT economy of the United States is still as big as that of the rest of the world combined. A much bigger question, in fact, is whether knowledge economies in the West can simply live off patents and intellectual property rights while the rest of the world supplies them with physical goods.

Under the post-industrial paradigm, the old industrial problems of rising labour costs and pollution were largely resolved by moving those activities overseas. Nonetheless, the need for industrial labour and goods does not dissipate and post-industrial coun-tries must find something to trade for them. By the logic of the knowledge economy, the relative advantages of hosting industrial production are offset by the greater value of the commercial rights exercised over the intellectual content of all economic, social and biological processes held in repository (Thomas and Servaes 2006; Thomas 2010: 117–77). Thus, the balance of trade between the developed and developing worlds was to be maintained to the enduring advantage of the West through the payments of royal-ties on all intellectual products, from films to genetic sequences. This is why corpora-tions and individuals from the United States file more patents in India than Indians do. However, even with an army of lawyers, it was always questionable whether such a powerline could be effectively maintained in a world increasingly defined by decentred flows of information. In their foundational obsession with cutting labour costs and increasing efficiency, with reducing the bottom-line and increasing short-term prof-its, the proponents of the knowledge economy significantly under-played the West's diminishing advantages in knowledge production (and in productive capacity overall). Consequently, due to an inherent bias towards the highest 'value-added' knowledge processes, many commentators under-estimated the full extent to which the new mobil-ity of 'bread-and-butter' activities would inevitably transfer technology, wealth and jobs across the world (Brewer and Nollen 1998). This may not, in the final analysis, turn out to be a bad thing. However, this less one-sided view of globalization means that every-thing will not come to us on our terms. In order to pursue employment opportunities in a global economy, more and more of us will be drawn into the space of flows.

Going with the Churn

In the gloomy environment of the present, it is easy to lose sight of the many new opportunities that have arisen in the workplace during the past twenty years. Despite the current dissatisfaction with offshoring strategies of various kinds, it is important to remember that the job market that has arisen around information technology has given rise to a wide range of new opportunities that have compensated for the passing of older professions. Digital technologies have created large numbers of new jobs, and not just in the high-profile media sector. Information work has increased the efficiency of private- and public-sector operations, resulting in a far greater range of services for consumers. The rise of information work means that most of us now work in cleaner and safer work environments than the previous generation. The creative skills developed through the use of computers have broadened the intellectual horizons of many people, and brought greater fulfilment not just to their working lives but to their lives as a whole. Information technology has significantly enhanced the capacity of higher education to reach ever larger numbers of people, making an informed society a realistic prospect for the first time in history. In the jobs market, the increasingly 'user-friendly' nature of IT applications is allowing a higher degree of mobility in employment. Computer work of all kinds, coupled with telecoms advances, promises increased flexibility in terms of where, when and how much we want to work.

It is not reasonable, however, to expect a world of endless positives or continuous improvements in all aspects of employment. Gains in organizational efficiency have consistently entailed the loss of jobs. Innovation in information processing has also tended to eliminate particular roles, and the new flexible jobs that have been created in the knowledge economy have not fully compensated for the loss of jobs elsewhere. Unemployment remains persistently high in the most technologically advanced economies, presaging the sci-fi dystopia of the 1970s British comic book *2000AD* more than the leisurely society envisioned by Daniel Bell. Large numbers of people unable, for whatever reason, to become 'lifelong learners' have been impoverished and undervalued. Unemployment and underemployment amongst young people is higher than it has been for decades. As a consequence of all this, workers at all levels of the economy suffer from a higher degree of job insecurity. For the vast majority, the increasing expendability of transferable knowledge workers results in lower wages in real terms, longer working hours, short-term contracts and reduced bargaining power over working conditions. For the lucky few able to match the mobility of the job market, career progression involves enormous commitments of financial and emotional resources, along with adherence to a round-the-clock regime of instrumental connectivity and decision-making. Thus, even the movers and shapers of the network live precarious lives that require a significant measure of self-absorption and ruthlessness over many years (Ross 2009). These 'battler' lifestyles direct our attention away from domestic and collective social bonds and thus cast their own inevitable affects over the pursuit of work as a means of fulfilment and self-expression (Standing 2011).

In the pursuit of a knowledge economy, the commercialization of education and research has profoundly changed the relationship between universities, students and the wider society. The increasing number of graduates that universities produce with great efficiency necessarily means additional competition for jobs and, for students, more time and money invested to obtain more qualifications for the same jobs. The financial costs of all this have been passed from business and government to the employees themselves. Similarly, the very notion of 'employability' could be seen to position employment as the sole responsibility of the jobseeker, rather than unemployment being a responsibility for either business or government. Consequently, rather than recognizing the present lack of employment opportunities as a failing of the economy as a whole, new textbooks on 'employability' encourage us to (self-)believe that we will get jobs by honing our impression-management skills and becoming more adept at selling ourselves (Cottrell 2003; Trought 2011). This may work for some, but it is in essence a game of numbers. Against the backdrop of this grand lottery, most (if not all) of the collective wealth created by the knowledge economy in the past two decades has recently disappeared in the 'creative' practices of de-regulated international banking. In that sense, the first sustained crisis of the post-industrial economy has finally arrived. Just as the digital economies of today were conceived by those who graduated amongst the industrial crises of the early 1970s, it will be those who graduate in the present recession (or its aftermath) who will ultimately identify the road ahead and shape the jobs of the future. This, of course, will be you.

Think and Discuss

1. Key Terms
Can you describe in simple language what is meant by the following terms found in this chapter?

- Creative industries
- Employability
- Flexible labour
- Lifelong learning
- Outsourcing

2. Critical Questions
Try answering the following questions, drawing upon your own understanding, experience and knowledge.

1. Based on your own experiences, how central have digital technologies become to the everyday culture of work?
2. To what extent do your future career plans entail a commitment to 'lifelong learning' and an 'employability' strategy?
3. What are the gains and losses of more flexible patterns of employment?
4. To what extent, and in what ways, have creative skills become valued in the professions in which you will be seeking employment?
5. What are the most compelling occupational opportunities on offer in a global knowledge economy?

Further Reading

Coyle, Diana (1999) *The Weightless World: Thriving in the Digital Age*, Oxford: Capstone
Deuze, Mark (2007) *Media Work*, Cambridge: Polity.
Florida, Richard (2002) *The Rise of the Creative Class*, New York: Perseus.
Gregg, Melissa (2011) *Work's Intimacy*, Cambridge: Polity.
Hesketh, Anthony and Brown, Phillip (2004) *The Mismanagement of Talent: Employability and Jobs in the Knowledge Economy*, Oxford: Oxford University Press.
Leadbeater, Charles (2000) *Living on Thin Air: The New Economy*, London and New York: Penguin.
McKercher, Catherine and Vincent Mosco (eds) (2007) *Knowledge Workers in the Information Society*, Lanham, MD: Lexington Books.
Ross, Andrew (2009) *Nice Work If You Can Get It: Life and Labor in Precarious Times*, New York: New York University Press.
Watson, Tony J. (2008) *Sociology, Work and Industry*, Abingdon: Routledge.

Go Online

Charles Leadbeater – http://www.charlesleadbeater.net/
Employability Alliance – http://www.employabilityalliance.eu/
International Labour Organization – http://www.ilo.org/global/lang--en/index.htm -
Peter Drucker Institute – www.druckerinstitute.com
United Nations Conference on Trade and Development – http://www.unctad.org/
Universitas 21 – http://www.universitas21.com/
US Department of Labor – http://www.dol.gov

Part IV

Digital Authorities

CHAPTER 13

Virtual Democracy

There are numerous activities through which we can interrogate the role played by digital media in the arena of personal communications and self-expression. On a larger scale, it is evident that the broader infrastructure of digital technologies is playing a central role in the operation of markets, the management of workforces and in the production and consumption of commodities more broadly. Nonetheless, despite a tendency to downplay the role of government in the emerging interface between consumers and free markets, there are a number of equally critical phenomena through which digital technologies become enmeshed within the political process. The usage of digital media in democratic societies (and even undemocratic ones) inevitably juxtaposes top-down and bottom-up modes of political participation. In the former case, the automation of state functions and the introduction of computerized efficiency into the business of government creates a new electronic apparatus of administration and communication. In the latter case, the interactivity of digital media technologies facilitates large-scale (and often real-time) participation of citizens in public debate. The advent of the Internet, therefore, has profound implications for the everyday practice of governance. Technically, at least, it makes democracy a more realistic proposition in a mass society.

The Democratic Ideal

In the early days of the 'Internet revolution', American technologist Howard Rheingold outlined his vision of 'virtual communities' on the 'electronic frontier' (1993). This model of social organization cast a universal and overarching technical system (the Internet) as the practical means for furthering what could be described as 'digital pastoralism'. By this model, social participation becomes intensely local in its conduct, while simultaneously operating on a mass scale due to the electronic connectivity between its constituents. An automated network of local inputs overwrites the institutionalized politics of the mass society and reinscribes the ideal of direct democracy upon the pattern of social organization. This idealistic account of an active and self-governing citizenry was predicated upon the romanticizing of the Internet itself and of the westward expansion of the United States. Arguably, this requires an elision of the largely complementary history of colonial expansion and political centralization. The lost 'self-government' of the frontier era was only the precursor to extending the formal sovereignty of the state and the arrival of 'responsible' government. Nonetheless, the enduring ideal of the frontier in modern America, and the mourning of its loss, is indicative of the inherent difficulty of reconciling the founding ideals of liberalism and freedom with the subsequent reality of a powerful state apparatus. In that sense, there is inevitably a disjuncture in all societies between political ideals and political realities.

In the case of liberal democracies, this disjuncture is acute because 'rule by the people' inevitably requires a complex state bureaucracy. That is, in order to exercise the democratic principle, effective power must be vested in public agencies. Accordingly, there is always a thin line between a healthy popular democracy and an autocratic socialist state. An awareness of this fact has underpinned the anti-government ethos that has infused American politics over the past thirty years (for example, Reynolds 2007; Schweizer 2010). However, taking a less polarized line, it is important to recognize that there are inherent technical difficulties posed by the democratic ideal. It is not practical to formulate every law by referendum. Equally, it is not plausible to conduct government in a manner that accommodates the interests of all. This is true of a people's republic (like the United States) or a democracy amongst royal subjects (like the United Kingdom). The gap between public participation and coherent government is therefore filled by political parties who put competing ideological visions before the electorate at regular intervals. In a modern democracy, political parties institute a political landscape that functions between the state and the citizenry, taking its authority from a measure of both.

> More than a political system of governance, a democracy is a guarantee of equality, freedom, the possibility of civic virtue ... [yet] Democracy is often treated as a static concept that we either practice effectively, live up to honorably, or are unable to attain. Democracy, however, is imaginary. It is an abstraction. It is based upon an ideal, subject to many interpretations, which then influence how the abstraction is practiced by nation-centric political systems. As a concept, it is derived from the Greek dimos (public) and kratos (rule), which suggests that power lies with the people, a proposition that is both irrevocable and long-lasting. Without question, rule lies with the people, but when it comes to how that rule is exercised, the questions are many. Responses vary, depending upon the unique economic, social, cultural, and political conditions of each society.
>
> Zia Papacharissi (2010b), *A Private Sphere: Democracy in a Digital Age*, Cambridge: Polity, pp. 3, 11

When we talk about democratic government, we typically make only a loose reference to the ideal of a popular consensus forged through debate. More often, we are referring to the conjoined mechanisms of 'representative government' and 'majority rule' that underpin modern politics. 'Representative government' is any mechanism by which the citizenry vest their authority in a small number of individuals who pledge to speak for their interests. Majority rule is a political principle that is given legitimacy by the philosophy of utilitarianism (Mill 2001). By this formulation, the irreconcilable demands of rule by all the people and the arbitrary acts of government are subordinated in principle to the 'greatest good for the greatest number'. Even this pragmatic approach to the implementation of democracy is itself an ideal to which governance corresponds fitfully in matters of policy. It does, however, formally subscribe and submit to this principle via the regular staging of public elections. As politicians become simultaneously representatives of the citizenry, of the state and of their respective party, the practice of 'representative government' seeks to accommodate the competing logics of absolutism, oligopoly and democracy. This is not, however, the form of democracy enshrined within the ideal of an electronically mediated 'virtual democracy'. The interactive mechanism at the heart of digital technologies has instead been associated with a form of 'direct democracy', that is, a system through which the general population themselves institute or veto legislation. This is a significant difference.

The systems of government inherited by the liberal democracies of today were primarily organized around formal institutions of state. Nonetheless, even in the eighteenth century, the operation of democracy exceeded the boundaries of government. It was able to do so primarily because of new forms of social communication brought into being by media technologies. At that time, newspapers were emerging as the major forums for public debate. The expression of 'public opinion' in this form introduced various checks and balances upon the power of elected governments. It was a recognition of the new political power of the middle classes, and their close relationship to the newspaper, that led the British Lord Macauley to identify the press in 1828 as a 'fourth estate' (Conboy 2004). Previously, the traditional social formations (or estates) under the feudal system had been the three estates of the clergy, the nobles and the peasants, with their relations mediated through the arbitration of the monarch. In practical terms, the new fourth estate comprised of professional writers who shaped the opinions of the newly conceived middle classes. The notion of the fourth estate has endured, coming to encapsulate the ideal of a democratic scrutiny of power. It formalizes the political necessity of the press as an institutional force in modern society. An independent press becomes a prerequisite for free speech, which is in turn essential for the formation of democratic debates which provide the necessary balance against state power (see Jessop 2007; Martin and Copeland 2003). Perhaps more problematically, the role of the fourth estate also gives the popular media a sovereign claim over public opinion.

Jürgen Habermas and the Public Sphere

Because of their role in disseminating information across society, media technologies become integral to the political process. Prior to the development of digital technologies, mass media systems had already been given an institutional form which balanced their accountability to their readership and to the state (which assumed regulatory controls over their ownership and operation). In that sense, press, radio and television provided a diffusion of information and a forum for public debate (for which they were, in many ways, held accountable by the state). At the same time, media institutions also placed the state under scrutiny, and therefore provided the basis for an informed 'civil society' that was able to exercise its democratic rights and obligations. The most influential account of the terrain upon which the modern media are engaged in democratic deliberation has been provided by the German social philosopher, Jürgen Habermas (1992). As a student of, and successor to, the Frankfurt School of sociology, Habermas has been particularly active in critical theorizations that support a social democratic consensus in Germany. During the 1960s, Habermas posited the notion of a 'public sphere'. This was an arena of debate which effectively mediated between citizens and government and, as such, it was seen as the primary forum of modern democratic society.

By 'the public sphere' we mean first of all a realm of our social life in which something approaching public opinion can be formed. Access is guaranteed to all citizens. A portion of the public sphere comes into being in every conversation in which private individuals assemble to form a public body ... In a large public body, this kind of communication requires specific means for transmitting information and influencing those who receive it. Today, newspapers and magazines, radio and television are the media of the public sphere.

Jürgen Habermas (1974), 'The Public Sphere: An Encyclopedia Article', *New German Critique*, 3, p. 49

There are many facets to Habermas's account of the public sphere (and his explicit contrast of an ideal public sphere with the messy realities of modern politics). The founding proposition is that a 'public sphere' is both an arena for, and a cumulative effect of, social discourse. To put that more simply, the public sphere is where public talk occurs (and vice versa). In Habermas's formulation, the public sphere is, in principle, democratic and inclusive. That is, everyone should be able to participate in public discussion. The notion of the public sphere therefore claims that there is a public arena of communication that remains distinct from the communicative structures arising from the state and the market. Habermas also notes that in any industrial society, meaningful communication between vast numbers of public citizens necessarily requires specialized apparatus in the form of the mass media. The political principle that Habermas seeks to establish via the model of the public sphere is one by which individual members of society, through talking to each other, come to construct a social body (the public). In the process, a democratically active agenda (public opinion) is forged through societal-wide discussion (public debate). This agenda can then be given expression through acts of government. Thus, if we consider the notion of the public sphere offered by Habermas alongside the older idea of the fourth estate, we can see how the notions of a civil society (informed citizenry), public sphere (social communication) and fourth estate (media institutions) are all interdependent concepts. The primary difference between the two notions is that Habermas does not invest the authority of the public in journalists (or any other specialist class). Rather, Habermas calls for direct public participation in the shaping of debate.

The primary reason for this call for a more participatory fourth estate is Habermas's disillusionment with the rise of 'public relations' as a means of influencing public opinion. Habermas claimed that the emergence of the modern newspaper in the seventeenth and eighteenth centuries created a new 'civil society'. Better informed by their access to the printed media, the educated members of society were able to come together and engage in rational debate on social and political issues. Thus, for the first time, something called 'public opinion' began to have an impact on processes of reform. This ideal public sphere subsequently foundered in the twentieth century due to the rise of mass politics, mass media and the accompanying communication specialists. In the political domain, a largely uninformed and emotive citizenry began to make their voices heard. In the mass media, a range of vested interests from politicians to capitalists and trade unions sought to control public debates through various techniques of public relations. As a result, the modern public sphere becomes a good deal less reasonable than the classical one. Instead of working towards consensus as a basis for political action, the contemporary public sphere becomes something of a bun fight between various institutional interests. The remedy that Habermas proposes is a mechanism by which adequate regulation ensures that citizens are once again able to publish their own opinions and ideas. Therefore, it was logical that the emergence of interactive digital media systems would transform social communication and change the terms of this particular debate. As such, a number of scholars have recently revisited Habermas's model of the ideal public sphere in the Internet era (Chadwick 2006; Norris 2000; Papacharissi 2010b; Poster 1997).

Box 13.1 The Internet as a public sphere

- The Internet makes the arena of mass communication available to its users (enabling public participation)
- The Internet has become a major forum for social debate (reflecting public opinion)
- The Internet connects people globally in previously unimaginable ways (enlarging the public sphere)
- The Internet has become a major communications channel for institutions (enabling public relations)

Canvassing the Digital Divide

In order to relate the emergence of the Internet productively to the notion of the public sphere, we need to consider how the medium both enables and interacts with public debate. A prerequisite for the expansion of public participation in political life is the widespread diffusion of knowledge and an adequate technology for enabling the right of reply. The Internet, as a technology, is well suited to both of these tasks. However, technological possibilities do not of themselves institute a fully fledged system of social communication. At the outset, the ideal of a new interactive, electronic public sphere had to encounter the technical limitations and structural boundaries hindering inclusive public participation. In that sense, the political uses of the Internet were as reliant upon capacity-building and public uptake as were the commercial and technical uses of the medium. For this reason, alongside the rapid growth of the commercial Internet, the term 'digital divide' was employed to draw attention to the contours of public participation (Norris 2000). The advent of newspapers perpetuated the dominance of the 'educated classes' in the early modern period. Film, radio and television also created new media 'elites' who came to dominate the public sphere in the twentieth century. Thus, there was every reason to believe that the requirements of technological literacy and the cost of Internet access would naturally favour the most advantaged groups in the emerging digital society. The 'digital divide' debates therefore sought to illustrate the differential between groups within society in terms of their access to digital information systems.

In 1996, the Clinton administration in the US drew public attention to the widespread differences in access to IT provision in the American school system. Elite schools were already well provisioned for instruction in information technology, but poorer state schools did not have sufficient resources to institute similar programmes (Kahin and Wilson 1997). This constituted an in-built disadvantage for much of the upcoming generation, which would become more acute as digital technologies became more central to the economy of the near future. In 1998, Donna Hoffman and Thomas Novak produced an influential study which emphasized the greater relative access of white Americans to the Internet when compared to black Americans. Subsequent studies showed that the divide between online and offline populations corresponded with a number of factors, including household income, gender, colour, age and location (Katz and Rice 2002). All in all, affluent, young, white, educated, urban males were much likelier to be online in the first Internet decade than poor, black, elderly, rural women with only a basic education. In order to tackle the disparity between children's access to ICT, the US Vice-President Al Gore announced major public investments in an 'information superhighway' that would put a networked computer in every classroom. The UK and Australia also spent state funds on providing public library access to the World Wide Web. Getting everyone online thus became a goal shared by socially oriented governments, information technology companies and the investors in the dot.com boom. In public policy, worldwide Internet connectivity became elevated to a status usually reserved for the provision of water or sanitation. Since being online was predicted to become essential for social participation, being offline was considered just as likely to condemn individuals to social isolation and poverty.

As the era of the commercial software giants unfolded, a large number of information technology professionals sought to pre-empt various predictions of the looming digital divide by working collectively to develop free software, open-source programming resources and non-proprietary access to computing applications. These efforts were global in their scope, because while the term 'digital divide' was being used to refer to the disparity in access to information networks within developed societies, it was also applied to the obvious gap between the richest and poorest regions and countries of the world. During the mid-1990s when the Internet was being widely celebrated as the most democratic medium ever created, 95 per cent of Africans lacked access to a telephone (Cubitt 1999). Many poorer countries lacked the capital and infrastructure to keep up with the growing technical and educational requirements of a 'wired' world, placing them at a growing economic disadvantage. Those that could afford to 'keep up' inevitably did so at the expense of other development needs. Thus, the capacity of the richest countries to diffuse technical capacity and literacy amongst their populations for economic gain also appeared likely to exacerbate the global disparity in wealth in the era of the 'knowledge economy'. Under the heading of 'ICTs for Development', ongoing programmes are seeking to deliver scaled-down computers to children in Africa and India. Large volumes of aid money have been spent around the world on projects intended to introduce IT into disadvantaged and/or remote societies (Unwin 2009).

As you might expect, not all of these efforts are entirely altruistic. Information technology companies benefit directly from participating in publicly sponsored programmes and they also benefit indirectly with every extension of the global user-base for information technologies. Similarly, while governments express genuine concern about the future employability of their citizens, they tend to do so with the health of the national economy in mind. In that respect, the rapid contraction of the digital divide over the past decade is also intended to furnish the conditions under which governments can transfer numerous interactions with their citizens into the online environment. In an era where the cost of government has increased dramatically, the efficiency gains of putting government services online promise to be quite considerable. Presently, 'e-governance' constitutes a distinctive field within the digital domain, where various states deploy digital systems to overcome logistical and financial obstacles to the overall efficiency of the public sector (Budd and Harris 2009). Taking economic motives aside, however, there are also important political reasons for ensuring wide participation in the Internet medium. The implementation of various 'direct government' initiatives provides a new means of communicating with citizens directly. In what is widely perceived to be an era of 'voter apathy', 'out-of-touch' politicians and political disillusionment, interactive political communication offers a critical feedback mechanism that might reinvigorate established political institutions.

There are many benefits for citizens too, since direct government platforms also provide a more accessible means for constituents to relate their concerns directly to their elected representatives. In the UK, citizens can now make e-petitions to the Prime Minister via the Directgov portal. This introduces the culture of 'direct democracy' into a political culture that has been strictly representative throughout its long history. Further, this form of contact confers the sensorial intimacy of digital media upon political communication. As such, the increasing personalization of political communication works hand in hand with the predominance of personality politics in a media age (which paradoxically provides an imperative for the outflanking of powerful media interests by initiatives of this kind). Direct communication can also be far more selective in its targeting of voters, and this allows a multidimensional approach to building political constituencies. In an age where politicians are obsessed with opinion polls and the ebb and flow of public opinion, interactive applications provide an obvious means of taking the political temperature at any given moment. Real-time platforms such as Twitter and SNS have proved to be powerful tools of political communication in the broader context of fast-moving media campaigns. In that regard, there is obvious scope for tech-savvy politicians to engage the digital generation in their 'home' environment, as Barrack Obama famously did in his run for the US Presidential nomination in 2008 (Harfoush 2009). Nonetheless, the mere fact of these digital engagements with the public may prove to be more compelling than the actual content of such platforms. In that respect, interactive portals are very consciously intended to give the impression of public engagement, accessibility and accountability.

Open Publishing

Approaches to the digital divide and direct government initiatives all highlight the roles played by government in furnishing, expanding and utilizing the infrastructure of a digital public sphere. The inclusive and interactive ambitions of such programmes do much to address Habermas's critiques of earlier mass-media systems and, to varying extents, they hold out the promise of bringing citizens closer to the political arena. Nonetheless, it is equally true that these tend to be top-down initiatives that have their own attendant class of communications specialists. In that regard, we could say that they generally engage citizens on terms set by government. The other constituent feature of the electronic public sphere, which we might see as the counterpoint to these measures, is the meteoric rise of open publishing amongst the citizens themselves. The potential of digital technologies for allowing millions of people to publish their own thoughts and viewpoints has consistently been seen as a source of enormous democratic, or even radical, potential (Jenkins and Thorburn 2004; Lievrouw 2011; Rettburg 2008). The processes of intermediation intrinsic to earlier forms of mass media placed information exchange in the hands of media specialists and regulators. These roles face potential erasure in a world of do-it-yourself publishing.

In the early years of the Internet, 'news groups' provided a rudimentary system by which users could post messages to topic related threads. Anyone could publish their own text on the listing, and UseNet groups were highly popular in the early 1990s.

With popularity came problems of scale, however, and many UseNet lists had to be 'moderated' by an overseeing team to deal with an increase in abusive postings (known as 'flaming') and the clogging up of groups with commercial or obscene content ('spamming'). The subsequent arrival of the graphical browser in 1993 made pictorial content a central part of the Internet medium. The commercial development of web authoring programs allowed users to design their own 'Internet pages' in a word-processing interface and publish their material on the World Wide Web. A majority of the pages that initially appeared were highly personal in nature, representing the hobbies and interests of their authors. Subsequently, however, the personal homepage developed in two different arenas. First, some personal pages were extended into larger websites, containing essays, poems, photographs and personal diaries. These, then, were public expressions of private lives (and the forerunners of SNS). Second, the concept of personal homepages was adopted by major institutions with a public relations motive in mind. This gave rise to the convention where employees are encouraged to publish personal homepages which include their image and explain their professional role, thereby giving a 'human face' to their company or employer. These 'personal' pages tend to be more standardized in format and sanitized in nature, making this usage of the format akin to an electronic CV.

The growing use of 'interactive scripting' within the coding of Internet pages saw new dynamic features being added to personal pages in the 2000s. Common applications included online forms, 'hit counters', bulletin boards, chatrooms and automated news listings. With both personal and corporate websites employing these new tools, the World Wide Web offered instant personal publishing alongside dynamic user-generated content produced by site visitors. As such, the function of the old UseNet newsgroups was superseded by site-specific discussion lists which allowed site creators to gather feedback from, and generate discussion amongst, their readership. The rise of interactive publishing in this form was noted by traditional publishers of information, who in the most part decided to do nothing. One important exception was the BBC, which launched its online news service in 1997. Traditional commercial news providers, by contrast, had to mull over whether online editions would diminish their 'real' sales or whether they would increase their readership. Crucially, they were without a viable model for collecting a fee for access to information. This did not become available until the second Internet decade, when the growth of the online advertising industry made commercial news a profitable proposition. The intervening period allowed amateur and activist news and commentary to carve out a visible space for citizen-authored news sources on the World Wide Web.

The Blogosphere

The era of the weblog began in 1998 with the launch of online platforms (such as OpenDiary) that allowed users to publish their own updateable Internet Content within an indexed collection. Since these services were fully automated and coded 'server-side', there was no need for users to possess specialized web-editing or coding skills. By simply adding their content into the 'shell' provided by the host application, authors could generate new content and update content quickly, as well as opt to include common interactive tools such as bulletin boards and newsfeeds. Visitors to blogs could comment on what they read and contribute links to other sites. All of this served to make Internet publishing more accessible to the general public. Once the popularity of automated personal publishing applications became apparent, various platforms followed, including: LiveJournal, DiaryLand and Blogger.com. Somewhere in the process, the term 'weblog' was shortened to just 'blog'. Thus, 'blogs' were written by 'bloggers', and by 2000 the era of popular blogging was under way. By 2007, there were over 20 million blogs on the Internet. More recently, it has been estimated that there are 70 million blogs online (Technorati 2011). Many bloggers remain content to focus their Internet publishing on their personal experiences of life or share photos of their holidays or of their favourite cat. Others use the format to enthuse on particular hobbies and lifestyles, or to sell their home-made products or expertise. However, some prominent blogs have been produced by voluntary organizations, political activists and other civil society groups. Thus, a significant number of bloggers are using the platform to offer political comment and to share their own views on news and current events.

It is this kind of citizen-based journalism that has increasingly drawn attention from the professional realms of journalism and academia, primarily because it appears to represent a novel manifestation of Habermas's description of a democratic public sphere. As with other earlier Internet formats, the blog started out as a primarily North American format, and blogging continues to be most prevalent in the United States. In the context of the politically charged atmosphere since 2000, bloggers from across the political spectrum have used the medium to share their views on the major events shaping American life. Debates over the atrocities of 9/11, the Iraq War, political corruption, and the perceived bias of the mainstream American media have all become hotly debated topics with a large readership (Matheson and Allen 2009). For those on the left of American politics, the narrow corporate interests that control America's traditional media offer up a diet of propaganda and deception about the real events taking place in the world today. For those on the right, the mainstream media are staffed with a coterie of politically correct, left-liberal intellectuals who manipulate information and exclude the common-sense views of the people. For both of these reasons, bloggers of many different persuasions have taken up public commentary in a personal idiom. The grassroots perspective of these commentaries, and their typically anonymous authors, makes blogging culture distinctly different from the protocols of professional journalism. This hotbed of partisan commentary on public life has been favourably related to Habermas's account of public debate via the notion of the 'blogosphere'.

The concept of the blogosphere recalls the public sphere idea of Habermas, a provocative if elusive way to think about the social geography of public communication – the realm of reason, argument and dialogue where public opinion emerges . . . the public sphere is often thought to be a mediated space, with the news media providing this visible forum of public voices. In this regard, the range of sources and perspectives permitted by professional news gatekeepers establishes the limits of the public sphere they manage. Alternatively, we may conceptualise the blogosphere as a conversation distributed more broadly across citizens and journalists. Where traditionally journalism was charged with monitoring and reflecting public expression, citizens can now hold these conversations amongst themselves.

Stephen D. Reese, Lou Rutigliano, Kideuk Hyun, Jaekwan Jeong (2007), 'Mapping the Blogosphere: Professional and Citizen-based Media in the Global News Arena', *Journalism*, 8(3): 237

One of the central problems facing bloggers who want to reach a wide public audience is that many Internet search engines favour high-traffic, large and frequently updated websites. Thus, in order to achieve visibility for their blogs in search returns, bloggers collectively invented the tactic of 'Google-bombing'. It was observed that the Google algorithm favoured recently updated and heavily interlinked websites, but was less concerned with overall size and traffic volumes. By consciously promoting cross-linking between blogs and by linking their own blogs to the most popular search terms, crafty bloggers were able to amplify this effect and get on to the first page of Google returns for almost any search. This gave them the necessary means to gain massive public exposure in an era where search portals increasingly dictate the browsing habits of Internet users (see Halavais 2009). The conscious manipulation of search algorithms is, of course, as old as the World Wide Web itself, but the particular effectiveness of 'Google-bombing' has been significant in gaining blogs the public prominence they have enjoyed in recent years. A negative version of the same technique is to create multiple links to official websites using a negative phrase, which has the result of making that website appear in Google when the phrase is used.

Employing both tactics, bloggers from both sides of the political debate have scored high-profile 'hits' on the established media in recent years. In 2002, Senate Republican Leader Trent Lott made remarks suggesting a failed Presidential candidate who ran for the White House on a racist platform in the 1940s would have 'saved America a lot of trouble' if he had been victorious. This comment, made in the presence of the mainstream media, was largely ignored, with only a minor report on his remarks appearing in the back pages of the *New York Times*. However, the story came to the attention of bloggers who debated it vociferously, attacking Lott repeatedly and publicizing the remarks until he was forced to resign, along with the editors of the *New York Times* (Khan and Kellner 2004: 92). In 2004, CBS aired a story in which President Bush's service in the National Guard was placed in disrepute on the basis of what they claimed were authentic official documents of the time. Conservative bloggers challenged the claims, assessing that the documents were false. Their media campaigns forced CBS to investigate further into the documents, which, as it turned out, could not be verified. This led to the ousting of the show's anchorman and producer and retraction of the claims made in the story. Both of these incidents illustrate a new dynamic in which established media professionals are challenged and deposed by popular blogging campaigns. They could be seen as exemplars of the 'people power' of blogging, but they are equally indicative of an adversarial relationship between the blogosphere and established journalism. In response to these challenges, professional news providers are quick to point out the lack of editorial control, checking of facts or gate-keeping of quality in the blogosphere.

The Bloggerati

The blogging phenomenon has challenged the established media at the very moment when they were consolidating their own presence in online news. It is an unequal battle at many levels, with the mainstream press enjoying privileged access to information, and the bloggers enjoying the privilege of unregulated bias and unaccountability. One logical response has taken the flavour of 'if you can't beat them, join them'. As such, blogging is now being widely adopted as a news format by professional journalists, either alongside their traditional presentation or in a personal capacity. Similarly, politically minded academics (no longer content to be confined to low-circulation academic journals) have embraced blogging with enthusiasm. Politicians and public servants have started writing blogs as a more 'personal' way of communicating with their constituents. Various lobby groups have funded the setting up of blogs and mobilized their members to 'flame' the online opposition, rig Internet polls and swamp the bulletin board forums now being routinely offered by mainstream news outlets. As a result of all this activity, the division between professional news media, organized politics and amateur blogging is becoming somewhat blurred. As such, it is clear that the mainstream media have been seriously rattled by these developments and that the world of journalism is taking the blogosphere very seriously indeed.

> In twentieth-century democratic societies, people wishing to have their words and ideas published or broadcast had to contend with editorial policies that were generally based upon ideology or what advertisers would support or the public buy . . . The Internet changed one of the great obstacles to true freedom of the press by eliminating or greatly reducing the cost of production and distribution . . . This new freedom to publish at will has caused journalists and editors to reevaluate the role of mainstream, professional media. If you want more information about a current event today, you can easily search across blogs, newspapers and other sources, finding stories far more diverse and extensive than those traditionally printed in a newspaper or relayed on television news . . . As blogs became a familiar genre, the mainstream media began to discuss whether blogging was a threat to journalism and to the media . . . Journalists began to ask a question that kept recurring: is blogging journalism?
>
> Jill Walker Rettberg (2008), *Blogging*, Cambridge: Polity, pp. 84–5

Whilst the blogosphere is commonly associated with an abundance of information along a pluralist model, Stephen Reese et al. (2007) have argued that the world of blogging is highly compartmentalized. Most bloggers provide hyperlinks to other sources of a similar disposition, pointing readers towards an information trail that tends to affirm existing views rather than broadening viewpoints within a debate. Although this is also true of traditional media to some extent, blogs tend to favour a more extreme polarization of viewpoints, since they lack the formal centralizing mechanism established by traditional media controls (and the 'professional' tones of objectivity). Similarly, traditional news sources are rarely involved in inciting their readership to direct action, and this has been a marked feature of the blogging culture. Such incitement may range from urging readers to vote in certain online polls in order to influence public perception, to lobby politicians or to assemble digitally connected activists in 'smart mobs' who take their mutual consensus out on to the streets (Rheingold 2003). Thus, while the increasing levels of public participation in the media apparatus might please Habermas, it seems likely that he would also see the polarization and compartmentalization of communication as a negative development (see Habermas 1984, 1987). In that respect, the world of citizen media typically appears more ideological than reasonable, and far more partisan than consensual in its immediate goals.

> The online world, while making possible easy exchange among citizens and journalists, also supports the creation of balkanized subgroups that form around any idea of interest. These cyber-communities raise similar issues of political insularity: the ideological equivalent to 'ethnic

cleansing'. If reasoned dialog among perspectives marks a healthy community and public sphere, the potential for 'link interbreeding' to produce such echo chambers is worrisome . . . Online overlap is often an automated media-driven process through links, recommendations, and blogrolls (lists of permanent links to other websites/weblogs on the homepage of a weblog) that will send readers to a variety of sources based on their interests they express . . . websites link to sources that support the sites argument, and blogrolls normally follow a conservative/liberal litmus test . . . this structure suggest a polarized linking pattern, with conservative and liberal blogs linking most to their own communities . . . in a reciprocal cycle of mutual affirmation.

Stephen D. Reese, Lou Rutigliano, Kideuk Hyun and Jaekwan Jeong (2007), 'Mapping the Blogosphere: Professional and Citizen-based Media in the Global News Arena', *Journalism*, 8(3): 240

Another compelling genre of blogging has been the personal accounts of professional life produced by 'insiders' within various industries. Sometimes this has entailed naked self-promotion (careerism), being designed to get the attention of superiors with only a veneer of anonymity. More problematically for employers, it has sometimes involved conscious 'whistle-blowing' of malpractice or the premeditated public sharing of company secrets. Companies have generally been alarmed by the appearance of employee blogs and have taken moves to crack down on this form of blogging. Given the amount of information that is typically made available through blogging over time, it is very hard for the authors to retain their anonymity. Employers can and do track down employees who blog their inside knowledge freely on the Web, resulting in a slew of lawsuits in the US in the past decade. It seems that while the 'personal homepage' is seen as a useful tool for giving an enterprise a human face, the more frank accounts that emerge when employees start publishing a public diary are generally not the sort of thing that the public relations department approves of. Of course, there are also numerous 'approved' blogs intended to promote a positive image for a range of occupations and organizations, but these legally cleared and more contrived endeavours make for less enjoyable reading than the fly-on-the-wall accounts which get frantically chased down by company lawyers. Thus, occupational blogging raises a further question regarding which bits of our professional life actually belong to us and which bits are suitable to the public domain.

Many accounts of the blogging craze take note of the celebrity status achieved by a handful of the most popular bloggers (whether they are political commentators or knitting enthusiasts) (Humphreys 2008). Every field produces a few 'winners' and some of the more entrepeneurial bloggers have been able to translate the popularity of their web forums into book contracts and substantial incomes from online advertising. This, of course, has led to a rush of pulp publications divulging the secrets of getting rich by blogging (e.g., Rowse and Garrett 2010). In a world of 70 million bloggers, this is both statistically unlikely and an inevitable occurrence. When we assay the elite group of bloggers, however, the most popular blogs almost invariably relate to topics that can draw upon substantial political or consumer bases already existing in society. As such, the professional production of blogs serving the pervasive field of celebrity culture has developed rapidly, with stars offering personal blogs and tweets as a publicity tool and fans reworking the 'fan site' into a diary format (Burns 2009). Not everyone is of equal interest in public debate, as Alexander Halavais notes: 'Of the millions of blogs in the blogosphere and videos on you tube, most get viewed by only one or two people, while a small number get millions of hits, far from equal access to the greater web audience' (2009: 59). For this reason alone, the egalitarian nature of the blogging craze can be significantly overstated, a celebratory tendency which has been true of Internet publishing from the outset. In the case of online diaries, success also relates to a number of factors including technical skills, network access, professional contacts, political affinity, financial acumen and available time. The quality of writing also continues to be significant, although few accounts of blogging take note of the import of this 'old media' skill. Samuel Pepys was not the only diarist of the Restoration period, but the longevity of his work suggests he was one of the most accomplished (2003). The same might be said of the leaders within the contemporary field of rhetoric being deployed on the Internet.

Box 13.2 Blogging the question (by 'dr. media')

- Is blogging evidence of citizens taking matters into their own hands, challenging old monopolies on public expression and old hierarchies of knowledge?
- Is blogging the electronic equivalent of writing on toilet walls, where bloggers can engage in smear campaigns without bearing any of the consequences?
- Is blogging evidence of a flowering of personal expression with a potential for recording and sharing the rich tapestry of human lives and experiences, across classes, cultures, nations and generations?
- Is blogging evidence of the paucity of human subjects, and their willingness to be confined to a single generic format for the benefit mostly of market researchers, sociologists and Internet advertisers?
- Is blogging building new networks of collaborative knowledge and new communities of association within electronic space that are turning the tide against social isolation and self-alienation?
- Is blogging simply providing enclaves where we can gather with those most like ourselves to the deliberate exclusion of others, with this herd instinct providing evidence of our continuing deficiency as empathic social agents?
- Is blogging giving us access to a new political forum that is richer, safer and more satisfying than the mainstream 'circus' of political life?
- Is blogging a self-indulgent substitute for an unrealized modern society, primarily intended to make up for the failure of democratic ideals?

Participatory Journalism

There is a very obvious disjuncture between the multivocal world of unregulated and partisan commentary championed through Internet publishing and the historically privileged conventions and traditions of the old fourth estate. Nonetheless, it would be a mistake to draw arbitrary distinctions between an 'objective' field of journalism and a 'subjective' domain of grassroots commentary. Scholars over many years have noted how the operation of the media institutions has been subordinated to the interests of the state and a 'professionalized' civil society recruited from a distinct social class (Beharrell, Davis, Eldridge and Hewitt 2009a/b). It is equally well known that the editorial line taken by mainstream media is heavily influenced by the interests and political agendas of their owners and proprietors (Curran and Seaton 2003; Doyle 2002). At the same time, the pursuit of advertising revenues and circulation figures imposes its own influence on the conduct of the profession, with an increasingly provocative, scandalous and partisan news culture (tabloidization) also becoming a target of criticism (Biressi and Nunn 2007). These distinctive 'framings' of information undermine the ideal of the fourth estate serving the interests of public accountability (D'Angelo and Kuypers 2010). These problems are not news in themselves, but they provide a ready means for justifying the 'disintermediation' of public information and an assault upon the mainstream. In the blogosphere, however, the delivery of information is equally, if not more, subject to partisan influence. On a regular basis, the 'genuine' voices of blogging turn out to be professional public relations consultants and employees of political organizations. Advertising is also beginning to play a crucial role in the economy of blogging. In that sense, blogging is not immune to any of the ills that it identifies in the media 'mainstream'.

A more critical distinction that can be made between the public authority of the mainstream media and the emerging domain of participatory journalism concerns their adherence to different models of democracy itself. The traditions of the press are firmly grounded in the traditions of representative democracy. In that respect, professional journalists are invested with authority over the domain of public opinion. They are quasi-official representatives acting for the general public. In practice, this means deciding what is in the public interest as well as responding to the demands of the public. By contrast, the blogging culture ascribes more or less explicitly to the operation of direct democracy. It seeks to express the interests and views of private individuals across a broad spectrum, and without any representative mediation. The accessibility of open publishing provides for a much wider terrain of interests and opinions than the established parameters of mainstream journalism. The blogosphere lays claim to an authentic subjectivity in place of public objectivity, since bloggers speak on their own behalf and not on the behalf of others. Consequently, the blogosphere is naturally disposed to engage in stronger and more emotive rhetorics. Their antagonism to the established fourth estate mirrors its own function, by demanding public accountability from those formally charged with the same task (Bruns 2005). In that sense, the blogging culture is not just 'for the people' but also 'of the people'.

The politics of citizen media via the Internet are inextricably caught up in the broader tradition of a radical press (Earl and Kimport 2011). In its present form, the blogging culture is aligned with a shared adherence to social movement theory that can be seen throughout contemporary digital culture. Manuel Castells saw popular movements driven by single issues as the primary drivers of social reform in network society (1997). Pippa Norris saw the digital media as providing the tools by which digital 'insurgents' would take on the political establishment (2000). Henry Jenkins promotes the rise of fan culture as a democratic intervention in the public domain (2006). The practice of blogging encapsulates all of these tendencies in contemporary public culture. Leah Lievrouw locates blogs accordingly as part of a wider domain of 'new media activism' that includes open-source software, Indymedia, hackers, file-sharers and smart mobs (2011). In light of this consensus upon the merits of grassroots activism and participatory culture, it becomes necessary to cast a critical eye over the radical rhetoric deployed by the proponents of digital culture. Even a cursory overview of the subject matter of blogs reveals that the politics of the digital public sphere are not overwhelmingly radical in nature. Indeed, the majority of content is apolitical and many of the most prominent political bloggers are card-carrying conservatives (of both left and right). In that sense, the form of open publishing is more radical in itself than the majority of its content. What is most telling about the rise of a 'DIY' publishing culture is the extent to which it reveals a broad suspicion of public professions in almost every aspect of life. This position chimes with a foundational commitment to personal expression that eschews any form of censorship or accountability.

> Established political actors, just like major corporations, can be expected to adapt the internet to their usual forms of communication, providing information online but not really reinventing themselves or rethinking their strategy in the digital world, unless successfully challenged. In contrast, insurgent organizations traditionally have fewer political assets, fewer traditional advantages, but also fewer inhibitions about adapting flexibly to the opportunities for information and communication via the internet . . . digital politics can be expected to have most impact in levelling the playing field, not completely but at least partially, for a diverse range of insurgent movements and challenger's such as transnational advocacy networks, alternative social movements, protest organizations and minor parties, such as those concerned with environmentalism, globalization, human rights, world trade, conflict resolution and single-issue causes from all shades of the political spectrum . . . The internet does not drive these insurgent movements – these causes are triggered by deeper passions – but it facilitates their organization, mobilization and expression.
>
> Pippa Norris (2000), *Digital Divide: Civic Engagement, Information Poverty and the Internet Worldwide*, New York: Cambridge University Press, p. 281

The Future of Public Authority

In responding to the effective emergence of an interactive public sphere, governments everywhere are forced, to some extent at least, to demonstrate their public authority by entering this turbulent domain of public discussion under new terms and conditions. Their motives are necessarily different from bloggers and activists. This becomes evident from the motives, scope and application of various initiatives in e-governance. At the same time, 'direct government' initiatives mark an important concession to a powerful public medium without any obvious owner. These experiments with direct democracy must necessarily balance the politics of 'being in touch' with the perils of 'being on call' to the whims of the blogosphere. This untidy medium marks the new terrain on which the political establishment seeks to engage its digital citizens. A stranglehold over media institutions is no longer a guarantee of controlling information. This is also a context, however, in which an easily corrected falsehood can spread so rapidly that it takes on more significance than the most carefully researched exposé. A fully Twitter-literate Barrack Obama has had his own experiences with this phenomenon. Interactivity guarantees a right of reply, but defensive and corrective statements encounter a stone wall of public scepticism. Indeed, the ingrained antagonism towards experts in the blogosphere habitually deflects the 'authoritative' voices that have traditionally monopolized the public sphere. Accordingly, a fundamental problem for the establishment of public authority in the digital medium is that the notionally democratic mandate of representative government makes it nigh impossible to make any overt criticism of the wisdom of 'the grassroots'.

Nonetheless, it is important to remember that the technorati are not the general public. At best, they are the loudest, most invested (and arguably narcissistic) personalities within the body politic. There is no doubt, however, that they have power-fully reinvigorated the operation and scope of the public sphere. Certainly, we may have to reconsider the predominant theme of 'political disengagement' identified by profes-sional commentators (on the basis of declining electoral turnouts, party memberships and newspaper circulations). This decline is given the lie by the obvious passion with which the writers of political blogs assail their opponents and champion their causes. This frenetic activity suggests a very significant measure of political commitment amongst the general population (every bit as much as it suggests disenchantment with traditional political forums and media institutions). The enthusiasm with which people engage in bulletin-board politics, and the floods of readers' comments that characterize every kind of public announcement illustrate a passionate need to be heard. All of this indicates that democracy is alive and well at the 'end of history' and that it flies 'in the face' of mainstream political consensus. Consequently, new questions inevitably arise for the interface between public discussion and public authority.

If we assess the present situation against Jürgen Habermas's ideal of a public sphere, we can identify effective progress in participatory mechanisms, the disintermediation of specialists and the unprecedented expansion of the depth and scope of public debate. It is equally critical that the public sphere is being reconfigured at an international scale. However, this extension of democratic participation in public communication has not revived the age of 'reasonable' consensus. It has in fact exacerbated the pre-vailing tendencies towards polarization and fragmentation that Habermas identified as the primary ill of public life. The reason for this is simple. The ethos of the digital medium is powerfully committed to direct expression, diversity and argument. Citizen media are reformist in their ambitions, but they show little inclination to take up the responsibilities of representative mediation and forging public consensus. As such, the enlargement of the public sphere reveals a significant shift towards direct democracy as an expressive practice.

In an era of public disenchantment with representative government, it has become clear that personal and political expression and private and public speech are becom-ing inextricably intermeshed. This will have great importance in shaping the opera-tion of political life in the years to come. We could see the apparent diminishing of detached consensus as a failing of public responsibility, but it is equally valid to argue that this is 'real' democracy in action. We could see the elevation of personal agendas as being the very ill that representative government was designed to contain, but it is equally valid to argue that the integrity of public institutions cannot be maintained without such scrutiny. This is as true of the professional news media as it is of civil servants and market makers. In that sense, it is important to note that Habermas's public sphere is an ideal which public communication is only ever likely to achieve in part. It is akin, therefore, to the conjoined notions of democracy, civil society and the fourth estate. Nonetheless, in an era when the volumes of public communica-tion have increased on such a scale as to recast the terms of debate, these ideals may prove to be more important than ever in making any reasonable assessment of public authority.

Think and Discuss

1. Key Terms
Can you describe in simple language what is meant by the following terms found in this chapter?

- Direct democracy
- E-governance
- Public sphere
- Grassroots
- Blogosphere

2. Critical Questions
Try answering the following questions, drawing upon your own understanding, experience and knowledge.
1. How much faith do you place in the objectivity of professional news media?
2. In what ways do digital media provide for public engagement in representative democracy?
3. What are the benefits and drawbacks of blogs and open publishing as information sources?
4. How crucial is the Internet for your own participation in democratic politics?
5. What criteria do you apply to the credibility and authority of news, information and commentary?

Further Reading

Beckett, Charlie and Ball, James (2012) *Wikileaks: News in the Network Era*, Cambridge: Polity.

Bruns, Axel (2005) *Gatewatching: Collaborative Online News Production*, New York: Peter Lang.

Budd, Leslie and Harris, Lisa (eds) (2009) *e-Governance: Managing or Governing?*, London and New York: Routledge.

Davis, Richard (2005) *Politics Online: Blogs, Chatrooms and Discussion Groups in American Democracy*, New York: Routledge.

Habermas, Jürgen (1992) *The Transformation of the Public Sphere: an Enquiry into a Category of Bourgeois Society*, Cambridge: Polity.

Lievrouw, Leah A. (2011) *Alternative and Activist New Media*, Cambridge: Polity.

Matheson, Donald and Allan, Stuart (2009) *Digital War Reporting*, Cambridge: Polity.

Norris, Pippa (2000) *Digital Divide: Civic Engagement, Information Poverty and the Internet Worldwide*, New York: Cambridge University Press.

Papacharissi, Zia (2010b) *A Private Sphere: Democracy in a Digital Age*, Cambridge: Polity.

Rettburg, Jill Walker (2008) *Blogging*, Cambridge: Polity.

Go Online

Blogger – http://www.blogger.com/
Directgov (UK) – http://directgov.uk/en/index.htm
Directgov e-petitions (UK) – http://epetitions.direct.gov.uk/
Open Government Initiative (US) – http://www.whitehouse.gov/open
Press Association (UK) – http://www.pressassociation.com/
Technorati – http://www.technorati.com
White House (US) – http://www.whitehouse.gov/

CHAPTER 14

Under Scrutiny

One of the most fundamental features of authority is a disposition for keeping an eye on things. Throughout history, the organizing forces within human societies have monitored their populations in the interest of reducing crime, suppressing dissent and raising revenues. In the close world of co-presence we have a natural capacity for mutual observation, but the larger societies that arose with the advanced agricultures of the ancient world predicated a need for more systematic and impersonal methodologies for assaying individuals within the larger society. Subsequently, the era of modern and industrial societies from the eighteenth century onwards naturally encouraged the widespread operation of surveillance activities by formal state bureaucracies. Within the productive mechanisms of the economy, the rise of industrial capitalism also gave birth to new surveillance techniques intended to manage and discipline the workforces assembled for factory production. The rise of mass participation in political systems in the late nineteenth century made the monitoring of organized dissent an increasing preoccupation of authority. The ensuing ideological conflicts of the twentieth century provided obvious justifications for constructing expansive institutions devoted to intelligence gathering on the activities and ideas of the home population (both in the communist East and the capitalist West). At the beginning of this century, a desire to finesse the consumption patterns of the general populace, and to pre-empt the growing reach of groups engaged in extra-governmental violence, saw further innovations in information-gathering technologies led by governmental, military and commercial concerns.

Michel Foucault on Disciplinary Society

The nature of surveillance in the modern world has a number of critical aspects. First of all, it becomes a domain over which the state claims prerogative. Second, it becomes rationalized and institutionalized. Third, it becomes increasingly automated and technological in its function. Finally, its operation becomes diffused throughout the social structure, enabling mutual surveillance on a mass scale. It is another, more corrective, version of the global village (McLuhan and Fiore 1968). It is also, however, a prerequisite for any democratic society which demands the public scrutiny of governance itself. In that sense, the ideal of an informed public sphere implies the application of techniques of observation and record that touch upon, potentially at least, every positioning of public interest (Habermas 1992). A legal consensus on the privileges of a 'private domain' subsequently demarcates the boundaries of public interest. Even at this stage, however, the private has become a privilege to be afforded by a collective mechanism of surveillance. In that sense, the surveillance apparatus claims sovereignty over all social life, but by its own rules elects to become selective in its application. This is what gives us the modernist notion of 'privacy', a set of boundaries that are inherently contingent and disciplinary in nature (Papacharissi 2010b; Schoeman 2008; Wacks 2010).

Box 14.1 Evolution of surveillance techniques

Spies and informers
The census
Censorship of printers
Formal constabulary
Social science
Modern passports and identity papers
Personal financial records
Radio intercepts
Wiretapping
Market research
CCTV cameras
Speed cameras
Population databases
Point of sale data
Online monitoring
Spyware and data mining
Data profiling
DNA records
Biometrics

During the 1970s, the French social philosopher Michel Foucault provided the most influential set of references for conceptualizing surveillance in modern society. Foucault was a key thinker in the 'poststructuralist' philosophy that surpassed the 'structuralism' (and existentialism) that had dominated the French humanities before 1968. His seminal work, *Discipline and Punish,* traces the evolution from feudal practices of grotesque physical torture to the rational, psychological techniques of modern 'correctional' institutions (1977). This work can be seen more broadly as part of Foucault's larger 'post-structuralist' project of deconstructing the historical narratives of progress. In that sense, many of Foucault's works can appear deeply contradictory. They offer a critique of any useful application of historical knowledge, yet they achieve this through largely historical accounts. They seek to perpetuate the foundational philosophical tradition of Immanuel Kant (2007), but do so in a form that chimes more with the nihilistic precision and moral equivalence of Friedrich Nietzsche (2003). *Discipline and Punish,* however, is one of Foucault's more accessible works, and it has informed a broad series of debates in sociology about the operation of power in the modern world. One common historicist reading (and thus one Foucault would most likely have rejected) marks a transition from physical to psychological forms of coercion in the evolution of the modern world. Another, more expansive, reading focuses on the dispersal of disciplinary techniques from the prison to the factory and, ultimately, across the society as a whole. The implication of this is that the rationalization of public institutions, modes of correction and modes of production becomes coterminous and, as a result, correctional methods become widely diffused. The disciplinary society, then, is a prison both within and without walls. One outcome of disciplinary action on this mass scale is 'governmentality', a new form of impersonal, rationalized, authoritarian rule. Another, quite different, outcome of this blanketing of discipline across society is that the imperatives of coercion become internalized by all social subjects and applied collectively in daily life.

The disciplinary society describes a situation where power is no longer concentrated in the hands of a few absolutists, but instead becomes diffused amongst the entire social structure. As such, controls are enforced by the entire population (both upon others and upon themselves). The disciplinary society is a social formation in which we become both jailor and the jailed. The primary mechanism for the rise of 'self-discipline' of this kind is not the old medieval regime of torture and confinement, but rather a new set of techniques that are essentially intangible and visual. Foucault argues that modern societies engage in perpetual observation, where the act of watching is necessarily combined with the experience of being watched. This permanent operation of visibility restricts and regulates the occurrence of deviant acts, as well as our responses to them. To illustrate this model, Foucault employs the example of a new form of prison architecture developed by the British utilitarian philosopher Jeremy Bentham in the eighteenth century. At the heart of Bentham's 'panopticon' design was the recognition that the best way of controlling the behaviour of prison inmates was to give them the impression that they were under constant observation. This was, with the technology of the time, physically impossible. Bentham's proposed innovation, however, was to organize the cells in his jail in a brightly lit circle around a central observation tower, from which guards who were themselves shielded from view could monitor the actions of each inmate. They still could not watch everyone at once, but each prisoner would be unable to tell whether they were being watched at any given time. Thus, the *potential* of observation would of itself cast a disciplining effect over its subjects.

> The major effect of the panopticon is to induce in the inmate a state of conscious and permanent visibility that assures the automatic functioning of power. So to arrange things that the surveillance is permanent in its effects, even if it is discontinuous in its action; that the perfection of power should tend to render its actual exercise unnecessary; that this architectural apparatus should be a machine for creating and sustaining a power relation independent of the person who exercises it; in short, that the inmates should be caught up in a power situation of which they themselves are the bearers . . . Bentham laid down the principle that power should be visible and unverifiable. Visible: the inmate will constantly have before his eyes the tall outline of the central tower from which he is spied upon. Unverifiable: the inmate must never know whether he is being looked at at any one moment; but he must be sure that he may always be so.
>
> The panoptic schema, without disappearing as such or losing any of its properties, was destined to spread through the social body; its vocation was to become a generalized function . . . [the Panopticon] has a role of amplification; although it arranges power, although it is intended to make it more economic and more effective, it does so not for power itself, nor for the immediate salvation of a threatened society: its aim is to strengthen the social forces – to increase productivity, to develop the economy, spread education, raise the level of public morality; to increase and multiply . . . On the whole, therefore, one can speak of the formation of a disciplinary society.
>
> Michel Foucault (1977), *Discipline and Punish: The Birth of the Prison*, New York: Random House, pp. 201 and 208

The Orwellian Nightmare

Our experience of the impersonal operation of state-sponsored surveillance goes far beyond the moral complexities of modern philosophy and correctional systems. The rise of modern media systems cannot in practice be separated from the innovations in surveillance practices that have gone with them. It is well known that the totalitarian regimes of the mid-twentieth century instigated an unprecedented regime of discipline upon their subjects, and even democratic and liberal societies came to incorporate and naturalize mass observation as a core function of modern government. The state-sanctioned horrors of the 1930s and 1940s, carried out with such rational and efficient brutality, relied upon an enforced consensus for which surveillance was both essential and pervasive. These tendencies did not end with the political and military defeat of fascism and they subsequently provided the inspiration for George Orwell's famous novel, *1984*, that describes the life of an individual within a society where 'Big Brother', the authoritarian persona of the state, monitors every aspect of its citizens' lives (1949). This omniscient (all-seeing) presence not only worked ceaselessly to detect acts of political resistance and criminality, but also sought to pre-empt mental dissent ('thought crime') that might lead to subversive actions in the future. Individuals within Orwell's fictional (or rather allegorical) society were thus perpetually disciplined by the constant surveillance made possible by the electronic apparatus of the 'ministry of truth'. Orwell's account was inspired both by the totalitarian regimes of the 1940s and by his own experiences of producing propaganda for the BBC during the Second World War. Orwell's book was deeply resonant with a public readership horrified by the recent memory of state systems where library records were used to hunt down potential subversives and send them off to labour camps (and worse).

Nonetheless, the advent of the Cold War in the early 1950s saw institutions of internal surveillance strengthened in all the countries of the 'free world'. Suspected 'sympathizers' on both sides were vigorously pursued, censured or purged by government agencies (Gorlizki and Khlevniuk 2006; Schrecker 2002). Postal communications were intercepted and daily routines and meetings were photographed by various 'agents' of government. Along with established methods of observation and 'keeping files' on people 'of interest', the growth of mass-media systems enabled many new surveillance techniques. With the spread of telephones into private homes during the 1950s and 1960s, telephone calls could easily be monitored through the use of 'wiretaps'. Famously, it was the use of surveillance for domestic political purposes that led to the resignation of US President Nixon in 1974 (Kutler 2010). In the other direction, the British intelligence services began bugging the offices of British Prime Ministers from the 1960s onwards. This atmosphere of paranoia and suspicion took its toll on leaders such as Harold Wilson, and was also reflected in the wider mythology of 'secret agents', 'brainwashing' and shadowy plots that infused the popular culture of the Cold War decades (McKnight 2002; Field 2005). Following the spate of demonstrations and strikes that spread throughout the Western world in the late 1960s, another form of mass-media surveillance that grew in usage was closed circuit television (CCTV) (Armstrong and Norris 1999). This application of television technology, pioneered by Nazi Germany in 1942, was directed to the monitoring of activities in public space.

Not all of this deepening culture of surveillance was state-sponsored, however, since the 'free press' also became increasingly assertive in its pursuit of 'investigative reporting', using many of the self-same techniques of espionage. Moreover, outside of the realm of 'public life', an entirely new industry for gathering information about individuals in society had become firmly established during the 1950s and 1960s. This was the world of 'market research', where the intended perfection of mass consumption as the central plank of the economic system encouraged manufacturers to invest large sums in finding out as much as they could about the people who bought, or who might buy, the goods that they produced (McPhee 1963; Cohen 2004). In this context, the emergence of market researchers as an influential professional group saw the industrial application of social research methods for the purposes of monitoring the behaviours of the modern shopper (McGivern 2005; Poynter 2010). At the outset, gathering this kind of information through surveys and consumer panels was time-consuming and expensive and the relatively small samples always made projections unreliable. Nonetheless, the scope of the practice, and its attendant linkages to social psychology and the advertising industry were well established immediately prior to the incoming tide of digitization (Kahle and Kim 2006; Harris and Sanborn 2009; Shrum 2003).

The Rise of the Database

The era of digital surveillance began in earnest with the institutional mainframe computers of the 1960s and 1970s. The various existing paper archives of information held by government departments were transferred into digital records that made storing and accessing information far more efficient (or at least, it did so when those systems were functioning reliably). In this initial stage, however, the information being digitized was mostly information that was already routinely collected (such as tax records and registrations of births, marriages and deaths). The databases that were created by different arms of government remained separate. These repositories were not networked and access to them remained a privilege of the originating departments. The architecture of these early databases was also primitive, lacking many of the more complex sorting and collating techniques ('relational algorithms') that would be developed in the decades to come. Nonetheless, the era of the database began some forty years ago, and this has subsequently proved to be a development that transforms the relationship between citizens and government (Miller 1971; Garfinkel 2000). As a somewhat authoritarian government publicity campaign sought to remind UK citizens in the late 2000s: 'You're in the Database'.

An equally significant development was the introduction of the 'credit card' (beginning in the 1960s). These new personal account devices allowed the purchasers of goods to spend freely without carrying large sums of cash. This was considered revolutionary at the time, since it allowed access to funds even when banks were closed (there were no ATMs for another decade). A significant by-product of these 'convenient' payment methods, however, was the creation of 'point-of-sale data' that matched individual purchasers to actual sales. This produced a parallel revolution in market research practices, because it automated the creation of detailed consumer profiles for each and every cardholder (Tadajewski and Jones 2008). For the first time, there was a wide-scale set of data concerning where, when and on what individuals spent their money. As credit cards became available to more and more people during the 1980s, the information collected about consumption patterns became a major commercial resource. The subsequent introduction of debit cards steadily displaced cheque books and cash as the primary means of payment in routine transactions, extending the wider virtualization of money into everyday life. This process vastly increased the power of banks over the rest of the economy, and it went hand in hand with the growth in personal credit facilities that drove the consumption bubble of the 1990s and 2000s. For the longer term, it also institutionalized a largely unregulated mechanism for recording the consumption habits of individual citizens, and thereby revealing their wealth, movements and interests.

Policing the Web

The spread of microcomputers throughout public and commercial workplaces led to an exponential increase in the production, storage and transferability of electronic information of all kinds. That is, beyond collecting and storing all manners of records on an unprecedented scale, networking allowed for the bringing together of disparate pieces of information from a wide range of information resources. Because so much of this information was attributed at the level of the individual, a remarkably rich profile of any citizen could now be collated by assembling the various pieces of data associated with them. Because the utility of this form of surveillance was obvious to both institutional and commercial interests, 'data-mining' applications for sifting and collating the information held in databases saw extensive development. This more dynamic form of information management provides an ideal combination with the routine collection of data. If someone becomes of interest, a large volume of their personal information is already available for retrieval. There is less of a need for targeted surveillance operations in the Cold War model, because everyone is already under surveillance. Database experts, rather than 'spooks' are in high demand.

Nonetheless, network technologies have not remained the preserve of expert technicians. The advent of the public Internet in the early 1990s saw millions of computer users link up to the largest information architecture the world had ever seen. The global configuration of the Internet and the search algorithms offered by the World Wide Web protocols gave the general public, for the first time in history, access to an unparalleled quantity of information about the world they lived in. If the credit card revolution had given market researchers access to information about people's spending habits, and electronic databases enabled governments to become more sophisticated in the way that they managed the information they held about their citizens, then the Internet gave the power of information (effectively, the power of seeing the world) to ordinary people. Moreover, in the initial phase of development, the information published and read via the Internet was an entirely anonymous and untraceable exchange. On this basis, utopian commentators such as Mark Poster predicated that the Internet would herald a new era where censorship and information control would become a thing of the past (1995).

If the technological basis of the media has habitually been viewed as a threat to democracy, how can theory account for the turn toward the construction of a technology (the internet) which appears to promote a decentralization of discourse, if not democracy itself, and appears to threaten the state (unmonitorable conversations), mock at private property (the infinite reproducibility of information) and flaunt moral propriety (the dissemination of images of unclothed people often in awkward positions)?

Mark Poster (1997), 'Cyber Democracy – Internet and the Public Sphere', in D. Porter (ed.), *Internet Culture*, London and New York: Routledge, pp. 210

This state of affairs, however, ran contradictory to the guiding logic of the 'information society'. It was not to last. With the rapid growth in Internet usage, law enforcement agencies became keenly aware of the potentials of the Internet for criminal activity. One area of concern that received widespread publicity was the use of the Internet to disseminate pornography. Pornography was restricted by laws in most countries in the world, which made this problematic in itself, but the nature of some of these images circulating on the World Wide Web was of even more serious concern. Early public discussions of the anonymous nature of Internet communication (arising from 'floating' IP addresses) centred upon the use of the Internet by paedophiles to exchange images (Akdeniz 2008). A further concern for many national governments was the use of the Internet by criminals, political dissidents and terrorists to conduct clandestine communications (Taylor et al. 2010). In light of these issues, police task forces were set up to monitor illegal activity on the Internet and legal experts began to work on the thorny issues surrounding illegal activity and legal jurisdiction in the new 'cyberspace'. Considerable pressure was applied to software manufacturers and to companies 'hosting' the file servers used by the Internet to pass on information about Internet users and to make Internet use an activity that could be effectively monitored.

These efforts to regulate Internet use bore fruit quickly. By 1996, Internet browsers were redesigned to store the pages that had been accessed by users in folders 'hidden' within the operating system used by their computer. The development of Internet 'cookies' created a mechanism where small files were invisibly downloaded to computers from the pages that their users visited. These cookies not only logged browsing activity but also identified the computer user each time they returned to a website. This allowed website managers to track the browsing activities of their users and to recognize them individually. The companies hosting Internet servers were generally less forthcoming than the software giants and initially resisted pressure to monitor and share information about their clients. Nonetheless, successive legislation introduced by various countries constructed a regime that by the early 2000s required Internet hosts to retain the data they handled for several years and to make it available to the relevant authorities upon request. This included the content of individual websites, users' surfing habits, financial transactions and electronic communications, including emails. Thus, within the space of a decade, the Internet went from being an unprecedented experiment in anonymous communication to being the most comprehensive mechanism of surveillance ever put into operation.

Box 14.2 The argument for digital surveillance

- That the Internet provides its users with the potential to circulate materials that undermine the codes of morality that guarantee our way of life
- That the capacity to communicate internationally through digital media is providing the

opportunity for transnational criminal networks and violent terrorist organizations to coordinate activities that threaten human life
- That the harvesting of information about citizens is crucial for the production of knowledge about society, which is essential for the planning of government services to provide for people's needs
- That the gathering of consumer data is the means by which the market is able to discern the personal desires and tastes of consumers and cater to them more efficiently
- That digital surveillance is an essential measure for combating identity theft in the era of e-commerce, and that electronic profiling highlights irregularities in commercial transactions and protects consumers and businesses alike
- That only those with 'something to fear' should worry about the extension of digital surveillance techniques

Spyware and Data Mining

As early as 1995, the first piece of software designed to harvest information from users' computers and transmit it to third parties was disseminated across the Internet. Since then, there has been intensive development of programs designed to exploit security loopholes in Internet browsers in order to install themselves on users' computers and transmit information about the data held on their hard drives, and about their browsing habits along with their personal details (Wall 2007). It has been estimated that 89 per cent of computers connected to the Internet are 'infected' with spyware of one kind or another (Webroot 2006). Some of these programs are clearly criminal in intent and are intended to uncover passwords and redirect financial information during online shopping, but for the most part the spyware industry is underwritten by the online advertising industry which uses the information gathered for 'targeted advertising'. Spyware programs are also commonly 'bundled' with free-to-download software applications. In recent years, the major commercial operating systems available for personal computers have also been reconfigured to gather substantial bodies of information about the habits of computer users. This entails making records of their usage of copyrighted materials (programs, media files, etc.) as well as their browsing habits and machine configuration. Unless these features are disabled by users, this information is automatically returned to the software companies in order to 'enhance the experience' of their customers. In the worst cases, some pieces of software cannot be operated without accepting the activation of these 'feedback' mechanisms

While legal institutions, law enforcements agencies and software providers were getting to grips with criminal activity on the Internet, the massive public uptake of the technology encouraged the development of major commercial platforms on the Internet. The use of the Internet for online catalogue-style shopping and as a distribution system for digital content was pioneered in the 1990s by companies like Amazon. com. Realizing the potential of the Internet as an interactive system, Amazon (and others) quickly saw that online shopping would automatically produce electronic records of consumers' preferences and habits and that this would become a major commercial asset. The use of payment records derived from the digitization of credit and debit cards was already transforming the market research industry. The Internet took this one step further, since the new combination of user-identification and interactivity allowed Amazon to target individual users with alternative products according to the profiles that they established through their purchasing patterns. Beyond this auto-mated 'sales assistant' function, the ever larger volumes of information being obtained as online shopping became popular meant that this body of data became a significant commercial property in itself. It has since become common practice to collect consumer profiles that are either shared with partner companies or exchanged for profit amongst commercial businesses.

Because consumer profiles are now being created and stored for such a large propor-tion of the population, and across such a wide field of activities, there is obvious util-ity in searching and collating these bodies of information. Simultaneously, the rise of 'e-governance' has also produced large stores of retrievable information about individu-als that can be matched with commercial data. Increasingly, there is formal interaction between state and market-sponsored forms of surveillance. Amazon UK will, for exam-ple, routinely notify the Television Licensing Authority (TVLA) whenever a customer purchases a TV display or recorder. This is a common-sense and pragmatic approach to the legal obligations that come with owning a TV set in British society. At another level, it is also one symptom of a new arrangement between government and the private sector by which the government is routinely notified of the purchasing habits of citi-zens. Into this merging of extensive commercial and state-operated surveillance prac-tices via the Internet, we must also account for the new bodies of data produced by GPS systems (or SatNavs), mobile phones, the electronic ticketing of most transport systems and numerous other forms of digitization that collectively produce a comprehensive body of information about almost every aspect of an individual's daily life. It is this body of data that is the raw material for the sophisticated techniques of data-mining that increasingly mark us out as creditworthy, in need of a computer upgrade or as a threat to national security (Ayres 2008; McCue 2006). It is equally significant, then, that the practice of data-mining is not conceived of as an historical review of past activity for its own sake, but rather as a mathematically precise technique for predicting the future actions of individuals.

Every message we write, every video we post, every item we buy or view, our time-space paths and patterns of social interaction all become data points in algorithms for sorting, predicting and managing our behaviour. Some of these data points are spontaneous – the result of the intentional action of consumers; others are induced, the result of ongoing, randomized experiments . . . The complexity of the algorithms and the opacity of correlation render it all but impossible for those without access to the databases to determine why they may have been denied a loan, targeted for a particular campaign message, or saturated with ads at a particular time and place . . . Much of this will hinge on whether the power to predict can be translated into the ability to manage behaviour, but this is the bet that marketers are making. Or more accurately, this is the bet that a society makes when it turns to a monitoring-based system of data-mining and predictive analysis.

Mark Andrejevic (2011), 'Surveillance and Alienation in the Online Economy', *Surveillance and Society*, 8(3): 278–87

The Surveillance Society

David Lyon is a Scottish sociologist who became a prominent figure in the establish-ment of a broad interdisciplinary field of 'surveillance studies' during the 1990s. Lyon's argument, laid out in a series of works during the first decade of the Internet, was that the conjoined rise of digital media and mass consumption had instituted a new regime of surveillance that was sufficiently totalizing to warrant the description of a 'surveillance society' (1994, 2001). A surveillance society is an environment in which the primary technologies, the focus of productive capacity and the major forms of social organization all revolve around the collection of data on the society itself. For Lyon, the surveillance society in its present form is woven from five major strands: the military techniques of reconnaissance and discipline, the bureaucratic management techniques of the modern state, the supervision and disciplining of workforces, the investigative methods of law enforcement and, finally, the fine-grained observation of consumer behaviours for commercial advantage (2007). Lyon's contemporary description of the surveillance society works hand-in-glove with Foucault's historical account of the disciplinary society, because it also recognizes that surveillance is inherently disciplinary in nature, as opposed to being purely managerial and functional. Equally, Lyon also recognizes surveillance as a productive mechanism that perpetuates its own operation. The more data we collect, the more central that data becomes in formulating the focus for further surveillance (2001).

> The Panopticon offers a powerful and compelling metaphor for understanding electronic surveillance. The prison-like society, where invisible observers track our digital footprints, does indeed seem panoptic. Bentham would surely smile wryly if he saw us complying with institutional norms as we use barcoded library books or note telephone callers' IDs before accepting a call. The familiar distinctions between public and private life dissolve as both government and corporation ignore old thresholds and garner personal data of the most mundane and intimate kinds. Beyond the metaphor, a model of power also lies in the concept of the panoptic, and it takes us well beyond the Orwellian jackboots and torture, or even the rats. The normalizing discipline, the exaggerated visibility of the subject, the unverifiability of observation, the subject as bearer of surveillance, the quest for factual certainty – all are important aspects of the panoptic as model of power.
>
> Lyon, David (1994), *The Electronic Eye: The Rise of Surveillance Society*, Minneapolis, MN: University of Minnesota Press, p. 71

Lyon seeks to emphasize that no regime of surveillance is an inevitable or immutable apparatus. Rather, surveillance regimes are an intrinsic aspect of social organization that crystallizes around particular historical occurrences and the technologies that are applied in that context. In this regard, as the latest round of the multipolar Middle East War accelerated from 2000 onwards, governments across the world have moved to extend their powers of surveillance. Many new information-gathering operations and processes have commenced through military investments in robotic drones, satellite surveillance and various forms of espionage and 'information warfare'. However, as a consequence of the spectacularly brutal terrorist attacks upon the United States in 2001 (and subsequent atrocities in Spain and the UK), the boundaries between military conflict and threats to distant civilian populations are considered to have been effectively eliminated. Because of the reach of terrorist organizations in an era of asymmetrical warfare (small versus the big) and the concealment of terrorists amongst the general population, considerable efforts are being made to profile citizens who might represent a potential threat (Lyon 2003b). At the same time, ostentatious displays of security are intended to reassure other citizens of the robustness of civil defence. In order to support these twin objectives, a raft of new legislation has removed much of the residual legal status of privacy within Western societies (Rosen 2000).

[A]s many commentators have noted, contemporary surveillance systems, increasingly rely on personal information in order to make inferences about individuals without taking into considera- tion the contextual integrity of the available information . . . especially with the penetration of the Internet, as well as other types of digital and/or interactive media, such as personal video recorders (PVR) and video on demand, information about individuals' media consumption habits make up an increasingly large share of the stock of data that institutions compile about individuals. This is largely due to the architecture of interactive media, which makes collecting data about individuals' media use habits considerably easier than collecting data about individuals' use of more traditional forms of media.

Lemi Baruh (2007) 'Read at your Own risk: Shrinkage of Privacy and Interactive Media', *New Media and Society*, 9(2): 187–211.

In an era where an invisible threat has to be met with the most feasibly visible response, we have seen tanks parked in airport terminals and the introduction of biometric screening. Against this backdrop, the routine usage of DNA databases has encountered far less opposition than it arguably should have. Similarly, the auto- matic collation of all email and phone records operates without restraint or notable opposition (over a quarter of a million accounts are scrutinized in the UK each year). Nonetheless, despite the overarching context of the 'war on terror' through which these activities are rationalized, it is important to remember that all of these techniques were anticipated, developed and on-hand for deployment prior to 2001. Working in paral- lel, the expanding apparatus of state-security has also requisitioned the considerable surveillance powers of the commercial sector in the pursuit of the overall war effort. As a consequence, market research techniques for consumer prediction have become cen- tral instruments of national defence. Consequently, the books that you buy on Amazon, the things you search for on Google and the comments you make on Twitter all have a direct impact upon whether or not you are allowed to board a plane or enter sensitive areas of employment. Thus, the technology that gives us YouTube and iTunes becomes a major apparatus of social observation and an integral part of a global military cam- paign. For this reason, there is good reason to be conscious of what you read, what you buy and who you phone in a digital society.

As Lemi Baruh points out, the nature of predictive data-mining is that it seeks to correlate the occurrence of events without any access to the context of those events (2007). For example, when you buy gifts for others on Amazon, you appear to express an investment in something in which you may not be interested in the slightest. There is no way for the assessor of your personal profile to know that you bought a flight simu- lator game for your brother, and a book on Internet activism because it was a set text at college. Taken out of context, however, this pairing of events can mark you out as a potentially dangerous radical. At the same time, our growing awareness of the perva- sive and militarized nature of consumer surveillance prompts us to think twice about reading politically contentious materials or letting others borrow our mobile phone. Thus, we institute a form of reflexive self-discipline that internalizes the conflict in the outside world within our personal domain. These protective strategies come to the fore, not simply amongst those who have 'something to fear', but amongst the entire population, because 'the data subject does not know when data is collected; who collects the data; who has access to the data; and who (or what) distinguishes acceptable behaviour from risky behaviour' (Baruh 2007: 205). We can relate this phenomenon of behavioural 'shrinkage' directly to David Lyon's observation that digital media technologies necessarily precipitate the era of the electronic panopticon (1994).

Debates on Privacy

Central to Foucault's theorization of power is his recognition that wherever power operates, it generates acts of resistance. Thus, if power is applied selectively, resistance to that power becomes specifically situated. If, however, power becomes infused throughout the social system, then it will inevitably produce dissent across society as a whole. Even amongst the intense hurt, anger and panic of the 2000s, dissenting voices pointed repeatedly to the various negative implications of automatic and unaccountable surveillance. In the relative calm of the last five years, the present and future status of privacy in the information society has become a central topic of public debate (Allen 2011; Andrejevic 2007a; Lyon 2003a; Solove 2004). Broadly speaking, we could place criticism of pervasive digital surveillance into three broad categories. In the first category, there are pragmatic difficulties raised for established surveillance practices which are inevitably transformed by the abundance of information. For example, practical issues can be identified concerning how information about pharmaceutical purchases is easily collated into individualized profiles that might cause medical or life insurers to consider someone a risk and refuse insurance. With the digitization of public health records adding to this body of knowledge, we may soon reach a situation where only those with very little chance of ever being ill will get medical insurance. This will render our present public health systems more or less inoperable in the hands of the private sector, since it hardly provides sufficient incentive to pay for the insurance in the first place. Insurance is a business built upon the overall balance of occurrence and numbers, but it is quickly becoming a selectively applicable business based upon surveillance and prediction.

Another largely pragmatic objection to the extension of digital surveillance relates to the security of data. The large volumes of information now being collected at every level of social life lead to the existence of concentrated and easily transferable information resources. Within a networked system, collecting information in this way gives rise to new substantive risks. Large volumes of sensitive data go missing when civil servants leave their laptops on trains, when hackers steal the account details of Amazon or Facebook users and when whistle-blowers like Bradley Manning send a quarter of a million US diplomatic cables to Wikileaks with a press of a button. In this respect, the pragmatic objections to ubiquitous surveillance lead us to the second category of objections, where we can outline various critiques surrounding the accountability of surveillance. If the state is to watch all of its citizens, then who is going to watch those employed within the state itself? Here, arguments for more stringent protections for private individuals are coupled with equally vocal demands for 'Freedom of Information' legislation that allows the citizenry to keep public figures under scrutiny. Mitt Romney, candidate for the Republican presidential nomination in 2012, is publicly pressured to release his private tax records into the public domain, with no prior allegation of any legal transgression having occurred. It is inconceivable that such a request would have been made of Harry Truman or Lyndon Johnson. Elsewhere, as it becomes apparent that British newspapers have been routinely 'hacking' into the mobile phones of celebrities and the victims of crime, a public outcry demands full scrutiny of the affairs of Rupert Murdoch's News Corporation. In the process, it comes to light that illegal surveillance is endemic in British journalism and that law enforcement agencies have long been aware of this, but effectively redirected by bribes and influence.

Photographs of social events and records of unofficial meetings reveal that there is an unhealthy relationship in the UK between mainstream politics, law enforcement and particular newspapers. The executives under investigation are seen hastily dumping their laptops into rubbish bins, which are subsequently retrieved and given to police by members of the public. Politicians, policemen and journalists scramble to defend themselves from scrutiny every bit as readily as they have imposed it upon others. As a consequence, privacy and surveillance become a conjoined battleground between the many and the few, where professional reputations and government policies can founder on the contents of a single 'leaked' email. Surveillance, it seems, moves both up and down the social system. Accordingly, a third category of critique emerges from the question of who is entitled to exercise the privilege of surveillance and who is not. Although few citizens have anything positive to say about the disciplinary gaze of the state, many people simultaneously recognize that this is a necessary part of an organized society, and that it leads to the (more or less) efficient resolution of numerous social problems. That is, people tend to believe in the ideal of law and order, as much as they expound cynicism surrounding its actual operation. When it comes to the privatization of surveillance privileges, however, there is little evidence of any public support for commercial data-mining or targeted advertising (Andrejevic 2007b). In this area, there are growing demands for greater statutory protection for individuals pertaining to the ways in which information about them is obtained and the ways in which their media usage is collected and shared by commercial companies. As it stands, if an individual conducted actions of this kind, they would be liable to arrest. Why are software companies and Internet portals sanctioned to sell personal information as a precondition of access to a public communications infrastructure?

Box 14.3 Arguments against digital surveillance

- The freedom to access information without fear of punishment is a prerequisite for free thought (and for a free society)
- That the widespread gathering of online user-behaviour data represents a systematic and unwarranted investigation into the lives of innocent citizens
- That the secure storage of electronic data is by no means assured, and that its concentration in databases represents a substantial risk to the public
- That the unfettered access to large bodies of personal information in a digital indexed form constitutes an unaccountable form of power, and this inevitably leads to the abuse of surveillance systems
- That the accumulation of circumstantial, harmless facts about individuals when collated into overall 'profiles' can lead to a misreading of potentials with very serious consequences for innocent individuals
- That the commercial exploitation of user-data being obtained without consent constitutes identity theft on a grand scale

Tales From Facebook

At present social networking sites are a central area of debate for the negotiation of privacy and surveillance. As a consequence, they have scarcely been out of the news in the past three years. Social networking inevitably becomes a privacy issue because the exposure of large volumes of highly personal information is intrinsic to this media format. The central paradox of social networking sites is that they require self-disclosure as their primary content, but most users nonetheless regard the public displays that they create as a private domain (being something halfway between a diary and a mobile phone). Thus, a situation comes into being where users offer a large volume of personal information as public speech, thereby constituting an enduring record of their interpersonal communications. They do this without being required or obligated to do so, and without paying for the service itself. As such, the content they produce is freely given into the public domain, subject only to the degree of public access that each user stipulates when they set up their pages. Against the contradictory backdrop of general suspicion about the extent of state surveillance, the popularity of social networking demonstrates a remarkable degree of faith in the integrity and security of SNS platforms. In many ways this is counterintuitive, since SNS portals are designed quite specifically to disperse information widely along complex chains of social relations. Sharing 'with friends only' is actually, and inevitably, a very wide transmission of information.

In that sense, an obvious area of risk associated with social networking relates to criminal intrusion. Social networking sites have become a prime target for various 'identity theft' scams. The security of the leading SNS platforms has been frequently compromised with hackers gaining access to user profiles in large numbers. In 2008, Facebook was targeted specifically by a number of viruses that intended to systematically harvest information from user profiles, and to use the interlaced connectivity of social networking sites to 'go viral' and spread themselves throughout the network (BBC News Online 2009e). Needless to say, the operators of the site are doing all they can to prevent any criminal misuse of user profiles. At the same time, however, their own economic model is itself predisposed upon their own capacity to harvest information from user profiles and turn the content of social networking into a commercial resource. Consequently, the data retention policy of Facebook has come under sustained criticism. Updates to the site's terms and conditions in February 2009, which gave the operators of the site authority to retain personal profiles indefinitely and to pass them to third parties, were met with stiff resistance by the user base of the site, leading to a temporary retraction of the new contractual conditions (BBC News Online 2009b). These conditions subsequently returned with a range of limited 'opt out' functions available to site members (BBC News Online 2011c). Fundamentally, Facebook's social networking platform is a free-to-use service, and as the business maxim goes: 'If something is free, you're the product'. Thus, the central problem in this case is that the economic worth of social networking sites has been assessed almost solely through their capacity to harvest personal information and facilitate targeted advertising.

This is where the money is, with the valuation of Facebook in 2012 estimated at $100 billion (BBC News Online 2011d, 2012b). For many of us, however, targeted advertising based upon an algorithmic assessment of our needs and wants is hardly sinister, and not an unreasonable price to pay for such a useful social tool. Similarly, data harvesting via SNS is entirely commensurate with its operation in almost every other commercial domain on the Internet. Surveillance in that sense is not only socially productive, but also economically productive. The real problem, perhaps, is the inherent permanence of digital content. This characteristic has made many users anxious in recent years because they were able to deactivate their profiles, but not able to delete them. The most common problem with this is that the various forms of 'public intimacy' that have arisen with social networking do not always lend themselves to impression management in the professional domain. For example, a 'party-hard' image (questionably) appropriate to college life becomes highly inappropriate to graduate employment as various employers in the United States begin to routinely check SNS platforms for information on potential hires. In 2009, a young woman in Essex, England, was dismissed from employment because she complained of the tedium of her job on her Facebook page. Having unwisely sent a 'friendship request' to another employee at work, her complaint was subsequently passed on to the owner of the business. The employer was moved to dismiss this employee because the time-honoured complaints of workers in the offline world become a libel offence when 'published' on the Internet (BBC News Online 2009d).

At the start of the twenty-first century it is clear that communication and information technologies have become central to understanding social change. Computer dependence has become a feature of both global connections and of everyday life. Indeed, globalization and daily living in the contemporary world are in part constituted by our relation with computers. No country wishes to miss out on the establishment of an information infrastructure. Few citizens or consumers wish to be excluded from the network of information flows, at least as far as having access to telephones, televisions and the Internet is concerned. But the obverse of the information society is the surveillance society. The world of electronic connectivity works both ways. It brings the global village to our doorstep. And at the same time it extracts personal data from us that are then processed, manipulated, traded and used to influence us and to affect our life chances.

David Lyon (2001) *Surveillance Society: Monitoring Everyday Life*, Buckingham: Open University Press, pp. 107–25

In the wider arena of law enforcement, the culture of 'self-disclosure' via social networking has proved to be a useful arena for gathering evidence. British police forces began sifting through Facebook content for evidence of criminal behaviour in 2008 (BBC News Online 2009d). Facebook has also been used to build up an interactive network of concerned citizens through neighbourhood watch mechanisms. Following the rioting that spread across Britain in 2011, several prosecutions were laid on the basis of incitements to riot made by defendants on social networking forums (BBC News Online 2011b). Thus, just as the mobile phone has provided an everyday mechanism for tracking the whereabouts of individuals and discovering their associates, social networking has become a rich field for harvesting loose talk about criminal activities and intentions. In the United States, the FBI have been sufficiently impressed by the potentials of this form of digital police work that they have recently commissioned a 'scraping' application that will harvest evidence of potential acts of criminality from social networking sites and map this data against the digital geographic resources provided by Google (BBC News Online 2012a). As a counterpoint, the 'democratic' revolution in Egypt in

2011 saw extensive use of social networking sites to publicize the atrocities committed by the state, to mobilize the population and to attract international sympathy, a pattern repeated throughout the so-called 'Arab Spring' (BBC News Online 2011a; Ghonim 2012).

Surviving in Surveillance Society

Social networking sites provide the perfect example of the convergence of personal communications and mutual surveillance, public relations and workplace surveillance, criminality and opportunistic surveillance, data-mining and state surveillance, social movements and activist surveillance – all of these actions being enabled in this instance by platforms that are themselves predicated upon the commodification of surveillance for profit (Andrejevic 2007b). Surveillance as a fully fledged commercial commodity is a recent historical development, and one which of itself rewrites established ideals of privacy and accountability. Although there is a significant volume of objections being raised towards this dimension of the digital economy, it has in the most part been tolerated as a necessary evil by those equally attracted to the model of a medium with 'free' content. The contours of this model have been predisposed by earlier mediums such as radio and television, but it is the interactivity of digital media that produces an entirely new set of conditions. In this context, surveillance is not only commercialized, but its subjects themselves play an active role in its operation. More broadly, the increasingly coercive nature of consumerism represents the widespread privatization of the rationalization of public life that came with the institutions of state. The self-replicating imperatives of bureaucracy were famously referred to by Max Weber as the 'iron cage' of modernity, and the binary exchanges of digital media have facilitated the diffusion of these systematic tendencies across the entire social domain (1958).

To respond to the present state of affairs with a trace of 'Orwellian' paranoia is a natural and instinctive response, albeit one which runs the risk of being placed under suspicion (as Orwell himself was). To demand privacy and protection from scrutiny is taken as an admission of guilt, and this is increasingly the case whether you are an ordinary citizen, a wealthy entrepreneur or a state official. In that sense, it is important to recognize that surveillance is not simply an authoritarian prerogative. It is also a political necessity, since democracy does not operate effectively behind closed doors. There is an inescapable fact that must be accounted for in any discussion of privacy in the present era: an information society is a surveillance society, and it cannot be otherwise. What is really at issue, therefore, is the formulation of appropriate terms and conditions under which the fruits of digital surveillance become applicable to social action. At the same time, it is a mistake to cast any surveillance mechanism as an apparatus exterior to the social system. Surveillance is embedded in everyday life, and the disciplinary effect that it creates is an integral feature of social organization. In that sense, a surveillance society is inevitably a disciplinary society where the unprecedented visibility of our actions shapes our behaviour. Our intense awareness of digital surveillance, from speed cameras to cookies to credit records, institutes a continuous strategic assessment of social participation. This 'reflexivity' in our daily conduct is just one example of the ways in which we negotiate the inherent risks of digital society.

Think and Discuss

1. Key Terms
Can you describe in simple language what is meant by the following terms found in this chapter?

- Privacy
- Data-mining
- Consumer profile
- Predictive analysis
- Panopticon

2. Critical Questions
Try answering the following questions, drawing upon your own understanding, experience and knowledge.

1. What forms of personal information are produced by your own everyday usage of digital media?
2. To what extent is it acceptable to you that your 'consumer profile' is collated and stored for future use by third parties?
3. What acts of 'digital surveillance' do you yourself engage in during the course of your daily affairs?
4. What are the advantages and limitations of predicting the future on the basis of 'data-mining'?
5. Is the perceived existence of an 'electronic panopticon' sufficient to reduce the likelihood of crimes and misdemeanours occurring?
6. Should we regard the collation of personal information for commercial purposes in a different light from the use of personal information by the state?

Further Reading

Andrejevic, Mark (2007a) *iSpy: Surveillance and Power in the Interactive Era,* Kansas: University Press of Kansas.

Ayres, Ian (2008) *Super Crunchers: How Anything Can Be Predicted*, New York: Bantam.

Foucault, Michel (1977) *Discipline and Punish: The Birth of the Prison*, New York: Random House.

Lyon, David (1994) *The Electronic Eye: The Rise of Surveillance Society*, Minneapolis, MN: University of Minnesota Press.

Lyon, David (2003a) *Surveillance as Social Sorting: Privacy, Risk and Digital Discrimination,* London and New York: Routledge.

Lyon, David (2007) *Surveillance Studies: An Overview,* Cambridge: Polity.

Rosen, Jeffrey (2000) *The Unwanted Gaze: The Destruction of Privacy in America*, New York: Random House.

Solove, D. J. (2004) *The Digital Person: Technology and Privacy in the Information Age*, New York: New York University Press.

Wacks, Raymond (2010) *Privacy: A Very Short Introduction*, New York: Oxford University Press.

Go Online

Electronic Privacy Information Center – http://www.epic.org/
Freedom of Information Act (US) – http://www.foia.state.gov/
Freedom of Information Act (UK) – http://www.legislation.gov.uk/ukpga/2000/36/contents
Liberty – http://www.liberty-human-rights.org.uk/
Loginworks – http://www.loginworks.com/
News Corporation – http://www.newscorp.com/
Privacy International – https://www.privacyinternational.org/
Surveillance Studies Centre – www.sscqueens.org/

CHAPTER 15

Managing Risk

The machinery of digital surveillance achieves legitimacy through a commonly held belief that it is necessary for 'keeping us safe' from a whole host of perceived dangers arising from the interface of advanced technologies and mass society. These might be threats to state institutions, to commercial interests or to individuals engaged in the practices of everyday life. In this sense, there are risks to be managed at every scale of human affairs. In the world of today, technology is overwhelmingly seen as the most likely source of remedies for forestalling adverse occurrences of all kinds. Information technologies, in particular, play a central role in seeking solutions and resolutions to problems. Computerized logic appears, on the face of it, to provide a ready means through which potential threats can be anticipated and thus systematically contained. At the same time, it is also widely perceived to be the case that advanced technologies of all kinds are themselves giving rise to new sources of threats to individual, collective and institutional well-being. As both power and responsibility over these domains are diffused throughout the social structure, it becomes increasingly imperative for mass media stakeholders to maintain and manage a visible field of discourse around specific threats. At one level, this is a straightforward matter of 'public awareness' by which warnings about identified threats can be widely diffused. However, as knowledge of a potential threat becomes dispersed, society as a whole becomes increasingly engaged in seeking a resolution to the problem or, at least, shaping the process of containment.

Ulrich Beck on Risk Society

As new dangers are identified, isolated and discussed across the length and breadth of society, the extent and vitality of the public sphere is brought into productive action. At a deeper level, however, the 'networking' of perceived threats via the mass media becomes a structuring force in the social world. Consequently, society itself is encountered primarily through the arena of risk management (and thus becomes understood implicitly as a 'problem' to be managed). Through the mass media, the sheer scale of public discussion around a whole series of threats tends to form the overall impression that potential risks are more likely to occur than they really are. We also get the sense that the volume and scale of risks to our well-being are increasing day by day. This 'media multiplier' effect has been described extensively in George Gerbner's 'cultivation of fear' thesis, by which the intrinsically dramatic nature of media representation fosters widespread anxiety amongst a mass public (Gerbner and Gross 1976). At the same time, however, the digital media provide the only available and effective means by which the large-scale problems that exceed our everyday experience can be encountered and resolved by a broad social base. Consequently, the German sociologist Ulrich Beck has written extensively on the ways in which a growing awareness of global scale and the sheer extent of scientific intervention in our own environment has tended to coalesce around the notion of a 'risk society' (1992, 1995, 1997).

There are a number of component parts to Beck's hypothesis, some of which he holds in common with other contemporary sociologists (Beck, Giddens and Lash 1994). In the first place, Beck takes a stagist approach by which he assesses shifts in the allegiances of citizens and in the framing of social consensus. By this measure, there are three historical alignments of social life: a 'traditional society' and an 'early modern' and 'late modern' society' (Beck 1992). In the former scenario, people lived in small-scale conurbations and tended to organize their lives around those who were co-present (see Giddens 1990). The worldview of these individuals was oriented towards overarching symbolic institutions such as the church and monarchy, in whom they placed their faith for managing both spiritual and material dangers to the social order. In early modern society, however, the division of the public and private domains effectively separates spiritual and secular allegiances. With the Enlightenment, the spread of rationalism subsequently replaced the feudal system with modern institutions of state, in which citizens now placed their faith in regard to matters of science, law, war and business. Thus, in the sprawling cities of the 'early modern' world, social authority was vested in public bureaucracies and political systems. In the last decades of the twentieth century, however, the prevailing consensus around modernist institutions began to weaken.

The systematic progress of science had given rise to advanced technologies, such as nuclear power and industrial chemicals, which appeared to threaten the fabric of life itself. The political institutions that had overseen the making of a mass society had also become implicated in numerous instances of totalitarian rule and in ruinous wars. As a consequence, citizens were becoming less inclined to place their faith in the large impersonal institutions of science and law, and instead began to internalize their participation in social life with regard to their own life-stories. Each citizen came to self-manage their own role in social life through an intellectual capacity to assess their own place in the larger scheme of things (Giddens 1991). In this era of 'late' or 'reflexive' modernity, the reorientation of social life around the individual creates new freedoms, but it also recasts collective responsibilities upon each of us. The many problems facing mass society as a whole are necessarily internalized via a more personalized understanding of risk (Beck 1992). Every one of us must now anticipate the likely consequences of our own social actions, on an individual and collective scale. This is by no means an easy thing to do, and in doing it, we must also account for the new kinds of dangers that only become comprehensible through large-scale technical systems operating beyond our own experience.

Risks such as those produced in the late modernity . . . induce systematic and often irreversible harm, generally remain invisible, are based on causal interpretations, and thus initially only exist in terms of the (scientific or anti-scientific) knowledge about them. They can thus be changed, magnified, dramatized or minimized within knowledge, and to that extent they are particularly open to social definition and construction. Hence the mass media and the scientific and legal professions in charge of defining risks become key social and political positions . . . As the risk society develops, so does the antagonism between those afflicted by risks and those who profit from them. The social and economic importance of knowledge grows similarly, and with it the power over the media to structure knowledge (science and research) and disseminate (mass media). The risk society in this

> sense is also the science, media and information society. Thus new antagonisms grow up between those who produce risk definitions and those who consume them.
>
> Ulrich Beck (1992), *Risk Society: Towards a New Modernity*, Cambridge: Polity, pp. 22–3, 46

Information technologies occupy a unique position within a 'risk society'. They constitute the major means by which risks are calculated, whether by prediction of events or by subsequent risk assessment and publication. The information visualization provided by digital data presentation methods gives the arcane mathematics of risk an accessible visual form. This graphical rendering subsequently provides the symbolic and emotional register for any given danger. Data on every conceivable threat can now be used to produce its own 'weather map' of occurrence and severity. Once this symbolic rendition of risk is diffused widely, again via the digital media, it produces a range of responses that drive awareness of the issue and perpetuate our attention to the matter across the public sphere. The 'informational' qualities of any digital risk map give us apparently rational grounds for debating the origins, faults and strategic positionings that surround the present danger. Information technologies thereby make the wider world of science tangible in public life. Thus, even as our overarching faith in scientific progress is diminished, we continue to give significant credence to the digital technologies by which the risks of science are managed. Information technologies produce a unique class of experts in themselves, as do the media formats that make use of these channels to distribute information. Thus, each form of scientific expertise (including that of social science) is necessarily augmented by these other classes of expert in the course of its public life (Cottle 1998). Thus, as Beck notes, risks 'deepen the dependency on experts' at many levels (Beck 1997: 123). As the grassroots and vested interests alike seek to contest any given pronouncement or dataset, these additional layers of expertise tend to go unnoticed, and consequently embed themselves further into the operations of the risk society.

Defining Cyber-crime

Information technologies provide the technological means for recording, processing, assessing, disseminating and debating all forms of risk. They are the 'natural' medium of risk assessment and risk management. However, in keeping with the broader sweep of Beck's arguments, it is worth noting that information technologies also produce new unfathomable risks of their own. This leaves us struggling to incorporate the simultaneous potentials of digital media for both enabling and managing the risks that are inherent to the technology itself. The most obvious, and therefore best-known, example of this arises with the various phenomena associated with 'cyber-crime'. Since the advent of the public Internet in the early nineties, there has been a growing unease amongst public officials and private citizens concerning the risks posed by criminal activities enacted in the virtual domain of cyberspace. In many respects, these concerns have been borne out by where we find ourselves today. The list of recorded cyber-crimes now encompasses a spectrum of criminality that ranges from the pursuit of gross perversion to the pursuit of easy money. With the ever-increasing commercialization of the Internet, new virtual forms of financial crime are now part of our everyday computer experience. Periodically, rarer and more sinister crimes against persons have also high-lighted the inherent dangers of anonymous communications. Cautious of 'identity theft', electronic scams, 'data phishing' and 'viral infections', and increasingly wary of strangers online, we have learned to occupy cyberspace with a measure of caution in recent years.

Beyond the threat to individuals, sophisticated cyber-crimes have also targeted commercial and government institutions and their information infrastructures. In response, software providers have constantly upgraded information security products to protect us from online threats. Enforcement agencies too have evolved new processes and techniques for tracking down criminals on the World Wide Web. Nonetheless, as a descriptive category, the concept of cyber-crime remains somewhat vague (or at best uncommonly broad). This is because the widespread application of information technologies in so many fields of life makes any misuse of digital devices a potential cyber-crime. As cyber-crime becomes a widely identified risk for all us, however, it is imperative that we more clearly illuminate what actually lies behind the term itself. In making the specific nature of cyber-crime apparent in this way, we can then begin to assess its impact upon an increasingly mediated society and formulate the requisite programmes of strategic risk management. Before we seek solutions, however, there are a number of legal, moral and socially constituted frames of reference that inevitably influence our underlying judgement of what constitutes criminality in the first place. For sociologists and legal professionals alike, this implies a practical necessity for a set of differential categorizations of cyber-crime that might facilitate an objective measure of risk. Only then can this knowledge be logically extended to investigative action and punitive outcomes.

Box 15.1 Potential cyber-crimes

Illegal financial transactions
Blackmail and intimidation
Trafficking and slavery
False impersonation
Sedition
Unauthorized surveillance
Flaming and crimes of netiquette
Computer infection
Data theft
Political humour
Online hate crimes
Online credit card fraud
Viewing and/or disseminating pornography
Media piracy
Identity theft
Promoting democracy
Website defacement
Dissemination of paedophile materials
Cyber-stalking
Treason
Online dating

> Releasing viral computer programs
> Online soliciting
> Cyber-terrorism
> Information warfare and espionage
> Publication of restricted information

Constructing a universally accepted categorical scheme for cyber-crimes is no easy task, for a number of reasons. One major challenge to establishing a universal definition of cyber-crime is the complexity of the various legal jurisdictions that exist across the world. Laws remain overwhelmingly national in character, even with the influence of international and regional lawmaking bodies. Each legal system inevitably makes its assessment of crime with different reference points and varying severity. Indeed, in many cases, a cyber-crime in one territory may be a legal activity in another. Plainly, this raises questions for all technical descriptions of international crime, but the combination of the virtual and the global aspects of the new media has also produced entirely new challenges for our legal frameworks. National criminal laws have traditionally assumed the physical presence of the perpetrator(s) within their jurisdiction (or at least within another national jurisdiction from which they can be extradited). By contrast, a cyber-crime takes place within a disembodied electronic space that cannot be easily defined as anyone's legal territory. This supra-national crime also operates at a global level in the technical sense, and thus frequently involves actions that are criminal in some countries but not in others. An internationally agreed set of laws for policing cyberspace is presently beyond the legal capacity and political will of the international system. Even where there is consensus on the nature and occurrence of a cyber-crime, the global reach of the Internet means that it is not always clear whose jurisdiction should prevail over that crime. This is often the case with political crimes or commercial crimes, but it also applies to personal crimes of a socially constructed nature.

Beyond the complexities of these political realities, there are also conceptual challenges to a clear categorical understanding of cyber-crime. When you look at the long list of potential cyber-crimes, you should also take time to think about how you would yourself choose to order that list. What frames of reference would you make use of? What should provide the dominant logic for understanding these various actions in relation to social norms and to each other? One approach would be to order this list as a deep category, where crimes are ranked vertically (for example, in terms of the severity of the crime). Alternatively, cyber-crime could be described as a wide category, including many different forms of criminal behaviours organized horizontally around their relationship to each other (for example, digital property crimes, crimes of violence etc.). Cyber-crimes can also be classified in a more strictly technological sense, in terms of the relative 'virtuality' of the criminal practice involved. These competing vectors of categorization all imply the arbitrage of various technological, ethical, legal, procedural and social conventions. They all have some validity and methodological usefulness, and that is one of the reasons why cyber-crime is a term that remains under negotiation or contestation.

Understanding cyber-crime from a technological perspective gives us a starting point. In taking this approach, Susan Drucker and Gary Gumpert provide an account that ranges from very serious and malicious crimes to online behaviours that are generally perceived as rude. Nonetheless, they make an important distinction between 'pure' cyber-crimes and what are previously established 'offline' actions that are now enhanced by digital communication. Planning an armed robbery, for example, is likely to involve digital communication in today's society, but the crime itself still takes place in the physical world. Drucker and Gumpert also identify that there are certain 'virtual crimes' that may have previously existed in a non-digital form, but that now take place almost solely through the computer medium. Fraud, for example, is an ancient crime, but it is now most likely to occur in cyberspace. Beyond this upgrading of established criminal behaviours, Drucker and Gumpert also categorize the violations of both formal and informal Internet regulations as crimes that are entirely contingent upon the computer environment. We could define these latter actions, therefore, as 'purely' cyber-crimes.

Box 15.2 Typology of cyber-crime 1: technology

- **Crimes using email and the Internet as an instrument or agency:** electronic connection is the means by which the violation is actualized, but the crime itself exists externally to computer environment
- **Virtual crimes – mediated felonies, misdemeanours and violations committed in cyberspace:** resembles and is characterized by the existence of the crime in non-mediated circumstances, but in this instance takes place solely in a computer environment
- **Violations of regulation governing email, the Internet or a regulated medium administered by a regulatory agency(ies) transmitted via the Internet:** computer-enabled violations of laws and regulations governing Internet usage as determined by government
- **Ethical violations of cybercodes of conduct:** no law is violated, but ethical impropriety does occur

Susan Drucker and Gary Gumpert (2000), 'CyberCrime and Punishment', *Critical Studies in Media Communication*, 17(2): 133–58

For Sarah Gordon and Richard Ford (2006), it is this demarcation between digital information crimes (type 1) and computer-enhanced crimes (type 2) that distinguishes their two primary categories of cyber-crimes. Type 1 cyber-crimes are essentially crimes of data that are undertaken online. These include 'phishing attempts, theft or manipulation of data or services via hacking or viruses, identity theft, and bank or e-commerce fraud based upon stolen credentials' (2006: 14). Type 2 cyber-crimes are essentially existing, material crimes that now employ online methods or have an online component. These include 'cyberstalking and harassment, child predation, extortion, blackmail, stock market manipulation, complex corporate espionage, and planning and carrying out terrorists activities online' (ibid.). This distinction is echoed by the 'computer-assisted crime' versus 'computer-focused crimes' model (offered by Furnell 2002) and 'old crime–new media' versus 'new crime–new media' adopted by the UK National Hi-Tech Crime Unit (NHTCU 2004). Majid Yar (2006), however, sees this kind of categorization as focusing overmuch on the technological dimension of the crime. Instead, Yar directs us to David Wall's more legalistic definition of cyber-crimes, which is organized in terms of their correspondence with existing and established legal categories (2001).

Box 15.3 Typology of cyber-crime 2: legality

- **Cyber-trespass** – crossing boundaries, entering into other people's virtual property and/or causing damage(for example, hacking, defacement, viruses)
- **Cyber-deceptions and thefts** – stealing financial property (for example, credit card fraud, phishing, intellectual property violations)
- **Cyber-pornography** – breaching laws on obscenity and decency
- **Cyber-violence** – doing psychological damage to, or inciting physical harm against others, thereby breaching laws relating to the protection of the person (for example, hate crimes, stalking, slander and harassment)

David Wall (2001), *Crime and the Internet*, London: Routledge, pp. 3–7

The notions of criminality employed by Wall are more orthodox, and their technological dimension as 'cyber-crimes' is much less important than the ethical conventions that are being transgressed in any given case. There is no explicit vertical arrangement to Wall's categories, implying a horizontal scheme of subcategories that denote cyber-crimes of varying nature and severity. While these distinctions may seem somewhat abstract and technical, they are actually quite fundamental to a practical understanding of cyber-crime. If, for example, we take Drucker and Gumpert's definitions we could well argue that almost everyone going online was likely to be a victim of cyber-crime on a daily basis. This would suggest a public risk of epidemic proportions. If we follow Gordon and Ford's model we might be inclined to concentrate cyber-crime enforcement strategies on the type I data crimes at the expense of the severe, material crimes which are seen as being 'merely' digitally enhanced regular crimes. By contrast, the more legalistic set of categorizations offered by Wall directs our attention away from the perpetrator of the crime and towards the victim in order to understand the harm caused by cyber-crime. This emphasizes the social consequences of cyber-crimes over and above the transgressive nature of the actions themselves. In taking this approach, however, the particular qualities of cyber-crimes as something more than computer-enhanced variations of existing crimes are relatively downplayed, and so it becomes possible at least that we will lose sight of 'pure' cyber-crime in favour of a technological upgrading of the wider established field of criminality.

Cyber-criminals

Clearly, there is a need to balance the remediation of crime in general with an awareness of the specific risks posed by new forms of crime in the information domain. In order to advance our investigation of cyber-crime in this way, it becomes useful to extend the typology of cyber-crime by means of a series of ideal types. By this device, legal and technical categories become populated by a whole range of 'cyber-criminals' seen as the perpetrators of the various illegal activities recorded online over the past two decades. In order to avoid the lengthy legal complexities of citing individual cases, the task here will be to match these various popular conceptualizations of the cyber-criminal with a broad definition of related crimes. We will also take note of the overall prevalence of each category of cyber-crime and the associated risks. These risks tend to be identified from the perspective of the victim of these crimes, rather the perspective of the instigator of the crime. While this is an acceptable and conventional approach, it is worth noting that criminality and victimhood are not mutually exclusive experiences, with many victims of crime themselves being instigators of various misdemeanours. Given the mundane nature of many digital crimes, you could well be one of them. Accordingly, it is the broad risks to society as a whole that we will seek to assess via this pantheon of digital miscreants.

The hacker

The term 'hacker' was originally used to refer to a member of a loose grouping of computer programming specialists with a commitment to a liberal information society (Jordan 2008; Levy 2010; Taylor 1999). More recently, however, the term has increasingly carried negative connotations as a verb; 'hacking' being used to refer to practices of intrusion carried out through digital information systems (Nissenbaum 2004). Since many cyber-crimes are predicated upon gaining access to information held by others, 'hacking' has become a principal technique of electronic crime. The 'hacker' associated with this activity is not generally imagined as a political progressive, but as a distant aggressor intent on recovering the financial details of individuals or companies, or retrieving and making criminal use of official information stores (Milone 2003). As such, 'hacker' and 'hacking' are now commonly used to denote the broader practice of criminal intrusion. However, these terms are still used to refer to the competitive 'testing' of new security systems by amateur programmers (Allsop 2009). To deal with this, the term 'hactivism' has been employed in recent years to refer to the use of hacking to pursue a particular political agenda that is closer to the counter-culture traditions of the term (Jordan and Taylor 2004). Hacking per se is a technical activity that can be seen as more or less a prerequisite for most forms of cyber-crime where virtual trespassing is a necessary component of the crime (Mitnick and Simon 2005). While hacking is illegal in its own right, it is typically conducted in the perpetration of another crime.

The viral coder

Related to the figure of the hacker in terms of the need for a mastery (albeit at an ever decreasing level) of computer skills, is the category of the viral coder. Viral coders produce and disseminate a range of softwares that attack the functions of computer systems (Hughes and DeLone 2007). This is also a form of cyber-crime that takes place almost wholly within the virtual realm, but which nonetheless has wide-ranging material effects in terms of massive disruption of public and commercial institutions. The definitive cyber-crime in this form is the dissemination of viruses and worms, 'malicious' programs that exploit loopholes in common computer software in order to disable operating systems and spread themselves across networks, causing disruption on a wide scale. Viruses are normally comprised of malicious code hidden within a host program, while worms are independent self-replicating programs. Another common form of viral cyber-crime concerns denial of service (DoS) attacks that disable online and network services by jamming or clogging their communication channels with an automated barrage of incoming messages.

Box 15.4 Definition of hacking crimes

- Gaining access to computer hardware owned by individuals, commercial companies and/or public institutions in order to gain criminal benefit from the information retrieved through intrusion (data theft)
- Gaining access to computer hardware owned by others in order to disable their functions or to alter, corrupt or delete information for criminal benefit (vandalism)
- Gaining access to computer hardware owned by others in order to make use of its capacity to store, disseminate or process information (resource theft)
- Gaining access to computer hardware owned by others in order to alter or vandalise online content for amusement, political expression or criminal benefit (graffiti)

Consequences of hacking and viral crimes
- Millions of dollars are siphoned off from online bank accounts every year using illegally obtained access
- A significant proportion of the millions of instances of online credit card fraud to date have resulted from hacking into commercial websites and stealing credit card information for many thousands of people
- Some 21% (U.S.) / 9% (UK) of business organizations report instances of digital sabotage over the course of a year
- Thousands of websites are defaced every year through illegally gained access, with government and commercial institutions being heavily targeted
- It has been estimated that more than $30 billion of commercial damage has been caused by a series of worms attacking common operating systems over the past decade
- DoS attacks are high in incidence with 42% of US and 20% of UK-based organizations reporting attacks during 2002–3

Majid Yar (2006), *Cybercrime and Society*, London: Sage, pp. 45–62

The digital pirate

We can identify digital piracy of music, books, television, computer games and movies as by far the most widespread and commonplace form of cyber-crime. The 'content-producing' industries (such as Hollywood) are keen to point out the ways in which piracy is often organized and linked to criminal interests of a more sinister nature (Valenti 2003). At the same time, the full extent of amateur piracy of cultural works for personal consumption is not known. It has at least been widely recognized that this is a very commonplace activity, especially amongst the under twenty-fives. However, the formal classification of a digital pirate is usually given to those involved in the mass dissemination of materials via illegal copying or the administration of content-sharing platforms that facilitate large-scale piracy (see Andersson 2009). Effective enforcement of intellectual property laws is hampered by the widespread sympathy for such offences amongst much of the public. Because of their intangible nature, crimes of piracy are generally not seen as morally comparable to material thefts. There is a commonly held perception that these are victimless crimes, and the sheer scale of user piracy means that this crime is also seen as low risk to the perpetrator. In that sense, most computer users do recognize that piracy is an illegal practice, but less than a quarter of them see piracy for personal use as unethical. Many people regard illegally downloading music and software as being socially acceptable. This leaves rights holders and enforcement agencies with an uphill task in terms of persuading the public of the full consequences of these crimes. Legal actions taken against file-sharers have failed to produce a significant deterrent effect. In an atmosphere redolent of the prohibition era, there continues to be a public backlash against expanding copyright controls that serves to legitimate the endemic theft of cultural works using computers (Lessig 2005a).

Box 15.5 Consequences of digital piracy

- Intellectual property organizations in the US attribute some $20–22 dollars lost to piracy via the Internet per annum
- It is estimated that 44 per cent of under twenty-five-year-olds have illegally copied copyright materials
- 81 million people illegally download music each year
- $13 billion worth of computer games are pirated each year
- More than one in three digital audio recordings sold is a counterfeit copy
- In some parts of the world more than 70 per cent of computer software in use is pirated (24 per cent in North America and 35 per cent in Western Europe)
- Despite increasingly strong legislation that has made copyright violation a criminal, rather than civil, offence in most countries, digital piracy continues to grow

Sources: RIAA 2005; MPAA 2005 ; IFPI 2009; BSA 2003

The cyber fraudster

The Internet has quickly become the foremost mechanism by which crimes of confidence are undertaken (Wells 2010). In these crimes, victims are persuaded to voluntarily make a payment to another person for goods or services on the basis of promises that subsequently turn out to be fraudulent. There have been many online scams that have netted millions of dollars for their perpetrators. These range from fraudulent websites that extract personal information to email scams that request electronic transfers or personal details, and to the auctioning of stolen and counterfeit goods via sites like eBay. It is estimated that online frauds increased sevenfold between 2000 and 2004, making this the fastest-growing cyber-crime (Yar 2006). As with many cyber-crimes, it is rare to catch criminals while the activity is taking place. Most cyberfrauds are reported after they have occurred and it also estimated that the embarrassment of victims leads to massive under-reporting of these crimes. These crimes are increasingly international in nature, making the pursuit of fraudsters difficult and time-consuming. An extremely common and well-known cyberfraud of recent years has been one of the oldest and simplest forms of fraud. The victim is contacted by email and told of a large sum of money held offshore (usually in West Africa) that the owners need desperately to transfer to another location. The victim is then asked to supply their bank details and/or pay a processing fee in order to hold the money for a substantial percentage share (Glickman 2005). Another adaptation of a classic model of fraud would be the online investment frauds where victims are contacted online and invited to take part in favourable investments, either in non-existent companies or in fraudulent shares for legitimate companies. Although response rates to such invitations are low, individuals may sometimes invest considerable amounts in these attractive schemes, making losses per victim quite considerable.

The advantage of digital communications for these activities is the speed and automation of the process of cultivating victims. By contrast, the rise of 'phishing' as a theft of an individual's digital signature for the purposes of fraud is a crime relatively specific to the digital era (Jakobsson and Myers 2007). Commonly, victims are contacted via email and directed to a fake website that mimics an official site (such as an online banking service). Here, they are asked to verify their personal login information, and this data is then collected and used by fraudsters to gain access to the victims' accounts and withdraw funds (Dhamija et al. 2006). The growing popularity of e-commerce has also extended opportunities to conduct trade frauds. For example, online auction sites are frequently used to sell stolen or fake goods. Similarly, non-existent items are auctioned and do not arrive after payment is made. The remote seller then typically disappears, only to reappear later under another identity. Even more commonplace is the practice of electronic 'shilling', where multiple identities are used to bid against the items under auction and thus increase the price paid by legitimate bidders (Yokoo, Sakurai and Matsubara 2004). All in all, it is estimated that perhaps a million frauds per year take place on eBay, although many suspect the incidence to be much higher (Chua and Wareham 2004).

The voyeur

Crimes of a sexual nature are extremely widespread in cyberspace. This is due to the opportunities offered by the anonymity of the medium as well as the tight regulation of sexual behaviours in most societies. Pornography has always been one of the major uses of the Internet, constituting 12 per cent of all Internet content and the subject of 25 per cent of Internet searches (Lane 2001). Whilst pornography is not illegal in many countries, there are large parts of the world where viewing pornography is illegal. This alone makes the viewing of pornography one of the most prevalent cyber-crimes. Even where access to pornography is legal, there are typically age restrictions to this kind of activity that are often circumvented by underage surfers and, implicitly, by pornography providers. The large numbers of children going online in the past decade has also weakened parental control over media access and this has raised considerable anxieties concerning what our children may be exposed to in cyberspace (Kuipers 2006; Littlewood 2003; Livingstone and Bober 2005). Furthermore, there are certain types of pornography that are considered obscene in almost all societies and that are subject to criminal prosecution. Thus, viewing pornography (as one of the major uses of the Internet) is considered criminal in some contexts and a legitimate private matter in others. However, the social stigma that surrounds these materials in almost all cultures makes pornographic websites fertile ground for various other crimes of deception and enticement in which the voyeur becomes victim.

Box 15.6 Digital sex crimes

Given the widespread prurient interest in all things sexual, the conduct of sex-related crimes via the Internet has been fairly commonplace. These have occurred:

- Where pornography is itself an illegal practice
- Where financial scams and cyberfrauds have used sexual materials to lure their victims
- Where materials of a sexual nature have been used for the purposes of harassment

- Where materials of a sexual nature are used for website defacement attacks
- Where the production of pornographic images has entailed coercion and other criminal activity
- Where pornographic materials have transgressed the boundaries between the erotic and the obscene according to legal definitions
- Where the intellectual property of pornographers has been violated by piracy of their materials

The paedophile

By far the most high-profile form of cyber-criminal is the figure of the 'Internet pae-dophile'. Discussions about children going online invariably gravitate towards the widespread fear of men who impersonate children in online spaces. They do so in order to gain the confidence of those minors who they will then conspire to meet in the real world and molest sexually. Internet paedophiles are also associated with the production and dissemination of digital images of criminal sexual acts against minors, commonly referred to as 'child pornography' (Renold et al. 2003; Taylor and Quayle 2003; Akdeniz 2008). The online communities formed for this purpose are known as 'paedophile rings'. These are crimes that have seen considerable international police actions resulting in large numbers of arrests worldwide. These cases invariably receive a higher degree of publicity than other forms of cyber-crime and, in recent years, certain celebrities who have been charged with these kinds of offences have received a high degree of media attention. It is the shadowy figure of the 'online stranger' that is now most commonly associated with these crimes in the popular imagination. Nonetheless, it remains the case that most sexual crimes against children are commit-ted by those who have offline access to them through familial and institutional roles. It is also notable that the discourse associated with paedophilia awareness focuses almost solely upon the vulnerability of female children, despite an equal prevalence of these crimes being committed against male children. Whilst these vile crimes pre-date the rise of the new media, there is no doubt that the digital media have greatly increased opportunities for paedophiles to circulate obscene images of children, particularly at the international scale (Jewkes and Andrews 2005). Conversely, digital information retrieval techniques and online surveillance have also made it much easier for police forces to detect and prosecute paedophiles, and this newfound capac-ity for identifying these sorts of crimes is also a contributor to the perceived rise of a paedophile 'epidemic' (Krone 2005).

The cyber-stalker

'Stalking' is a contemporary term for practices of harassment directed against an indi-vidual, typically by another individual. Stalking first became a matter of widespread public concern during the 1980s, and the spread of electronic communications and virtual social spaces has greatly increased the opportunities for unwarranted intrusions into other people's lives (Goode 1995). Cyber-stalking involves harassment using emails, mobile phones and the verbal targeting of a particular individual in online social forums (Bocij 2004). Whilst some cases of cyber-stalking may involve infatuation, these are more commonly acts of aggression against individuals. The British Crime Survey has revealed that around 2 million UK Internet users have been victims of online harassment and/or cyber-stalking at some point (UK Home Office 2010). As with other forms of stalking, the victim will often be known to the perpetrator in the real world. However, the greater incidence of anonymous dislocated interaction via the Internet means that a higher proportion of cyber-stalking cases involve perpetrators who are strangers to their victims. Cyber-stalking can lead to further crimes against the victim in the material world, with a small number of murders being the most extreme cases recorded. Some, however, describe cyber-stalking as a trivial matter which generally entails behaviours that occur in the real world and which are rarely considered as crimes in that context. Others claim that the incidence of cyber-stalking is commonly over-exaggerated, partially due (once again) to its extremely broad definition (see Reyns 2010).

Cyber-bullies and hate gangs

The virtual nature of online spaces means that most instances of cyber violence take on a virtual form. Aggressive language, threats, intimidation, sexual communication and cyber-stalking are all forms of violent behaviours (Barak 2005). The publication of hate materials on the Internet by individuals, groups or by governments are also acts of symbolic violence against their intended victims. Some would also argue that the prevalence of Internet pornography represents an act of collective violence against women. Victims of cyber-bullying may well suffer from considerable psychological and material consequences due to being targeted online (Finn 2004). It is rare for instances of cyber violence to lead to direct acts of violence in the real world, although various cases have occurred where cyber-stalkers do go on to molest and/or murder their victims. Perhaps the most extreme case on record is an Internet user in Germany who ate another man he met online. Such gruesome instances naturally receive widespread press attention, but are extremely rare. More generally, we understand cyber-bullying as a spiteful practice that targets specific individuals, often systematically. Aggression towards particular social groups or communities is more commonly referred to as a 'hate crime'. In that respect, the Internet is now the major site for the conduct of hate crimes of all political persuasions (Kaplan and Moss 2003; Schafer 2002).

Hate crimes single out particular social groups for vilification, threats and ridicule. Many perpetrators seek to mask their crimes behind arguments for free speech, but the criminalization of hate crimes by a number of countries has opened up legal avenues for challenging some of the most offensive content to be found on the Internet. Nonetheless, hate gangs remain commonplace on the net, and typically target specific racial and faith groups, and particular genders and sexualities, as well as those with physical and mental disabilities (Gerstenfeld et al. 2003). They may also target well-known individuals, often on the basis of their connection to the above categories (see Deirmenjian 2000). While individual posters may engage in hate crimes using the technique of abusive postings (or 'flaming'), hate crimes are more commonly group activities. Here, a virtual gang of haters will assemble online in order to articulate their grievances, seek collective support from like-minded bigots and disseminate literature that legitimates their agenda. There is, of course, a fine line between hate crimes that can be proscribed by law, and mainstream politics. Although most hate crimes are treated as crimes of expression, it is worth noting that online discussion amongst hate gangs can and does lead to real-life violence and intimidation (Tresis 2002).

Cyber-terrorists

Since 2001, accounts of cyber-crime have commonly incorporated discussion of the phenomenon of cyber-terrorism. Here the perpetration of information infrastructure attacks, online frauds and hate crimes is tentatively linked to a wide number of groups engaged in various forms of political violence (Gordon and Ford 2002; Taylor et al. 2010). However, there is little in the way of hard evidence for these assertions. Rather, it is in the context of violent struggles between sovereign states and non-state actors that the distinction between criminality and warfare has become increasingly blurred. In an era of 'information warfare', the remote control of robotic military vehicles, operational command and reconnaissance and the winning of 'hearts and minds' are all activities that are heavily reliant upon information technologies. Therefore, it is a point of debate whether the existence of a political agenda affords the various activities associated with cyber-terrorism the status of acts of war in certain cases, or whether they should be regarded simply as criminal acts. We might take one of two approaches here: we could either consider the illegitimacy of non-state political groupings associated with violence as sufficient cause to define all their online activity as cyber-crimes, or we could reserve this definition for the instances where their use of the new media corresponds with the procedural categories of cyber-crime in general, thereby recognizing political terrorism as a motive rather than being the crime itself. In taking either approach, we must still contend with the partisan nature of the various state actors that sponsor and/or proscribe terrorist organizations.

Since 2001, the asymmetric nature of various ongoing conflicts has highlighted the paradox of high-technology warfare. Whilst the incomparably sophisticated IT systems of the US military make it the most advanced army in history, the increasing reliance on IT networks also means that the US is the country most vulnerable to information attacks. The computerization of financial, industrial and public service infrastructures makes them susceptible to intrusion and sabotage. Accordingly, there has been increasing concern that terrorist groups will be successful in targeting America's information infrastructure (Taylor 2006). Certainly, terrorist groups have already used the Internet extensively for the purposes of coordinating violent attacks, organizing their operations, hacking government databases and spreading propaganda. Equally, there have been numerous instances during the past decade of 'information infrastructure attacks' being carried out by state agencies, with countries such as China, Russia and the United States being the most frequently accused. These activities are designed to disable and degrade scientific programmes, defence infrastructure and critical public services. Other 'information warfare' activities are more straightforward acts of interstate espionage, which are both illegal and normative in international relations. Most of the digital stores of classified information in government repositories have been hacked at some stage, and teams of 'official' hackers continue to breach scores of government systems during test attacks. In response to these threats, vast sums are now spent trying to secure the interlocking computer networks on which states increasingly depend. Comparable efforts are being made to breach the 'cyber defences' of other states.

Risk, Harm and Frequency

This roster of cyber-crimes is impressive in scope, ranging from the mundane (and almost unavoidable) breach of copyright law to apocalyptic destruction via information attacks on nuclear infrastructure. In this broad framing, it becomes almost impossible to make any meaningful assessment of the scale of the problem to be addressed. It follows, then, that cyber-crimes are distinctively different problems that happen to involve information technologies (much like online gaming, photographic manipulation and derivatives trading all rely on algorithms). Approached in a more piecemeal fashion, we can actually make more informed risk assessments about cyber-crimes in the conduct of everyday life. Were we to remain engaged at the overarching level, we would actually be required to assess the much larger question of the risks posed by information technology across the board (this is a valid, but far more expansive, undertaking). In focusing on cyber-crimes in more specific terms, we can begin to assess the relative severity of each risk. A proportionate response of this kind is necessary because losing thirty dollars on eBay is not the same as being murdered. To mitigate the general predilection with the rarest and most terrible crimes, we should also plot the relative occurrence of the various cyber-crimes. Having performed this (both abstract and reflexive) exercise, we can locate the relative risks of cyber-crime within a matrix that accounts for severity and occurrence. This then allows us to calculate the level of personal risk via an informed understanding of potential harm and frequency. It sounds very complicated, and it is, but we also do this each and every day.

Box 15.7 Typology of cyber-crime 3: occurrence

1. **Speech crimes** – these are crimes that involve the use of communication as a means of aggression, deception or for the subversion of social values. This would include: false impersonation and identity theft, flaming and crimes of etiquette, advocacy of treason and sedition, hate crimes conducted through public expression, political activism (in certain societies), slander and defamation, viewing and/or disseminating pornography and website defacement. Occurrence: endemic.
2. **Crimes of property** – these are forms of cyber-crime that are motivated by the desire to acquire the property of others, whether that property exists in a material or digital form. This would include: illegal financial transactions, online credit card fraud, online scams, data theft, media piracy, disposal of illegal goods. Occurrence: commonplace.
3. **Information infrastructure crimes** – these are crimes that involve the sabotage, corruption or other damage to information systems. This would include: computer intrusion, releasing viral computer programs, information infrastructure attacks, data theft and espionage, deliberate corruption of databases, destruction of data. Occurrence: frequent.
4. **Crimes of violence** – these are forms of cyber-crime, regardless of their motivation, that entail violence against others (either against their physical or virtual selves): this would include: online coordination of human trafficking, cyber-stalking with menace, blackmail and intimidation, production and dissemination of paedophile materials, coordination of terrorism and other violent material crimes, physical coercion of others for the purpose of cyber-crime. Occurrence: marginal.

As with most accounts of criminality in popular discourse, the societal discussion of cyber-crime has displayed a tendency to emphasize the most serious criminal acts that make use of the new media. The popular image of the Internet paedophile and the cyber-stalker as the definitive cyber-criminals is consistent with the longstanding tendency of media accounts to foreground the most frightening crimes at the expense of the more common ones (Gerbner and Gross 1976). In that sense, we can equate these terrifying figures with the phenomenon of modern 'folk devils' that inhabit our social imagination (Carrabine 2008; Littlewood 2003). That does not mean that such people do not exist, because it is very clear that they do, but overall it is readily apparent that a far greater proportion of the cyber-crimes taking place every day are financially motivated actions. Taken overall, the most frequently occurring cyber-crimes are invariably those that inhabit the grey area between legitimate self-expression and crimes of expression. This is also the domain where the legal frames of reference are most variable. A fully democratic society, for example, may permit political expression that would be considered a crime in a more autocratic society. A liberal society would permit sexual expression that would be counted as a crime in a more conservative society. Even the expression of violent, threatening viewpoints is openly tolerated in many societies, provided that such expressions are not causally linked to actual recorded physical violence.

The moral and legal ambivalence of speech crimes is not a marked feature of crimes of property. Variation in intellectual property laws and jurisdictions has played a very significant role in the epidemic of copyright violations, but the general principle of copyright is widely recognized throughout the world. For this reason, financial crimes and crimes of property are by far the most common forms of recorded cyber-crimes resulting in legal actions. Information infrastructure attacks have also been a long-standing feature of distributed computing. This apparently widespread inclination to sabotage computer systems is sometimes motivated by commercial competition or by political beliefs, but in many cases it is undertaken as a test of programming skill or even as a leisure pastime (Taylor 1999). Generally speaking, these forms of crime have not been treated with the same gravity that sabotage of, say, a national railway system would be. However, as the scale and density of digital technologies has increased, we have reached a point where essential infrastructures have become more vulnerable to these acts of remote sabotage. In the emerging digital economy, even the temporary disabling of a commercial or institutional website has very real material consequences for those depending upon that service. In that sense, it is important to recognize that the less sensational forms of cyber-crime are far from trivial matters. They have considerable social impact, both individually and collectively, and they are also everyday risks.

By contrast, the category of violent crimes covers the most high-profile, but by far the less frequently occurring, forms of cyber-crime. These are crimes that typically, if not always, have fewer victims than other forms of cyber-crime. For this reason, the risk to individuals is statistically negligible and their overall social impact is actually somewhat less than that of the more mundane forms of cyber-crime. However, this is not to say that the terrible consequences of the most vile crimes for their victims should not be issues of major concern for those charged with protecting the public. Over time, law enforcement agencies have developed new procedures and techniques for identifying such crimes and gathering evidence of their occurrence. These have included extensive surveillance resources, information retrieval and digital forensics along with greater inter-agency and international cooperation (Goel 2009; Krone 2005; Sommer 2004). Entrapment by investigators posing as cyber-criminals or as potential victims is another successful mechanism (although this is proscribed in some legal systems). Growing linkages between international politics and cyber-crime have also brought national security agencies into cyber-crime investigations. The vast majority of cyber-crimes, however, fall into mundane 'low-harm' categories that do not receive priority from law enforcement agencies. Instead, these activities have been accounted for in a wide range of new legislation across the world that is concerned specifically with digital property rights, legal jurisdiction, tax collection, investigative privileges, data retention, public surveillance and orders enforcing moral and social codes of behaviour (Akdeniz 2008; Grabosky 2007).

Law and enforcement are only ever one part of resolving the risks arising from crime. A large part of any societal response to cyber-crime must come from the public itself. The harms caused by cyber-crime to both individual users and to society as a whole can be described as: emotional, political, financial, functional and physical. This would also most likely be an accurate descending order of occurrence. Such a broad range of risks, inflicted through a dispersed media system offering ready anonymity to perpetrators, inevitably raises considerable challenges for societies trying to counter cyber-crime. For this reason, a number of public education campaigns and risk assessments associated with personal safety online have also been undertaken in recent years. An increased awareness of digital intrusion crimes and online frauds has subsequently prompted individuals, commercial and public institutions to invest large sums in electronic security systems designed by the software industry. Increasingly sophisticated firewalls and encryption systems mark an ongoing battle between security programmers and criminal hackers. Ultimately, however, it is the capacity of everyday Internet users to detect fraudulent approaches online and to report incidences of illegal material that is most critical for reducing the overall incidence of cyber-crime. At the most fundamental level, each and every Internet user needs to understand the inherent risks involved in anonymity, connectivity, public speech and data storage. If they are able to do so, our society will become more adept at the reflexive management of risk in cyberspace, reducing the human fallibilities that make cyber-crime an easy proposition for the casual criminal.

Think and Discuss

1. Key Terms
Can you describe in simple language what is meant by the following terms found in this chapter?

- Flaming
- Virus
- Cyber-stalking
- Phishing
- Identity theft

2. Critical Questions
Try answering the following questions, drawing upon your own understanding, experience and knowledge.

1. Have you ever been a victim of a cyber-crime? If so, how did it happen, what harm did you suffer and what did you learn from the experience?
2. Have you ever committed any one of the offences described in this chapter? If so, would you consider yourself a cyber-criminal?
3. Can we make practical distinctions between different forms of cyber-crime that will enable us to prioritize certain areas for law enforcement?
4. What impact does a reflexive awareness of cyber-crime have upon your own daily usage of networked media?
5. What is your assessment of the overall level of risk to society as a whole from cyber-crime?

Further Reading

Akdeniz, Yaman (2008) *Internet Child Pornography and the Law*, Farnham: Ashgate.

Clough, Jonathon (2010) *Principles of Cybercrime*, Cambridge: Cambridge University Press.

Beck, Ulrich (1992) *Risk Society: Towards a New Modernity*, London: Sage.

Beck, Ulrich, Giddens, Anthony, Lash, Scott (1994) *Reflexive Modernization: Politics, Traditions and Aesthetics in the New Social Order*, Cambridge: Polity.

Jewkes, Yvonne (ed.) (2003) *Dot.cons: Crime, Deviance and Identity on the Internet*, Cullompton: Willan.

Livingstone, Sonia and Haddon, Leslie (eds) (2009) *Kids Online: Opportunities and Risks for Children*, Bristol: The Policy Press.

Wall, David (2007) *Cybercrime: The Transformation of Crime in the Information Age*, Cambridge: Polity.

Wells, Joseph T. (ed.) (2010) *Internet Fraud Casebook: The World Wide Web of Deceit,* Hoboken: John Wiley

Yar, Majid (2006) *Cybercrime and Society*, London, Thousand Oaks and New Delhi: Sage.

Go Online

Australian Federal Police – http://www.afp.gov.au/policing/e-crime.aspx

Federal Bureau of Investigation – http://www.fbi.gov/about-us/investigate/cyber/cyber

Interpol – http://www.interpol.int/public/TechnologyCrime/default.asp

Symantec – http://us.norton.com/cybercrime/index.jsp

UK Cyber Crime Strategy 2010 – http://www.official-documents.gov.uk/document/cm78/7842/7842.pdf

United States Department of Justice – http://www.cybercrime.gov/

CHAPTER 16

Living in a Cloud

No examination of the nature of authority in a digital society can be completed without recognizing the unprecedented influence of an information technology elite over the conduct of markets, governments and the mundane pleasures of billions of people. This power is recognized instinctively by all of us in a myriad of small ways, but the 'technorati' have yet to face any meaningful challenge or substantial oppositional criticism to their systemic operation of technical privilege. There have, of course, been high-profile charges of monopolistic practices (against Microsoft, for example), the violation of privacy laws (against Google) and numerous suits charging commercial espionage and theft in the present patent wars (between Apple, Samsung, Facebook, Yahoo and others). Nonetheless, the legal challenges faced by the information technology giants are grounded in conservative wisdom. That is, they are overwhelmingly drawn from moral and philosophical legacies laid down in the eighteenth and nineteenth centuries. The sabotages of various hacking collectives are a much more contemporary form of critique native to digital society. These direct actions have, on occasion, been highly effective in imposing undemocratic judgements on the ethics of IT corporations, service providers and government agencies. On other occasions, hacking sprees have been childish, destructive and effective only insomuch as inspiring a further tightening of controls over the information infrastructure. By their very calling, of course, the digital pranksters do not take umbrage with the notion of technical privilege itself.

In that respect, the technical, commercial and legal nexus of the digital society has remained insulated from serious public questioning to an extent that even the most powerful states, corporations and the wealthiest individuals must surely envy. This power filters down into the everyday operation of the digital society. When the IT department issues a decree or implements a major structural change, entire institutions comply with hardly a murmur. Similarly, when a major software producer changes the status of a program, entire industries have to reorganize their workflows around the new production interface. When governments undertake information technology projects, they write open cheques. When a major innovator in Silicon Valley dies, there is public mourning. When a yet-to-see-profit Internet 'start-up' goes public, investors flood the company with billions of dollars without seeking to understand the fundamentals of the business in any great detail. Thus, in so many ways, the effective authority of the edifice of information technology is inverse to the extent that the mechanics of information technologies remain ineffable to the average citizen, politician or managing director.

Optimists, Pessimists and Sceptics

Why does the most pervasive technology of our times continue to occupy a mystical black box, when millions of us labour in its design and operation? Most of its manifestations are out in the open, or are at least open secrets. Most of us are well aware that there is a fuller history to account for than the rhetorical 'buzz' around digital media tends to suggest. For the most part, however, we have readily adapted to the regular directives of the new technology. This pressing of the 'reset' button occurs regularly across a broad range of fields, from avant-garde arts practice to development economics. Nonetheless, the broader reconfiguration of theoretical orthodoxies in the digital society did not appear entirely 'out of the blue'. The founding debates over the domain of 'cyberspace' were given shape by a number of emergent discourses that had themselves gathered momentum over the preceding decades. These included (amongst other things) the political primacy of personal expression, the techno-theology of futurism, the diminishing of institutional authority and the neoliberal ideal of efficient markets. Thus, the framing of the digital society was historically situated at the end of the millennium, without being simply 'of the moment'. Within this competing field of prophecies, the incipient possibilities of digital technologies were powerfully associated with far-reaching social changes seen as being on the immediate threshold of our experience. The World Wide Web, in particular, was seen as both cause and symptom of a new pattern of social relations. It was a catalyst for social change that was consciously designed for that very purpose.

Against this backdrop, Pippa Norris identified three broad schools of thought, which she associated with distinct cohorts of like-minded thinkers and commentators. Norris described these as the cyber-optimists, the cyber-pessimists and the cyber-sceptics (2000). Cyber-optimists, in general, believed that the Internet heralded a new era of unparalleled citizen participation in public life (Negroponte 1995; Rheingold 1993; Poster 1995). The new plenitude of information available via networked resources would revolutionize education, cultural production and political accountability. The functional interactivity of digital media technologies would empower individuals within society by giving them a far-reaching public voice, along with equal access to the many economic benefits of a single digital economy. The disintermediation of old monopolies via information technologies would open up entry to the fruits of the marketplace and usher in an era of entrepreneurship where new forms of intellectual creativity would flourish in the fertile ground of the 'knowledge economy' (Drucker 1993; Gates 1996; Leadbeater 2000). A growing culture of participation fostered amongst the 'grassroots' of a technologically enhanced society would alleviate the alienation of mass society and make the top-down autocracy of industrial society a thing of the past. Economic exploitation would become unworkable in an era where the producers and consumers of goods were in direct contact, and where they would become inseparable as social categories. Political conflict throughout society would diminish as the democratization of the means of production accelerated the rise of the consumer voter. As technical literacy became increasingly diffused throughout society, we could also expect to see a large number of people engaged in a collective and reiterative design process that would constantly monitor and improve the design of a self-sustaining socio-technical system.

Cyber-pessimists, in general, rejected the utopian proposition of an efficient commercial democracy arising on the base of a digital communications infrastructure (Baudrillard 1994; Lyon 1994; Virilio 2000; Webster and Robins 1986). Their more dystopian prophecies claimed that information technologies would reproduce, or even worsen, the hegemony of the dominant interests in society. Taking note of its military and industrial origins amongst the vital organs of state power, the Internet was set to become a powerful tool of state interests. A new elite of technical specialists, working in close alliance with multinational capitalists, would fix the usage of digital technologies in such a way as to maximize their combined control over the medium. They would, through the implementation of monopoly structures, direct information technologies towards the extraction of profits above all else. This pursuit of profit would require the extension of commodity rights over digital media content (via software, media formats and stores of data). An open system would soon give way to a proprietary system via a technical and legal process of 'digital enclosure' determined in the interests of multinational corporations (Boyle 2003). Thus, the Internet would steadily increase the divide between the haves and have-nots in a 'pay-per-view' society (Mosco 1989). The natural duopoly between state power and market makers would eventually dominate the online realm in a manner analogous to its previous stranglehold over social communication. If anything, the interactivity of digital media was likely to underwrite an era of unprecedented surveillance and the fine-tuned control of individuals in the workplace, on the streets and in the home.

A third grouping of cyber-sceptics can be associated with a general tendency to regard the entire digital revolution as being somewhat overstated (Margolis and Resnick 2000; Standage 1998). From this viewpoint, there was simply not enough empirical evidence to justify the 'hype' surrounding digital media, and the Internet in particular. In that sense, it was held that most of what people could and would do on the Internet would simply be things that they were already doing via other media (reading mail, watching movies, playing video games, chatting to friends). The exuberant investment flows into web platforms were thus regarded as speculative exercises preceding any evidence of a sustainable economic basis for online business models. The first collapse of the dot. com boom in 2000, tended to reinforce this sceptical viewpoint of the digital economy, even as its appeal began to broaden amongst the general public. The overarching prediction of cyber-sceptics was 'more of the same' across the fields of culture, business and politics. Genuine new multimedia forms would remain secondary to the remediation of earlier forms (Bolter and Grusin 2001). The aggregation of content would, if anything, reinforce the hegemony of our existing popular culture. Companies that had a viable business in the 'real world' would simply add online ordering mechanisms, and 'virtual' businesses would simply replicate existing commercial models (such as advertising, cable TV or catalogue shopping). Mainstream politics would balance a broader commentary from the public with more extensive public relations exercises. Political activists would put publications online without necessarily widening their existing readership or meaningfully expanding their political base.

Luddites and Revolutionaries

Over the turn of the millennium, it was the optimistic view of digital media that won out. Arguably, it did so because it corresponded with the varying agendas of a number of interested parties, including IT companies, governments, venture capitalists and academics. However, we must also take into account the fact that this optimistic view was also a reflection of a much broader enthusiasm for digital devices and new media platforms amongst the general public. Flying in the face of this popular sentiment, those taking a pessimistic view of digital media were often accused of being techno-Luddites (see Flew 2005). 'Luddites' historically were a group of English workers who vandalized new industrial machineries that threatened their livelihoods. The term has since become a byword for anyone seen to be 'afraid' of new technology. In the language of the digital revolution, pessimists were also derided as defenders of the status quo. They were accused of being attentive to the interests of various 'specialists' and therefore opposing the democratization of information processes (Jenkins 2006). Alternatively, they were habitual 'radicals' who simply opposed any kind of innovation. Thus, not only were they wedded to obsolete technologies, they were also wedded to an obsolete politics (such as liberalism or socialism). Luddites were 'non-technical' people, and typically offered plenty of critique without proffering any usefully designed correctives for the dangers that they identified. They were nonetheless widely heard, in part because they fulfilled the useful role of 'strawmen' for public rebuttal in the pages of *Wired* magazine.

While the optimist–pessimist face-off was a useful rhetorical mechanism for allaying public anxieties about the digital revolution, the sceptical position received far less attention. In many respects, it was ignored because the veracity of the digital revolution was simply taken as a given by most participants in the debate. Professional commentators on digital media naturally have an underlying commitment to the central importance of those technologies. Where sceptical views were recognized at all, it was typically assumed that their adherents simply lacked the capacity of projection. As such, they were unable to understand the technology in ways that allowed them to identify its unique characteristics and thereby imagine its potentials across the broad social canvas. Sociology itself has, over a much longer time span, witnessed a similar polarization between pessimistic and optimistic accounts of the social structure and between radical and sceptical responses to social change. Order can be seen as being oppressive or enabling (Durkheim 1895; Marx and Engels 1888). In reality, it is always both. Nonetheless, sociologists in the majority remain committed to the idea of social change. This is also a natural bias, because an unchanging social order has a lesser need for sociologists. It has also become a political matter since Karl Marx argued that the point was not to describe society, but to change it (1938). Ever since then, whether any instance of social change is for better or for worse has always been a matter of contention between optimists and pessimists. Revolution (whether sharp or slow) can be seen as being threatening or empowering (Mason 2012). In reality, it is always both. This holds true for the recent uprisings that have been closely associated with social media (Ghonim 2012; Taylor and Gessin 2012). In that respect, a sceptical view is better supported in sociology due to a long-term historical record that allows scholars to identify consistencies in human behaviour and social change (Arendt 2009; Burke 1968; Hobsbawm 1988).

Web 2.0: the Maturation of a Medium

At the turn of the millennium, most of us elected to remain optimistic about the digital revolution. Time, however, moves on. We are now twelve years into the twenty-first century. As such, this book speaks to a time when the 'new media' are no longer new. It is likely, in fact, that much of what has been discussed here has already been a feature of your daily experience for a number of years. If you are under twenty, then the radical experiment of the public Internet is already older than you are. If you are under forty, then personal computers have been around since you were a toddler. Today, digital technology can be found in almost every corner of our social environment. Personal computing devices have become portable in numerous forms. In-built computers drive our phones, televisions and cars. Silicon chips are embedded in train tickets, price tags and people. Like the World Wide Web, these are all implementations of what Mark Weiser called 'ubiquitous' (everywhere) computing (1991). Those who have been born into this socio-technical interface have been described recently by John Palfrey and Urs Gasser as 'digital natives' (2008). Back in the 1960s, Marshall McLuhan noted that 'the kids' understood electronic media like television, but their print-trained parents did not (1964). Similarly, Palfrey and Gasser address a 'parent' reader struggling to understand the umbilical connection between the young and personal media devices, SNS and participatory culture. Thus: 'These kids are different. They study, work, write and interact with each other in ways that are very different from the ways that you did growing up' (2008: 2).

Palfrey and Gasser's larger point is that, for digital natives, the 'new media' are hardly novel. They are no longer imminent. They are now. For the young, they are simply taken for granted as a pervasive social environment, where 'Major aspects of their lives – social interactions, friendships, civic activities – are mediated by digital technologies. And they've never known any other way of life' (ibid.). It is, of course, possible to overstate any large-scale typification of a generation, and the trend towards furnishing 'psychographic' profiles of every generation since the baby boomers has produced a somewhat confused field of overlapping claims (for example, the so-called generations 'X', 'Y', 'C'). In reality, there are always overlaps between generations. This is as true for their adoption and adaptation of technology as it is with pretty much everything else. Equally, the homogeneity of youth culture is readily apparent, but also ephemeral. Every generation produces its dissidents, and the substance of what we say and do online is more difficult to discern than the general activity itself. Nonetheless, Palfrey and Gasser are making a valid and important statement in noting, implicitly at least, that what we are actually talking about now is a relatively 'mature' medium. This signals an important change in our frames of reference. Raymond Williams wrote his definitive account of television at a similar stage in its development trajectory (1974). By the seventies, television technology had existed for forty years, and had been widely used for twenty years. During that time, the medium had been given institutional form by regulation, seen technological improvements in design and manufacturing, and had adopted the various formats of programming and content that are recognizable today.

The World Wide Web as it stands can be located along a similar timeline of development, implementation and maturation. The radical novelty of the system gave rise to an early period of frenetic and haphazard experimentation in the early 1990s. In the process, various usages were established and demands for particular kinds of content and services became apparent. Technical experts and government regulators worked throughout the decade to establish legal and technical jurisdictions. Simultaneously, investors and programmers joined together in numerous efforts to produce commercially viable platforms. By the 2000s, the users themselves had developed the literacy necessary for them to make full use of the technology. At the beginning of the 2010s, there is a range of broadly understood functional and semantic conventions in place characterizing the predominant generic forms of Internet content. This current iteration of web culture is seen as being coherent enough for the era of 'Web 2.0' to be announced (O'Reilly 2005). Web 2.0 is a domain in which user-produced content comes to the fore, replacing 'elite' sources of information. Web 2.0 is a configuration in which database-driven websites replace 'hand-coded' ones. It is a medium in which interactive search and communication services predominate over 'reading' distinct pieces of content. It is also a remediation by which the static computer is replaced by roaming access via a wide range of mobile devices. Web 2.0 is an operating system where software is not located on the user's computer, but is instead run 'server-side' and accessed by everyone. Consequently, Web 2.0 is a culture dominated by new social media formats such as SNS, blogs, Twitter, YouTube and Wikipedia. There is a familiar 'stagism' to this proposition, which seeks to imply that the now redundant 'Web 1.0' was a read-only environment locked into desktop computers and dominated by a web-designer elite. These are astonishing claims, which have drawn a rebuke from World Wide Web creator Tim Berners Lee, and from others who believe that Web 1.0 was actually a far more democratic environment than the environment of proprietary commercial platforms that characterizes Web 2.0 (Lanier 2010). In this recent past, you designed your own applications for the Web, as opposed to feeding content into monolithic compilers. In many respects, however, Web 2.0 marks not so much a technical shift as a commercial relaunch. The central problem is that unlike television at a comparable stage, the maturation of the World Wide Web continues to lack a sustainable commercial basis. Much of what is presently occurring on the Web is therefore oriented towards putting this final piece into the puzzle. There are many components to the overall challenge of achieving this goal, including the inherent interactivity of the medium, its diffusion across a much broader range of applications than earlier media 'delivery' systems and the 'free culture' of plenitude on which its popularity was originally founded. Competing interests also remain in play between the manufacturers of consumer electronics and the software industries, between the aggregators and creators of content, and between the technical community and the user base. In the past five years, the more commercially astute logic of Web 2.0 has sought to institute operating models drawn from other media. Various services based upon the subscription model associated with the mobile phone industry have been trialled (for example, online radio platforms like 'spotify'). There has also been a very public embrace of the advertising income that has long formed the bedrock of commercial television.

What's Behind the Cloud?

As the number of users has surpassed critical mass, and the upcoming generation of 'digital natives' turns to the Web as its major point of access to all forms of social communication, it makes sense for the advertising industry to redirect its efforts and expenditure towards appropriate platforms on the Web. To date, search giant Google has been the major beneficiary of this business (Halavais 2009). At the same time, the vast array of content being created by users and the material collected about their usage is also becoming the primary focus for sustainable commercialization. Google has also led the charge in the collection of user data from search requests, digital mapping and webmail services. This information provides valuable market and social research data, while also allowing for the delivery of targeted online services to individuals regardless of their location. The constant proximity of the mobile phone and the boundless resources of the information society are stitched together by wireless transmission and hyperactive databases. These innovations rest upon the investment flows coming from the consumer economy. It is by this mechanism that 'targeted advertising' makes integrated interactive services a realistic proposition that can be delivered cheaply to the user (or even for 'free'). At the same time, as other service providers follow the Google model, there is a noticeable shift away from the idea of the Internet as a content delivery vehicle and towards the idea that the actions of users will become the primary commodity underpinning the Internet economy.

There is, nonetheless, more than monetization at work in the reshaping of interactive services. The advent of Web 2.0 also marks a critical shift in the predominant ecology of computer science. For forty years, we have organized our understanding of digital technologies around the interface of the personal computer. At the back-end, the prevailing logic of 'personal distributed computing' was that the possession of a customizable, single-user device with its own processing resources was the most efficient and powerful way to widely disseminate the benefits of information technology. At the beginning of the 2010s, however, we are witnessing an emerging model of so-called 'cloud computing' where processing power, software functions and data storage are being redesigned for dispersal across the Internet. You will no longer own and operate your own data storage devices and software, but will instead access 'free' software applications and storage facilities online via a handful of web-based portals available from an infinite spread of devices and locations. As you roam around a world of 'pervasive' access with various contact devices in your bag or pocket, you will be able to uplink to a vast range of software applications and data services as and when you need them. This greater efficiency and convenience will lower the cost of maintaining software licenses, and it will also come with a large quota of data storage which will enable you to put your 'life' in the 'cloud' for safekeeping and ready access.

This is the prevailing vision of the next phase of computing, and it is being promoted heavily by information technology consultants, software houses and hardware manufacturers. Driven by online versions of core computing applications (such as word processing, gaming and image editing), the obvious advantage of cloud computing is that it frees us to roam without carrying our own processing equipment and data. Proponents of the cloud are also claiming that this model will allow individuals to harness the collective processing power of distributed computing for themselves. Rather than being an autonomous node (single computer) at the end of a communications network, the user will be able to make use of the combined capacity of the entire network (all computers). In that sense, the era of 'cloud computing' posits the 'time-sharing' of resources in a similar fashion to the long-gone days of the mainframe. One big difference, of course, is that packet-switching, fibre-optics and the Internet will allow everyone to time-share at the same time. Another crucial difference is that your access to the 'big' computer will actually be access to a single, global computer network (which is about as big as you can get). In that sense, the model of 'cloud computing' constitutes a drastic reversal of the logic of distributed computing to which we have become accustomed for so long. Your computer devices may be personal in size and feel, but they will not be standalone devices. They will all be integrated components of an enormous social computer.

The Hive Mind

In technology circles, Web 2.0 applications and the cloud model correspond because they give priority to the collective capacity of the system. This utilization of aggregated inputs is evidenced by collective knowledge-production platforms like Wikipedia. It is also deployed in the collective efforts of the open-source programming community. It finds yet another expression in the rapid rise of YouTube and Facebook on the back of content produced by vast numbers of end-users. Whilst the contributions made by each user may be small, when they are aggregated across the entire Web they constitute an enormous resource that far outstrips what even the most gifted individual could achieve. This is increasingly seen as providing the basis for harnessing the power of 'collective intelligence'. Here, the sum of our individual creativity becomes greater than the parts. Because our efforts online inevitably produce an indelible record of data suitable for any number of independent, dynamic informational processes, this collective creativity is predicted to become a self-sustaining mechanism. In that respect, the pursuit of cloud computing is also pertinent to John Von Neumann's historic commitment to creating a sentient machine (1958). At some point, it is assumed that the 'hive mind' of aggregated human activity replicated amongst the circuitry of the Internet will achieve a sentient autonomy from its creators (the so-called 'singularity' of artificial intelligence programs). This informational 'consciousness' sounds like a far-fetched proposition, but it is no more so than many of the goals that have guided the development of computer science over the past half-century (Clynes and Kline 1960; Licklider 1960; Wiener 1962).

Self-improving intelligent machines have long been seen as an imminent possibility. The logic, as laid down by Irving John Good in 1965, is that we will inevitably reach a stage where we design a computer that is smarter than we are. Such a machine will subsequently be able, and in fact required, to work on its own improvement. This capacity will increase exponentially, as the super-intelligent machine begins to design its own successors, which go on to do the same. This is the digital application of Von Neumann's *Theory of Self-Replicating Automata*, where machines make machines (1966). At a purely functional level, this goal is presently being pursued in the microscopic domain of nanotechnology. However, with the coming of the Internet, a new approach to achieving technological singularity was inspired by a broad notion of collective intelligence emerging in online communication (Levy 1997; Smith 1994). The thinking behind this is also deceptively simple: large numbers of people are smarter than any one individual could ever be. Where this greater social intelligence can be put to use, we can expect to see much higher productive efficiency in informational tasks. The most common analogy is with the insect world, where thousands of individuals work collectively to complete tasks that far exceed the capacity of any individual member. At their own scale, termites build enormously tall and climate-controlled buildings that humans cannot. They do so, not simply because of their tightly regimented labour, but also because of the cumulative capacity for problem-solving that informs the division and specialization of tasks.

In general terms, swarm intelligence can be defined as a phenomenon which arises from the social structure of interacting agents over a period of time if the sum of the problems solved collectively is higher than the sum of the problems solved individually. Two preconditions must be fulfilled in order for swarm intelligence to develop: The agents must interact with each other and they must be capable of problem-solving. Characteristics of swarm intelligence are self-organization, robustness, and flexibility. The members of the swarm interact without supervision or centralized control. The swarm is capable of achieving its goal even if some members fail and is able to adapt to a changing environment. The phenomenon of collective intelligence cannot only be observed in colonies of social insects but also in collaborative groups of humans. By exchanging experiences, correcting mistakes, and inspiring one another, collaborative groups are in a better position of solving problems than individuals. Collaboration can be understood as an act of collective information processing . . . Web 2.0 platforms increase this effect of knowledge enhancement. A wider range of people can connect more easily and more rapidly to reach a common opinion in online discussion.

Carolin Kaiser, Johannes Krockel, Freimut Bodendorf (2010), 'Swarm Intelligence for Analyzing Opinions in Online Communities', Proceedings of the 43rd Hawaii International Conference on System Sciences, viewed 16 June 2010 at: http://www.computer.org/portal/web/csdl/doi/10.1109/HICSS.2010.356

It has been argued that the Internet could well serve as an enabling mechanism for a powerful form of swarm intelligence in humans, provided that there is a practical means of directing the simultaneous activities of that vast collective. For this to happen, there needs to be a feedback mechanism as well as a set of processes through which tasks can be fed forward to the hive. The point at which the setting of tasks and the monitoring and assessment of responses becomes autonomous of human control would be the point (perhaps) at which a technological singularity might occur. An algorithmic hive mind capable of harvesting, collating and processing the intellectual output of millions of human beings would, by definition, be smarter than any single human being. This is, of course, a proposition entirely antithetical to the networked individualism which has been consistently promoted as the cause célèbre of digital society since the 1970s. It is, however, a proposition that has been taken seriously by a number of technologists and futurists (Kurzweil 2005; Szuba 2001).

Working the Crowd

A less ambitious, if no less instrumental, version of hive logic can be found in the comments of James Surowiecki on the *Wisdom of Crowds* (2004). Here the operation of collective intelligence is detected in the statistical averages of human responses to simple queries. The primary example employed is a commercial one: a hundred or so years ago, 800 people at a market in Plymouth were asked to guess the weight of an ox. The statistical average of their responses was a single integer away from being correct, and it was closer than any one of the individual guesses. Statisticians have subsequently explored this wisdom-of-crowds effect through many different variants, finding that it works best with simple requests that require a correct response along a single continuous scale. The scale and interactivity of the Internet make it a perfect mechanism for systematically harvesting the wisdom of crowds in a business environment (Tapscott and Williams 2006). Taking a similar tack, Clay Shirky has argued that the amount of human processing power connected to the Internet is vastly underutilized (2008). Given that the majority of users on the World Wide Web are engaged in exercises of distraction most of the time, their intellectual resources are largely untapped. If one were able to persuade people to give up just 1 per cent of their time online to wisdom-of-the-crowd exercises, then this enormous 'cognitive surplus' would transform the intellectual capacity of the digital society. The argument that Shirky makes for a participatory culture of networked volunteerism is a liberal one, although the structural effect of those actions would be akin to a cognitive socialism.

Scale is a big part of the story, because the surplus has to be available in aggregate . . . people must be able to donate their free time to collective efforts and produce a cognitive surplus, instead of making just a bunch of tiny, disconnected individual efforts. Part of the story of aggregate scale has to do with how the educated population uses its free time, but another part of it has to do with aggregation itself, with our being connected together in a single, shared media landscape. In 2010 the global internet-connected population will cross two billion, and mobile phone accounts already number three billion . . . We live, for the first time in history, in a world where being part of a globally interconnected group is the normal case for most citizens . . . The cognitive surplus, newly formed from previously-disconnected islands of time and talent, is just raw material. To get any value out of it, we need to make it mean or do things.

Clay Shirky (2008), *Cognitive Surplus: Creativity and Generosity in a Connected Age*, New York: Penguin Press, pp. 23–4, 29

As it stands, the best-known example that we presently have of harnessing a cognitive surplus is Wikipedia. Here, thousands of individuals record, edit and maintain thousands of pages of information on a vast range of topics. The same application also invites comparison with Surowiecki's arguments about the wisdom of crowds. Despite the fact that anyone can register to edit a page and there is no independent editorial control, the accuracy of most Wikipedia entries remains relatively high. When mistakes are made, they are quickly spotted and rectified by others. Similarly, when falsehoods are published or vandalism is conducted on Wikipedia pages, they are very quickly repaired by a small army of anonymous caretakers. The bias of individual authors is also mitigated by the corrections of others, producing entries that are appropriately neutral in tone. Shirky's central argument is that, even by modestly tapping the cognitive surplus amongst Internet users, we could have a hundred new projects of this size and scope running on the Web each year. This leads us, of course, to the contemporary popularity of 'crowdsourcing'. This term, coined by Jeff Howe of *Wired* magazine, describes the practical use of the Internet to recruit anonymous, collective talent in the solving of complex problems or the conduct of routine tasks (Brabham 2008; Howe 2009).

[C]rowdsourcing represents the act of a company or institution taking a function once performed by employees and outsourcing it to an undefined (and generally large) network of people in the form of an open call. This can take the form of peer-production (when the job is performed collaboratively), but is also often undertaken by sole individuals. The crucial prerequisite is the use of the open call format and the large network of potential laborers.

Jeff Howe (2006), 'Crowdsourcing: A Definition', *Crowdsourcing: Tracking the Rise of the Amateur*, viewed 4 April 2008 at: http://crowdsourcing.typepad.com/cs/2006/06/crowdsourcing_a.html

Crowdsourcing has proved to be an attractive concept for people engaged in many different endeavours. In some cases, the crowd is recruited to help search for aliens or to contribute spare processing capacity to solving complex problems in meteorology or experimental physics. More prosaically, various forms of crowdsourcing have been employed by start-up companies seeking technical advice, amateur musicians seeking collaborators and image libraries aggregating amateur photography. A much more systematic usage of the concept has been undertaken for a number of years by the

Internet retailer Amazon. Since 2005, Amazon has offered a 'Mechanical Turk' service to its clients. Here, simple information tasks that are either difficult to automate or low in volume are offered to a user-base as Human Intelligence Tasks (HITs). Those volunteering to undertake these tasks are paid very low sums for their completion, from a few cents to a few dollars. Some of these tasks might be challenging prospects, while others may be mundane exercises. A large army of mechanical Turks has been formed, ranging from straightforward enthusiasts to people (increasingly in the developing world) trying to make a living from 'Turking' (Ross et al. 2010). The name of the service comes from a famous chess-playing robot that toured Europe in the eighteenth century (which actually had a human player concealed inside). Although the client puts their HIT before an anonymous crowd, the tasks are undertaken by individuals rather than through mobilizing 'the hive'. For this reason, crowdsourcing applications like this are sometimes referred to as 'artificial artificial intelligence'.

Another manifestation of collective intelligence operating via digital networks has been highlighted in Howard Rheingold's work on 'smart mobs' (2003). Here the environment of pervasive social communication and personal media devices leads to seemingly spontaneous social actions being undertaken by citizen-collectives formed, and then coordinated, by mobile information technologies. In recent times, we have seen such phenomena operating on a large scale in the Middle East (the so-called 'Facebook' revolutions in Egypt and Tunisia), in the financial districts of American cities (the 'Occupy' movements) and on the streets of British cities (the 'social media' riots). These are single-issue virtual communities on the street in considerable numbers. Mobile connectivity facilitates these unpredictable concentrations of common purpose, where mutually anonymous individuals are rapidly mobilized in collective actions. In that respect, the affordances of crowdsourcing are equally applicable to direct action by citizens and sabotage by cyber-terrorists. Rheingold is nonetheless very explicit in noting that motivation is a critical factor in any understanding of smart mobility. The phenomenon itself may be value neutral in its mathematics, but there are important value judgements at play in differentiating between smart civic activists and rioters with mobile phones. The wider social structure also comes into play, since these phenomena illustrate an inevitable conflict being played out between those seeking to harness the potentials of the cloud from below and those seeking to direct it from above.

Lords of the Cloud

The hive, mobs and mechanical Turks all take us back to the question of where the power lies in this emergent configuration of the socio-technical interface. Does it reside in the network technology and the disembodied intelligence that it aggregates, as the singularity-enthusiasts would have us believe? Does it belong to the users and the cumulative effects of expressive democracy, as liberal cultural theorists assert? Or does it remain beholden to the small group of decision-makers who enjoy overarching access to the bird's eye view of the cloud, and who possess the technical capacity to structure its operation? It is too early to answer this question decisively, not least since it requires us to adopt a clear position on the nature of power, which is no easy task in itself. Perhaps the most logical starting point is to ask: who is presently harnessing the power of the cloud most effectively?

Google is probably the most obvious contender. This company has the capacity to monitor and analyse the information retrieval requests of the vast majority of users. It has the capacity to observe each and every point in global space via the combination of GPS, street photography and cartography. It is compiling human knowledge through the digital compendium of all the world's books. It has the capacity to apply relational algorithms to the disparate contents of public webmail systems and online office applications. This extensive aggregation of dynamic information resources puts Google in possession of a vast chunk of malleable data, which implies that it already holds a readily applicable source of power in any configuration of an information society or knowledge economy. The very notion of any contest, compromise or collusion between Google and the People's Republic of China demonstrates how significant this technical capacity is. As Alexander Halavais notes, we have yet to make a full assessment of 'what happens when the putatively natural, rational exercise of power by search technologies comes into conflict with the equally naturalized power of the state' (2009: 117).

Mark Zuckerberg's Facebook is another platform whose commercial value relies on extracting value from its users. In this form of crowdsourcing, the user constitutes the product that is on sale. That is why the company's stated adherence to the 'hacker ethic' does not get in the way of the huge data-mining operation from which it derives its income. The business model is itself a massive, centralized, top-down hack. The present ambition of Facebook is to expand its range of services in ways that will make it a one-stop shop for accessing the Web 2.0 environment. With 800 million users, the Facebook cloud could easily become one of the predominant weather features of our immediate future. Amazon and eBay also continue to be very important portals in the commercial domain of the information society. Like Facebook and Google, their core business is centred upon the aggregation of content produced by others. The key difference, of course, is that they match buyers and sellers on a commission basis, rather than relying on external revenues from advertising. All of these companies enjoy a market dominance in their respective domains that has few comparisons outside of information technology. They are all actively pursuing new applications that will leverage their respective positions to diversify and integrate their holdings in the cloud. The desired combination of controlling key access portals, managing everyday applications and overseeing personal data storage offers many practical opportunities to direct the inhabitants of the cloud. Where does this leave, as Jose Van Dijk puts it, 'users like you'?

To illustrate the complexity of user agency, the recent development of YouTube serves as a case of enquiry. Started as a video-sharing site in 2005 and run by three students from a silicon valley garage, the financially failing but hugely popular site was bought up by Google in October of 2006 for the unprecedented sum of $1.6 billion . . . In less than a year, YouTube became an (independent) subsidiary of a commercial firm whose core interest is not in content per se, but in the vertical integration of search engines with content, social networking and advertising . . . User agency is cast by cultural theorists as participatory engagement, in contrast to the passive recipients of earlier stages of media culture. Economists and business managers phrase user agency in the rhetoric of production rather than consumption. And in terms of labour relations, users are appraised in their new roles as amateurs and volunteers . . . If we want to understand how socio-economic and technological transformations effect the current shake-up in power relations between media companies, advertisers and users, it is important to develop a multifarious concept of user agency. Users like 'you' . . . have a rather limited potential to 'wrest power from the few', let alone to 'change the way the world changes'.

Jose Van Dijk (2009), 'Users Like You: Theorizing Agency in User-Generated Content', *Media, Culture and Society*, 31(1): 41–58

The metaphor of the cloud is particularly well chosen because of its heavenly manifestation and its benign (and fluffy) associations. It makes a more compelling case for a reconfiguration of personal computing than saying: 'why don't you stick all your stuff into a bunch of our servers in undisclosed remote locations'. Similarly, 'roaming access' via beautifully designed personal devices has more appeal than saying: 'you will have to pay various subscription fees, and put up with a wall of advertising, in order to get at your stuff, which I will also be sifting through and selling to other people as I see fit'. Even this blunt statement of the economics of aggregation is a more viable proposition for public up-take than saying: 'I want to suck your thoughts into my hive mind, in order to produce a world more fitting for my machines'. Better, perhaps, to stick with the fluffy white stuff and avoid such sinister science fictions. Having said this, there remains plenty to be sceptical about in all the hype surrounding the cloud, hive and crowd. The Internet is big and users have repeatedly proved to be fast-moving and fickle. Neither Mark Zuckerberg of Facebook nor Eric Schmidt of Google are in clear possession of the cloud just yet. As to the notion of a singularity triggered by aggregate Internet activity, it is, in all likelihood, a long way from Search adverts and SNS to an electronic godhood. Nonetheless, amongst the general celebration of 'participatory culture' and the 'democratization' of creativity, we should remain attentive to the underlying objectives of the people Jaron Lanier has recently described as the self-proclaimed 'lords of the cloud' (2010).

Watching the Weathermen

As a card-carrying Californian technologist, Lanier's overarching criticism is that the prevailing ethos of the 'technorati' has become fundamentally anti-human and that it now systematically devalues the contribution of individuals. Mobs are smart, it seems, but individuals are dispensable. Mathematical aggregates are given credence over philosophical judgement. Mashups are more valuable than artistic genius. Together, we approach technological divinity, but alone we serve no useful purpose in a world being reorganized around programmatic exploitation. Positioning himself as a digital dissident, Lanier makes the counter-claim that the hive fails to deal with true complexity in ways that a human being can. Politically and socially, he describes aggregated online behaviour as more akin to a herd than a hive. Lanier also supports Andrew Keen's argument that the logics of Web 2.0 are more likely to create a cultural 'grey ooze' than a creative economy of any standing (2008). In that sense, more will be lost in the generic formats of social media than will be gained statistically by their increasing membership. Thus, the crowd is not without its discontents; nor has its wisdom gone unchallenged.

Intellectual dissidents are not the only challengers to the lords of the cloud, however. In recent months, the US government has moved to introduce legislation that will see

US legal jurisdiction (in the form of copyright prosecutions and censorship) applied to the entire global Internet. Many leading Internet companies blacked out their websites in a symbolic protest. In the wake of the 2011 street riots, the UK government is presently initiating legislation that will give government agencies real-time 'live' access to all digital communications (commercial, personal or otherwise) (BBC News Online 2012). This is a powerful reminder that technology companies can own clouds, but the blue sky remains a government domain. As such, the shift to the cloud (and the story of the Internet in general) may well prove to be 'a normalized revolution . . . where new technologies create deeply significant, perhaps wholesale changes to the function of *established* political institutions without overthrowing those institutions' (Wright 2012: 253). Events may yet prove otherwise, but either way, all revolutions constitute a power play, and that includes technical ones. Thus, at the risk of sounding like digital dinosaurs, some of us may want to direct our attention towards what effectively constitutes the 'forces of participation' and the 'relations of participation' in the Web 2.0 reworking of the digital society.

The means themselves seem clear enough. The benefits of interoperability and automated systems that sideline the literacy gap are very clear. People can access and do more things online than ever before, from the most mundane acts of registration to the most immersive journeys of personal realization. Cloud applications mean that we can be, and often are, present anywhere and everywhere in a manner that was simply inconceivable not so long ago. The commercial innovations of Web 2.0 allow us to do this without bearing the cost of developing and maintaining the necessary infrastructure. As such, the motivations of those seeking to direct the cloud may not be a straightforward matter of megalomania and control freakery. At this point in the history of the World Wide Web, clouding may provide the foundation for firmly establishing the future of digital culture, in much the same way that movie studios and television networks did at similar points in the development trajectories of those technologies. Nonetheless, it also has to be said that the economics of aggregation bear more than a hint of the cynical exploitation of a 'prosuming' culture. This is by no means the only, or even the most practical, way of making the digital infrastructure pay for itself or to serve some useful social purpose.

Parallel attempts to harness collective intelligence are posited as a technical augmentation of social knowledge production. Humanity presently faces a number of highly complex challenges, and the scale and capacity of networked collectives offer one of the most readily available means for maximizing human potentials in response. In that respect, the good or evil of swarm intelligence really depends upon who is putting the questions to the hive. Nonetheless, even if we are able to maintain our commitment to 'do no evil' (which is doubtful), the significance of the shift away from personal computing should not be understated. In effect, we are surrendering the ownership of our personal data. We are also accepting the necessity of uninterrupted web connectivity, and paying for it (paying more, I suspect, as time goes by). We are conceding the loss of capacity to compute as a standalone activity (with the attendant intellectual privacy and creative autonomy). We are rapidly consigning the knowledge produced by millions worldwide to a supra-national storage facility administered by a handful of opaque corporations who already control key web portals and applications. In making any judgements on the utility of the cloud model, therefore, it is useful to review the predictions made by the optimists, pessimists and sceptics of the 1990s. All but the most ardent ideologues (and there are always a few of those amongst us) would concede that there was a measure of truth in all those positions. At the very least, this suggests that there needs to be a critical debate on the sociological significance of a collective global computing resource in the twenty-first century.

Think and Discuss

1. Key Terms
Can you describe in simple language what is meant by the following terms found in this chapter?

- Digital natives
- Crowdsourcing
- The hive mind
- Mechanical Turks
- Cloud computing

2. Critical Questions
Try answering the following questions, drawing upon your own understanding, experience and knowledge.

1. Would you describe yourself as a cyber-optimist, pessimist or sceptic and, if so, on what basis?
2. To what extent do your own experiences of digital communication provide evidence of swarm intelligence in operation?
3. Can you think of any examples where you rely upon the wisdom of crowds to obtain practical information?
4. Where would you locate the balance of power in Web 2.0?
5. In what ways can we expect digital natives to change the world?
6. Is intelligent machinery a proposition that you expect to encounter in the next twenty years?

Further Reading

Barnatt, Christopher (2010) *A Brief Guide to Cloud Computing: An Essential Introduction to the Next Revolution in Computing*, London: Constable and Robinson
Halavais, Alexander (2009) *Search Engine Society*, Cambridge: Polity.
Howe, Jeff (2009) *Crowdsourcing: How the Power of the Crowd is Driving the Future of Business*, New York: Penguin.
Kurzweil, Raymond (2005) *The Singularity is Near: When Humans Transcend Biology*, New York: Viking Penguin.
Lanier, Jaron (2010) *You Are Not a Gadget: A Manifesto*, London: Allen Lane.
Palfrey, John and Gasser, Urs (2008) *Born Digital: Understanding the First Generation of Digital Natives*, New York: Basic Books.
Rheingold, Howard (2003) *Smart Mobs: The Next Social Revolution*, Cambridge, MA: Perseus.
Shirky, Clay (2008) *Cognitive Surplus: Creativity and Generosity in a Connected Age*, New York: Penguin Press.
Surowiecki, James (2004) *The Wisdom of Crowds: Why the Many Are Smarter Than the Few and How Collective Wisdom Shapes Business, Economies, Societies and Nations*, New York: Doubleday.
Tapscott, Don and Williams, Anthony (2006) *Wikinomics: How Mass Collaboration Changes Everything*, New York: Penguin.

Go Online

Amazon Mechanical Turk – https://www.mturk.com/mturk/welcome
Google – http://www.google.com
Smart Mobs – http://www.smartmobs.com/
SOPA and PIPA Protests – http://sopablackout.org/learnmore/
Wikipedia Foundation – http://www.wikipedia.org/
Wired Magazine – http://www.wired.com/

Postscript: Towards a Digital Sociology

Over the course of this work, the notion of a digital society has led us to explore the role played by computing technologies across a broad range of human endeavours. In that sense, the usefulness of this notion lies in the permission it gives us to explore the socio-technical interface between computer technologies and everyday life using any number of frames and scales. Nonetheless, we should always remain attentive to the ways in which the foundational terms of our analysis inevitably shape our view of the subject matter, as well as the conclusions we draw. Thus, I will remind you one final time that the very term 'digital society' implies that binary computing is the central technology defining social organization and personal interaction in the world today. In this book, we have identified plenty of evidence to support such a claim. It is also, however, worth noting that there are other technologies which may prove to have equally critical importance for our species (neither biotechnology nor nuclear physics can be omitted as a concern for the ways in which we will live). Similarly, there is much that we can find in the existing usage of digital technologies that is not determined by the technologies themselves, but is instead contingent upon various human factors that put all manners of technologies to use in particular ways. The term 'digital society' is therefore deployed upon a qualified basis, claiming only that the significance and usage of these technologies is expansive enough to warrant a wide-ranging discussion that correlates how 'we shape our tools and our tools shape us'.

Within this particular context, we have encountered various other frames of reference that each cast their own inflections upon the wider discussion. Some are similar macro-sociological metaphors with an overlapping set of purposes (such as 'the information society', 'the surveillance society', 'the risk society'). Other key terms that we have encountered seek to concentrate our attention upon specific phenomena, but do so in a manner which suggests (more or less explicitly) that those practices lie at the heart of social life (such as 'the efficiency of free markets', 'the ideals of participatory culture' or 'the interface between technological mobility and individuation'). For our purposes, these are all jigsaw pieces within the puzzle of the digital society, but they could be (and indeed often are) used to provide overarching explanations of social interaction in their own right. In taking up their relative positions within this particular account, however, these various framings serve to remind us that there is no single standpoint from which we can observe social life. Given their critical role in the very making of the digital society, they also serve to remind us how sociological framings exert an influence upon how we plan, administer and assess interventions in society, with the domain of digital technology being no exception to this general rule. In describing things in certain ways, we provide a rationale for bringing particular sets of social relations into being and for making things anew. Sociology is not merely a descriptive practice. It is also a productive mechanism. This is a duality that it shares with information technologies, which amplify both the observational power and interventionist tendencies of the discipline.

A digital society needs a digital sociology, and it would be difficult to argue otherwise. David Beer and Roger Burrows have made the case that the present environment requires an updating of terminology, and a renewed sociology of description that captures the complexity of the digital society (Beer and Burrows 2007). Media studies has already led the charge with the pronouncement of a '2.0' variant designed to encapsulate a particular attentiveness to the moment (Gauntlett 2007b). A 'sociology 2.0' in this form would, however, be a disingenuous device for two major reasons. The first reason is that it is late in the day to suggest that sociological thinking might cross an event line imposed by interactive digital technologies. The digitization of sociological practice has already occurred over a long period. Quantitative research has undergone several decades of computerization and the rendering of social life in the form of dynamic datasets has already become an established focus for undergraduate courses in social research methods. Certain variants of sociology (such as panel data analysis) find a natural home in the era of the database. In that sense, we are already lords of our own cloud. In other areas, it has become increasingly common to research social life without leaving our computer terminal. The era of social media provides us with expansive new collections of material for interpretative analysis. As such, the steady refinement of techniques for virtual ethnography and anthropology indicates that the possibilities of interactive digital research have been recognized for some time. The problem, then, is not so much one of catching up with technological change, but rather one of avoiding any confusion between digital data and the social world that produces it. Sociology could be equally prone to the fallacy of the hive mind.

The second reason that sociology 2.0 appears to be an unlikely proposition is that the social sciences have consistently informed the development of information technologies. This contribution has not only been at the level of human–computer interaction analysis in the lab or social impact studies in the field, important as these may have been. The sociological imagination necessarily operates at the foundational level of technological development. The implementation of IT applications has always drawn heavily on a diverse sociological canon from behavioural psychology to social network analysis. The contemporary expression of digital culture is itself heavily informed by a wide range of sociological traditions from political economy to cultural studies and psychoanalysis. Consequently, there is no significant rupture between the broader legacy of sociology and the present iteration of digital technologies. So, again, the problem is not a matter of catch-up, so much as a problem of achieving critical distance (Latour 2007). Arguably, there can be no objective separation between positivist research and the information society, between political economy and intellectual property, or between social psychology and the surveillance society. The digital society is a universal lab, and in that respect, the advantage that sociology has over other inhabitants of the hive is that it has its own programming language. At the same time, we face the subsequent problem of finding ways to translate this language into forms that are effective in informing public debates over the usage of technology.

Sociologists tend to be consulted about practices that are associated with risk, but such consultations frequently come after the fact. Nonetheless, many sociologists are presently concerned with getting on the front foot in discussions about the future development of 'social media'. The aims of this book, however, have been far more modest. As a starting point, I have attempted to demonstrate some (hopefully) useful relationships between social theory and our everyday encounters with digital media. In the process, we have begun to re-examine various things that we already do within a set of framings that draw our attention to questions of determination, typification, selfhood, morality, social interaction and social structure. Along the way, I have attempted to balance the perennial 'newness' of computing as we experience it with a sketchpad rendition of its modern history. As this field of enquiry matures alongside the major applications of digital technologies you may want to direct yourself towards more detailed accounts of the various phenomena covered here. The suggestions that I have provided for that purpose (good as I think they are) should not be taken as the only pathways into the various discussions that I have opened up. If we are serious about this, we will have to do more than follow hyperlinks.

If you discern any particular bias in this overview of the field, then it most likely stems from a residual humanism on my part. I paid early attention to the macrological scale of personal experience for precisely that reason. At the same time, I see no value in neglecting the influence of collective social structures over daily conduct, and this is where the major iterations of conflict and consensus within digital society have been canvassed. Technological forms also exert a structuring effect (Web 2.0 is a good example of this) and I have tried to draw your attention to such inputs via a number of specific applications. Understanding the relationships between all these different actors is no easy task, and is perhaps best approached via a series of small steps. Nonetheless, these are steps that we are all taking in one way or another. This is how we presently live and, as a consequence, not all computer scientists are anti-human and not all humanists are Luddites. In the final analysis, the problems that we identify and resolve through technological innovation will always be essentially human concerns which engender characteristically human solutions. Much the same can be said for the practice of sociology.

Adrian Athique
March 2012

Bibliography

Acquisti, Alessandro, Gritzalis, Stefanos, Lambrinoudakis, Costos and Vimercati, Sabrina de (eds) (2007) *Digital Privacy: Theories, Technologies and Practices*, Boca Raton: Auerbach.

Adorno, Theodor (1991) *The Culture Industry: Selected Essays on Mass Culture*, London: Routledge.

Adorno, Theodor and Horkheimer, Max (1944) 'The Culture Industry: Enlightenment as Mass Deception', in Meenakshi Gigi Durham and Douglas M. Kellner (eds) (2006), *Media and Cultural Studies: Keyworks*, Malden, MA: Blackwell, pp. 41–72.

Adorno, Theodor and Horkheimer, Max (1993) *The Dialectic of Enlightenment*, New York: Continuum.

Agar, Jon (2004) *Constant Touch: A Global History of the Mobile Phone*, Cambridge: Icon.

Akdeniz, Yaman (2008) *Internet Child Pornography and the Law*, Farnham: Ashgate.

Akdeniz, Yaman, Walker, Clive, Wall, David (eds) (2000) *The Internet, Law and Society*, Harlow: Longman.

Allen, Anita (2011) *Unpopular Privacy: What Must We Hide?*, New York: Oxford University Press.

Allsop, Will (2009) *Unauthorised Access: Physical Penetration Testing for IT Security Teams*, Hoboken, NJ: John Wiley.

Althusser, Louis (1971) 'Ideology and Ideological State Apparatus: Notes Towards an Investigation', in Meenakshi Gigi Durham and Douglas Kellner (eds) (2006), *Media and Cultural Studies: Keyworks*, Oxford: Blackwell, pp.79–87.

Anderson, Benedict (1991) *Imagined Communities: Reflections on the Origin and Spread of Nationalism (Revised Edition)*, London: Verso.

Anderson, Chris (2006) *The Long Tail: How Endless Choice is Creating Unlimited Demand*, New York: Random House.

Anderson, Craig, Gentile, Douglas, and Buckley, Katherine (2007) *Violent Videogame Effects on Adolescents and Children: Theory, Research and Public Policy*, Oxford: Oxford University Press.

Andersson, Jonas (2009) 'For the Good of the Net: The Pirate Bay as a Strategic Sovereign', *Culture Machine*, 10: 64–108.

Andrejevic, Mark (2007a) *iSpy: Surveillance and Power in the Interactive Era*, Kansas: University Press of Kansas.

Andrejevic, Mark (2007b) 'Surveillance in the Digital Enclosure', *The Communication Review*, 10: 295–317.

Andrejevic, Mark (2011) 'Surveillance and Alienation in the Online Economy', *Surveillance and Society*, 8(3):278–87.

Ang, Ien (1991) *Desperately Seeking the Audience*, London and New York: Routledge.

Appadurai, Arjun (1996) *Modernity at Large: Cultural Dimensions Of Globalisation*, Minneapolis, MN, and London: University of Minnesota Press.

Arendt, Hannah (2009) *On Revolution*, London: Penguin.

Armstrong, Gary and Norris, Clive (1999) *The Maximum Surveillance Society: The Rise of CCTV*, London: Berg.

Arvidsson, Adam (2005) *Brands: Meaning and Value in Media Culture*, London and New York: Routledge.

Arvidsson, Adam (2006) '"Quality Singles": Internet Dating and the Work of Fantasy', *New Media and Society*, 8(4): 671–90.

Atkins, Barry (2003) *More Than A Game: The Computer Game as a Fictional Form*, Manchester: University of Manchester Press.

Ayres, Ian (2008) *Super Crunchers: How Anything Can Be Predicted*, New York: Bantam.

Bales, Robert Freed (1950) *Interaction Process Analysis: A Method for the Study of Small Groups*, Reading, MA: Addison-Wesley.

Balsamo, Anne (1997) *Technologies of the Gendered Body: Reading Cyborg Women*, Durham, NC, and London, Duke University Press.

Barak, Azy (2005) 'Sexual Harassment on the Internet', *Social Science Computer Review*, 23(1): 77–92.

Bardini, Thierry (2000) *Bootstrapping: Douglas Engelbart, Coevolution and the Origins of Personal Computing*, Palo Alto, CA: Stanford University Press.

Bardini, Thierry and Horvath, A. (1995) 'The Social Construction of the Personal Computer User', *Journal of Communication*, 45(3): 40–66.

Barnatt, Christopher (2010) *A Brief Guide to Cloud Computing: An Essential Introduction to the Next Revolution in Computing*, London: Constable and Robinson.

Baron, Nancy (2008) *Always On: Language in an Online and Mobile World*, New York: Oxford University Press.

Baruh, Lemi (2007) 'Read at Your Own Risk: Shrinkage of Privacy and Interactive Media', *New Media and Society*, 9(2): 187–211.

Baudrillard, Jean (1988) *Selected Writings* (ed. and introduced by Mark Poster), Stanford, CA: Stanford University Press.

Baudrillard, Jean (1994) *Simulacra and Simulation*, Ann Arbor, MI: University of Michigan Press.

Baudrillard, Jean (1995) *The Gulf War Did Not Take Place*, Bloomington, IN: Indiana University Press.

Baym, Nancy K. (1995) 'The Emergence of Community in Computer-Mediated Communication', in Steven Jones (ed.), *Cybersociety: Computer-Mediated Communication and Community*, Thousand Oaks, CA: Sage, pp. 138–63.

Baym, Nancy K. (1999) *Tune In, Log on: Soaps, Fandom and Online Community*, London and Thousand Oaks, CA: Sage.

Baym, Nancy (2006) 'Interpersonal Life Online', in L. A. Levrouw and S. Livingstone (eds), *The Handbook of New Media*, London: Sage, pp. 35–54.

Baym, Nancy (2010) *Personal Connections in the Digital Age*, Cambridge: Polity.

BBC News Online (2009a) 'Facebook Used to Target Gang Crime', at: http://news.bbc.co.uk/today/hi/today/newsid_7852000/7852763.stm; viewed 27 January 2009.

BBC News Online (2009b) 'Facebook "Withdraws" Data Changes', at: http://news.bbc.co.uk/2/hi/technology/7896309.stm; viewed 19 February 2009.

BBC News Online (2009c) 'Facebook Offers Control To Users', at: http://news.bbc.co.uk/2/hi/technology/7913289.stm; viewed 26 February 2009.

BBC News Online (2009d) 'Facebook Comments Girl Sacked', at: http://news.bbc.co.uk/1/hi/england/7915212.stm; viewed 27 February 2009.

BBC News Online (2009e) 'Facebook Users Suffer Viral Surge', at: http://news.bbc.co.uk/2/hi/technology/7918839.stm; viewed 2 March 2009.

BBC News Online (2010) 'US May Shares Crash Caused by a Single Trader', 1 October 2010; at: http://www.bbc.co.uk/news/business-11456941.html; viewed 1 October 10.

BBC News Online (2011a) 'Egypt Unrest: Bloggers Take Campaign to Tahrir Square', at: http://www.bbc.co.uk/news/world-middle-east-12381295; viewed 7 February 2011.

BBC News Online (2011b) 'Social Media Talks About Rioting Constructive', at: http://www.bbc.co.uk/news/uk-14657456; viewed 25 August 2011.

BBC News Online (2011c) 'Facebook to Seek Consent for Privacy Changes', at: http://www.bbc.co.uk/news/technology-15692542; viewed 27 November 2011.

BBC News Online (2011d) 'Can Facebook Turn 800m Users Into a $100bn Dollar Business?', at: http://www.bbc.co.uk/news/business-15962476; viewed 1 December 2011.

BBC News Online (2012a) 'FBI Plans Social Network Map Alert Mash-Up Application', at: http://www.bbc.co.uk/news/technology-16738209; viewed 26 January 2012.

BBC News Online (2012b) 'Facebook To Go Public with $10bn Share Offering'', at: http://www.bbc.co.uk/news/business-16779779; viewed 29 January 2012.

BBC News Online (2012c) 'Irish Privacy Watchdog Calls for Facebook Changes', at: http://www.bbc.co.uk/news/technology-16289426; viewed 21 December 2011.

BBC News Online (2012d) 'Email and Web Use "To Be Monitored" Under New Laws', at: http://www.bbc.co.uk/news/uk-politics-17576745; viewed 1 April 2012.

Beck, Ulrich (1992) *Risk Society: Towards A New Modernity*, London: Sage.

Beck, Ulrich (1995) *Ecological Politics in the Age of Risk*, Cambridge: Polity.

Beck, Ulrich (1997) *The Reinvention of Politics: Rethinking Modernity in the Global Social Order*, Cambridge: Polity.

Beck, Ulrich (1999) *World Risk Society*, Cambridge: Polity.

Beck, Ulrich, Giddens, Anthony, Lash, Scott (1994) *Reflexive Modernization: Politics, Traditions and Aesthetics in the New Social Order*, Cambridge: Polity.

Beckett, Charlie and Ball, James (2012) *Wikileaks: News in the Network Era*, Cambridge: Polity.

Beer, David (2008) 'Social Network(ing) Sites . . . Revisiting The Story So Far: A Response to danah boyd and Nicole Ellison', *Journal of Computer-Mediated Communication*, 13: 516–29.

Beer, David and Burrows, Roger (2007) 'Sociology and, of and in Web 2.0: Some Initial Considerations', *Sociological Research Online*, 12(5): 17, at: http://www.socresonline.org.uk/12/5/17.html, viewed 03/01/2012.

Beharrell, Peter, Davis, Howard, Eldridge, John and Hewitt, John (2009a) *Bad News*, London and New York: Routledge.

Beharrell, Peter, Davis, Howard, Eldridge, John and Hewitt, John (2009b) *More Bad News*, London and New York: Routledge.

Bell, Daniel (1973) *The Coming of Post-Industrial Society: A Venture in Social Forecasting*, New York: Basic Books.

Bell, David (2006) *Science, Technology and Culture*, Maidenhead: Open University Press.

Benjamin, Walter (1972) *Illuminations*, London: Fontana Press.

Benkler, Yochai (2006) *The Wealth of Networks: How Social Production Transforms Markets and Freedom*, New Haven, CT: Yale University Press.

Ben-Ze'ev, Aaron (2004) *Love Online: Emotions on the Internet*, Cambridge: Cambridge University Press.

Berry, David (2008) *Copy, Rip, Burn: The Politics of Copyleft and Open Source*, London: Pluto Press.

Biressi, Anita and Nunn, Heather (eds) (2007) *The Tabloid Culture Reader*, Maidenhead: Open University Press.

Biro, George M. (1999) *Marshall McLuhan Meets the Millennium Bug: The First 100 Years of Computers, and How We Can Make It*, Kingston, Ontario: Uplevel.

Blomberg, Jeanette (1995) 'Ethnography: Aligning Field Studies of Work and System Design', in A. F. Monk and N. Gilbert (eds), *Perspectives on HCI: Diverse Approaches*, London: Academic Press, pp. 175–97.

Blomberg, Jeanette, Giacomie, Jean, Mosher, Andrea and Swenton-Wall, Pat (1991) 'Ethnographic Field Methods and Their Relation To Design', in Douglas Schuler and Aki Namioka (eds), *Participatory Design: Perspectives on System Design*, Hillsdale: Lawrence Erlbaum, pp. 123–55.

Bloor, David (1991) *Knowledge and Social Imagery*, Chicago, IL: University of Chicago Press.

Blumer, Herbert (1969) *Symbolic Interactionism: Perspective and Method*, Chicago, IL: University of Chicago Press.

Bocij, Paul (2004) *Cyberstalking: Harassment in the Internet Age and How to Protect Your Family*, Westport, CT: Praeger.

Bohemia Interactive (2011) 'Virtual Battlespace 2', viewed 24 March 2011, at: http://www.bistudio.com/index.php/english/company/simulations.

Boldrin, Michele and Levine, David (2008) *Against Intellectual Property*, Cambridge: Cambridge University Press.

Bolin, Goran (2011) *Value and the Media*, Farnham: Ashgate.

Bolter, Jay David and Grusin, Richard (2001) *Remediation: Understanding New Media*, London and Cambridge, MA: MIT Press.

Bourdieu, Pierre (1993) *The Field of Cultural Production: Essays on Art and Literature*, Cambridge: Polity.

boyd, danah and Ellison, Nicole (2007) 'Social Network Sites: Definition, History and Scholarship', *Journal of Computer-Mediated Communication*, 13: 210–230.

Boyle, James (2003) 'The Second Enclosure Movement and The Construction of the Public Domain', *Law and Contemporary Problems*, 66(33): 147–78.

Brabham, Daren C. (2008) '"Crowdsourcing as a Model for Problem Solving": An Introduction and Cases', *Convergence: The International Journal of Research Into New Media Technologies*, 14(1): 75–90.

Branscomb, Lewis (1999) *Industrializing Knowledge: University-industry Linkages in Japan and the United States*, Cambridge, MA: MIT Press.

Brewer, Thomas L. and Nollen, Stanley D. (1998) 'Knowledge Transfer to Developing Countries after WTO: Theory and Practice in Information Technology in India', Working Paper 98-14, Carnegie Bosch Institute.

Brousseau, Eric and Curien, Nicolas (2007) *Internet and Digital Economics*, Cambridge: Cambridge University Press.

Bruns, Axel (2005) *Gatewatching: Collaborative Online News Production*, New York: Peter Lang.

Bruns, Axel (2008) 'The Future is User-Led: The Path Towards Widespread Produsage', *The Fibreculture Journal*, 11, at: http://eleven.fibreculturejournal.org/fcj-066-the-future-is-user-led-the-path-towards-widespread-produsage/; viewed 11 March 2012.

BSA (2003) *Eight Annual BSA Global Software Piracy Study*, Business Software Alliance, at: http://www.bsa.org/country/Research%20and%20Statistics.aspx; viewed 14 July 2006.

Budd, Leslie and Harris, Lisa (eds) (2009) *e-Governance: Managing or Governing?*, London and New York: Routledge.

Bull, Michael (2005) 'No Dead Air! The iPod and the Culture of Mobile Listening', *Leisure Studies*, 24(4): 343–55.

Bull, Michael (2007) *Sound Moves: iPod Culture and Urban Experience*, London and New York: Routledge.

Bunnel, David and Luecke, Richard A. (2000) *The eBay Phenomenon: Business Secrets Behind the World's Hottest Internet Company*, New York: John Wiley.

Burgess, Jean and Green, Joshua (2009) *YouTube: Online Video and Participatory Culture*, Cambridge: Polity.

Burke, Edmund (1968) *Reflections on the Revolution in France*, London: Penguin.

Burns, Kelli (2009) *Celeb 2.0: How Social Media Foster Our Fascination with Popular Culture*, Santa Barbara, CA: Praeger.

Bush, Vannevar (1945) 'As We May Think', *Atlantic Monthly*, 176(1): 101–8.

Butler, Judith (1990) *Gender Trouble: Feminism and the Subversion of Identity*, New York: Routledge.

Byron, Tanya (2008) *Safer Children in a Digital World: Report of the Byron Review*, Nottingham: Department of Children Schools and Families.

Campbell-Kelly, Martin (2003) *From Airline Reservations to Sonic the Hedgehog: A History of the Software Industry*, Cambridge, MA: MIT Press.

Careny Davis, Richard (2005) *Politics Online: Blogs, Chatrooms and Discussion Groups in American Democracy*, New York: Routledge.

Carmel, Erran and Tija, Paul (2005) *Offshoring Information Technology: Sourcing and Outsourcing to a Global Workforce*, Cambridge: Cambridge University Press.

Carnoy, Martin (2000) *Sustaining the New Economy: Work, Family and Community in the Information Age*, Cambridge, MA: Harvard University Press.

Carr, Diane, Buckingham, David, Burn, Andrew and Schott, Gareth (2006) *Computer Games: Text, Narrative and Play*, Cambridge: Polity.

Carrabine, Eamonn (2008) *Crime, Culture and the Media*, Cambridge: Polity.

Castells, Manuel (1977) *The Urban Question: A Marxist Approach*, London: Edward Arnold.

Castells, Manuel (1996) *The Information Age: Economy, Society and Culture, Vol. I: The Rise of the Network Society*, Cambridge, MA, and Oxford: Blackwell.

Castells, Manuel (1997) *The Information Age: Economy, Society and Culture, Vol. II: The Power of Identity*, Cambridge, MA, and Oxford: Blackwell.

Castells, Manuel (1998) *The Information Age: Economy, Society and Culture, Vol. III: The End of Millennium*, Cambridge, MA, and Oxford: Blackwell

Castells, Manuel (1999) 'Information Technology, Globalization and Social Development', UNRISD Discussion Paper No. 114, New York: United Nations Research Institute for Social Development.

Castells, Manuel (2002a) An Introduction to the Information Age', in G. Bridge and S. Watson (eds), *The Blackwell City Reader*, Oxford: Blackwell, pp. 40–8.

Castells, Manuel (2002b) *The Internet Galaxy: Reflections on the Internet, Business and Society*, Oxford: Oxford University Press.

Castells, Manuel, Fernandez-Ardevol, M., Lichuan Qui, J. and Sey, A. (eds) (2007) *Mobile Communication and Society: A Global Perspective*, Cambridge, MA: MIT Press.

Cavanagh, Allison (2007) *Sociology in the Age of the Internet*, Buckingham: Open University Press.

Caves, Richard (2002) *Creative Industries: Between Art and Commerce*, Cambridge, MA: Harvard University Press.

Cerf, Vint and Kahn, Bob (1974) 'A Protocol for Packet Network Communication', *IEEE Transactions on Communications*, 22(5): 637–47.

Chadwick, Andrew (2006) *Internet Politics: States, Citizens and New Communications Technologies*, New York: Oxford University Press.

Chandler, Alfred D. (2005) *Inventing the Electronic Century*, Cambridge, MA: Harvard University Press.

Chua, Cecil and Wareham, Jonathon (2004) 'Fighting Internet Auction Fraud: An Assessment and Proposal', *Computer* , 37(10): 31–7.

Clough, Jonathon (2010) *Principles of Cybercrime*, Cambridge: Cambridge University Press.

Clynes, Manfred and Kline, Nathan (1960) 'Cyborgs and Space', *Astronautics* (September): 26–76.

Cohen, Lizabeth (2004) *A Consumer's Republic: The Politics of Mass Consumption in Postwar America*, New York: Vintage Books.

Coleman, James (1994) *Foundations of Social Theory*, Cambridge, MA: Harvard University Press.

Conboy, Martin (2004) 'The Discourse of the Fourth Estate', in *Journalism: A Critical History*, London: Sage, pp.109–27.

Copeland, B. Jack (2004) *The Essential Turing*, Oxford: Oxford University Press.

Copeland, B. Jack et al. (2006) *Collosus: The Secrets of Bletchley Park's Code-breaking Computers*, Oxford: Oxford University Press.

Cottle, Simon (1998) 'Ulrich Beck, "Risk Society" and the Media', *European Journal of Communication*, 13(1): 5–32.

Cottrell, Stella (2003) *Skills for Success: The Personal Development Planning Handbook*, Basingstoke: Palgrave Macmillan.

Coyle, Diana (1999) *The Weightless World: Strategies for Managing the Digital Economy*, Cambridge MA: MIT Press.

Cronin, Blaise and Davenport, Elisabeth (2001) 'E-Rogenous Zones: Positioning Pornography in the Digital Economy', *The Information Society*, 17(1): 33–48.

Cubitt, Sean (1999) 'Orbis Tertius', *Third Text*, 47 (Summer): 3–10.

Curran, James (2002) *Media and Power*, London: Routledge.

Curran, James and Seaton, Jean (2003) *Power Without Responsibility: The Press and Broadcasting in Britain*, London and New York: Routledge.

Daft, Richard and Lengel, Robert (1984) 'Information Richness: A New Approach to Managerial Behaviour and Organizational Design', *Research in Organizational Behaviour*, 6: 191–233.

D'Angelo, Paul and Kuypers, Jim (eds) (2010) *Doing News Framing Analysis: Empirical and Theoretical Perspectives*, London and New York: Routledge.

DCMS (1998) *Creative Industries Mapping Document*, London: Department of Sports Media and Culture.

Debord, Guy (1967 [1995]) *The Society of the Spectacle*, Cambridge, MA: Zone Books.

Deirmenjian, John (1999). 'Stalking in Cyberspace', *Journal of American Academic Psychiatry Law*, 27: 407–13.

Deirmenjian, John (2000) 'Hate Crimes on the Internet', *Journal of Forensic Sciences*, 45(5): 1020–22.

Derrida, Jacques (1973) *Speech and Phenomena and Other Essays on Husserl's Theory of Signs*, Evanston, IL: Northwestern University Press.

Dery, Mark (1996) *Escape Velocity: Cyberculture at the End of the Century*, London: Hodder and Stoughton.

Deuze, Mark (2007) *Media Work*, Cambridge: Polity.

Dhamija, Rachna, Tygar, J. D. and Hearst, Marti (2006) 'Why Phishing Works', CHI 2006 Proceedings, 22–27 April 2006, Montréal.

Doggett, Peter (2008) *There's A Riot Going On: Revolutionaries, Rock Stars and the Rise and Fall of '60s Counter-culture*, Edinburgh: Canongate Books.

Dossani, Rafiq and Kenney, Martin (2007) 'The Next Wave of Globalization: Relocating Service Provision to India', *World Development*, 35(5): 772–91.

Doyle, Gillian (2002) *Media Ownership: The Economics and Politics of Convergence and Concentration*, London: Sage.

Drucker, Peter (1959) *Landmarks of Tomorrow*, New York: Harper and Row.

Drucker, Peter (1969) 'Knowledge Society', *New Society*, 13(343): 629–31.

Drucker, Peter (1993) *Post-capitalist Society*, Oxford: Heinemann.

Drucker, Susan and Gumpert, Gary (2000) 'CyberCrime and Punishment', *Critical Studies in Media Communication*, 17(2): 133–58.

Durkheim, Émile (1893 [1984 edn]) *The Division of Labour in Society*, London: Macmillan.

Durkheim, Émile (1895 [1982 edn]) *The Rules of Sociological Method*, London: Macmillan.

Durkin, Kevin and Barber, Bonnie (2002) 'Not So Doomed: Computer Game Play and Positive Adolescent Development', *Applied Developmental Psychology*, 23: 373–92.

Dyer-Witheford, Nick (1999) *Cyber-Marx: Cycles and Circuits of Struggle in High Technology Capitalism*, Urbana, IL: University of Illinois Press.

Earl, Jennifer and Kimport, Katrina (2011) *Digitally Enabled Social Change: Activism in the Internet Age*, Cambridge, MA: MIT Press.

Eco, Umberto (1986) *Travels in Hyperreality*, Orlando, FL: Harcourt Brace & Company.

Edgell, Stephen (2006) *The Sociology of Work: Continuity and Change in Paid and Unpaid Work*, London: Sage.

Elberse, Anita (2008) 'Should You Invest in the Long Tail?', *Harvard Business Review*, July–August 2008, Reprint R0807H, pp. 1–10.

Engelbart, Douglas (1963) 'A Conceptual Framework for the Augmentation of Man's Intellect', in P. Howerton and D. Weeks (eds), *Vistas in Information Handling Vol. 1*, Washington: Spartan, pp. 1–29.

Enslinn, Astrid and Muse, Eben (eds) (2011) *Creating Second Lives: Community, Identity and Spatiality as Constructions of the Virtual*, Abingdon and New York: Routledge.

Ensmenger, Nathan (2010) *The Computer Boys Take Over: Computers, Programmers and the Politics of Technical Expertise*, Cambridge MA: MIT Press.

Epstein, Richard (2005) 'The Creators Own Ideas', *Technology Review*, 108(6): 56–60.

Ess, Charles (2009) *Digital Media Ethics*, Cambridge: Polity.

Farrell, Diana (2007) *Offshoring: Understanding the Emerging Global Labour Market*, Cambridge, MA: Harvard Business School Press.

Featherstone, Mike (1990) *Global Culture: Nationalism, Globalization and Modernity*, London, Thousand Oaks, CA, and New Delhi: Sage.

Featherstone, Mike and Burrows, Roger (eds) (1996) *Cyberspace, Cyberbodies, Cyberpunk: Cultures Of Technological Embodiment*, London: Sage.

Ferguson, Niall (2007) *The War of the World: History's Age of Hatred*, London: Penguin.

Fetveit, Arild (1999) 'Reality TV in the Digital Era: A Paradox In Visual Culture?' *Media, Culture & Society*, 21(6): 797.

Field, Douglas (2005) *American Cold War Culture*, Edinburgh: Edinburgh University Press.

Field, John (2008) *Social Capital*, London and New York: Routledge.

Finn, Jerry (2004) 'A Survey of Online Harassment at a University Campus', *Journal of Interpersonal Violence*, 19(4): 468–83.

Fiske, John (1989) *Understanding Popular Culture*, London and New York: Routledge.

Flew, Terry (2002) *New Media: An Introduction*, Melbourne: Oxford University Press.

Flew, Terry (2005) *New Media: an Introduction*, Oxford: Oxford University Press.

Flew, Terry (2011) *The Creative Industries: Culture and Policy*, London, Thousand Oaks, CA, and New Delhi: Sage.

Florida, Richard (2002) *The Rise of the Creative Class*, New York: Perseus.

Ford, Martin (2009) *The Lights in the Tunnel: Automation, Accelerating Technology and the Economy of the Future*, Acculent Publishing.

Foucault, Michel (1969) *L'archéologie du savoir*, Paris: Gallimard.

Foucault, Michel (1977) *Discipline and Punish: The Birth of the Prison*, New York: Random House.

Foucault, Michel (2002) *Archaeology of Knowledge*, London: Routledge.

Friedman, Milton (1962) *Capitalism and Freedom*, Chicago, IL: Chicago University Press.

Friedman, Thomas (2005) *The World is Flat: A Brief History of the Twentieth Century*, New York: Farrar, Straus and Giroux.

Frisby, David P. and Featherstone, Mike (1997) *Simmel on Culture: Selected Writings*, London: Sage.

Fuchs, Christian (2008) *Internet and Society*, London and New York: Routledge.

Fukuyama, Francis (1992) *The End of History and the Last Man*, New York: Free Press.

Furnell, Steven (2002) *Cybercrime: Vandalizing the Information Society*, London: Addison-Wesley.

Garfinkel, Simson (2000) *Database Nation: The Death of Privacy in the 21st Century*, Cambridge: O'Reilly.

Gates, Bill (1995) *The Road Ahead*, 2nd edn, London and New York: Penguin.

Gauntlett, David (2007a) *Creative Explorations: New Approaches to Identities and Audiences*, London and New York: Routledge.

Gauntlett, David (2007b) 'Media Studies 2.0', *Theory.org.uk*, at: http://www.theory.org.uk/ mediastudies2.htm (viewed 2 January 2012).

Gee, James Paul (2003) *What Have Videogames to Teach Us about Learning and Literacy?*, London and New York: Palgrave Macmillan.

Gerbner, George and Gross, Larry (1976) 'Living With Television: The Violence Profile', *Journal of Communication*, 26: 172–99.

Gerstenfeld, Phylis, Grant, Diana, Chiang, Chua-Pu (2003) 'Hate Online: A Content Analysis of Extremist Internet Sites', *Analyses of Social Issues and Public Policy*, 3: 29–44.

Ghonim, Wael (2012) *Revolution 2.0*, New York: Fourth Estate.

Gibson, William (1984) *Neuromancer*, London: Grafton.

Giddens, Anthony (1984) *Constitution of Society: Outline of the Theory of Structuration*, Cambridge: Polity.

Giddens, Anthony (1990) *The Consequences of Modernity*, Cambridge: Polity.

Giddens, Anthony (1991) *Modernity and Self-Identity*, Cambridge: Polity.

Giddens, Anthony (1999) *Runaway World: How Globalisation is Reshaping Our Lives*, Cambridge: Polity.

Giddens, Anthony (2002) *Runaway World*, London: Routledge.

Giddings, Seth and Lister, Martin (2011) *The New Media and Technocultures Reader*, London and New York: Routledge.

Glickman, Harvey (2005) 'The Nigerian "419" Advance Fee Scams: Prank or Peril?', *Canadian Journal of African Studies*, 39(3): 460–89.

Glucksmann, Miriam (1982) *Women on the Line*, London and New York: Routledge (under pseudonym).

Goel, Sanjay (ed.) (2009) *Digital Forensics and Cyber Crime*, Albany, NY: Springer.

Goffman, Erving (1959) *The Presentation of the Self in Everyday Life*, Garden City, NY: Doubleday.

Goggin, Gerard (2006) *Cell Phone Culture: Mobile Technology In Everyday Life*, New York: Routledge.

Goggin, Gerard (2010) *Global Mobile*, New York: Routledge.

Goldberg, Adele (ed.) (1988) *A History of Personal Workstations*, Reading: Addison-Wesley.

Good, Irving John (1965) 'Speculations Concerning the First Ultraintelligent Machine', in F. Alt and M. Rubinoff (eds), *Advances in Computers, Vol. 6*, New York: Academic Press, pp. 31–88.

Goode (1995) 'Stalking: Crime of the 90's?', *Criminal Law Journal*, 19(1): 1–10.

Gordon, Sarah and Ford, Richard (2002) 'Cyberterrorism?', *Computers and Security*, 21(7): 636–47.

Gordon, Sarah and Ford, Richard (2006) 'On the Definition and Classification of Cybercrime', *Journal of Computer Virology*, 2(1): 13–20.

Gorham, Michael and Singh, Nidhi (2009) *Electronic Exchanges: The Global Transformation from Pits to Bits*, Berlington: Elsevier.

Gorlizki, Yoram and Khlevniuk, Oleg (2006) *Cold Peace: Stalin and the Soviet Ruling Circle, 1945–1953*, New York: Oxford University Press.

Gow, Gordon and Smith, Richard (2006) *Mobile and Wireless Communications: An Introduction* , Maidenhead: Open University Press.

Grabosky, Peter (2007) 'Requirements of Prosecution Services to Deal With Cyber Crime', *Crime Law and Social Change*, 47(4–5): 201–23.

Granovetter, Mark (1973) 'The Strength of Weak Ties', *American Journal of Sociology*, 78: 1160–80.

Granovetter, Mark (1974) *Getting A Job: A Study of Contacts and Careers*, Cambridge, MA: Harvard University Press.

Green, Nicola (2002) 'On the Move: Technology, Mobility, and the Mediation of Social Time and Space', *The Information Society*, 18: 281–292.

Gregg, Melissa (2011) *Work's Intimacy*, Cambridge: Polity.

Guertin, Carolyn (2012) *Digital Prohibition: Piracy and Authorship in New Media Art*, London and New York: Continuum.

Habermas, Jürgen (1974) 'The Public Sphere: An Encyclopedia Article', *New German Critique*, 3, p. 49-54.

Habermas, Jürgen (1984) *The Theory of Communicative Action, Vol. 1: Reason and Rationalization of Society*, Boston, MA: Beacon Press.

Habermas, Jürgen (1987) *Theory of Communicative Action, Vol. 2*, Cambridge: Polity.

Habermas, Jürgen (1992) *The Transformation of the Public Sphere: An Enquiry into a Category of Bourgeois Society*, Cambridge: Polity.

Halavais, Alexander (2009) *Search Engine Society*, Cambridge: Polity.

Hale, Constance (ed.) (2006) *Wired Style: Principles of English Usage in the Digital Age*, San Francisco, CA: Hardwired.

Hall, Stuart (1980) 'Encoding/Decoding', in Stuart Hall, Dorothy Hobson, Andrew Lowe and Paul Willis (eds), *Culture, Media, Language: Working Papers in Cultural Studies 1972–79*, London: Routledge, pp. 128–38.

Hall, Stuart (1981) 'Notes on Deconstructing the Popular', in Raphael Samuel (ed.), *People's History and Socialist Theory*, London: Routledge and Kegan Paul, pp. 227–39.

Hall, Stuart, Hobson, Dorothy, Lowe, Andrew and Willis, Paul (1980) *Culture, Media, Language: Working Papers in Cultural Studies 1972–79*, London: Routledge.

Hall, Stuart, Du Guy, Paul, Janes, Linda and Mackay, Hugh (1983) *Doing Cultural Studies: The Story of the Sony Walkman*, Milton Keynes: Open University Press, p. 17.

Handy, Charles (1994) *The Empty Raincoat: Making Sense of the Future*, London: Hutchinson.

Harfoush, Rahaf (2009) *Yes, We Did: An Inside Look at How Social Media Built the Obama Brand*, Berkeley, CA: New Riders.

Haraway, Donna (1991) *Simians, Cyborgs and Women*, New York: Routledge.

Harris, Richard Jackson and Sanborn, Fred (2009) *A Cognitive Psychology of Mass Communication*, Mahwah, NJ: Lawrence Erlbaum.

Hartley, John (ed.) (2009) *Creative Industries*, Oxford: Blackwell.

Harvey, David (2005) *A Brief History of Neoliberalism*, Oxford: Oxford University Press.

Harvey, David (2010) *The Enigma of Capital and the Crises of Capitalism*, London: Profile Books.

Hassan, Robert (2008) *The Information Society*, Cambridge: Polity.

Hayek, Friedrich August Von (1944) *The Road to Serfdom*, New York: Routledge.

Hayles, Katharine (1999) *How We Became Posthuman: Virtual Bodies in Cybernetics, Literature and Informatics*, Chicago, IL: University of Chicago Press.

Haynes, Richard (2005) *Media Rights and Intellectual Property*, Edinburgh: Edinburgh University Press.

Heath, Joseph and Potter, Andrew (2006) *The Rebel Sell: How the Counterculture Became Consumer Culture*, Chichester: Capstone.

Hebdige, Dick (1979) *Subculture: The Meaning of Style*, London: Methuen and Co.

Held, David and McGrew, Anthony (eds) (2007) *Globalization Theory*, Cambridge: Polity.

Hesketh, Anthony and Brown, Phillip (2004) *The Mismanagement of Talent: Employability and Jobs in the Knowledge Economy*, Oxford: Oxford University Press.

Hildreth, Paul and Kimble, Chris (2004) *Knowledge Networks: Innovation Through Communities of Practice*, Hershey: Idea Group Publishing.

Hillis, Ken, Petit, Michael, Epley, Nathan Scott (2006) *Everyday eBay: Culture, Collecting and Desire*, New York and London: Routledge.

Hiltz, Star Roxanne and Turoff, Murray (1978) *The Network Nation: Human Communication Via Computer*, Reading, MA: Addison-Wesley.

Hiltzik, Michael (2000) *Dealers of Lightning: Xerox PARC and the Dawn of the Computer Age*, New York: HarperCollins.

Hind, David and Moss, Stuart (2005) *Employability Skills*, Houghton-le-Spring: Business Education Publishers.

Hobsbawm, Eric (1988) *The Age of Revolution: Europe 1789–1848*, London: Abacus.

Hobsbawm, Eric (1995) *The Age of Extremes: The Short Twentieth Century*, London: Abacus.

Hobsbawm, Eric and Ranger, Terence (eds) (1992) *The Invention of Tradition*, Cambridge: Cambridge University Press.

Hoffman, Donna and Novak, Thomas (1998) 'Bridging The Racial Divide On The Internet', *Science*, 280: 390–1.

Hoggart, Richard (1957) *The Uses of Literacy*, London: Chatto and Windus.

Hopson, Barrie and Ledger, Kate (2009) *And What Do You Do?: 10 Steps to Creating A Portfolio Career*, London: A & C Black.

Horrocks, Christopher (2000) *Marshall McLuhan and Virtuality*, New York: Totem Books.

Howe, Jeff (2006) 'Crowdsourcing: A Definition', *Crowdsourcing: Tracking the Rise of the Amateur*, viewed 4 April 2008 at: http://crowdsourcing,typepad.com/cs/2006/06/crowdsourcing_a.html

Howe, Jeff (2009) *Crowdsourcing: How the Power of the Crowd is Driving the Future of Business*, London: Random House.

Howkins, John (2002) *The Creative Economy: How People Make Money From Ideas*, London: Penguin.

Hughes, Lorine A. and DeLone, Gregory J. (2007) 'Viruses, Worms and Trojan Horses: Serious Crimes, Nuisance, or Both?', *Social Science Computer Review*, 25(1): 78–98.

Humphreys, Sal (2008) 'Grassroots Creativity and Community in New Media Environments:

Yarn Harlot and the 4000 Knitting Olympians, *Continuum: Journal of Media and Cultural Studies*, 22(3): 419–33.

Husserl, Edmund (1965) *Phenomenology and the Crisis of Philosophy*, New York: Harper Torchbooks.

Husserl, Edmund (1970 [1936]) *The Crisis of European Sciences and Transcendental Philosophy*, trans. D. Carr, Evanston, IL: Northwestern University Press.

IFPI (2009) *Digital Music Report*, International Federation of the Phonographic Industry, at: http://www.ifpi.org/content/library/dmr2009.pdf; viewed 15 January 2010.

Inkson, Kerr (2007) *Understanding Careers: The Metaphors of Working Lives*, London: Sage.

Innis, Harold (1951) *The Bias of Communication*, Toronto: University of Toronto Press.

Innis, Harold (1952) *Changing Concepts of Time*, Toronto: University of Toronto Press.

Isbister, J. N. (1985) *Freud: An Introduction to His Life and Work*, Cambridge: Polity.

Jackson, Tim (2011) *Prosperity Without Growth: Economics for a Finite Planet*, London and New York: Routledge.

Jakobsson, Markus and Myers, Steven (2007) *Phishing and Countermeasures: Understanding the Increasing Problem of Electronic Identity Theft*, Hoboken, NJ: John Wiley.

Jameson, Fredric (1991) *Postmodernism, or, The Cultural Logic of Late Capitalism*. Durham, NC: Duke University Press.

Jankowski, Nicholas W. and Prehn, Ole (2001) *Community Media in the Information Age*, New York: Hampton Press.

Jarvis, Peter (2010) *Adult Education and Lifelong Learning*, London: Routledge.

Jeffcutt, Paul and Pratt, Andy (2009) (eds) *Creativity and Innovation in the Cultural Economy*, London and New York: Routledge.

Jenkins, Henry (1992) *Textual Poachers: Television Fans and Participatory Culture*, New York: Routledge.

Jenkins, Henry (2004) 'The Cultural Logic of Media Convergence', *International Journal of Cultural Studies*, 7(1): 33–43.

Jenkins, Henry (2006) *Convergence Culture: Where Old and New Media Collide*, New York: New York University Press.

Jenkins, Henry and Thorburn, David (2004) *Democracy and New Media*, Cambridge, MA: MIT Press.

Jessop, Bob (2007) *State Power*, Cambridge: Polity.

Jewkes, Yvonne (ed.) (2003) *Dot.cons: Crime, Deviance and Identity on the Internet*, Cullompton: Willan.

Jewkes, Yvonne and Andrews, Carol (2005) 'Policing the Filth: The Problems of Investigating Online Child Pornography in England and Wales', *Policing and Society*, 15(1): 42–62.

Jewkes, Yvonne and Yar, Majid (2009) *Handbook of Internet Crime*, Cullompton: Willan.

Johns, Andrew (2011) *Piracy: The Intellectual Property Wars from Gutenberg to Gates*, Chicago, IL: Chicago University Press.

Johnson, J. David (2009) *Managing Knowledge Networks*, Cambridge: Cambridge University Press.

Johnson, Steven (1997) *Interface Culture: How New Technology Transforms the Way We Create and Communicate*, New York: HarperEdge.

Johnson, Steven (2001) *Emergence: The Connected Lives of Ants, Brains, Cities and Software*, New York: Simon and Schuster.

Jones, Steven (2002) 'Music that Moves: Popular Music, Distribution and Network Technologies', *Cultural Studies* 16(2): 213–32.

Jordan, Tim (2008) *Hacking: Digital Media and Technological Determinism*, Cambridge: Polity.

Jordan, Tim and Taylor, Paul (2004) *Hacktivism and Cyberwars: Rebels with a Cause?*, London and New York: Routledge.

Juul, Jasper (2005) *Half-Real: Video Games Between Real Rules and Fictional Worlds*, Cambridge, MA: MIT Press.

Kafai, Yasmin (1994) *Minds in Play: Computer Game Design as a Context for Children's Learning*, London and New York: Routledge.

Kahin, Brian and Wilson, Ernest (1997) *National Information Infrastructure Initiative: Vision and Policy Design*, Cambridge, MA: MIT Press.

Kahle, Lynn and Kim, Chung-Hyun (2006) *Creating Images and the Psychology of Marketing Communication*, Marwah, NJ: Lawrence Erlbaum.

Kaiser, Carolin, Krockel, Johannes and Bodendorf, Freimut (2010) 'Swarm Intelligence for Analyzing Opinions in Online Communities', *Proceedings of the 43rd Hawaii International Conference on System Sciences* at: http://www.computer.org/portal/web/csdl/doi/10.1109/HICSS.2010.356; viewed 16 June 2010.

Kant, Immanuel (2007) *Critique of Pure Reason*, London: Penguin.

Kaplan, James E. and Moss, Margaret P. (2003) *Investigating Hate Crimes on the Internet*, Washington, DC: Partners Against Hate.

Katz, James E. and Aakhus, Mark (2002) *Perpetual Contact: Mobile Communication, Private Talk, Public Performance*, Cambridge: Cambridge University Press.

Katz, James E. and Rice, Ronald E. (2002) *Social Consequences of Internet Use: Access, Involvement, and Interaction*, Cambridge, MA: MIT Press.

Katz, James E. and Sugiyama, S. (2006) 'Mobile Phones as Fashion Statements: Evidence from Student Surveys in the US and Japan', *New Media and Society*, 8(2): 321–37.

Keen, Andrew (2008) *The Cult of the Amateur: How Today's Internet is Killing Our Culture and Assaulting Our Economy*, London and Boston, MA: Nicholas Brealey.

Keynes, John Maynard (1936) *The General Theory of Employment, Interest and Money*, Cambridge: Cambridge University Press.

Khan, Richard and Kellner, Douglas (2004) 'New Media and Internet Activism: From the "Battle of Seattle" to Blogging', *New Media and Society*, 6(1): 87–95.

Kingsepp, Eva (2003) 'Apocalypse the Spielberg Way: Representations of Death and Ethics in *Saving Private Ryan*, *Band of Brothers* and the Videogame *Medal of Honor: Frontline*', in M. Copier and J. Raessens (eds), *Level Up Conference Proceedings*, Utrecht: University of Utrecht Press, CD-ROM.

Kingsepp, Eva (2007) 'Fighting Hyperreality with Hyperreality: History and Death in World War II Digital Games', *Games and Culture*, 2(4): 366–75.

Klapper, Joseph (1960) *The Effects of Mass Communication*, New York: Free Press.

Kling, Rob (ed.) (1996) *Computerization and Controversy: Value Conflicts and Social Choices*, San Diego, CA: Academic Press.

Kobayashi-Hillary, Mark (2005) *Outsourcing to India: The Offshore Advantage*, Berlin: Springer Verlag.

Kroker, Arthur (1997) 'Digital Humanism: The Processed World of Marshall McLuhan', in Arthur Kroker and Marilouise Kroker (eds), *Digital Delirium*, New York: St Martin's Press.

Krone, Tony (2005) 'International Police Operations Against Online Child Pornography', *Crime and Justice International*, 21: 11–20.

Kucklich, Julian (2006) 'Literary Theory and Digital Games', in Jason Rutter and Jo Bryce (eds), *Understanding Digital Games*, London: Sage, pp. 95–111.

Kuhn, Thomas (1962) *The Structure of Scientific Revolutions*, Chicago, IL: University of Chicago Press.

Kuipers, Giselinde (2006) 'The Social Construction of Digital Danger: Debating, Defusing and Inflating the Moral Dangers of Online Humour and Pornography in the Netherlands and the United States', in *New Media and Society*, 8(3): 379–400.

Kumar, Krishnan (2005) *From Post-Industrial to Post-Modern Society: New Theories of the Contemporary World*, Oxford: Blackwell.

Kurzweil, Raymond (2005) *The Singularity is Near: When Humans Transcend Biology*, New York: Viking Penguin.

Kutler, Stanley (2010) *Watergate: A Brief History With Documents*, Chichester: John Wiley.

Lacan, Jacques (1953) 'Some Reflections on the Ego', *International Journal of Psychoanalysis*, 34: 11–17.

Lacity, Mary and Rottman, Joseph (2008) *Offshore Outsourcing of IT Work: Client and Supplier Perspectives*, Houndmills: Palgrave Macmillan.

Landow, George (1997). *Hypertext.2.0*. Baltimore, MD: Johns Hopkins University Press.

Lane III, Frederick (2001) *Obscene Profits: The Entrepreneurs of Pornography in the Cyber Age*, London: Routledge.

Lanier, Jaron (2010) *You Are Not a Gadget*, London: Allen Lane.

Lash, Scott (1990) *The Sociology of Postmodernism*, London: Routledge.

Latour, Bruno (2007) *Reassembling the Social: An Introduction to Actor-Network Theory*, Oxford: Oxford University Press.

Law, John and Hassard, John (eds) (1999) *Actor-Network Theory and After*, Oxford: Blackwell.

Leadbeater, Charles (2000) *Living On Thin Air: The New Economy*, London and New York: Penguin Books.

Lee, Hye-Kyung (2005) 'When Arts Met Marketing: Arts Marketing Theory Embedded in Romanticism', *International Journal of Cultural Policy*, 11(3): 14–27.

Lessig, Lawrence (2002) *The Future of Ideas: The Fate of the Commons in a Connected World*. New York: Vintage Books.

Lessig, Lawrence (2005a) *Free Culture: The Nature and Future of Creativity*, New York: Penguin.

Lessig, Lawrence (2005b) 'The People Own Ideas', *Technology Review*, 108(6): 46–53.

Lessig, Lawrence (2009) *Remix: Making Art and Commerce Thrive in the Hybrid Economy*, New York: Penguin.

Levay, Simon and Nonas, Elisabeth (1995) *City of Friends: A Portrait of the Gay and Lesbian Community in America*, Cambridge, MA: MIT Press.

Levinson, Paul (1999) *Digital McLuhan: A Guide to the Information Millennium*, London and New York: Routledge.

Levy, Pierre (1997) *Collective Intelligence: Mankind's Emerging World in Cyberspace*, New York: Plenum.

Levy, Steven (2010) *Hackers: Heroes of the Computer Revolution*, Sebastopol: O'Reilly Media.

Levy, Steven (2011) *In The Plex: How Google Thinks, Works and Shapes Our Lives*, New York: Simon and Schuster.

Lewis, Elen (2008) *The eBay Story Phenomenon: How One Brand Taught Millions of Strangers to Trust One Another*, Tarrytown, NY: Marshall Cavendish.

Licklider, J. C. R. (1960) 'Man–Computer Symbiosis', *IRE Transactions on Human Factors in Electronics*, vol. HFE-1, pp. 4–11.

Lievrouw, Leah A. (2011) *Alternative and Activist New Media*, Cambridge: Polity.

Lievrouw, Leah A. and Livingstone, Sonia (2005) *The Handbook of New Media: Social Shaping and Social Consequences of ICTs*, London and New Delhi: Sage.

Lindner, Rolf (1996) *The Reportage of Urban Culture: Robert Park and the Chicago School*, Cambridge: Cambridge University Press.

Ling, Richard and Donner, Jason (2009) *Mobile Phones and Mobile Communication*, Cambridge: Polity.

Lister, Martin (1995) *The Photographic Image in Digital Culture*, London and New York: Routledge.

Littlewood, Anne (2003) 'Cyberporn and Moral Panic: An Evaluation of Press Reactions to Pornography on the Internet', *Library and Information Research*, 27(86): 8–18.

Livingstone, Sonia (2008) 'Taking Risky Opportunities in Youthful Content Creation: Teenagers Use of Social Networking Sites For Intimacy, Privacy and Self-Expression', *New Media and Society*, 10(3): 393–411.

Livingstone, Sonia and Bober, Magdalena (2005) *UK Children Go Online: Final Report of Key Project Findings*, London: LSE.

Livingstone, Sonia and Haddon, Leslie (eds) (2009) *Kids Online: Opportunities and Risks for Children*, Bristol: The Policy Press.

Lowood, Henry and Nitsche, Michael (2011) *The Machinima Reader*, Cambridge, MA: MIT Press.

Lyon, David (1994) *The Electronic Eye: The Rise of Surveillance Society*, Minneapolis, MN: University of Minnesota Press.

Lyon, David (2001) *Surveillance Society: Monitoring Everyday Life*, Buckingham: Open University Press.

Lyon, David (2003a) *Surveillance as Social Sorting: Privacy, Risk and Digital Discrimination*, London and New York: Routledge.

Lyon, David (2003b) *Surveillance After September 11*, Cambridge: Polity.

Lyon, David (2007) *Surveillance Studies: An Overview*, Cambridge: Polity.

Lyotard, Jean (1984) *The Postmodern Condition: A Report on Knowledge*, Manchester: Manchester University Press.

McCue, Colleen (2006) *Data Mining and Predictive Analysis: Intelligence Gathering and Crime Analysis*, Burlington: Elsevier.

McDermott, John (1997) 'Technology: The Opiate of the Intellectuals', in Kristin Sharon Shrader-Frechette and Laura Westra (eds), *Technology and Values*, Lanham, MD, and Oxford: Rowman and Littlefield, pp. 87–106.

McDowell, Linda (2003) *Redundant Masculinities?: Employment Change and White Working Class Youth*, Malden, MA, and Oxford: WileyBlackwell.

McDowell, Linda (2009) *Working Bodies: Interactive Service Employment and Workplace Identities*, Malden, MA, and Oxford: WileyBlackwell.

McGivern, Yvonne (2005) *The Practice of Market and Social Research*, Harlow: Pearson Education.

Mackay, Hughie and Gillespie, Gareth (1992) 'Extending the Social Shaping of Technology Approach: Ideology and Appropriation', *Social Studies of Science*, 22(4): 685–716.

McKercher, Katharine and Vincent Mosco (eds) (2007) *Knowledge Workers in the Information Society*, Lanham, MD: Lexington Books.

McKnight, David (2002) *Espionage and the Roots of the Cold War*, London and New York: Frank Cass.

McLuhan, Marshall (1962) *The Gutenberg Galaxy: The Making of Typographic Man*, Toronto: University of Toronto Press.

McLuhan, Marshall (1964) *Understanding Media: The Extensions of Man*, New York: McGraw Hill.

McLuhan, Marshall (2001 edn) *Understanding Media: The Extensions of Man*, New York: Routledge.

McLuhan, Marshall and Fiore, Quentin (1968) *War and Peace in the Global Village*, New York: Bantam.

McPhee, William (1963) *Formal Theories of Mass Behaviour*, New York: The Free Press.

McQuail, Denis (2005) *McQuail's Mass Communication Theory*, London, Thousand Oaks, CA, and New Delhi: Sage.

Margolis, Michael and Resnick, David (2000) *Politics as Usual: The 'Cyberspce' Revolution*, Thousand Oaks, CA: Sage.

Marshall, P. David (1997) *Celebrity and Power: Fame in Contemporary Culture*, Minneapolis, MN: University of Minnesota Press.

Marshall, P. David (2006) 'New Media–New Self: The Changing Power of Celebrity', in P. David Marshall (ed.), *The Celebrity Culture Reader*, London and New York : Routledge, pp. 634–44.

Martin, Shannon E. and Copeland, David A. (2003) *The Function of Newspapers in Society: A Global Perspective*, Westport, CT: Greenwood Publishing Group.

Marx, Karl ([1867] 1990) *Capital Vol. 1*, London: Penguin.

Marx, Karl ([1927] 2009) *The Economic and Political Manuscripts of 1844*, New York: Dover Press.

Marx, Karl (1938) *The German Ideology*, London: Lawrence and Wishart.

Marx, Karl and Engels, Fredrich ([1888] 1968) *The Communist Manifesto*, London: Penguin.

Mason, Paul (2012) *Why It's Kicking Off Everywhere: The New Global Revolutions*, London: Verso.

Masuda, Yoneji (1980) *The Information Society as Post-Industrial Society*, Bethesda: World Future Society.

Masuda, Yoneji (1990) *Managing the Information Society: Releasing Synergy Japanese Style*, Oxford: Blackwell.

Matheson, Donald and Allan, Stuart (2009) *Digital War Reporting*, Cambridge: Polity.

Mead, George Herbert (1934) *Mind, Self and Society: From the Standpoint of A Social Behavourist*, Chicago, IL: University of Chicago Press.

Mill, John Stuart (2001) *Utilitarianism*, Indianopolis, IN: Hackett.

Miller, Arthur R. (1971) *The Assault on Privacy: Computers, Databanks and Dossiers*, Ann Arbor, MI: University of Michigan Press.

Miller, Daniel (2011) *Tales from Facebook*, Cambridge: Polity.

Milone, Mark (2003) 'Hacktivism: Securing the National Infrastructure', *Knowledge, Technology and Policy*, 16(1): 75–103.

Mitnick, Kevin and Simon, William (2005) *Intrusion: The Real Stories Behind the Exploits of Hackers, Intruders and Deceivers*, Indianapolis, IN: John Wiley.

Mosco, Vincent (1989) *The Pay-Per Society: Computers and Communication in the Information Age*, Norwood, NJ: Ablex.

Mosco, Vincent and Wasko, Janet (eds) (1988) *The Political Economy of Information*, Madison, WI: University of Wisconsin Press.

MPAA (2005) *Anti-Piracy Report*, Movie Picture Association of America, at: http://www.mpaa.org; viewed 23 March 2008.

Nadeem, Shehzad (2011) *Dead Ringers: How Outsourcing is Changing the Way that Indians Understand Themselves*, Princeton, NJ: Princeton University Press.

Nakamura, Liza (2007) *Digitizing Race: Visual Cultures of the Internet*, Minneapolis, MN: University of Minnesota Press.

Napoli, Philip (2010) *Audience Evolution: New Technologies and the Transformation of Media Audiences*, New York and Chichester: Columbia University Press.

Narayan, Brinda (2011) *Bangalore Calling*, India: Hachette India.

Negroponte, Nicholas (1995) *Being Digital*, Rydalmere: Hodder and Stoughton.

Nelson, Ted (1974a) *Computer Lib*, South Bend, IN: The Distributors.

Nelson, Ted (1974b) *Dream Machines*, South Bend, IN: The Distributors.

NHTCU (2004) 'What is Hi-Tech Crime?', at: http://www.nhctu.org/nqcontent.cfm/a_id=12334&tt=nhctu; viewed 24 June 2007.

Nielsen, Jakob and Loranger, Hoa (2006) *Prioritizing Web Usability*, Berkeley, CA: New Riders.

Nietzsche, Friedrich (2003) *Beyond Good and Evil*, London: Penguin.

Nightingale, Virginia (2011) *Handbook of Media Audiences*, Malden, MA, and Oxford: Wiley-Blackwell.

Nissenbaum, Helen (2004) 'Hackers and the Contested Ontology of Cyberspace', *New Media and Society*, 6(2): 195–217.

Norman, Donald A. (1988) *The Psychology of Everyday Things*, New York: Basic Books.

Norman, Donald A. (2002) *The Design of Everyday Things*, New York: Basic Books.

Norman, Donald and Draper, Stephen (eds) (1986) *User Centred System Design: New Perspectives on Human/Computer Interaction*, Hillsdale, NJ: Lawrence Erlbaum.

Norris, Pippa (2000) *Digital Divide: Civic Engagement, Information Poverty and the Internet Worldwide*, New York: Cambridge University Press.

Ong, Walter (1982) *Orality and Literacy: The Technologizing of the World*, London and New York: Routledge.

O'Reilly, Tim (2005) 'What is Web 2.0: Design Patterns and Business Models for the Next Generation of Software', O'Reilly Media, at: http://www.oreilly.com/web2/what-is-web-20.html (viewed 15 December 2011).

Ornstein, Allan (2007) *Class Counts: Education, Inequality and the Shrinking Middle Class*, Lanham, MD: Rowman and Littlefield.

Orwell, George (1949) *Nineteen Eighty-Four*, London: Secker and Warburg.

Oshri, Ilan, Kotlarsky, Julia and Willcocks, Leslie (2009) *The Handbook of Global Outsourcing and Offshoring*, Houndmills: Palgrave Macmillan.

Page, William and Bud, Andrew (2008) 'The Long Tail Interrogated', Performing Rights Society, at: http://www.prsformusic.com/creators/news/research/Pages/default.aspx (viewed 16 February 2009).

Palfrey, John and Gasser, Urs (2008) *Born Digital: Understanding the First Generation of Digital Natives*, New York: Basic Books.

Papacharissi, Zia (ed.) (2010a) *The Networked Self: Identity, Community and Culture on Social Network Sites*, London and New York: Routledge.

Papacharissi, Zia (2010b) *A Private Sphere: Democracy in a Digital Age*, Cambridge: Polity.

Park, Robert (1923) 'The Natural History of the Newspaper', *American Journal of Sociology*, 29(3): 273–89.

Park, Robert (1929) 'Urbanization As Measured by Newspaper Circulation', *American Journal of Sociology*, 35(1): 60–79.

Pepys, Samuel (2003) *The Diaries of Samuel Pepys – A Selection*, London: Penguin Classics.

Perlin, Ross (2011) *Intern Nation: How to Earn Nothing and Learn Little in the Brave New Economy*, London: Verso.

Pettinger, Lynne (2011) 'Knows How to Please A Man: Studying Customers to Understand Service Work', *The Sociological Review*, 59(2): 223–41.

Pettinger, Lynne, Parry, Jane, Taylor, Rebecca and Glucksmann, Miriam (2006) *A New Sociology of Work?*, Oxford: Blackwell.

Petzold, Charles (2008) *The Annotated Turing: A Guided Tour Through Alan Turing's Historic Paper on Computability and the Turing Machine*, Indianapolis, IN: Wiley.

Philo, Greg (1990) *Seeing and Believing: The Influence of Television*, London: Routledge.

Pinkard, Terry (2000) *Hegel: A Biography*, Cambridge: Cambridge University Press.

Polanyi, Karl (1957) *The Great Transformation*, New York: Rinehart and Company.

Poster, Mark (1995) *The Second Media Age*, Cambridge: Polity.

Poster, Mark (1997) 'Cyber Democracy – Internet and the Public Sphere', in David Porter (ed.), *Internet Culture*, London and New York: Routledge, pp. 201–17.

Poynter, Ray (2010) *Handbook of Online and Social Media Research: Tools and Techniques for Market Researchers*, Chichester, John Wiley.

Price, Charlton. (1975) 'Conferencing Via Computer: Cost Effective Communication for the Era of Forced Choice', in Harold Linstone and Murray Turoff (eds), *The Delphi Method: Techniques and Applications*, Reading, MA: Addison-Wesley, pp, 291–324.

Putnam, Robert (1995) 'Bowling Alone: America's Declining Social Capital', *Journal of Democracy*, 6(1): 65–78.

Putnam, Robert (2000) *Bowling Alone: The Collapse and Revival of American Community*, New York: Simon and Schuster.

Quah, Danny (1999) 'The Weightless Economy in Economic Development', Discussion Paper, Centre for Economic Performance, London: London School of Economics.

Quayle, Ethel and Taylor, Max (2003) *Child Pornography: An Internet Crime*, Hove: Brunner Routledge.

Radway, Janice (1991) *Reading the Romance: Women, Patriarchy and Popular Literature*, Chapel Hill, NC: University of North Carolina Press.

Rainie, Lee and Wellman, Barry (2012) *Networked: The New Social Operating System*, Cambridge, MA: MIT Press.

Reese, Stephen D., Rutigliano, Lou, Hyun, Kideuk and Jeong, Jaekwan (2007), 'Mapping the Blogosphere: Professional and Citizen-based Media in the Global News Arena', *Journalism*, 8(3): , 235–61.

Renold, Emma, Creighton, Susan, Atkinson, Chris, Carr, John (2003) *Images of Abuse: A Review of the Evidence on Child Pornography*, London: NSPCC.

Rettburg, Jill Walker (2008) *Blogging*, Cambridge: Polity.

Reynolds, Glenn (2007) *An Army of Davids: How Markets and Technology Empower Ordinary People to Beat Big Media, Big Government and Other Goliaths*, Nashville, TN: Nelson Current.

Reyns, Bradford (2010) 'Being Pursued Online: Nature and Extent of Cyberstalking Victimization from a Lifestyle/Routine Activities Perspective', Unpublished PhD thesis, Cincinnati: University of Cincinnati.

Rezabek, Landra and Cochenour, John (1998) 'Visual Cues in Computer-Mediated Communication: Supplementing Text With Emoticons', *Journal of Visual Literacy*, 18(2): 201–15.

Rheingold, Howard (1993) *The Virtual Community: Homesteading on the Electronic Frontier*, Reading, MA: Addison Wesley.

Rheingold, Howard (2000) *The Virtual Community: Homesteading on the Electronic Frontier: Revised Edition*, Cambridge, MA: MIT Press.

Rheingold, Howard (2003) *Smart Mobs: The Next Social Revolution*, Cambridge, MA: Perseus.

RIAA (2005) *Annual Commercial Piracy Report*, Recording Industry Association of America, at: http://www.riaa.org/; viewed 15 April 2006.

Richmond, W. Kenneth (2011) *The Education Industry*, London and New York: Routledge.

Rivlin, Gary (1999) *The Plot to Get Bill Gates*, London: Quartet Books.

Robertson, Roland (1994) 'Globalization or Glocalization?', *Journal of International Communication*, 1(1): 33–52.

Rogers, Everett M. (2003) *Diffusion of Innovations*, New York: Free Press.

Rose, Ellen (2003) *User Error: Resisting Computer Culture*, Toronto: Between the Lines.

Rosen, Jeffrey (2000) *The Unwanted Gaze: The Destruction of Privacy in America*, New York: Random House.

Ross, Andrew (2009) *Nice Work If You Can Get It: Life and Labor in Precarious Times*, New York: New York University Press.

Ross, Joel, Irani, Lilly, Silberman, M. Six, Zaldivar, Andrew and Tomlinson, Bill (2010) 'Who are the Crowdworkers? Shifting Demographics of the Mechanical Turk', *Proceedings of CHI 2010*, Atlanta, GA, USA, 10–15 April 2010, pp. 2863–72.

Roszak, Theodore (1995) *The Making of a Counter-culture: Reflections on the Technocratic Society and its Youthful Opposition*, Berkeley, CA: University of California Press.

Rowse, Darren and Garrett, Chris (2010) *Problogger: Secrets for Blogging Your Way to a Six Figure Income*, Indianapolis, IN: Wiley.

Rutter, Jason and Bryce, Jo (eds) (2006) *Understanding Digital Games*, London: Sage.

Sandvoss, Cornell (2005) *Fans: The Mirror of Consumption*, Cambridge: Polity.

Scase, Richard (1989) *Industrial Societies: Crisis and Division in Western Capitalism and State Socialism*, London: Routledge.

Schafer, Joseph A. (2002) 'Spinning the Web of Hate: Web-Based Hate Propagation by Extremist Groups', *Journal of Criminal Justice and Popular Culture*, 9(2): 69–88.

Schiller, Daniel (2000) *Digital Capitalism*, Cambridge, MA: MIT Press.

Schoeman, Ferdinand David (2008) *Privacy and Social Freedom*, Cambridge: Cambridge University Press.

Schott, Gareth (2005) 'Sex in Games: Representing and Desiring the Virtual', *Proceedings of DiGRA 2005 Conference*, viewed 17 August 2007 at: http://www.digra.org/dl/.

Schott, Gareth (2009) '"I'm OK": How Young People Articulate "Violence" in Videogames', *Refractory: A Journal of Entertainment Media* (16 (November), viewed 24 December 2010 at: http://refractory.unimelb.edu.au/2009/11/18/%E2%80%98i%E2%80%99m-ok%E2%80%99-how-young-people-articulate-%E2%80%98violence%E2%80%99-in-videogames-gareth-schott/.

Schrecker, Ellen (2002) *The Age of McCarthyism*, Houndmills: Palgrave Macmillan.

Schutz, Alfred (1972) *The Phenomenology of the Social World*, London: Heinemann.

Schweizer, Peter (2010) *Architects of Ruin: How Big Government Liberals Wrecked the Global Economy – and How They Will Do It Again if No One Stops Them*, New York: HarperCollins.

Scott, John P. and Carrington, Peter (eds) (2011) *The Sage Handbook of Social Network Analysis*, London, Thousand Oaks, CA, and New Delhi: Sage.

Search Engine Watch (2011) 'What People Search For', viewed 1 December 2011 at: http://searchenginewatch.com/article/2066257/What-People-Search-For-Most-Popular-Keywords.

Sears, Andrew and Jacko, Julie (eds) (2007) *The Human–Computer Interaction Handbook*, New York: Lawrence Erlbaum.

Segal, Howard P. (2012) *Utopias: A Brief History From Ancient Writings to Virtual Communities*, Malden:, MA Wiley-Blackwell.

Seldman, Marty and Seldman, Joshua (2008) *Executive Stamina: How to Optimize Time, Energy and Productivity to Achieve Peak Performance*, Hoboken, NJ: John Wiley.

Shaw, Jenny (2010) *Shopping: Social and Cultural Perspectives*, Cambridge: Polity.

Shirky, Clay (2008) *Cognitive Surplus: Creativity and Generosity in a Connected Age*, New York: Penguin Press.

Short, John, Williams, Ederyn and Christie, Bruce (1976) *The Social Psychology of Telecommunications*, Chichester: Wiley.

Shrum, L. J. (ed.) (2008) *The Psychology of Entertainment Media: Blurring the Lines Between Entertainment and Persuasion*, Mahwah, NJ: Lawrence Erlbaum.

Smith, John (1994) *Collective Intelligence in Computer-based Collaboration*, Hillsdale, NJ: Lawrence Erlbaum.

Solove, Daniel J. (2004) *The Digital Person: Technology and Privacy in the Information Age*, New York: New York University Press.

Sommer, Peter (2004) 'The Future for the Policing of Cybercrime', *Computer Fraud and Security*, 1: 8–12.

Stallman, Richard and Gay, Joshua (2009) *Free Software, Free Society: Selected Essays of Richard M. Stallman*, CreateSpace.

Standage, Tom (1998) *The Victorian Internet*, New York: Walker Publishing.

Standing, Guy (2011) *The Precariat: The New Dangerous Class*, London: Bloomsbury Academic.

Steffens, John (1994) *New Games: Strategic Competition in the PC Revolution*, Burlington, VT: Elsevier.

Stiglitz, Joseph (2010) *Freefall: Free Markets and the Sinking of the Global Economy*, London: Penguin.

Suppes, Patrick (1966) 'The Uses of Computers in Education', *Scientific American*, 215: 207–20.

Surowiecki, James (2004) *The Wisdom of Crowds: Why the Many Are Smarter Than the Few and How Collective Wisdom Shapes Business, Economies, Societies and Nations*, New York: Doubleday.

Swade, Doron (2001) *The Cogwheel Brain*, London: Abacus.

Szuba, Tadeusz (2001) *Computational Collective Intelligence*, New York: John Wiley and Sons.

Tadajewski, Mark and Jones, Brian (2008) *The History of Marketing Thought*, London: Sage.

Tapscott, Don and Williams, Anthony (2006) *Wikinomics: How Mass Collaboration Changes Everything*, New York: Penguin.

Taylor, Astra, Gessin, Keith et al. (2012) *Occupy!: Scenes from Occupied America*, London: Verso.

Taylor, Ethel and Quayle, Max (2003) *Child Pornography: An Internet Crime*, Hove: Brunner-Routledge.

Taylor, Marcus (ed.) (2008) *Global Economy Contested: Power and Conflict Across the International Division of Labour*, Abingdon: Routledge.

Taylor, Paul A. (1999) *Hackers: Crime in the Digital Sublime*, New York: Routledge.

Taylor, Robert W., Fritsch, Eric J., Liederbach, John R. and Holt, Thomas J. (2010) *Digital Crime and Digital Terrorism*, New Jersey: Prentice Hall.

Taylor, T. L. (2006) *Play Between Worlds: Exploring Online Game Culture*, Cambridge, MA: MIT Press.

Technorati (2011) 'Technorati', viewed 11 November 2011 at: http://www.technorati.com/.

Thomas, Douglas and Loader, Brian (2000) *Cybercrime: Law Enforcement, Security and Surveillance in the Information Age*, London: Routledge.

Thomas, Michael (ed.) (2011) *Deconstructing Digital Natives: Young People, Technologies and New Literacies*, New York: Routledge.

Thomas, Pradip Ninan (2010) *Political Economy of Communications in India: The Good, The Bad and the Ugly*, New Delhi: Sage.

Thomas, Pradip Ninan and Servaes, Jan (eds) (2006) *Intellectual Property Rights and Communications in Asia: Conflicting Traditions*, New Delhi: Sage.

Thussu, Daya and Sarikakis, Katharine (eds) (2006) *Ideologies of the Internet*, New Jersey: Hampton Press.

Toffler, Alvin (1970) *Future Shock*, New York: Random House.

Toffler, Alvin (1980) *The Third Wave*, New York: Bantam Books.

Toffler, Alvin and Toffler, Heidi (2007) *Revolutionary Wealth: How It Will Be Created and How It Will Changes Our Lives*, New York: Currency.

Tonnies, Ferdinand (2011) *Community and Society*, New York: Dover Publications.

Trepte, Sabine and Reinecke, Leonard (eds) (2011) *Privacy Online: Perspectives on Privacy and Self-Disclosure in the Social Web*, Berlin: Springer.

Tresis, Alexander (2002) *Destructive Messages: How Hate Speech Paves the Way for Harmful Social Movements*, New York: New York University Press.

Trought, Frances (2011) *Brilliant Employability Skill: How to Stand Out From The Crowd in the Graduate Job Market*, Harlow: Pearson Education.

Tuchman, Gaye (2009) *Wannabe U: Inside the Corporate University*, Chicago, IL: University of Chicago Press.

Turkle, Sherry (1996) *Life on the Screen: Identity in the Age of the Internet*, New York: Simon and Schuster.

Turkle, Sherry (2005) *The Second Self: Computers and the Human Spirit: 20th Anniversary Edition*, Cambridge, MA: MIT Press.

Turner, Graeme (2002) *British Cultural Studies: an Introduction*, London and New York: Routledge.

Turner, Graeme (2004) *Understanding Celebrity*, London and Thousand Oaks, CA: Sage.

Turner, Graeme (2011) *What's Become of Cultural Studies?*, London: Sage.

UK Home Office (2010) *British Crime Survey*, London: Home Office, HM Govt.

UNCTAD (2008) *Creative Economy Report 2008*, Geneva: United Nations Conference on Trade and Development.

Unwin, Tim (ed.) (2009) *ICT4D: Information and Communication Technology for Development*, Cambridge: Cambridge University Press.

Valenti, Jack (2003) 'International Copyright Piracy: Links to Organized Crime and Terrorism', *Testimony of Jack Valenti, President and CEO Motion Picture Association of America, before the Subcommittee on Courts, the Internet, and Intellectual Property*, Committee on the Judiciary, US House of Representatives.

Van Der Veer, G. and Melguizo, M. (2003) 'Mental Models', in Andrew Sears and Julie Jacko (eds) (2007) *The Human–Computer Interaction Handbook*, New York: Lawrence Erlbaum, pp. 52–80.

Van Dijk, Jan (2006) *The Network Society: Social Aspects of New Media*, London: Sage.

Van Dijk, Jose (2009) 'Users Like You?: Theorizing Agency in User-Generated Content', *Media, Culture and Society*, 31(1): 41–58.

Virilio, Paul (2000) *The Information Bomb*, London: Verso.

Virilio, Paul (2002) *Desert Screen: War at the Speed of Light*, London: Continuum.

Von Neumann, John (1958) *The Computer and the Brain*, New Haven, CT, and London: Yale University Press.

Von Neumann, John (1966) *Theory of Self-Replicating Automata*, Champaign, IL: University of Illinois Press.

Wacks, Raymond (2010) *Privacy: A Very Short Introduction*, New York: Oxford University Press.

Wall, David (ed.) (2001) *Crime and the Internet*, London: Routledge.

Wall, David (2007) *Cybercrime: The Transformation of Crime in the Information Age*, Cambridge: Polity.

Walther, J. B. (1992) 'Interpersonal Effects in Computer Mediated Communication', *Communication Research*, 19(1): 52–90.

Wasko, Janet, Murdock, Graham and Soussa, Helena (eds) (2011) *The Handbook of Political Economy of Communications*, Malden, MA: Wiley-Blackwell.

Wasser, Frederick (2002) *Veni, Vidi, Video: The Hollywood Empire and the VCR*, Austin, TX: Texas University Press.

Watson, Tony J. (2008) *Sociology, Work and Industry*, Abingdon: Routledge.

Weber, Max (1947) *The Theory of Economic and Social Organization*, New York: Free Press.

Weber, Max (1949) *The Methodology of the Social Sciences*, New York: Free Press.

Weber, Max (1958) *The Protestant Ethic and the Spirit of Capitalism*, New York: Free Press.

Weber, Max (1978) *Economy and Society: An Outline of Interpretive Sociology*, Berkeley, CA: University of California Press.

Webroot (2006) 'Spyware Infection Rates Return to Peak 2004 Levels', at: www.ebroot.com/en_US/pr/state-of-internet-security/corp/spyware-infection-rates-return-to-peak-levels.html (viewed 12 January 2008).

Webster, Frank (2006) *Theories of the Information Society*, London and New York: Routledge.

Webster, Frank and Robins, Kevin (1986) *Information Technology: A Luddite Analysis*, New York: Ablex.

Webster, Frank et al. (eds) (2005) *The Information Society Reader*, London and New York: Routledge.

Weiser, Mark (1991) 'The Computer for the 21st Century', *Scientific American* (draft), at: http://www.ubiq.com/hypertext/weiser/SciAmDraft3.html (viewed 4 January 2012).

Wellman, Barry (1979) 'The Community Question: The Intimate Networks of East Yorkers', *American Journal of Sociology*, 84: 1201–31.

Wellman, Barry (1999) *Networks in the Global Village: Life in Contemporary Communities*, New York: Perseus.

Wellman, Barry and Berkowitz, S. D. (1988) *Social Structures: A Network Approach*, Cambridge: Cambridge University Press.

Wellman, Barry and Gulia, Milena (1999) 'Virtual Communities as Communities: Net Surfers Don't Ride Alone', in P. Kollock and M. Smith (eds), *Communities in Cyberspace*, Berkeley, CA: University of California Press, pp. 167–94.

Wellman, Barry and Hampton, K. (1999) 'Living Networked in a Wired World', *Contemporary Sociology*, 28(6): 648–54.

Wellman, Barry et al. (2003) 'The Social Affordances of the Internet for Networked Individualism', *Journal of Computer-Mediated Communication*, 8(3), at: http://onlinelibrary.wiley.com/doi/10.1111/jcmc.2003.8.issue-3/issuetoc; viewed 12 February 2012.

Wells, Joseph T. (ed.) (2010) *Internet Fraud Casebook: The World Wide Web of Deceit*, Hoboken, NJ: John Wiley.

Wenger, Etienne (1999) *Communities of Practice: Learning, Meaning and Identity*, Cambridge: Cambridge University Press.

Werding, Martin (ed.) (2006) *Structural Unemployment in Western Europe: Reasons and Remedies*, Cambridge, MA: MIT Press.

Wetherall, Margaret, Lafleche, Michellyn and Berkeley, Robert (eds) (2007) *Identity, Ethnic Diversity and Community Cohesion*, London and Thousand Oaks, CA: Sage.

Whitty, Monica, Baker, Andrea and Inman, James (eds) (2007) *Online Matchmaking*, Houndmills: Palgrave Macmillan.

Whyte, William (1963) *The Organization Man*, Harmondsworth: Penguin.

Wiener, Norbert (1962) *The Human Use of Human Beings*, London: Free Association.

Wikstrom, Patrick (2006) *The Music Industry: Music in the Cloud*, Cambridge: Polity.

Wilden, Anthony (1968) *The Language of the Self: The Function of Language in Psychoanalysis*, Baltimore, MD: Johns Hopkins University Press.

Williams, Raymond (1961) *The Long Revolution*, London: Chatto and Windus.

Williams, Raymond (1962) *Communications*, Baltimore, MD: Penguin.

Williams, Raymond (1974) *Television: Technology and Cultural Form*, London: Collins.

Williams, Raymond (1988) *Resources of Hope*, London: Verso.

Williams, Robin and Edge, David (1996) 'The Social Shaping of Technology', *Research Policy*, 25; 865–99.

Williams, Sam (2006) *Free as in Freedom*, Sebastopol: O'Reilly Media.

Willis, Paul (1978) *Learning to Labour*, Farnham: Ashgate.

Wolf, Mark and Bernard Perron (2003) *The Video Game Theory Reader*, New York and London: Routledge.

Wolf, Martin (2007) *The Videogame Explosion: A History from Pong to Playstation and Beyond*, Westport, CT: Greenwood Press.

Wright, Erik Olin (1985) *Classes*, London: Verso.

Wright, Scott (2012) 'Politics as Usual?: Revolution, Normalization and a New Agenda for Online Deliberation', *New Media and Society*, 14(2); 244–61.

Yar, Majid (2006) *Cybercrime and Society*, London, Thousand Oaks, CA, and New Delhi: Sage.

Yokoo, Makoto, Sakurai, Yuko, Matsubara, Shigeo (2004) 'The Effect of False-Name Bids in Combinatorial Auctions: New Fraud in Internet Auctions', in *Games and Economic Behavior*, 46(1); 174–88.

Zyda, Michael (2005) 'From Visual Simulation to Virtual Reality to Games', *IEEE Computer Society* (September);25–32.

Index